MAY 03 2017

Fiji

**Vanua Levu &
Taveuni**
(p150)

**Mamanuca &
Yasawa Groups**
(p113)

**Nadi, Suva &
Viti Levu**
(p52)

**Ovalau & the
Lomaiviti Group**
(p138)

**Kadavu, Lau &
Moala Groups**
(p180)

D0179550

THIS EDITION WRITTEN AND RESEARCHED BY
Paul Clammer, Tamara Sheward

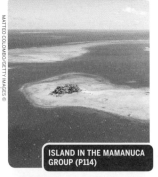

ISLAND IN THE MAMANUCA
GROUP (P114)

A WARM WELCOME AWAITS
VISITORS (P215)

MATTEO COLOMBO/GETTY IMAGES ©

CULTURA RM EXCLUSIVE/STUART WESTMORLAND/GETTY IMAGES ©

Contents

Welcome to Fiji

*Set your internal clock to 'Fiji time':
exploring the archipelago's exquisite
beaches, undersea marvels, lush
interiors and fascinating culture
shouldn't be rushed.*

Beachy Keen

Dazzling sands, perfect palm trees and waters so blue they glow – Fiji's beaches look airbrushed. While stunning stretches abound, it's on the islands of the Mamanucas and Yasawas that you'll find heavenly heavyweights. These beaches are the poster-child for paradise, luring thousands of visitors keen to discover their own South Sea idyll. The appeal of the islands stretches beyond holiday snaps; the reefs, bays and sublime sands have provided cinematic eye candy to films including *Cast Away* with Tom Hanks and 1980 teen-dream classic *The Blue Lagoon*.

Subsurface Showstoppers

Fiji's calm seas belie the riot of life going on within. With seemingly endless stretches of intensely coloured reefs and more than 1500 species of fish and colossal creatures Fiji's underwater world is worth the plunge. Seasoned divers and snorkellers will find plenty to thrill them, while first-timers will be bubbling excited exclamations into their mouthpieces. Anywhere a fin flashes or coral waves, you'll find a diving or snorkel day trip, and there are excellent live-aboard journeys for those after a truly immersive experience.

Dry-Land Drawcards

While it's easy to spend your holiday in, on or under the water, those who take the time to towel off will be rewarded by treasures on dry land. Fiji offers ample opportunities for hikers, birdwatchers, amblers and forest-fanciers, particularly on the islands of Taveuni – known as the Garden Island for its ludicrously lush interiors – and Kadavu, a less-travelled slice of prehistoric paradise with almost no roads to speak of. If urban wildlife is your thing, Suva boasts a surprising nightlife scene, while towns such as Savusavu entice with rollicking taverns and meet-the-locals haunts.

A Warm Welcome

Fijian life revolves around the church, the village, the rugby field and the garden. While this may sound insular, you'd be hard-pressed to find a more open and welcoming population. Though the realities of local life are less sunny than the country's skies – many regions are poor and lack basic services – Fijians are famous for their hospitality and warmth, which makes it easy to make friends or immerse yourself in Fijian culture on a village homestay.

Why I Love Fiji

By Tamara Sheward, Writer

What makes Fiji exceptional isn't any must-see sights or unforgettable experiences (though those are pretty thick on the ground): for me, it's the people. Whether I'm visiting a village, dodging coconuts on the beach or walking the big cities, nary a moment goes by without being dazzled by genuine smiles, greetings of *bula* or having a shower of smooches land on my baby daughter. I get goosebumps recalling traditional, eerily beautiful songs of welcome and farewell. Even though we're just passing through, I always come away feeling like a member of a big family. Fijians greet guests with a rousing 'Welcome home!'...and they mean it.

For more about our writers, see page 256

Above: Local woman, Tokoriki (p122), Mamanuca Group

Fiji

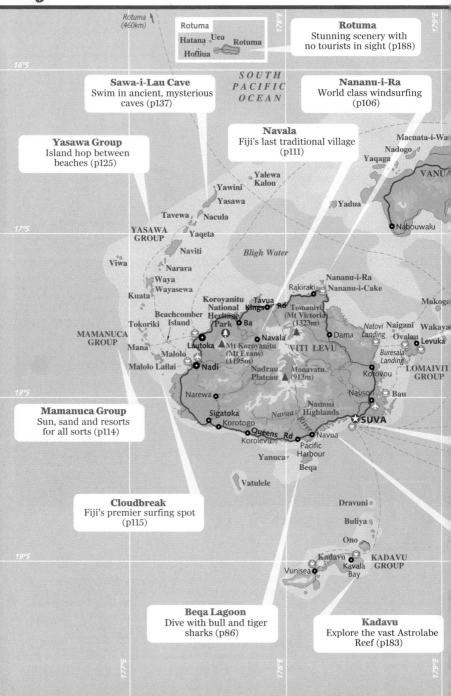

Rotuma
Stunning scenery with no tourists in sight (p188)

Sawa-i-Lau Cave
Swim in ancient, mysterious caves (p137)

Nananu-i-Ra
World class windsurfing (p106)

Navala
Fiji's last traditional village (p111)

Yasawa Group
Island hop between beaches (p125)

Mamanuca Group
Sun, sand and resorts for all sorts (p114)

Cloudbreak
Fiji's premier surfing spot (p115)

Beqa Lagoon
Dive with bull and tiger sharks (p86)

Kadavu
Explore the vast Astrolabe Reef (p183)

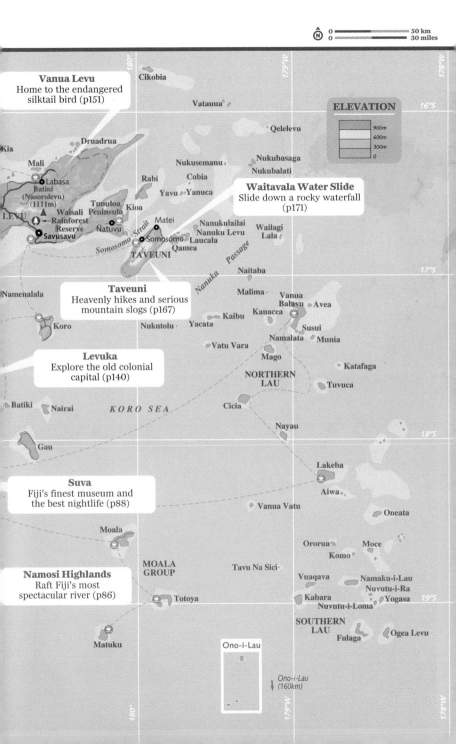

Vanua Levu
Home to the endangered
silktail bird (p151)

Cikobia

Vatauua

ELEVATION

Qelelevu

900m
600m
300m
0

Nukubasaga
Nukubalati

Kia

Druadrua

Mali

Nukusemanu

Waitavala Water Slide
Slide down a rocky waterfall
(p171)

Labasa
Batini
(Nasorolevu)
(111m)

Rabi
Cobia
Yavu Yanuca

LEVU

Waisali
Rainforest
Reserve
Savusavu

Tunuloa
Peninsula
Kioa

Natuvu

Matei

Nanukulailai
Nanuku Levu
Laucala

Wailagi
Lala

Somosomo Strait

Somosomo
Qamea

TAVEUNI

Naitaba

Nanuka Passage

Taveuni
Heavenly hikes and serious
mountain slogs (p167)

Malima
Vanua
Balavu Avea

Kanacea

Namenalala

Koro

Kaibu

Nukutolu Yacata

Susui

Namalata Munia

Vatu Vara

Mago

Katafaga

Levuka
Explore the old colonial
capital (p140)

**NORTHERN
LAU**

Tuvuca

Batiki Nairai

KORO SEA

Cicia

Gau

Nayau

Lakeba

Aiwa

Suva
Fiji's finest museum and
the best nightlife (p88)

Oneata

Moala

Vanua Vatu

Ororua Moce
Komo

Namosi Highlands
Raft Fiji's most
spectacular river (p86)

**MOALA
GROUP**

Tavu Na Sici

Vuaqava Namaku-i-Lau
Nuvutu-i-Ra
Kabara Yogasa
Nuvutu-i-Loma

Totoya

**SOUTHERN
LAU** Ogea Levu
Fulaga

Matuku

Ono-i-Lau

Ono-i-Lau
(160km)

Fiji's Top 15

1

Mamanucas & Yasawas

1 The 50-odd islands of the Mamanuca and Yasawa Groups are Fiji's come-hither call to paradise-hunters from across the globe. Ringed by reef and surrounded by impossibly blue seas, the chains each have their claims to fame. The Mamanucas (p114; Tavarua, pictured), a quick hop from Viti Levu, offer water sports galore, resorts for all budgets and unforgettable day trips taking in celebrity islands (*Cast Away* was shot at tiny Modriki) and further-flung islets considered sacred by locals. Up north, the Yasawas (p125) beckon with crystal-clear lagoons, handsome volcanic landscapes, remote villages and heavenly beaches.

Diving & Snorkelling

2 With warm, clear waters, friendly fish and ravishing reefs, underwater Fiji lures divers and snorkellers of all skill levels. Billed as the 'soft-coral capital of the world', the archipelago is home to such attractions as Rainbow Reef (p167; pictured) – home to the famous White and Purple Walls – and the huge Great Astrolabe Reef (p183). The Nasonisoni Passage drift dive (p154) is a thrillseeker's delight. Snorkellers will find bliss around the Mamanucas, Yasawas and the southern end of Taveuni; for something different, snorkel the oyster lines at pearl farms on Vanua Levu and Taveuni.

MATTEO COLOMBO/GETTY IMAGES ©

PETE OXFORD/MINDEN PICTURES/GETTY IMAGES ©

Hiking Taveuni

3 Lush, green and humid, Fiji's 'Garden Island' of Taveuni is heaven for hikers, where even the shortest trails lead to rare endemic birdlife, gargantuan trees and bizarre rock formations. About 80% of the island is protected by the Bouma National Park, home to the Lavena Coastal Walk (p176; pictured), which takes trekkers on a 5km journey past beautiful beaches and jungle villages and over a suspension bridge to hidden waterfalls. Serious sloggers can head up the steep Des Voeux Peak or to the muddy mountain crater of Lake Tagimaucia.

Navala Village

4 Nestled in a valley high in the Nausori Highlands, Navala (p111) is the best place in Fiji to witness authentic, age-old indigenous life up close. It's the country's last bastion of traditional architecture: from the chief's home to the outhouses, all of its 200 buildings are constructed using ancient techniques that make use of woven bamboo walls, thatched roofs and ropes made of fibre from the surrounding bush. Visitors are welcomed with a kava ceremony and stuffed full of locally caught, picked and harvested food cooked over an open fire.

Sawa-i-Lau Cave

5 A lone limestone island among the volcanic Yasawas, Sawa-i-Lau (p137) hides a mystery within its hollow caverns: carvings, paintings and inscriptions of unknown age and meaning. They're accessible with a torch and a guide (and a shot of courage) by swimming through a short underwater passage from the cave's main chamber. If your breath has already been taken away by the gorgeousness of the grotto, there's more placid paddling to be had in a clear pool beneath the cave's domed ceiling.

Local Life

6 '*Bula*', Fiji's ubiquitous greeting is more than a simple hi; it translates as 'Life', an apt salutation from a spirited people who seem to live theirs to the fullest. Fijians are genuinely friendly, and visitors will receive a warm welcome – often with open arms and song. The best place to experience this is at one of the villages that dot the countryside (p212): visits usually involve a kava ceremony (pictured), and possibly a *meke* (ceremonial dance) or *lovo* (feast from an underground oven), while homestays offer the chance to delve deep into local life.

Surfing & Windsurfing

7 Fiji is one of the best places in the world to hang 10, drawing surfers from all over. Its most famous breaks are the colossal Cloudbreak (p115; pictured) and Restaurants (p115), two mighty lefts that are most definitely not for the inexperienced. Surf resorts dot the archipelago, from the Mamanucas (p114) and Yanuca (p87) by Viti Levu, to the further-flung Qamea (p178) in the north and Kadavu (p182) to the south. Windsurfers also find plenty to whoop about: Nananu-i-Ra (p106) is exposed to consistent trade winds.

Indo-Fijian Culture

8 Indentured labourers from India were first brought to Fiji in 1879 to toil in British sugar cane and copra plantations. Their descendants, and the traditions they brought with them, remain. For a taste of Indo-Fijian culture, head to any of the ubiquitous curry houses or visit one of the brightly-painted Hindu temples on Viti Levu or Vanua Levu, such as Sri Siva Subramaniya Swami Temple (p56; pictured) in Nadi. Time your visit with Diwali, Holi or Suva's gasp-inducing South Indian Fire-Walking Festival (p95) if you can.

MACDUFF EVERTON/GETTY IMAGES ©

FEVERPITCHED/GETTY IMAGES ©

Suva

9 Steamy Suva (p88) offers a multicultural mix of contemporary and colonial Fiji. Gracious old buildings and monuments line a lively waterfront and harbour. Downtown Suva boasts slick, air-conditioned shopping malls and crowded handicraft stalls, both of which are ripe for exploring. Immerse yourself in the colourful chaos of the municipal market, learn about Fiji's wild history at the national museum, watch a game of rugby (pictured) and sip cocktails at the beautiful old Grand Pacific Hotel before exploring Suva's diverse restaurant scene.

Namosi Highlands

10 Geology looms large in the spectacular Namosi Highlands (p86). Sheer canyon walls crowd the Wainikoroiluva River and falls (pictured), and the dramatic curtains of rock form the backdrop to Fiji's most scenic river-rafting trip, taken aboard a *bilibili* (bamboo raft). The lower, longer, wider reaches of the palm-fringed waterway are usually covered in speedier style – in canoes with outboard motors – alongside villagers making their way to or from market on local boats laden with pigs, coconuts, taro and leafy green vegetables.

Birdwatching

11 You don't have to venture far to see beautiful birds: riotously coloured parrots parade through hotel gardens, and Suva's accessible Colo-i-Suva Forest Park (p91) is full of fluttering natives, such as the collared lory, (pictured). On other islands, Taveuni (p167) tops the list, with 100-plus species, including the rare orange dove, bright-red kula parrots and birds of prey; while the island's looming Des Voeux Peak (p171) is heaven for birdwatchers. Vanua Levu (p151) houses a silktail sanctuary, while to the south, Kadavu (p182) impresses with plenty of indigenous rainforest species.

Far-Flung Fiji

12 Though many come to Fiji to sit on beaches, the country also offers adventures. Adventurous, occasionally rough, sea voyages to the remote islands in the Lau and Moala Groups are just the beginning: once there, hardy travellers can blaze their own trail and discover pristine reefs, secluded swimming and snorkelling spots and lush interiors ripe for once-in-a-lifetime hikes. Those seeking ultimate isolation can make their way to Rotuma (p188), 460km off Viti Levu, a tiny outpost with perfect beaches and laid-back locals.

Waitavala Water Slide

13 Bruises, bumps and declarations of 'Most fun ever!' are the order of the day at this natural cascade of rock slides (p171) on the island of Taveuni. Start by watching the local kids to get an idea of what you're in for. They make it look easy, tackling the slides standing surfer-style, each turn more outrageously brave/crazy than the last; you, on the other hand, should go down on your bum (pictured above). Your (doubtless awkward) attempt will be rewarded by a cool plunge into the pools below.

Levuka Colonial Architecture

14 The Wild West meets the South Seas at Levuka (p140), the country's sleepy one-time colonial capital and Fiji's only World Heritage Site. You can almost imagine sailors rowdily bursting out from the frayed but colourful timber shopfronts. Women from the villages sell *dalo* and produce on the side of the road, a church rises, faded and cracked-white against the sky and the only sounds come from the occasional car chugging through town.

Manta Rays & Sharks

15 Fiji's large populations of manta rays and sharks provide the ultimate thrill for undersea explorers. Between May and October, manta rays cruise the channel between Nanuya Balavu and Drawaqa islands in the Yasawas (p131); resorts in the area drop guests in the passage, which has a no-touch, no-scuba policy designed to protect the graceful rays. Sharks patrol much of Fiji's waters; see them on a snorkel trip in the lower Yasawas or on a daring dive with bull and tiger sharks at Beqa Lagoon (p86; pictured above).

Need to Know

For more information, see Survival Guide (p221)

Currency
Fijian dollar ($)

Language
Fijian, English and Fiji-Hindi

Visas
Visas are given on arrival to most nationalities and are valid for three months.

Money
ATMs and banks are widespread in larger towns on the main islands but scarce or nonexistent on outlying islands. Top-end resorts accept credit cards.

Mobile Phones
Vodafone and Digicel are Fiji's mobile-phone carriers. With an unlocked phone, you can buy a SIM card and top up with pre-pay units.

Time
Fiji Standard Time (GMT/UTC plus 12 hours)

When to Go

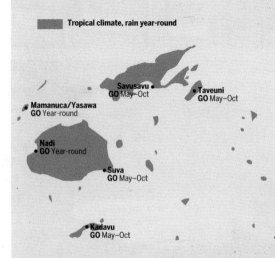

Tropical climate, rain year-round

Savusavu
GO May–Oct

Taveuni
GO May–Oct

Mamanuca/Yasawa
GO Year-round

Nadi
GO Year-round

Suva
GO May–Oct

Kadavu
GO May–Oct

High Season
(Jun–Sep; Dec & Jan)

➡ Peak seasons coincide with the school holidays in Australia and New Zealand.

➡ Prices go up by 10% to 20%; costs peak in June and July.

Shoulder
(May & Oct)

➡ The shoulder season includes the 'Fijian winter' or 'dry season' (May to October), bringing low rainfall, low humidity, milder temperatures and a lower risk of cyclones.

Low Season
(Nov & Feb–Apr)

➡ November to April is Fiji's 'wet season', with heavy rains and high humidity.

➡ Fewer tourists equal reduced rates, though discounts are hard to come by in December and January during Australian and New Zealand school holidays.

Useful Websites

Fiji Times (www.fijitimes.com.fj) Fiji's daily newspaper.

Fiji Village (www.fijivillage.com) Daily news and links to local events.

Fiji Visitors Bureau (www.fiji. travel) Fiji's official tourist site.

South Pacific Tourism Organisation (www.spto.org) Useful directory with info on South Pacific countries.

Important Numbers

There are no area codes in Fiji; within the country numbers can be dialled as they are presented.

Fiji's country code	☏679
International access code	☏00
Emergency	☏911
International directory assistance	☏022

Exchange Rates

Australia	A$1	$1.55
Canada	C$1	$1.61
Europe	€1	$2.31
Japan	¥100	$2.03
New Zealand	NZ$1	$1.48
UK	UK£1	$3.32
US	US$1	$2.78

For current exchange rates see www.xe.com.

Daily Costs

Budget: less than $180

➡ Dorm bed, with meals: $40–120

➡ Local transport and markets: good value on the main islands

➡ A half-day snorkelling excursion: $40–70

Midrange: $180–400

➡ Double room in a hotel: $140–300

➡ Local restaurants: $10–30 for a main dish

➡ Activities: at least $80 per day

High end: over $400

➡ Resorts: meals and activities often included in tariffs

➡ *Bure* (bungalows): $300 to $3000 per night

Opening Hours

Fiji shuts down on Sundays, though many eateries and a handful of shops will operate until the afternoon. 'Fiji time' is a real thing; the hours provided below may prove flexible.

Banks 9.30am to 4pm Monday to Thursday, to 3pm Friday

Restaurants 11am to 2pm and 6pm to 9pm Monday to Saturday

Shops 9am to 5pm Monday to Friday, until 1pm Saturday

Arriving in Fiji

Most travellers arrive at Nadi International Airport (p229).

➡ Local buses, just outside the airport cost $0.90 to downtown Nadi.

➡ Most hotels provide free pre-booked transport to and from the airport.

➡ A taxi downtown costs $15.

All yachts must call into an official Port of Entry (Suva, Lautoka, Savusavu or Levuka).

Getting Around

Cities and larger towns have paved roads, while island interiors are often criss-crossed by rough trails. There are no passenger trains in Fiji.

Car There are rental car agencies in heavily populated or touristed areas. A 4WD is a good idea if you're exploring out of town. Local carriers can also be chartered.

Taxis Cabs, commonplace in cities and towns, can be an inexpensive option for day trips, as well as for shorter commutes.

Bus Fiji's larger islands are well-served by long-distance buses. Cheap, often windowless local buses offer a friendly, truly Fijian experience (as in: timetables are erratic, but you'll have a good time riding them!).

Boat Ferries and cargo ships travel between Viti Levu and other islands. Be sure to check how often they return, especially to more remote destinations; some only run once a week. There are regular ferries between Nadi and the Mamanuca and Yasawa island groups.

Plane Fiji Airways (operating domestically as Fiji Link) and Northern Air fly from Viti Levu to many of the outer islands. Private seaplanes and helicopters are an option for island resorts.

Don't Leave Home Without...

➡ Insect repellent.

➡ Plenty to read: bookshops are only found in cities.

➡ Reef shoes to protect yourself and the reefs that surround most of Fiji's islands.

➡ A torch and batteries; many regions don't have power overnight.

➡ Your own snorkel and mask.

➡ A waterproof camera (or phone case).

➡ Sunscreen and a raincoat to combat tropical climate conditions.

➡ Seasickness tablets if you don't have sea legs.

For much more on **getting around**, see p230

If You Like...

Family Fun

Its soft sands and warm waters make Fiji one big beachy playground. But even away from the seaside, there are plenty of jollies for the knee-high crew.

Sabeto Hot Springs Kids large and small will love slinging mud at one another in these natural outdoor pools. (p69)

Kula Eco Park This wildlife park on the Coral Coast offers youngsters a chance to get nose-to-beak with rare birds. (p78)

Coral Coast Scenic Railway Chugging past jungle and villages to Natadola Beach, this former sugar train is tons of fun. (p74)

Robinson Crusoe Island Children will squeal in delight with all the activities in place. (p73)

Sawa-i-Lau Which kid can resist the storybook adventure of swimming in a mysterious cave? (p137)

Romantic Getaways

Beachside dinners, private plunge pools and candlelit massages – these intimate, adult-only resorts leave no pillow unplumped and provide honeymooners and lovebirds with some serious island-style pampering.

Likuliku Lagoon This resort boasts Fiji's first overwater bungalows, each beautifully appointed with traditional touches. (p121)

Matangi Island Resort For arboreous amour, Matangi's secluded tree houses can't be beaten. (p179)

Tokoriki Island Resort With its cute chapel, photogenic knee-dropping nooks and an on-site Romance Coordinator, Tokoriki is a lovers' lair par excellence. (p122)

Emaho Sekawa Luxury Resort Couples gets looked after by their own private staff – including a gourmet chef. (p158)

Nanuya Island Resort A short walk from the Blue Lagoon, the resort has cosy hilltop nests and a new, jaw-droppingly luxurious honeymoon villa. (p135)

Idyllic Beaches

While the main islands have surprisingly few world-class beaches, nearly all of the smaller islands have beaches so perfect that they're practically unreal. With so many to choose between, it seems miserly to single out just a few.

Modriki Ever since the Tom Hanks' film *Cast Away* was filmed here, this tiny island has become Fiji's biggest star. Its broad lagoon and gorgeous beach have most day-trippers wondering why Tom ever left. (p148)

Caqalai This itty-bitty island – a mere speck on most maps – has golden beaches backed by swaying palms. (p148)

Long Beach The finest beach on Nacula and one of the best in the Yasawa Group; it's but a short boat ride from the original Blue Lagoon. (p136)

'Sand bridge' between Waya and Wayasewa With twice the amount of sandy real estate than anywhere else, this strip is lapped by water on both sides. (p130)

Village Life

A homestay or village visit offers excellent insight into everyday life. Bring a *sevusevu* (gift) of *yaqona* (kava) root, and a loud barracking voice for the village rugby-field sidelines. Food generally comes straight from the garden and includes such starchy staples as *tavioka* (cassava) and *dalo* (taro) roots alongside seafood in *lolo* (coconut cream).

Lovoni Join Epi's Island Tours and trek to this village built inside the crater of an extinct volcano. (p147)

Navala Perched in Viti Levu's highlands, Navala is the only community that insists all homes are built using traditional materials and conform to traditional architectural styles. (p111)

Nabalasere Locals in one of Viti Levu's prettiest villages are the guardians of the spectacular Savulelele waterfall. (p103)

Viseisei Village Homestays According to oral tradition, Viseisei is Fiji's oldest village, established by Melanesian explorers hundreds of years ago. (p70)

Waya Island Leave the resorts behind and lap up island life, local-style, at Waya's friendly villages. (p130)

Koroyanitu National Heritage Park Getting to the two villages here is no cakewalk, but time spent with the welcoming locals makes the trip worthwhile. (p69)

Diving & Snorkelling

The archipelago's warm, clear waters and abundance of reef life make it a magnet for divers and snorkellers. Underwater visibility regularly exceeds 30m, and when the current flows, the corals bloom with flower like beauty.

Beqa Lagoon One of the few places in the world where it's possible to dive with bull and tiger sharks without a cage. (p83)

Snorkelling with manta rays Work your fins to keep up with the giant manta rays that cruise the nearby channel between Nanuya Balavu and Drawaqa islands. (p131)

Top: Likuliku Lagoon (p121), Malolo, Mamanuca Group
Bottom: Village children, Navala (p111), Viti Levu

E6, Bligh Passage, Lomaiviti Group A phenomenal seamount that brushes the surface; a magnet for pelagics. (p139)

Great White Wall, Taveuni Possibly the best soft-coral dive in Fiji; it's part of the famous Rainbow Reef. (p167)

Eagle Rock, Kadavu One of the many dives that can be had on the Great Astrolabe Reef, a 100km barrier reef with a vibrant assemblage of hard- and soft-coral formations. This dive is a maze of faults, canyons and tunnels. (p183)

Surfing

Fiji has some world-class breaks year-round, but from May to October southerly swells form colossal breaks that will have most surfers shivering in their wetsuit.

Cloudbreak Fiji's most famous break; for experienced riders only. (p115)

Namotu Left So named after the huge lefties the spot is renowned for. (p115)

Frigate Passage Consistently good, with waves that seldom drop below head height, this is one of the most underrated spots in the South Pacific. (p86)

Restaurants Fast left-hander that will chew you up and spit you out. (p115)

Natadola Beach In the right conditions a small break forms that's ideal for beginners. (p72)

King Kong Lefts Unlike most Fijian breaks, this is within paddling distance of land and holds great shape when small. (p183)

Sailing

A permanent fixture on the South Pacific 'Coconut Milk Run', Fiji has long drawn yachts from all over the globe. You must call into an official port of entry before fanning out through Fiji's extensive archipelago.

Savusavu With two top marinas and a boatload of facilities, Savusavu is now Fiji's best-resourced port for pleasure cruisers. (p155)

Musket Cove Home to Fiji Regatta Week – a weeklong party of fun and sun. Most skippers have this one pencilled in their cruising calendars every September. (p124)

Port Denarau Posh marina with excellent facilities; yachties can stock up with supplies and arrange repairs. (p65)

Royal Suva Yacht Club It's no longer the institution that it once was, but this is the first official port of entry for yachts arriving from Tonga and the east. (p93)

Birdwatching

A small but dedicated number of travellers come to Fiji in hope of seeing some of its rare and colourful birds. While some, such as the collared lory, can be seen in hotel gardens, others are more elusive.

Taveuni A top twitching site with abundant flora, the 'Garden Island' is home to more than 100 species, including the rare orange dove. (p169)

Kadavu This island enjoys a high diversity of birdlife, including such endemics as the Kadavu musk parrot. (p183)

Vanua Levu Birders should head to Tunuloa Peninsula, home to the rare silktail. (p161)

Colo-i-Suva Forest Park Only 11km from downtown Suva, a network of forest trails offers a good chance to see some of Fiji's more common native birds. (p91)

Hiking

Although walking for fun might strike most locals as a little odd, Fiji is home to some spectacular treks and trails.

Lavena Coastal Walk Skirting the forest's edge, this 5km walk links beautiful white- and black-sand beaches to isolated villages. Trekkers can cool off in a pool carved by twin waterfalls. (p176)

Koroyanitu National Heritage Park Go on rough-and-ready guided treks through dakua (kauri) forests in search of waterfalls, and tackle sweaty scrambles up mountain peaks for breathtaking views. (p69)

Colo-i-Suva Forest Park This park offers a network of trails between forest-fringed swimming holes, plus gorgeous views. (p91)

Des Voeux Peak Nature-lovers are rewarded for the challenging slog to the top of this peak with incredible birdwatching opportunities.(p171)

Mt Tomanivi Fiji's highest peak (1323m) is steep and rugged, but offers rewarding views; get there with Talanoa Treks, the country's only dedicated hiking company. (p103)

Month by Month

TOP EVENTS

Bula Festival, July

Hibiscus Festival, August

South Indian Fire-Walking Festival, August

Fiji Regatta Week, September

Uprising Festival of Music, Dance & Lights, October

January

Hot and wet. Although temperatures rise above 30°C at this time of year, Fiji's seasonal variations are not pronounced and this is only 5°C above the yearly average. Humidity, however, will make it seem hotter.

New Year's Day

New Year's Day is celebrated with much fervour in Fiji, with some parts of the country having festivities for the entire month. In Suva, the New Year is welcomed with fireworks and street parties.

February

Although only 10 to 15 cyclones strike Fiji each decade (usually between November and April), there is a greater risk of encountering one during February (along with January).

March

The wet season continues and this is usually Nadi's wettest month, with an average rainfall of 324mm.

Holi (Festival of Colours)

Holi (also called *Phagua* locally) is celebrated by Hindu Indo-Fijians by joyfully throwing coloured powder at one another. Most celebrate the day after the full moon in March.

Ram Naumi (Birth of Lord Rama)

A Hindu religious festival held in late March or early April, it is mainly celebrated in private homes, although you may see worshippers wade into the water at Suva Bay to throw flowers.

April

Heavier-than-average rains continue until mid-April, but by the end of the month, the wet season is officially over and humidity levels – thankfully – start to drop.

May

With the start of the dry season, water visibility increases and divers should enjoy excellent clarity from now until October. Fiji's easterly and southeasterly trade winds become more persistent.

Surfing

Consistent southerly swells make May a great time to surf; the best surfing is at Cloudbreak. This weather pattern keeps the breaks large until October. (p115)

June

Pleasant temperatures, low humidity and fine days kick off Fiji's peak tourist season.

🏃 Windsurfing

The trade winds that begin in May continue to provide perfect conditions for windsurfers and kiteboarders around Nananu-i-Ra. Favourable windsurfing conditions persist here well into next month. (p106)

July

July is one of Fiji's coldest and driest months; night temperatures sink to around 18°C. The pleasant days (around 24°C) make this an ideal time to visit.

🎊 Bula Festival

One of Fiji's biggest festivals, this week-long party is held in Nadi with rides, marching bands, shows and the crowning of 'Miss Bula'. (p59)

August

Winter temperatures continue, and a light sweater will be needed during the cooler nights. Days remain warm and dry. Ocean temperatures reach their lowest monthly average but are entirely swimmable at 23°C.

🎊 Hibiscus Festival

Held in Suva, this whopping nine-day festival has live music, floats, food stalls, fair rides and the crowning of 'Miss Hibiscus'. (p95)

🎊 South Indian Fire-Walking

At this festival usually held in August (sometimes July), Hindu devotees at Suva's

Top: Adi Senikau, Fiji's largest transgender pageant, is part of the Hibiscus Festival (p95)

Bottom: Preparing coals for fire-walking (*vilavilairevo*; p216), Beqa

Mariamma Temple walk across red-hot stones and pierce their bodies with metal skewers. (p95)

September

The reliably fine weather continues, although Fiji's peak tourist season begins to wind down.

🏃 Fiji Regatta Week

This annual regatta lures avid yachties and party people from around the world. Held at Musket Cove Marina. (p124)

✨ Sugar Festival

Sleepy Lautoka comes alive with fun fairs, parades and the crowning of the Sugar Queen (https://www.facebook.com/LautokaSugarFestivalAssociation).

✨ Friendly North Festival

Similar to Lautoka's Sugar Festival (with bonus Bollywood Night), this event (http://fnflabasa.wix.com/friendly-north-fes) is held in Labasa.

October

The cooler dry season ends and temperatures begin to climb as the Southern Hemisphere moves towards its summer.

✨ Bilibili Race

Coral Coast hospitality employees race one another down the Sigatoka River on *bilibilis* (bamboo rafts) on 10 October; hilarity (and large crowds) guaranteed.

✨ Fiji Week

Week long celebrations focus on the diversity of Fijian and Indo-Fijian cultures, culminating on Fiji Day (10 October), which marks the country's independence from British colonial rule. (p70)

✨ Diwali (Festival of Lights)

Hindu families decorate their homes, set candles and lanterns on their doorsteps, and pray to Lakshmi (the goddess of wealth and prosperity). This festival (www.diwalifestival.org/diwali-in-fiji.html) is held in late October or early to mid-November.

✨ Uprising Festival of Music, Dance & Lights

This 12-hour marathon of music and performing arts (http://uprisingbeachresort.com/music-festival) is timed to coincide with Diwali. More than 100 musicians and dancers make this one of Fiji's most popular festivals. It's held at Uprising Beach Resort (Pacific Harbour).

✨ Ram Leela (Play of Rama)

Primarily a Hindu festival; theatrical performances celebrate the life of the god-king Rama and his return from exile. It's held at the Mariamman Temple (in Vunivau, near Labasa) around the first week of October, and has been celebrated here for more than 100 years.

November

Fiji's wet season starts in November and continues across summer until April. The mountains of Viti Levu and Vanua Levu create wet climatic zones on their windward (southeastern) sides and dry climatic zones on their leeward (northwestern) sides.

✨ Balolo Rising

Blue, edible sea worms rise at midnight about a week after November's full moon. Many island communities celebrate the annual harvest with songs and feasts. (p189)

December

The rainy season arrives in earnest, though travel is still entirely possible. Rain showers are usually heavy but brief and followed by steamy, sunny spells.

✨ Fara

Six weeks of dancing and partying kick off on 1 December as Rotumans celebrate Fara; groups of performers visit villages and homes, entertaining their hosts. (p188)

Itineraries

Sawa-i-Lau Cave

Blue Lagoon

YASAWA GROUP

Nanuya Balavu — Drawaqa

Waya
Wayasewa

SOUTH PACIFIC OCEAN

MAMANUCA GROUP — Modriki — Beachcomber Island

Mana

Port Denarau

VITI LEVU

1-2 WEEKS The Eclectic Island Hop

Though it's easy to imagine the **Mamanuca** and **Yasawa Groups** as one long string of same-same paradisiacal islands, this hugely popular region is quite diverse. Board the *Yasawa Flyer* at **Port Denarau** and head first to **Beachcomber Island**; popular with party people (and increasingly, families), this is a great place to pick up tips from fellow travellers and to soak up the first of your island rays. Head onwards to **Mana** for a sharky scuba dive at the nearby Supermarket and a day trip aboard a schooner to **Modriki**, where *Cast Away* was shot. Say goodbye to the resorts of the Mamanucas and hello to a genuine look at local life, Yasawas-style, with a homestay at **Waya** island. After a couple of days of village food – and a steep host-led hike up a volcanic plug on neighbouring **Wayasewa** – you're now ready to keep up with the manta rays that ply the passage between **Nanuya Balavu** and **Drawaqa** islands; resorts in the area run snorkel trips here in season. Further north, give yourself a well-earned rest with a frolic in the **Blue Lagoon** before hopping a water taxi to the magnificent and mysterious **Sawa-i-Lau Cave**.

This trip is best undertaken with a Bula Pass (from five to 21 days) for the *Yasawa Flyer*. See page 127 for more information.

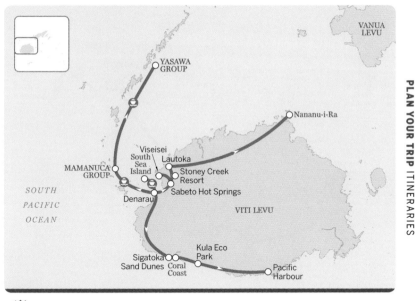

 **Family Fling**

Slow down and get into the slow swing of Fiji time with a relaxing couple of days at a family-friendly resort on **Denarau Island**. It's not all flopping by the pool (though it can be if you desire), with a nearby water park, family cooking classes and minigolf to keep everyone on the go. Head out of town – you can stay at the wonderful **Stoney Creek Resort** or take day trips from Denarau – and enjoy a bout of literal mud-slinging at **Sabeto Hot Springs**, whizzing over waterfalls on a zipline and bouncing through the forest on a buggy tour. Nearby, the friendly village of **Viseisei** offers homestays (though you can also just visit); the local kids love making new playmates.

But a boat ride away, the **Mamanuca** and **Yasawa Groups** seem purpose-built for families, with easy snorkelling, water sports and safe swimming on offer. Some popular family destinations include Treasure, Castaway, Malolo Lailai and Mana island resorts. If you're on limited time, a day trip out to **South Sea Island** (30 minutes from Denarau) is a must-do.

Back on Viti Levu, options abound. If you can't get enough of island escapades, head north, making a brief stop in **Lautoka** to watch the sugar trains (in season) clunking through town, then carry on to **Nananu-i-Ra**, a low-key island with great kayaking, windsurfing and oodles of friendly fish. Otherwise, head south to the **Coral Coast** for a ride on its scenic railway, a trek to the top of the **Sigatoka Sand Dunes** and awesome animal encounters at **Kula Eco Park**. Nearby **Pacific Harbour** offers all manners of adventurous outings, from horse-riding to fishing.

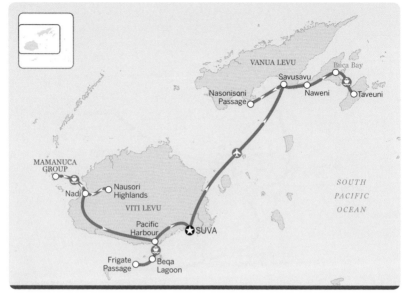

 ## Thrills & Spills

Hit the ground running – or riding – in **Nadi** by joining a fast-paced downhill cycling tour of the nearby **Nausori Highlands**. The next day, take a 14,000ft leap over the spine-tingling scenery of the **Mamanuca Group** with a tandem skydive. Continue your island journey with a few days of surfing some of the country's best breaks at Cloudbreak, Restaurants and Desperations.

Catch the *Yasawa Flyer* back to Nadi, but don't wash the salt from your hair just yet; travel south to **Pacific Harbour** for an exhilarating shark dive at **Beqa Lagoon**, then hop a boat for more surfing, this time at the underrated **Frigate Passage**. For freshwater thrills, head up to the nearby Navua River for rafting through deep canyons.

Make your way to **Suva** and indulge in some wild nightlife before hopping a flight bound for **Savusavu** on Vanua Levu (landing at this tiny airport can be a spine-tingling experience in itself). From your base in this rollicking port town, it's easy to access some superb dive sites, including an exhilarating, superfast drift dive through the narrow **Nasonisoni Passage**. Continue your underwater adventures at any of the remote dive resorts near **Buca Bay**. At **Naweni**, you'll encounter the legendary 'sacred prawns' that respond to locals' chants. Across the strait, **Taveuni** offers jungle kicks, including hurtling down the Waitavala Water Slide and clambering across slick boulders at the Tavoro Waterfalls.

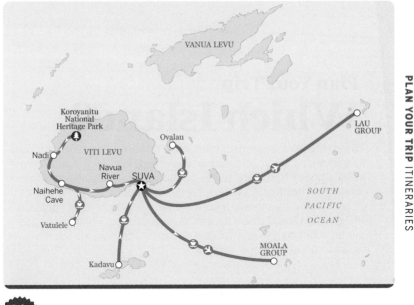

 **Fiji Rambler**

From Nadi, head up and inland to the **Koroyanitu National Heritage Park** for a few days of slow-going hiking: you'll need a guide, and your guide will need a machete! There are two small, friendly villages – Abaca and Navilawa – visitors are welcome to stay and take part in laid-back local life.

Take your time making your way towards the capital; there are lots of off-the-beaten-track destinations worthy of your time. The **Naihehe Cave**, north of Sigatoka, was once used by cannibals; down south, you can drift along the **Navua River** on a *bilibili* (bamboo raft) or head to any of the small islands lying off the coast, including **Vatulele**.

Once in **Suva**, explore the Fiji Museum, amble along the trails of Colo-i-Suva Forest Park and pick through the eclectic offerings at the Suva Flea Market. From there, catch a ferry to **Ovalau** off the coast of eastern Viti Levu; during colonial times the town of Levuka was the nation's capital, and it retains a good measure of its Wild West vibe. Time your return to Suva with the weekly ferry from there to **Kadavu**, a far-flung paradise encircled by the eminently diveable Great Astrolabe Reef; it's also a hiking and birdwatching mecca. If you've got the time to truly get away from it all, occasional ferries and flights leave Suva for Fiji's 'final frontier', the **Lau** and **Moala Groups**, home to spectacular nature and almost no infrastructure.

Plan Your Trip
Which Island?

Whether you're looking for relaxation, romance or rollicking adventure, chances are you'll discover the island holiday of your dreams in Fiji. Choose from bare-bones backpacker haunts and cultural-connection homestays to upscale beach bungalows and massive resorts. There's generally a lively scene in the tourist hot spots on Viti Levu and the Mamanuca and Yasawa Groups, while things are quieter – but no less enjoyable – on less-visited islands such as Kadavu, Vanua Levu and Taveuni.

Top Five Luxury Resorts
Likuliku Lagoon (p121)

Emaho Sekawa Luxury Resort (p158)

Taveuni Palms (p175)

Turtle Island Resort (p121)

Wakaya Club (p149)

Top Five Backpacker Hangouts
Beachcomber Island Resort (p119)

Mantaray Island Resort (p132)

Bamboo (p61)

Mango Bay Resort (p81)

Uprising Beach Resort (p85)

Top Five Romantic Getaways
Tokoriki Island Resort (p122)

Savasi Island (p158)

Nanuya Island Resort (p135)

Navutu Stars (p133)

Matangi Island Resort (p179)

The Resort Experience

The term 'resort' is bandied around freely in Fiji and can refer to almost anything within a frisbee throw of a beach. Take note of the price and do your homework to make sure you know what you're getting yourself into. If the tariff is low, chances are you're not booking into a luxury establishment, though it may be a lovely budget choice.

Resort Islands
Viti Levu

➡ The gateway to the country and the largest of the Fijian islands; boasts a taste of everything the country has to offer.

➡ Denarau Island, despite having no actual beach, has a string of big-brand resorts; many packages include a night or two here.

➡ The Coral Coast and Pacific Harbour have a broad spectrum of resorts, including some good midrange options.

Mamanuca Group

➡ Most Mamanuca islands are around an hour's boat ride from Nadi.

➡ Reliably good weather and beautiful beaches ensure they remain Fiji's most famous islands.

➡ Most cater to families, honeymooners or romantically inclined couples, although

Beachcomber Island has earned its stripes over the years as *the* party destination in Fiji.

Yasawa Group

➡ Traditionally caters to either backpackers or the well-heeled, but there are now tons of options for midrange travellers.

➡ Well connected to the mainland by a high-speed catamaran, but it is nonetheless remote and has little infrastructure.

Ovalau & the Lomaiviti Group

➡ Most accommodation on the main island of Ovalau is in the form of small hotels, homestays and lodges.

➡ Four of the beach-blessed offshore islands have their own isolated resorts: there's something for all budgets.

➡ Midrangers will love Koro and Naigani, while you'd be hard-pressed to find any lodging more beautiful or luxurious than Wakaya's.

Vanua Levu

➡ There is a wide range of resorts near pretty Savusavu; choose between family-friendly, luxe, new-age or sustainable stays.

➡ The far east – and Namena to the south – are home to dive resorts accessible only by boat.

➡ Other remote getaways can be found northwest of Labasa at Palmlea Lodge and on the private island of Nukubati.

Taveuni

➡ There's something for all budgets here, plus affordable adventures by the bucketload.

➡ Most of the posh options are in the north, along with plenty of great-value dive and activity-oriented resorts.

➡ Resorts on Taveuni's offshore islands, including Matagi, Qamea and Laucala, are utterly sublime.

Kadavu

➡ Nearly all the resorts here are admirably conserving their environment and watching their social impact by growing their own organic vegetables, working in tune with the local villages and much more.

➡ Only Ono has a very luxurious option, while the rest of the group's options offer a good level of comfort without too many frills.

➡ Its location close to the Great Astrolabe Reef makes it ideal for scuba diving.

What to Expect

Organise pickups in advance, and you'll be met at the airport by a resort representative. Transport depends on where you're staying and could come in the form of a bus, car, speedboat, truck or seaplane. Upon registration, your bags will almost certainly be taken to your room for you (tipping is not obligatory in Fiji, though many people choose to make a donation to the staff Christmas fund). Most resorts have organised activities – many of them free – listed on boards that are updated daily.

➡ High-end resorts usually have day spas, landscaped pools and stylish restaurants.

➡ Midrange resorts will generally have a restaurant and bar and possibly a swimming pool; some but not all will have kids clubs or dive operators.

➡ Most resorts have rates that include nonmotorised (snorkelling, windsurfing and sailing) sports; diving, parasailing, waterskiing, jet-skiing, fishing and island-hopping excursions usually cost extra.

➡ Resorts nearly always feature some kind of *bure* (bungalow) accommodation, often with a thatched roof and hints of traditional architecture.

Food & Drink

At luxury resorts you'll usually find a sumptuous mix of Western, Fijian, Indian, Asian and fusion specialities, perhaps spread over several restaurants. The bar will be stocked and a good wine selection will be available. Most of the bigger hotels put on a Fijian dance performance (*meke*), and a *lovo* – traditional banquet with food prepared in an underground oven – a few times a week. Breakfast will often be buffet; other meals might be à la carte with more simple options such as burgers and sandwiches available at lunch.

Midrange and budget resorts on the bigger islands will almost always have a bar (or at least available alcohol) and a restaurant with a menu including Western, Fijian and Indian fare. In remote settings these types of places often only serve set meals that are eaten with the other guests, either at individual tables or family-style at one big table. Upon booking or check-in, you'll usually be asked if you have any special food requirements. If you have any serious allergies or dietary restrictions, let your hosts know as far in advance as possible so they can get the proper supplies.

Most resorts, regardless of price, offer guests a 'welcome drink': don't get too excited, especially if you're not staying somewhere super-upmarket. This is usually orange juice or, if you're lucky, a coconut with a straw in it.

The Budget Experience

Many of Fiji's hostels and backpacker accommodation are more resort-like than the cheaper hotels, not in terms of luxury, but for the (usually) beachside location and the activities on offer. To make the choice between a budget hotel or backpacker resort you'll have to decide what's more important to you: a hot-water bathroom, privacy and TV, or socialising, cheap activities, beach bumming and (better usually) snorkelling.

Which Island?

Viti Levu

➡ Nadi, the country's revolving door, is particularly well represented, and backpacker haunts often have their own restaurants, bars, laundries, internet access and tour desks.

➡ While Nadi rocks out with arriving and leaving tourists you can get your groove on with the locals in Suva.

➡ There are some good budget options outside of the main cities, including Stoney Creek Resort near the airport, Uprising Beach Resort in Pacific Harbour and a cluster of excellent beachside digs on Nananu-i-Ra in the north.

Mamanuca Group

➡ Partiers head for Beachcomber Island – the 84-bed dorm seems less daunting after partaking in the resort's plentiful buffet meals, well-stocked bar and relentless nightly entertainment.

➡ Quieter nights can be found at South Sea Island, with room for 32 overnighters in the resort's dorm.

➡ Bounty Island offers a good balance between wild and mild, plus the dorms are (blissfully) air-conditioned.

Yasawa Group

➡ Many young travellers head up the Yasawa chain in search of the perfect beach, but be prepared for the possibility of being the only guest at smaller budget resorts.

➡ For partying, it's hard to do better than the hypersocial Coralview Resort on Tavewa Island.

➡ Low-key Waya Lailai Resort offers a wider range of land-based activities than many, while Mantaray Island Resort ups the ante with its facilities, food and in-shore reef.

➡ Naqalia Lodge is a great place to mingle with both backpackers and the local families that run the resort.

Ovalau & the Lomaiviti Group

➡ Ovalau has midrange and budget hotels, a B&B and a village stay.

➡ The resort-cum-backpacker-hangouts on the outer islands of Caqalai and Leleuvia are the crème de la crème of all-to-yourself budget paradise.

Vanua Levu

➡ Savusavu has some good locally run guesthouses/hostels on the fringes of town – during low season you may feel like the only backpacker in town. Gecko Lodge is one of the best.

➡ Rabi Island, off Vanua Levu's east coast, has basic budget rooms available for those wishing to experience a different – and very remote – side of Fiji.

Taveuni

➡ There are some fabulous, fun and friendly backpacker choices around Matei – Bibi's Hideaway is fantastic – and on the outer island of Qamea; Beverley Campground in Matei lets you sleep in tents or dorms right on the beach.

➡ Wonderful, quiet village guesthouses are found in Lavena and Vuna.

What to Expect

➡ In a well-run establishment you can expect fan-cooled dorms – and very rarely, air-conditioned – and doubles that are clean and functional with few frills.

➡ At older establishments, rooms can come in a hodgepodge of configurations, many of them hot and airless with poor toilet-to-guest ratios.

➡ Facilities are generally shared, with cold-water showers.

NON-RESORT ACCOMMODATION

Camping

There are few campgrounds in Fiji – those that exist usually offer dorms, basic cabins and tents. Some budget resorts do cater for those with a proclivity for canvas, but as campsites are only a few dollars cheaper than dormitories, the hassle of carrying a tent hardly seems worth it.

Nor should you camp without permission. Most of Fiji's land, even in seemingly remote, unoccupied areas, is owned by the local *mataqali* (extended family) group or village. Before pitching a tent, present your *sevusevu* (gift) of kava root to the chief and ask for permission. Chances are, you will be invited to stay with a family anyway and to refuse this invitation will likely be interpreted to mean you find their home beneath you.

Village Homestays

Some villages offer homestays as a way of earning a little extra cash. Not only is this an affordable way to travel, but you'll also gain a real insight into Fijian traditions and make a village-worth of friends in the process. Viseisei, Navala, Namatakula, Rabi, Waya and Silana all see a trickle of inquisitive travellers. On remote islands, like those in the Lau, Moala and Rotuma Groups, homestays and village guesthouses may be your only option.

Couchsurfing

Couchsurfing has exploded in popularity in Fiji, with almost 600 Fiji-based host members. Couchsurfers may enjoy free accommodation, but the real reward lies in the chance to meet locals, interact with their families and join in their daily activities. Visit www.couchsurfing.com to join up.

Holiday Rentals

Renting privately owned holiday homes, particularly for those travelling in groups or as a family, can be good value – rates range from $850 to $3000-plus – and ideal for those looking for a fixed base from which to take day trips. Pacific Harbour on Viti Levu, Savusavu on Vanua Levu and Taveuni have Fiji's highest concentration of rentals.

Some helpful websites:
➡ www.harcourts.com.fj
➡ www.flipkey.com
➡ www.airbnb.com

➡ Dedicated single rooms are few and far between, so you'll usually have to fork out for a double if you are a solo traveller wanting privacy.

➡ Few budget resorts include activities in the rates (although these are almost always on offer), though not all charge for the use of their snorkelling equipment.

➡ Many cheapies are run by families or village communities and can often offer a better view of local life than the more upscale resorts.

➡ Outside of the larger backpacker haunts, Sundays are extremely quiet affairs; don't expect too much from your host (or sometimes, even be able to find them!) on these days.

Food & Drink

Many hostels, backpackers and cheaper hotels, particularly on the main islands, have their own simple restaurants. Budget lodging in the outer islands, where there are no other eating options, usually offer a plan of two to three meals a day where you'll eat a set meal with the other guests. Some inexpensive accommodations have communal kitchens; check before you arrive to see if shops are nearby, or if you should bring your own supplies.

While the *mekes* and *lovos* of the higher-end resorts aren't common at budget places, guests will often have the chance to try kava with locals, either in staged ceremonies or proper down-and-dirty (literally; it tastes like dirt) drinking sessions.

Activities

Resorts, upscale boutique places and even hard-core budget lodges will usually have plenty of activities available for guests or will work with trusted independent operators.

Action Sports

Viti Levu offers tons of activities to get your blood pumping. There are jet-boat trips down the Nadi and Sigatoka rivers, jet ski safaris out to the Mamanucas, zip-lining just north of Nadi and at Pacific Harbour, and wild buggy rides through the forest near the Sabeto Mountains.

The resorts of the **Mamanuca and Yasawa Groups** often have their own water sports equipment and offerings: in addition to banana boating, parasailing and the like, some resorts offer flyboarding, an extreme sport that lets thrill seekers 'surf the sky' attached to a water jetpack.

On **Vanua Levu**, the Vosa Ni Ua Lodge offers kitesurfing (and other) adrenalin sports; kiting is also gaining popularity on **Taveuni**.

Outrigger canoe expeditions are popular on **Kadavu**.

Birdwatching

There are well over a hundred species of birds in the Fijian islands, with many that are endemic to only one island. **Taveuni** and **Kadavu** have easy access to the interior, and you won't have to go far to see some of the species, as many have no predators and aren't shy. The former houses the rare orange dove, the Fiji goshawk and red-throated lorikeet; on the latter, you can tick the indigenous Kadavu honeyeater, Kadavu fantail, velvet fruit dove and Kadavu musk parrot off your list.

On **Viti Levu**, the accessible Colo-i-Suva Forest Park (near Suva) and Kula Eco Park on the Coral Coast offer birders a chance to get nose-to-beak with rare and exotic birds without slogging into the forest.

On **Vanua Levu**, the Tunuloa Peninsula is home to the rare silktail. Fiji's rarest

bird, the kacau (petrel), as seen on the back of the $50 note, is only found on Gau in the **Lomaiviti Group**.

In urban areas throughout the country, you're likely to see the chunky collared lory (a common parrot) and the brilliant emerald, red-headed parrot finch. Aggressive introduced species, such as Indian mynahs, have forced many native birds into the forest, where you'll hear barking pigeons and giant forest honeyeaters. Some 23 tropical sea birds are also present in the country.

Guides are available throughout Fiji – ask at your place of lodging.

For practical planning tips, field reports and inspiration – or even to find a 'birding pal' – have a look at the following websites:

➡ www.fiji-bird-watching.com

➡ www.fatbirder.com

➡ www.birdingpal.org

Diving & Snorkelling

Fiji is a rightfully famous diving and snorkelling destination, with colourful reef and marine life in all shapes and sizes patrolling its warm, generally clear waters. Many resorts have dive centres; those that don't can usually organise dives for you. See the Diving chapter (p36) for more detailed information.

Snorkellers are well catered for via boat trips and excursions, but it's a good idea to bring your own gear since rental or offered equipment may be in poor shape.

Fishing

Villages have rights over the reefs and fishing in Fiji, so you cannot just drop a line anywhere: seek permission first. Many of the more expensive resorts offer game-fishing tours and boat chartering and tend to favour surface lures and deep and shallow jigging. Budget resorts can organise boats and tackle, although this may be just a simple handline with baited hooks and sinkers.

SPECIES	SEASON	BEST MONTH
barracuda	Oct-Mar	Feb
black marlin	Jul-Nov	Aug-Sep
blue marlin	Mar-Aug	Jul-Aug
dogtooth tuna	Jun-Oct	Jul
dolphinfish	year-round	Nov
giant trevally	Oct-Mar	Feb

Waya (p130), Yasawa Group

SPECIES	SEASON	BEST MONTH
sailfish	year-round	Jun-Sep
skipjack tuna	May-Aug	Jun
striped marlin	Jun-Aug	Jul
tanguige	Oct-Mar	Feb
wahoo	Jun-Sep	Jul-Aug
yellowfin tuna	May-Jul	Jun

Hiking

Arguably the best hiking in Fiji is found on **Taveuni**, where a huge section of the island has been designated a national park. Hardcore hikers can tramp up Des Voeux Peak (1195m) or to Lake Tagimaucia (823m); other hikes and ambles include the Vidawa Rainforest Trail and the Lavena Coastal Walk.

While the **Mamanuca and Yasawa Groups** are better known for their offshore activities, there are good hikes to be had on Waya, Wayasewa, Tavewa and Nacula islands.

Viti Levu, **Kadavu**, **Vanua Levu** and **Ovalau** also have fantastic hiking, but it's imperative to hire a guide as most trails pass through village lands and you will need permission (and the proper etiquette)

to go through them. For the main island, start your research – and book a guided hike – at www.talanoa-treks-fiji.com or www.exoticholidaysfiji.net.

Horse-Riding

The locals around Natadola Beach on **Viti Levu** make a living out of saddling-up day trippers, while horse-riding is also a common resort activity along the Coral Coast. Other opportunities crop up at Bulou's Eco Lodge in the Nausori Highlands.

Some of the more upmarket resorts on **Taveuni** and **Vanua Levu** can arrange horse-riding trips.

Kayaking

Many resorts around Fiji have kayaks for guest use; they're almost always free of charge. The **Mamanuca and Yasawa Groups**, **Vanua Levu**, **Nananu-i-Ra** and **Kadavu** are all great for kayaking. Some keen kayakers paddle **Taveuni**'s rugged Ravilevu Coast, but generally the western sides of the islands are preferred as they're sheltered from the southeast trade winds.

Special sea-kayaking tours are available during the drier months, between May and

November. Some combine paddling with hiking into rainforests, snorkelling, fishing and village visits. For the Yasawas, try www.southernseaventures.com or www.worldexpeditions.com; for Kadavu, look up www.tamarillo.co.nz.

Island Tours & Cruises

Depending on the island, minibuses, tour buses, private cars or 4WDs may be used to take you around to see the sights. The most visited islands also offer opportunities for day cruises to smaller offshore islands with deserted beaches of unimaginable beauty – plus you'll often get a picnic and go snorkelling.

Surfing

Most surf pitches over outer reefs and in passages, and is for intermediate to advanced surfers only. For these reefs you need boats and guides. Marine safety can be lax, so ask to have oars, life jackets and drinking water as well as a mobile phone on board. Southerly swells are consistent from May to October, but there is surf year-round. The trade winds are southeast and offshore at the famous breaks. Northerlies, from November to April, are offshore **Viti**

Levu on the Coral Coast. Nearby, Frigates in **Beqa Lagoon** can be reached from the surf camp on Yanuca island or the more upmarket Waidroka Surf & Dive Resort near Pacific Harbour. Windsurfing is great up north at **Nananu-i-Ra**.

Cloudbreak, Restaurants and Namotu Left are easily accessed from the Mamanuca islands of **Malolo**, **Malolo Lailai**, **Namotu** or **Tavarua** (the latter two are private surf resorts). They can be reached just as easily by boat from the resorts near Uciwai Landing on Viti Levu.

To get away from the crowds, head to **Qamea**, off Taveuni, for its fickle breaks, or to the **Kadavu Group** for the excellent King Kong Lefts.

Village Visits

Tours across the country usually include a village visit in the itinerary. Some villages have become influenced by busloads of tourists parading through their backyard, and the *sevusevu* (gift) ceremony and *meke* (a dance performance that enacts stories and legends) can seem somewhat contrived. Other village tours, especially those run by the villagers themselves, are smaller in scale with perhaps not so much

---

FIJIAN WEDDINGS & HONEYMOONS

Many resorts cater to the almost-wed and newlywed with irresistible honeymoon and wedding packages; they can provide much of the information and planning you need. The obvious place for romance is the Mamanuca Group, although you'll find a number of romantic, adult-only affairs scattered throughout the country.

You'll need to bring the required documentation (including birth certificates and a statutory declaration signed by a justice of the peace, notary public or solicitor to prove you are not married) to a registry office prior to your actual marriage in order to obtain a marriage licence. The **Registrar General's office** (Map p90; ☑331 5280; www.bdm.gov.fj; Ground fl, Suvavou House, Victoria Pde; ☺8.30am-3.30pm Mon-Fri) is in Suva, but there are also **Divisional Registrars** in **Lautoka** (Map p108; ☑666 5132; 1st fl, Rogorogo-i-Vuda House, Tavewa Ave; ☺9am-3pm Mon-Fri) and **Labasa** (☑881 2477; www.bdm.gov.fj; Namuka House; ☺9am-3pm Mon-Fri). There's a $22 fee and you have 28 days to then get hitched.

The following websites can help you plan the perfect Fijian wedding or honeymoon, if not organise it outright:
➡ www.fijibride.com.au
➡ www.fijidreamweddings.com
➡ www.fijihoneymoon.com
➡ www.southpacificweddings.com.au/fiji
➡ www.fijiweddings.com

going on; however, the experience can feel more genuine. Do your research carefully.

If you come across a village during a hike, don't just barge in: ask the first local you see for permission and take it from there.

Planning & Choosing

Independent Travel

Outside of high season (June through September and mid-December through mid-January) you could arrive just about anywhere in Fiji without any idea of where you're going or what you're doing and have an amazing trip. During the seasonal rush, however, the better places will be booked and flights may be full, so it's wise to plan in advance.

Package Tours

A package tour can work out to be a financial godsend, but it doesn't give much leeway to explore at will. Although most tours offer the opportunity to visit more than one island, you will have to prebook one hotel or resort for each destination before departure (meaning you can't swap resorts halfway through if you're not happy).

There are a variety of tour packages available from travel agents and online booking agencies in all Western countries. If you want more than a straightforward combo package, a good travel agent is essential – they can negotiate better prices at the larger hotels and handle the internal flight bookings. In addition to the traditional travel operators, there are agencies that specialise in diving tours. These packages typically include flights, accommodation and diving trips.

There are also many cruises that visit and travel throughout Fiji.

Where to Book a Package

Plenty of agents book packages to Fiji, but a good place to search and get a feel for pricing is on the websites of the airlines that service the region, including **Fiji Airways** (www.fijiairways.com), **Air New Zealand** (www.airnewzealand.co.nz), **Jetstar** (www.jetstar.com), **Qantas** (www.qantas.com.au) and **Virgin Australia** (www.virginaustralia.com).

Note that most packages quote double-occupancy pricing. Solo travellers have to pay a 'single-person supplement'. Extra people can usually share a room, but there's a charge for the extra bed, which varies enormously from resort to resort.

Useful Accommodation Websites

➡ www.fiji-backpacking.com

➡ www.fiji.travel/accommodation

➡ www.myfiji.com

➡ www.awesomefiji.com

➡ www.fiji4less.com

➡ www.fiji.pacific-resorts.com

➡ www.fiji-budget-vacations.com

➡ www.travelmaxia.com

➡ www.fijibeaches.com

Plan Your Trip
Diving

It's not for nothing that Fiji has a global reputation for divine diving: some of the country's most spectacular scenery lies just below the surface. Fiji's waters are warm, clear and absolutely teeming with life. All the things that divers' dreams are made of can be found here, from multicoloured fish, stealthy sharks, magnificent macros (miniature marine life), canyon-like terrain and vertigo-inducing walls festooned with exquisite soft and hard corals resembling flower gardens in full bloom.

Best for Beginner Divers

Fiji is a perfect spot for new divers, as the warm water in the shallow lagoons is a forgiving training environment. Just about anyone in good health, including children aged eight years and over, can learn to dive.

Breath Taker, Viti Levu (p105) Great pelagic action on an incoming tide.

Gotham City, Mamanuca Group (p124) Reef species galore.

Yellow Wall, Kadavu (p182) An atmospheric site resembling a fairy-tale castle.

Lekima's Ledge, Yasawa Group (p127) A coral-studded underwater cliff.

Best for Experienced Divers

Great White Wall, Taveuni (p167) Possibly the best soft-coral dive in Fiji.

Beqa Lagoon, Viti Levu (p83) Bull and tiger sharks galore – a once-in-a-lifetime experience.

Nasonisoni Passage, Vanua Levu (p154) Exhilarating drift dive through a narrow passage.

E6, Lomaiviti Group (p139) A phenomenal seamount that brushes the ocean's surface.

Diving Conditions

Although Fiji is diveable year-round, the best season is from April to October. November to March tends to see the most rainfall, which can obscure visibility off the main islands with river run-off.

Keep in mind that many dives are subject to currents, which can vary from barely perceptible to powerful. Visibility varies, too, from a low of 10m at certain sites up to 40m at others. Water temperatures range from 23°C in August to 29°C in January. You probably won't need anything more than a thin neoprene or a 3mm wetsuit to remain comfortable while diving.

Top Dive Sites

Fiji is often dubbed the 'soft corals capital of the world', but there's more to its reputation for fantastic diving than that. You will also find majestic reefs ablaze with Technicolor critters, spectacular underwater topography, shark dives and thrilling drift dives. Fiji's only weak point is the dearth of impressive wrecks.

Viti Levu

The best diving is found off Nananu-i-Ra island to the north, although Viti Levu's most noteworthy dive site is undoubtedly Shark Reef in Beqa Lagoon, where divers can witness a phenomenal shark-feeding session.

Beqa Lagoon, Pacific Harbour (p83) Go nose-to-nose with massive bull and tiger sharks. Divers should also check out Caesar's Rocks, Side Streets and ET, which features a vast tunnel more than 30m long, densely blanketed with sea fans and soft corals.

Rakiraki reefs (p104) and **Nananu-i-Ra** (p106) This area has a good balance of scenic seascapes and elaborate reef structures, with easy access to the Bligh Passage. Dream Maker and Breath Taker are famous for their dense concentrations of colourful tropicals and good-quality corals. To the northwest, off Charybdis Reef, Spud Dome is renowned for its dramatic scenery while Heartbreak Ridge offers a chance of spotting pelagics.

Mamanuca Group

Due in part to its proximity to Nadi and Lautoka on Viti Levu, the Mamanucas are very popular with divers. Trips depart the mainland daily or you can base yourself at any of the island resorts; diving infrastructure is well-established throughout the region. Most dive sites are scattered along the Malolo Barrier Reef or off the nearby islets. Diving is probably less spectacular than in the more remote areas of Fiji, but it's still rewarding, with diverse marine life, good visibility and a varied topography, as well as a glut of easy sites that will appeal to novice divers.

Plantation Pinnacles Near Malolo Lailai, this site is notable for its three deep-water rock towers.

Sherwood Forest (p115) Near Tokoriki; home to beautiful gorgonian sea fans.

Gotham City, Malolo Barrier Reef (p124) Located inside the barrier-reef lagoon, the site comprises several coral heads surrounded by a smorgasbord of reef fish in less than 20m.

Salamanda (p115) The wreck of a 36m vessel sunk as an artificial reef near Treasure Island rests upright on a rubble seafloor at around 20m; it's partly encrusted with soft corals and anemones.

LIVE-ABOARDS

A handful of live-aboards ply the Fiji waters, usually with weeklong itineraries. These trips are recommended for those looking to experience uncrowded dive sites beyond the reach of land-based dive operations, especially the sites in Bligh Passage and off the Lomaiviti Group. Some also stop off at extremely remote islands, giving you a rare chance to explore very traditional villages. Give any of these operators a go:

Tui Tai Expeditions (p155)

Nai'a (☑345 0382; www.naia.com.fj; from $7500)

Siren Fleet (www.sirenfleet.com; from $6800)

Yasawa Group

The Yasawas are less crowded, with fewer dive boats and day trips. This chain of ancient volcanic islands offers excellent corals, pristine reefs and good visibility.

Lekima's Ledge (p127) A stunning underwater cliff off Vawa island, suitable for novice divers.

Maze (p127) Fun swim-throughs and tunnels off Nacula Island.

Passage between Nanuya Balavu and Drawaqa (p131) Frequented by giant manta rays. Although the use of scuba equipment is prohibited, this is an amazing snorkelling experience.

Lomaiviti Group & Bligh Passage

Central Fiji roughly covers the area between the country's two main landmasses – it extends from Bligh Passage in the west to Namenalala and the Lomaiviti Group in the east. Most sites in this 'golden triangle' can only be accessed by live-aboards and so remain largely untouched.

E6, Vatu-i-Ra Channel (p139) E6 is consistently rated as one of the best sites in Fiji. This seamount rises from 1000m to the surface and acts as a magnet for pelagics. A huge swim-through in the seamount, called the Cathedral, has a magical atmosphere.

Top: Diving, Namena
Marine Reserve (p154)

Bottom: View of Cloud
9 (p123), Malolo,
Mamanuca Group

MATTEO COLOMBO/GETTY IMAGES ©

Nigali Passage (p139) Also known as Shark Alley, this narrow channel off Gau island is home to an almost ever-present squadron of grey sharks as well as schooling trevally, barracuda, snapper and the occasional ray.

Chimneys (p162) At Namenalala Reef, off the southeastern coast of Vanua Levu; has several towering coral pillars, all coated with soft corals, sea fans and crinoids.

Blue Ridge, off Wakaya (p139) Notable for its abundance of bright-blue ribbon eels.

Vanua Levu

Arguably the best diving in Fiji – and certainly the best around Vanua Levu – is found at Namena Marine Park, a 70 sq km reserve with mindblowing corals and underwater life; it's about two hours from Savusavu. Closer to land, the island's top sites are in and around Savusavu Bay. The underwater scenery is striking, the walls are precipitous and the fish population (which includes pelagics) is diverse.

Nasonisoni Passage, Namena Marine Park (p154) A rip-roaring drift dive in a narrow, current-swept channel. During tidal exchange, divers are sucked into the passage and propelled through the funnel by the forceful current.

Dreamhouse, Namena Marine Park (p154) A small seamount that seems to attract a wealth of pelagics, including grey reef sharks, jacks and tuna.

Taveuni

The Somosomo Strait, a narrow stretch of ocean that is funnelled between Taveuni and Vanua Levu, has achieved cult status in the diving community, and for good reason: it houses some of the most spectacular soft-coral dive sites in the world. The only downside is that average visibility does not exceed 15m to 20m, and when the plankton blooms (January and February), it is further reduced.

Rainbow Reef (p167) Strong tidal currents push the deep water back and forth through the passage, providing nutrients for the soft corals and sea fans that form a vivid tapestry.

Purple Wall (p167) An impressive wall with a dense layer of purple soft-coral trees, whip corals and sea fans. Numerous overhangs and arches harbour soldierfish and squirrelfish.

> ### DIVING & FLYING
>
> Most divers get to Fiji by plane. While it's fine to dive soon *after* flying, it's important to remember that your last dive should be completed at least 12 hours (though many experts advise 24 hours) *before* your flight, to minimise the risk of residual nitrogen in the blood causing decompression. Careful attention to flight times, as compared with diving times, is necessary in Fiji because so much of the interisland transport is by air.

Great White Wall (p167) This is one of Fiji's signature drift dives, with a phenomenal concentration of white soft coral resembling a snow-covered ski slope when the current is running.

Annie's Bommies (p167) An explosion of colour, with several big boulders liberally draped with soft corals and surrounded by swirling basslets.

There are also superb dive sites around neighbouring Matagi, Qamea and Laucala islands and at Motualevu Atoll, some 30km east of Taveuni.

Kadavu

Kadavu's main claim to fame is the Great Astrolabe Reef, the world's fourth-largest barrier reef. Hugging the south and east coasts of the island for about 100km, it's home to a vibrant assemblage of hard- and soft-coral formations and breathtaking walls. Unlike Taveuni, currents are probably easier to handle in this area, but be prepared for rough seas and reduced visibility when it's raining or when the winds blow, especially from November to April.

Western side of the Great Astrolabe (p183) Recommended dive sites include Broken Stone, Split Rock and Vouwa. They more or less share the same characteristics, with scenic underwater seascapes of twisting canyons, tunnels, caverns and arches.

Naiqoro Passage (p183) Just off the east coast of Kadavu, this narrow channel is frequently swept by strong tidal currents and offers rewarding drift dives along steep walls.

Northwestern side of Kadavu (p182) This area is a bit overshadowed by the Great Astrolabe Reef, but novice divers will feel comfortable here. Mellow Reef, Yellow Wall and *Pacific Voyager,* a

PLAN YOUR TRIP DIVING

SHARK-FEEDING

A few kilometres off the Viti Levu coast near Pacific Harbour lies Shark Reef. In other parts of the world, shark-feeding usually involves grey reef sharks and, if you're lucky, lemon sharks and nurse sharks. Here, up to eight different types of shark turn up: tawny nurse sharks, white-tip, black-tip and grey reef sharks, sicklefin lemon sharks, silvertips, massive bull sharks (except from October to January, when they leave the spot to mate) and the heavyweight of them all – tiger sharks!

During the dives, divers form a line behind a purpose-built small coral wall. The feeder dips into a huge bin and pulls out hunks of dead fish. For several minutes, it may be hard to work out what is happening in the swirl of tails and fins as one shark after another materialises, ripping and tearing at the bait. It's definitely intense, but there's no frenzy to speak of. The sharks approach in surprisingly orderly fashion, even the ponderous-looking bull sharks. If the arena suddenly clears, brace yourself: a 4m-long tiger shark is about to appear.

While it's certainly thrilling, this is more a show than a dive, and fish-feeding is a controversial subject. On one hand, these artificial encounters undeniably disrupt natural behaviour patterns: sharks may grow dependent on 'free lunches' and can unlearn vital survival skills. On the other hand, some experts believe these displays have educational virtue, raising awareness among divers and helping sharks gain some much-needed positive press. We'll let you decide.

63m-long tanker that was intentionally sunk in 30m of water in 1994, are the best dives.

Responsible Diving

The Fiji islands are ecologically vulnerable. By following these guidelines while diving, you can help preserve the ecology and beauty of the reefs:

➡ Encourage dive operators to establish permanent moorings at appropriate dive sites.

➡ Practise and maintain proper buoyancy control.

➡ Avoid touching living marine organisms with your body and equipment.

➡ Take great care in underwater caves, as your air bubbles can damage fragile organisms.

➡ Minimise your disturbance of marine animals.

➡ Never stand on corals, even if they look solid and robust.

Dive Centres

There are at least 30 professional dive centres in Fiji. All of them are affiliated with one or more internationally recognised certifying agencies, usually PADI or Scuba Schools International (SSI). In general, you can expect well-maintained equipment, good facilities and knowledgeable staff, but standards may vary from one centre to another. Dive centres are open year-round, most of them every day, and offer a whole range of services, such as introductory dives, night dives, exploratory dives and certification programs. Many are attached to a resort and typically offer two-tank dive trips.

The country has only one recompression chamber, in Suva.

Costs

Diving in Fiji is rather good value, especially if you compare it to other South Pacific destinations. If you plan to do many dives on one island, multidive packages are usually much cheaper. Some sample prices:

Introductory dive: about $200

Two-tank dive: between $230 and $350, including equipment rental

Open-water certification course: between $800 and $975

Plan Your Trip
Travel with Children

Fiji is a kids' own adventure story writ large. The swimming is spectacular, the fish are friendly, there are caves and jungles to explore, and there are enough mangroves and mud pools to satisfy every get-grubby urge. And the Fijians – who famously adore children – have smiles and hugs for every little visitor.

Fiji for Kids

The unofficial adage of Fiji seems to be: children should be seen, heard, smooched and squeezed at every given opportunity. Children are cherished here, and local littlies seem unfamiliar with the concept of shyness: your kids will be quickly absorbed into their games and welcomed into their homes.

Not all resorts accept children in Fiji. Many that do have kids clubs (usually for children from 3 or 4 to 12 years) and child-friendly pools. Nannies and babysitting for babies and toddlers is easily arranged from about $7 per hour, or overnight at a fixed rate.

Food & Drink

Most eateries have kid-pleasing items such as hamburgers and pasta dishes on the menu, but it's worth encouraging them to try local specialities like fish in coconut milk, root vegetable 'chips', roti wraps or a mild dhal. Ice cream – often homemade – is frequently available, and in addition to the usual favourites, often comes in exotic local flavours.

Some restaurants in cities, touristed regions and well-equipped resorts have high chairs, but they're quite uncommon elsewhere. Travel high chairs make a good

Best Regions for Kids

Nadi, Suva & Viti Levu
Kids can run amok on the Coral Coast, exploring dunes, rivers, villages and a hill fort; good luck getting them to bed after a stimulating evening cultural show. Pacific Harbour has adventure sports, highland tours from nearby Navua and offshore island trips. Just north of Nadi, the mud pools, buggy tours and zipline are thrilling for all ages.

Mamanuca & Yasawa Groups
Safe swimming, awesome snorkelling and some of the most family-friendly resorts in the world, plus boat rides galore: what's not to love?

Vanua Levu & Taveuni
Fiji's wild islands offer jungle adventures, waterfall pools, village visits and raft rides. There are great resorts here, or you can rent your own rainforest bungalow. Jumping between days at Taveuni's International Dateline marker is a strangely thrilling buzz.

Kadavu, Lau & Moala Groups
Snorkel with manta rays, watch the kids catch their first big fish and wonder how you'll ever tear them away from their new village pals.

investment if you don't want someone squirming on your (doubtless splattered) knee at mealtimes.

Supermarkets aren't always that super when it comes to kids' food: if you've got a fussy eater, pack a few backup tins or pouches of their favourite meals. Long-life milk is readily available, as is bottled water and fruit juice. If you're not sure whether your formula brand is sold in Fiji, make room in the suitcase for a tin or two. While breastfeeding is common, you'll seldom see it: you'll probably want to follow locals' example and be discreet.

Splash Out

Babies and toddlers will be delirious with delight on most of Fiji's beaches. The sands are soft, the waters warm, and there are plenty of fish, hermit crabs and shells to play with and goggle at. Older kids wishing to explore the colourful world beneath the tranquil seas can go snorkelling or take their first underwater breaths on a Bubble-maker course (from age eight); good swimmers aged 10 and up can enrol in a Junior Open Water Diver course – see www.padi.com for information. Most resorts offer kayaks and stand-up paddleboards free of charge; many have superfun sea trampolines. Banana boat and jet-boat rides offer squeals and hilarity by the bucketload.

Land Lubbers

Contrary to popular belief, Fiji is not just a neverending series of stunning beaches; its tropical interiors are adventures unto themselves, with waterfalls, tangled jun-gle, natural waterslides and muddy trails, not to mention the brilliantly bumpy 4WD trips that are a requirement to get almost anywhere inland. Children will have fun looking out for spectacular native birds (including brightly coloured parrots), while critter-keen kids can spy on sleeping fruit bats, native lizards and snakes (there are no venomous land snakes in Fiji). Village visits often end with declarations of love and 'best friends forever!' between visiting kids and their local counterparts. Whatever your beliefs, Sunday church services provide enough fascinating, goosebumpy moments to hold the interest of even the squirmiest scallywag.

Children's Highlights
Swimming

Blue Lagoon (p135) Rightfully famous for its calm, sparkling waters.

Treasure Island (p119) Lightly sloping beaches, perfect for toddlers.

Kadavu (p182) The protected west side holds patches of perfect sandy-bottom lagoon.

Leleuvia (p148) Wade into shallow swimming straight from the beach.

Tavoro Waterfalls (p177) The first falls (there are three) have a superb natural pool.

Underwater Fun

Yasawa Group (p125) Plentiful corals, sea turtles and friendly (really!) sharks.

Mana (p120) Easy snorkelling from the beach; lots of colourful fish.

Caqalai (p148) Older kids who can get in the water over some reef will be awestruck by the amount of life here.

Kadavu (p182), and **Nanuya Balavu** and **Drawaqa** (p131) Snorkel with manta rays!

South Sea Island (p118) Check out sharks, starfish and other sea-dwellers in a semi-submersible.

Sandy Stretches

Long Beach, Nacula (p135) A sublime stretch, aptly named for its sandy length.

BEST RESORTS FOR KIDS
- **Castaway Island Resort** (p123)
- **Plantation Island Resort** (p125)
- **Treasure Island Resort** (p120)
- **Jean-Michel Cousteau Fiji Islands Resort** (p157)
- **Outrigger Fiji Beach Resort** (p79)
- **Hideaway Resort** (p81)
- **Leleuvia Island Resort** (p148)
- **Paradise Cove Resort** (p132)

PLANNING

Some hotels and resorts have no-children policies (especially under 12s); others let kids stay for free – always ask when booking. Some tours and activities are discounted for kids.

Nappies, wipes, formula, sterilising solution and baby food are available in pharmacies and supermarkets in the main cities and towns, but if you are travelling to remote areas or islands, take your own supplies. Top tip: pack nappies in 'space bags'; you'll never fit anything else in your suitcase otherwise!

Infant/child pain relievers and teething gels are hard to come by; bring your own. If your baby uses a dummy (pacifier), bring plenty, as well as a clip-on strap.

Check with your child's doctor about pretrip shots, especially if you're going to be spending time in remote areas. Some GPs recommend hep A and typhoid jabs (the latter is unsuitable for kids under two years old).

What to Pack

All ages need sunscreen, sunhat, insect repellent, warmer clothes for evenings and rain gear.

For babies and toddlers, consider packing a folding stroller (though a baby carrier is a better option if you plan on hiking or staying at a resort with terraced or sandy paths), a portable changing mat (baby-changing facilities are almost nonexistent) and inflatable 'floaties'.

For older kids you may want to pack binoculars, a snorkelling mask and field guides to Fijian flora and fauna.

Transport & Safety

Large-chain car-rental companies and some private drivers can provide baby seats (if arranged in advance), but local companies and taxis don't. Local buses have bench seating, no seat belts and can be fairly cramped; babies and small children will be expected to sit on your lap.

Many small boats don't carry enough life jackets and rarely have child-size ones; if you're using these to island-hop, consider bringing your own.

Octopus Resort, Waya (p130) Wide stretch of wonderful beach with never-want-to-leave charm.

Resort islands around Ovalau (p139) All of the resorts on outlying islands of the Lomaiviti Group are encircled by low-key, kid-friendly white beaches.

Lavena Beach (p176) A stunning strip framed by forest; its neighbouring black-sand beach is cool too.

Cultural Shows & Museums

Robinson Crusoe Island (p73) Everything from a 'cannibal attack' on arrival to hermit-crab racing and traditional performances at night.

Arts Village, Pacific Harbour (p82) Disneylike take on a Fijian village with performances including mock battles and dance.

Fiji Museum (p88) & **Thurston Gardens** Lots of big, eye-catching displays and a massive garden to run around.

Denarau (p65) The child-friendly resorts here have regular cultural shows and entertainment.

Village Visits & Homestays

Navala village (p111) Be welcomed into the traditional lifestyle of one of Fiji's most scenic villages.

Silana Ecolodge, Ovalau (p147) If you don't mind roughing it, you'll have a ball with the huge, friendly family here.

Waya (p130) There are heaps of homestay options on this beautiful, rugged island in the Yasawas.

Viseisei village (p70) Fiji's first settlement is easily accessible from Nadi; there are loads of kids to play with.

Plantation Island Resort (p125), Malolo Lailai, Mamanuca Group

Ocean Sports

Nananu-i-Ra (p106) Kiteboarding and windsurfing.

Natadola Beach (p72) Good for bodysurfing.

Natadola Inside Break (p72) Best bet for beginner surfers.

Inland Sports

Ziplining Near Pacific Harbour (p84) and Nadi (p69).

Jet-boating (p77) Down the Sigatoka River.

Rafting White-water or low-key *bilibili* (bamboo raft) thrills on the Navua River (p84) or around the Namosi Highlands (p86).

Trail-riding (p74) On the Coral Coast.

Buggy-riding (p58) Through the forests near Nadi.

Critter Encounters

Kula Eco Park (p78) Meet sea turtles, parrots and flying foxes.

Treasure Island (p119) Turtle- and iguana-feeding.

Mana (p120) Monthly 'Environment Day' with coral planting.

Kadavu (p182) Manta rays.

Takalana Bay (p103) Dolphinspotting.

Jungle Explorers

Navua River (p84) Inland villages, hiking and river activities.

Colo-i-Suva Forest Park (p91) Walking trails, swimming holes (one with a rope swing) and great birdlife.

Waitavala Water Slide (p171) Older kids love this natural slippery dip in the middle of the rainforest.

Lovoni (p146) Jungle village trek to an extinct crater.

Bouma National Heritage Park (p177) Seaside walks, steep treks and waterfall pools just begging to be splashed in.

Regions at a Glance

Nadi, Suva & Viti Levu

Adventure
Culture
Highlands

Exhilarating Escapades

Hike through tangled forest at Mt Koroyanitu, scramble up the Sigatoka sand dunes, partake in muddy mayhem near the Sabeto Mountains or dive with huge sharks at Beqa Lagoon.

Multicultural Mingling

The 'Big Island' is a melting pot of indigenous Fijian and Indo-Fijian cultures: take part in a *meke* (traditional dance performance) and a *lovo* (feast cooked in a pit oven) one night, and watch fire-walking while sweating over a curry the next. Experience traditional life with a village homestay.

Highland Life

The inland landscapes of the Nausori and Namosi Highlands sharply contrast with the coastal zone. High mountainous roads, tall forests, raftable rivers and remote villages make for a great self-drive adventure.

p52

Mamanuca & Yasawa Groups

Beaches
Activities
Wildlife

Beach-Bumming

If sprawling on white sands is your idea of a perfect holiday, head to the Yasawas: the sugar-soft beaches practically glow. Choose between long stretches framed by looming palms, small sheltered coves and secluded swimming bays.

Water Sports

Get off your towel and plunge into the splashy sports of the Mamanucas. If it's in or on the water – and gets your heart racing – it's on offer here. Choose between high-octane jet-skiing, paragliding, flyboarding and surfing, or delve deeper on snorkelling and diving trips.

Fabulous Fauna

Seasonal manta rays and whales add to the year-round attraction of resident armies of fish, sharks and dolphins. The islands themselves are home to native iguanas and soaring seabirds. Endangered turtles breed on several islands in the region.

p113

Ovalau & the Lomaiviti Group

Snorkelling
Hiking
Architecture

Dauntless Dips

Snake Island, off Caqalai, isn't for the faint-hearted: in addition to strong currents and a rough entry through a minefield of corals, expect to see the banded sea snakes that give the island its name. The payoff is a wonderland of soft corals, schools of fish and giant Napoleon wrasses.

Jungle Treks

Tramp through thick rainforest, splash through rivers and cool off in waterfalls en route to the Lovoni crater, home to a proud village.

Heritage Hamlet

World Heritage–listed colonial architecture makes Levuka one of the South Pacific's most picturesque towns. Marvel at weatherworn churches and shopfronts that look like something out of a John Wayne film.

p138

Vanua Levu & Taveuni

Diving
Hiking
Surfing

Rainbow Reef

The Somosomo Strait houses the Rainbow Reef, famous worldwide for its soft corals. Dive the Purple Wall, covered in violet coral trees, or the ethereal White Wall, where, in the right current, snowy corals open to feed on plentiful plankton.

Rainforest Rambles

Taveuni is dominated by the lush Bouma National Heritage Park, home to some of Fiji's best hiking. Other top treks include the strenuous scramble up Des Voeux Peak, where you can look for the rare *tagimaucia*, Fiji's emblem flower.

Clean Breaks

Qamea island, off Taveuni, offers a few fickle, but little-known, breaks. When they're working, expect clean, fun rides and no crowds.

p150

Kadavu, Lau & Moala Groups

Diving
Snorkelling
Walking

Endless Reef

The Great Astrolabe Reef is the world's fourth-largest barrier reef. It holds a tremendous stretch of impressive dive sites; many are yet to be discovered. Kadavu's west side holds other reef networks that are arguably as lovely and are better protected from trade winds.

Meet the Mantas

You don't have to dive to see one of the ocean's most spectacular species: manta rays. Off the Great Astrolabe Reef near Ono island, snorkellers are almost guaranteed the life-altering experience of swimming with these graceful creatures.

Assorted Ambles

Most resorts have walking trails leading to villages, waterfalls and prime birdwatching spots.

p180

TOM COCKREM/GETTY IMAGES ©

Celebrate Fiji

Fijians are a famously hospitable people, with personalities as sunny as the islands they live on, and few visitors escape without being befriended by at least some of the hotel staff. For those who dig a little deeper, a land rich with traditional etiquette and a fascinating history awaits. Blend this with the colourful Indo-Fijian culture, the influence of neighbouring South Pacific nations and a Christian inheritance courtesy of Western missionaries and it's easy to see why Fiji has such a rich cultural cocktail.

➡ Meeting the Locals
➡ Festivals & Arts

Local children, Vanua Levu (p151)

Meeting the Locals

Village life today is a far cry from the days of cannibalism and ritualised warfare, and it's ironic that the islands that were once feared by early sailors are now revered by today's travellers. To meet some of these friendly locals, ditch the poolside lounger and head to a local favourite.

Hindu Temples

For a gaudy slice of India in Melanesia, visit one of the country's many Hindu temples. Nadi's Sri Siva Subramaniya Swami Temple (p56) is a particularly fine example of traditional Dravidian architecture.

Sunday Church

Throughout Fiji, Sunday church services are filled with beautiful songs and skilfully harmonised vocals. Our favourite? The hymns sung by the congregation at Taveuni's Wairiki Catholic Mission (p171).

Rugby

Rugby is an integral part of the *vaka i taukei* (Fijian way of life; p211) and every village has a team. To enjoy a game, bring a loud, barracking voice and join the scrum of supporters on the sidelines of a village rugby field.

Suva Nightlife

Spending a night on the dance floors of Suva (p88) is not only fun but it may force you to re-evaluate your thoughts about Fijian youth and Fiji's cultural landscape.

The Market

Most markets are simple, open-air affairs where villagers gather to sell produce, swap stories and share jokes. Suva's Municipal Market (p91) is one of the biggest in the South Pacific and the perfect place to buy a *sevusevu (gift)* or sample local delicacies such as *bila* (fermented cassava).

1. Sri Siva Subramaniya Swami Temple (p56), Nadi, Viti Levu 2. Island church, Tokoriki (p122), Mamanuca Group 3. Rugby team, Suva (p88), Viti Levu 4. Suva Municipal Market (p91), Viti Levu

Lovo (pit oven) used for cooking meals (p213)

Festivals & Arts

Meke & Lovo

Many resorts have weekly *meke* (p215; a performance that enacts ancient lore) nights which include meals cooked in a *lovo* (pit oven) and traditional song-and-dance performances.

Indo-Fijian Fire-Walking

To witness the incredible commitment exhibited by Hindi devotees as they pierce their bodies with metal skewers and walk over hot embers, attend Suva's South Indian Fire-Walking Festival (p95).

Hibiscus Festival

Fiji's largest festival (p95) draws crowds that converge on Suva's Albert Park to partake of the stalls, carnival rides and free entertainment.

Fiji Museum

Fiji's traditional arts are best appreciated at the Fiji Museum (p88), with its treasure-trove of war clubs, cannibal utensils and chiefly ornaments.

On the Road

Nadi, Suva & Viti Levu

Best Places to Eat

➡ Taste Fiji (p63)

➡ Eco Café (p82)

➡ Governors (p98)

➡ Beach Bar & Grill (p80)

➡ Nadina Authentic Fijian
Restaurant (p68)

Best Places to Stay

➡ Stony Creek Resort (p69)

➡ Grand Pacific Hotel (p97)

➡ Safari Lodge (p107)

➡ Outrigger Fiji Beach
Resort (p79)

➡ Bamboo (p61)

Why Go?

Everyone passes through Viti Levu, Fiji's largest island, on their trip to the country, but too often it's looked at as just home to an international airport, an unavoidable transit stop for those en route to a palm-fringed resort. But those who skip the island too quickly are missing out, as there are plenty of attractions to make you linger longer.

Away from the gateway hub of Nadi, the southern Coral Coast offers a lively mix of resorts aimed at families and backpackers alike, and a host of adventure sports including scuba diving with massive tiger sharks.

While sultry Suva, the South Pacific's largest city, has a rich cultural heritage to explore, northern Viti Levu's best attractions are on the water, from the dolphin-spotting and kite-surfer paradise of Nananu-i-Ra, to the coral reefs of the Bligh Passage. Tie this in with visits to traditional villages and breathtaking waterfalls, and you will find that Viti Levu is easily the centrepiece of any Fijian trip.

When to Go
Suva

Dec–Mar Trips upriver to the Namosi Highlands can be wetter than planned.

May–Oct Roads to the scenic Nausori Highlands are most accessible in the dry season.

Year-round The Coral Coast offers activities for all seasons.

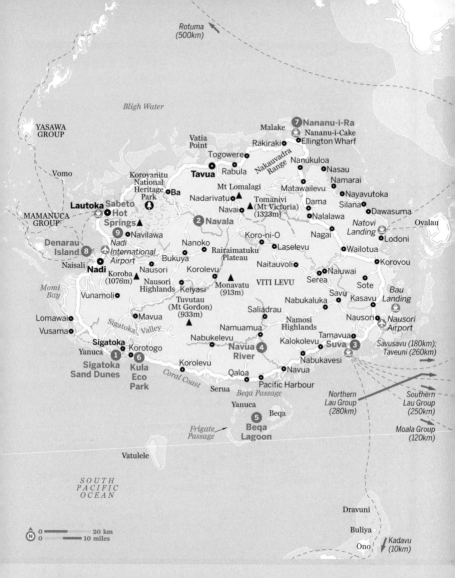

Nadi, Suva & Viti Levu Highlights

1 Sliding over the **Sigatoka Sand Dunes** (p75) on the lookout for ancient burial relics.

2 Heading into the highlands to **Navala** (p111), Fiji's sole remaining traditional *bure* (wood-and-straw hut) village.

3 Getting to grips with traditional culture on display at the Fiji Museum in **Suva** (p88).

4 Kayaking the mighty **Navua River** (p86) in the rugged Namosi Highlands.

5 Diving with resident tiger sharks in **Beqa Lagoon** (p83).

6 Watching parrots and stroking iguanas at the **Kula Eco Park** (p78).

7 Windsurfing and snorkelling on the island's best reefs at **Nananu-i-Ra** (p106).

8 Getting spoiled in serene surrounds at a **Denarau Island resort** (p57).

9 Slipping, slopping and laughing yourself silly in the wonderfully gloopy **Sabeto Hot Springs** (p69) mudpit.

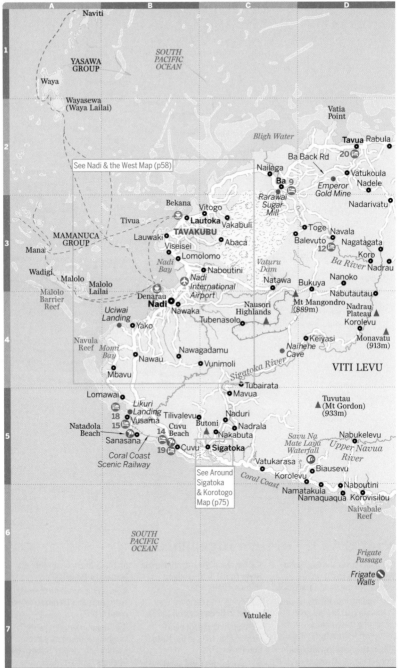

See Nadi & the West Map (p58)

See Around Sigatoka & Korotogo Map (p75)

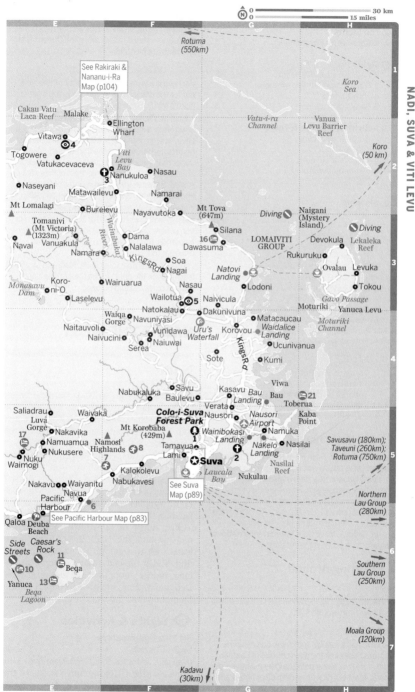

0 ———————— 30 km
0 ———————— 15 miles

Rotuma (550km)

Koro Sea

See Rakiraki & Nananu-i-Ra Map (p104)

Cakau Vatu Laca Reef   Malake

Vitawa ⦿4
Togowere
Vatukacevaceva
Ellington Wharf
Vatu-i-ra Channel
Vanua Levu Barrier Reef

Koro (50 km)

Viti Levu Bay
Naseyani
Nanukuloa ⚓3
Nasau

Matawailevu
Namarai

Mt Lomalagi ▲
Burelevu
Nayavutoka
Mt Tova (647m)
Diving 🤿
Naigani (Mystery Island)
Diving 🤿

Tomanivi (Mt Victoria) (1323m) ▲
Navai   Vanuakula
Dama
Nalalawa
Silana
16⦿
Dawasuma
LOMAIVITI GROUP
Devokula
Lekaleka Reef

Namara
Soa
Nagai
Natovi Landing
Rukuruku
Ovalau
Levuka

Koro-ni-O
Monasavu Dam
Laselevu
Wairuarua
Nasau
Wailotua ⦿5
Naivicula
Dakunivuna
Lodoni
Tokou
Gavo Passage
Moturiki   Yanuca Levu

Natokalau
Uru's Waterfall
Korovou
Matacaucau
Waidalice Landing
Moturiki Channel

Waiqa Gorge
Naitauvoli
Navuniyasi
Vunidawa
Naiuwai
Serea

Ucunivanua

Sote
Kumi

Kings Rd

Nabukaluka
Savu
Baulevu
Kasavu
Viwa
Bau Landing
Bau
Toberua 21

Saliadrau
Waivaka
Verata
Nausori
Colo-i-Suva Forest Park
Nausori Airport
Namuka
Kaba Point

Luva Gorge
17
Nakavika
Namuamua
Mt Korobaba (429m) ▲
Namosi Highlands 8
Tamavua
1 Wainibokasi Landing
Nakelo Landing
Nasilai

Savusavu (180km); Taveuni (260km); Rotuma (750km)

Nukusere
7
Lami
2

Waimogi
Nuku
Kalokolevu
Nabukavesi
⭐ **Suva**
Laucala Bay
Nukulau
Nasilai Reef

Nakavu
Waiyanitu
Navua
6
See Suva Map (p89)

Northern Lau Group (280km)

Pacific Harbour
Qaloa   Deuba Beach
See Pacific Harbour Map (p83)

Side Streets
Caesar's Rock
11
10
Beqa
13
Yanuca
Beqa Lagoon

Southern Lau Group (250km)

Moala Group (120km)

Kadavu (30km)

Viti Levu

❶ Getting There & Away

Most travellers arrive in Fiji at **Nadi International Airport** (Map p60; www.airportsfiji.com/nadi_airport.php; Queens Rd). Nadi is also a main domestic transport hub. From here there are flights to many of the other larger islands as well as reliable boat services and cruises. A more limited number of international flights – as well as domestic flights – leave from **Nausori International Airport** (Map p54) on the outskirts of Suva.

❶ Getting Around

AIR
There are regular light-plane flights between Nadi and Suva from around $180.

BUS
Viti Levu has a regular and cheap bus network. Express buses link the main centres of Lautoka, Nadi and Suva, along both the Queens and Kings Roads. Most will pick up or drop off at hotels and resorts along these highways. Slower local buses also operate throughout the island and even remote inland villages have regular (though less frequent) services. Minibuses and carriers (small trucks) also shuttle locals along the Queens Road and taxis are plentiful.

CAR & MOTORCYCLE
Viti Levu is easy to explore by car or motorcycle, but for the unsealed highland roads you'll generally need a 4WD.

Nadi and Suva are linked by the sealed Queens Road along the 221km southern perimeter of Viti Levu, which contains a scattering of villages and resorts and is known as the Coral Coast. Many minor roads lead off this road to isolated coastal areas and into the highlands; most of these are unsealed. Between the wetter months of November and April, some roads can become impassable.

Heading north from Suva, the Kings Road is mostly sealed and travels for 265km through Nausori (where Suva's airport is located), the eastern highlands, Rakiraki and Ba on the north coast, and on to Lautoka.

Three roads (beginning at Ba, Nadi and Sigatoka) lead up from the coast to the Nausori Highland villages of Navala and Bukuya.

NADI & THE WEST

Nadi

POP 42,285

Most travellers go to Nadi (*nan*-di) twice, whether they like it or not: its indecently warm air slaps you in the face when you first step from the plane, and kicks you up the backside as you board for home.

For some, this is twice too often and many people ensure their Nadi exposure is as brief as possible: this ramshackle town doesn't offer much, though it's a good place to stock up on supplies, plan trips and make use of facilities that may be lacking elsewhere.

Just north of downtown, between the mosque and the Nadi River, Narewa Rd leads west to Denarau island, where you'll find Nadi's top-end resorts. There's also a busy tourist shopping and eating area at Denarau Marina, where boats depart for the Mamanuca and Yasawa Groups.

◉ Sights & Activities

Sri Siva Subramaniya
Swami Temple   HINDU
(Map p62; admission $3.50; ⊗5.30am-7pm) This riotously bright Hindu temple is one of the few places outside India where you can

see traditional Dravidian architecture; the wooden carvings of deities travelled here from India, as did the artists who dressed the temple in its colourful coat and impressive ceiling frescos. Dress modestly and remove your shoes at the entrance; photos are okay in the grounds, but not the temple. The inner sanctum is reserved for devotees bringing offerings. The on-site temple custodian can help you make sense of it all.

Skydive Fiji SKYDIVING

(☏992 4079, 672 8166; www.skydivefiji.com.fj; jumps $495-735) Scream at some of the world's most beautiful scenery with a tandem jump (from 8000ft to 14000ft) on to Denarau Island; jumps over islands in the Mamanucas can also be arranged.

☞ Tours

Nadi is a good base to explore the west side of Viti Levu: it's possible to visit Koroyanitu National Heritage Park, Nausori Highlands and Namosi Highlands near Pacific Harbour. Most out-of-town tour companies will pick up and drop off in Nadi.

The Mamanuca and Yasawa island chains are the most popular day trips out of the Nadi area. Boats depart from Port Denarau several times daily and offer free hotel transfers. Organised trips to Robinson Crusoe Island just south of Nadi are also an easy, fun day excursion.

Stinger Bicycle Tours BICYCLE TOUR

(☏992 2301; www.stingerbikes.com; ◷8am-6pm) This local outfit runs a huge variety of scenic mountain biking tours, taking in villages, mountains, forests and 'Nanders' itself. The website has a full list of set trips; rides can also be tailored to suit skills and stamina. Speedfreaks should try the Cannibal Downhill ride, a blistering 500m descent from the top of the Nausori Highlands.

VITI LEVU FOR KIDS

Fiji's main island has plenty to offer families with little tackers in tow. If you're staying in the Nadi area, try a day cruise to one of the Mamanuca (p114) or Yasawa (p125) islands or the ever-popular Robinson Crusoe Island (p73). The Big Bula Inflatable Waterpark (p66) on Denarau Island is guaranteed to please. North of town, kids aged four and up can whiz through the rainforest on the Sleeping Giant Zipline (p69), while the nearby Sabeto Hot Springs (p69) is a squishy, squelchy mudfest (don't fret, parents: there are pools to clean off in). Kids also love grubby buggy rides through the forest with Westside Motorbike Tours (p58).

The Coral Coast is home to a number of attractions that will appeal to kids. A day on the Coral Coast Scenic Railway (p74) is a fun way to gain an appreciation of Fiji's landscape; nearby, the Kalevu Cultural Centre (p74) showcases Fijian singing, dancing and ceremonies. A little more kitsch are the demonstrations, boat tours and mock battles at the Arts Village (p82) in Pacific Harbour. You could also take the kids horse riding at Natadola Beach (p72) or show them Fiji's less-domesticated wildlife at the excellent Kula Eco Park (p78). Hot Glass Fiji (p78) lets kids aged seven and up blow their own glass souvenirs. If your little one is an adrenaline hound, give the jet boats of Sigatoka River Safari (p77) a go.

Suva's Fiji Museum (p99) is chock-full of exhibits (including cannibal utensils) that will capture inquisitive young minds; their monthly open day (last Saturday of the month) has live music, traditional dancing, fire-walking and more. Nananu-i-Ra (p106) is a short hop from the mainland's north coast and offers calm (and very fishy) seas for child-friendly swimming and snorkelling, plus self-catering accommodation. On the east coast, Dolphin Watch Fiji (p103) trips enjoy daily spottings of spinner dolphins.

Many resorts, especially at Denarau, have abundant activities to occupy children. Some kid-friendly resorts include the following:

➡ Shangri-La's Fijian Resort (p74)

➡ Hideaway Resort (p81)

➡ Sonaisali Island Resort (p71)

➡ Radisson Blu Resort Fiji (p67)

➡ Outrigger Fiji Beach Resort (p79)

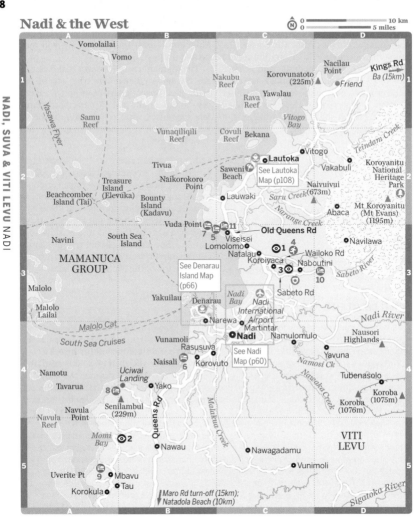

Map of Nadi & the West region showing Viti Levu, the Mamanuca Group, and surrounding areas including Lautoka, Nadi, Denarau, and various islands.

Individual bike hire ($50 to $80 per day) is also available; they'll deliver to wherever you're staying.

Westside Motorbike Tours
ADVENTURE TOUR
(☎672 6402; www.motorbikerentalsfiji.com) Leave your Sunday best behind for these grandly grubby rides through the nearby Sabeto valley. The aptly named Go Dirty tour zooms through the bush on a 1100CC, four-seater buggy, while the Go Trek trip makes use of bouncy 500CC quad bikes. It's brilliant fun any time of year, but it's best in the wet. From $269 per person.

Fiji Surf Company
SURFING
(Map p62; ☎992 8411; www.fijisurfco.com; Crown Investment Bldg, cnr Main St & Hospital Rd) Local surf legend Ian Muller and his team of local surf guides run both hardcore and family-friendly half-day surf tours (from $160) as well as private surf charters and five-night surf holidays. The surf school (one/two/three/four people per person $270/230/200/180) is endorsed by Surfing Australia. The shop sells, repairs, makes and rents boards ($40 to $70 per day) and paddle boards ($100 per day).

★☆ Festivals & Events

Nadi's Hindu festivals, such as Karthingai Puja (monthly), Panguni Uthiram Thirunaal (in April) and Thai Pusam (in January), attract worshippers from around the world. Devotees circle Sri Siva Subramaniya Swami Temple, offering bananas, smashing coconuts, burning camphor and receiving the priest's blessing. Nadi also hosts the Bula Festival each July, a week-long celebration of the Fijian spirit with rides, stalls galore and the crowning of 'Miss Bula'.

⌱ Sleeping

Regardless of what the websites or brochures promise, there are no appealing beaches in the Nadi area. That said, the resorts located at the grey-sand New Town and Wailoaloa beaches are fairly isolated and peaceful. Martintar is placed (conveniently and noisily) on the main bus route; walk a few metres down its side roads and you'll quickly get a sense of local life. Many of Nadi's midrange and top-end hotels are located along the Queens Road between downtown Nadi and the airport. Rates vary, depending on season and availability; there are likely to be sizeable discounts on rates quoted here for walk-ins or phone-a-day-ahead bookings.

Apartments are a good idea for families or those staying longer: check out **Hibiscus Apartments** (Map p60; ☑672 8009; www.hibiscusapartmentsfiji.com; Enamanu Road, Martinar; apt $195-235; ℗✳🖥) and **Rosie's Deluxe Apartments** (Map p64; ☑672 2755; fitres@rosie.com.fj; Queens Rd, Martintar; apt $110-184; ✳🖥). There are megaresorts on Denarau Island (p65).

⌱ Along the Queens Road

Rabosea Bed & Breakfast　　　　B&B $
(Map p64; ☑946 7857; www.raboseafiji.com; 2 Jalil's Drive, Martintar; shared/private bathroom $80/140; ℗✳🖥) This splendid, central B&B is a fantastic budget alternative to Nadi's hostels. With only three bedrooms, a communal kitchen and a comfy lounge, a stop here feels like a homestay, thanks in large to the amiable Fijian/German owners, who can whip your trip plans into shape, rent you a bicycle, or take you for a visit to their nearby 120-hectare farm.

Nadi Bay Resort Hotel　　　　RESORT $
(Map p64; ☑672 3599; www.fijinadibayhotel.com; Wailoaloa Rd, Martintar; dm $39-44, s/d without bathroom from $80/95, s/d with bathroom & air-con $130/180, apt from $220; ✳@✳) One of Nadi's best-equipped budget resorts, this sociable spot serves up a jovial mixed bag of package-tour guests and backpackers. The two **restaurants** (mains $8 to $35) and bars are outstanding, the rooms are comfortable and clean, and there's even a free mini movie theatre, games room and library. The day spa offers traditional Fijian treatments starting at $35.

Dulcinea Hotel Oasis　　　　APARTMENT $
(Map p64; ☑672 2044; www.dulcineahoteloasis.com; Ragg St, Martintar; s/d/tr $85/95/110; ℗✳🖥✳🖐) Formerly the Sandalwood Lodge, this is an oldie but a goodie. The complex has a retro-Fiji feel, and while the colourful apartments aren't for those after a 'resort' experience, they're wonderful for families and self-caterers: kids love the rambling grounds and cute pool. Kitchenettes are well-equipped; stock up at the huge supermarket a five-minute walk away.

Tanoa Skylodge　　　　LODGE $
(Map p60; ☑672 2200; www.tanoaskylodge.com; Queens Rd, Namaka; dm $35, r $85-140; ✳🖥✳🖐) Nestled amid 1.6 hectares of gardens with loads of facilities, this is a fine choice for families, budget travellers and businessfolk. For

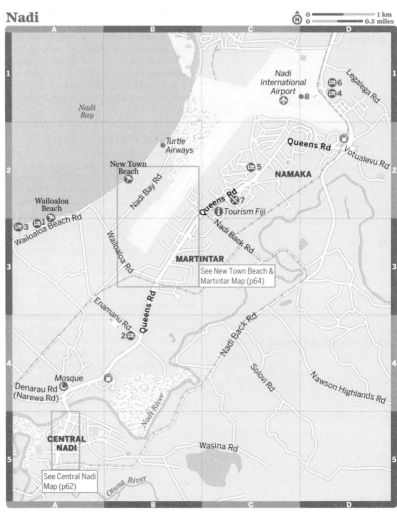

the little ones, there's an indoor soccer and basketball court, games room, kids' pool and on-site hair braider; grown-ups can recover at the CU cocktail bar. Rooms are spotless and sunny; family rooms have extra space and well-equipped kitchenettes.

Tokatoka Resort Hotel
RESORT **$$**

(Map p60; ☑672 0222; www.warwickhotels.com/tokatoka-resort; Queens Rd, Namaka; r $120-300; P❄@🛜🏊👪) This sprawling, low-rise resort is a 'village' of villas in varying sizes. The designer pool and waterslide are loads of fun (though safety-conscious parents will give the rickety playground a wide

berth). It's a popular stop for families flying in or out of Nadi, as it's right across from the airport (free transfers). Other facilities include a good **restaurant** (mains $18 to $55) and wheelchair-accessible rooms.

Raffles Gateway Hotel
RESORT **$$**

(Map p60; ☑672 2444; www.rafflesgateway.com; Queens Rd, Namaka; r $105-165, ste $320; P❄🛜🏊👪) Directly opposite the airport, Raffles is a sound choice behind its ostentatious entrance. A Nadi favourite since 1969 and recently refurbished, the cheaper rooms are small but serviceable; superior rooms offer more space, facilities and private patios.

Nadi

Kids love Raffles for their two pools, waterslide and tennis court; those under 16 stay free. There's a pool bar and two restaurants; one casual (mains $10 to $35) and one more upmarket (mains $15 to $50).

🛏 New Town Beach & Wailoaloa Beach

A haul from downtown and the main road, New Town Beach offers budget travellers a cluster of backpacker resorts amid a smattering of wealthy residential properties. It's a peaceful area with great views of the Sabeto Mountains across the water. Most New Town places are within five minutes' walk of each other, on the beachfront of Wasawasa Rd or just off it.

★ Bamboo
HOSTEL $

(Map p64; ☑672 2225; www.bambootravellers. com; 33 New Town Beach; dm $15-25, r with fan $60-75, with air-con $85-95, Bamboo Tropic r $80-120; ❋🐾⬛) Cheap and chilled, Bamboo is a wonderful old-school backpackers. A destination unto itself with a dedicated band of repeat visitors, Bamboo isn't fancy, but it is friendly and loads of fun. As well as breakfast, a variety of beach/sport/cultural activities and kava sessions come free. The more upmarket Bamboo Tropic – a beachfront mansion – is 100m from the hostel.

Smugglers Cove Beach Resort & Hotel
RESORT $

(Map p64; ☑672 6578; www.smugglersbeach fiji.com; Wasawasa Rd; dm $38-48, r $185-385; ❋🐾⬛) Fun, well-run and with major buzz, this is one of Nadi's most popular choices. Though it offers family rooms, it's geared towards young budget travellers looking for a social spot with facilities and activities galore: parties and programs (kava sessions, knife throwing, fire dancing) rock on through the night, while non-motorised water sports and golf gear come free for those functioning in the daytime.

The cheaper dormitory is fairly cramped, with 34 bunk beds divided into cubicles of four. The smaller, brighter dorms (including one women-only) are more expensive but offer better value and more privacy.

Aquarius on the Beach
RESORT $

(Map p64; ☑672 6000; www.aquariusfiji.com; 17 Wasawasa Rd; dm $35-45, d $145-160; ❋🐾⬛) Set in a former luxury home, the Aquarius swims with warm party vibes. There's a lively restaurant (mains $8 to $28) and, for those who overdo it on the nightly cocktail specials, the refreshing pool and beach hammocks are but a stagger away. The 12-bed dorm gets cramped: cough up a bit extra for a two-, four- or six-bedder. All rooms have attached bathrooms.

Oasis Palms Hotel
BOUTIQUE HOTEL $$

(Map p60; ☑777 7337; www.oasispalmshotel. com; Wailoaloa Beach Rd; dm $42, bungalow $168, r $183-365; ❋🐾⬛) Spanking new and utterly sparkling, this is a welcome addition to Nadi's by-the-beach options. Dorms are airy and slick, while polished bungalows and upmarket rooms have balconies and mountain views. It's a short walk to the beach, but dragging yourself from the two pools, hot tub and superb Japanese restaurant Mamasake (mains $13 to $32; try the ridiculously moreish 'Mama's Balls') takes supreme willpower.

Deals are available for longer stays, or those going on to the hotel's sister resorts in the Yasawas, Octopus, Paradise Cove or Blue Lagoon.

Club Fiji Resort
RESORT $$

(Map p60; ☑672 0150; www.clubfiji-resort.com; Wailoaloa Beach Rd; apt $174, bungalow $210-330; ❋🐾⬛) This smiley spot is less frenzied than some other budget beach options but has enough buzz to keep things interesting. Scattered among native gardens, the tidy *bures* (wood-and-straw huts) all have private verandahs. There's a great selection of daily activities; it also runs tours, including game fishing and surfing. The great restaurant (mains $15 to $50) changes menus throughout the week, with Fijian, Teppanyaki, Mongolian barbecue and Mexican theme nights.

Central Nadi

◉ 0 ▬▬▬▬ 100 m
0 ▬▬▬▬ 0.05 miles

Central Nadi

◉ Sights
1 Sri Siva Subramaniya Swami
  Temple A4

◈ Activities, Courses & Tours
2 Fiji Surf Company A3

⌷ Sleeping
3 Nadi Downtown Hotel A4

✕ Eating
4 Corner Café A2
5 Mama's Pizza B1
6 Market B3
7 Tata's B4
8 The Food Hub A1

◔ Drinking & Nightlife
9 New Nadi Farmer's Club A1

◉ Shopping
10 Handicraft market A3

ℹ Transport
11 Awesome Adventures Fiji B1

Good-quality meat is not so easy to come by (self-catering carnivores, gird yourself for frozen sausages). There are several large supermarkets and bakeries downtown and in Martintar: look out for RB Patel, New World and MH supermarkets.

✕ Central Nadi

★ Tata's
INDIAN $
(Map p62; Nadi Back Rd; mains $5-10; ◷8am-8pm Mon-Sat) This rough-looking joint just down from the temple dishes up some of the most authentic and flavoursome curries on Viti Levu: just ask the droves of locals crowding the open-air deck. There's a menu, but for the best experience, let the friendly staff pick for you (though the 'Uncivilised Chicken' curry is worth seeking out).

The Food Hub
FUSION $
(Map p62; 101 Sagayam Rd; mains $2-15; ◷9am-5pm; ✱) This little place, tucked behind the main street, dishes up top-notch Indian curries and thalis (plus Fijian and international dishes) at ludicrously low prices. It also specialises in freshly made exotic juices and lassis. This is a place to eat well and do good: the venture was set up to provide funds for medical charities and provide training to local students.

⌷ Central Nadi

Nadi Downtown Hotel
HOTEL $
(Map p62; ☎670 0600; www.fijidowntown hotel.com; Main St, Nadi Town; dm $15, r $105-135; P✱⌗) The name doesn't lie: this place is as downtown as it gets in Nadi, with bars, eateries, the handicraft market and the Hindu temple all within skipping distance. Though recently renovated, it's not flash, but for cheap and central, it can't be beaten. Free breakfast and airport transfers.

✕ Eating

Most Nadi eateries serve a mixture of traditional Fijian, Indian, Chinese and Western dishes, and there are lots of cheap lunchtime places downtown. The restaurants at most resorts welcome nonguests. Nadi has a large **produce market** (Map p62; Hospital Rd), which sells fresh fruit and vegetables.

Bulaccino and
Hemisphere Wine Bar
CAFE $$

(Map p60; ☏672 8638; www.bulaccino.com; Queens Rd, Namaka; mains $8-30; ☺7am-8pm Tue-Sun, to 3pm Mon; ⚹❄🛜) Rightfully famous for its coffee, this Western-style hangout is also gaining renown for its gigantic sandwiches, tasty mains and scrummy cakes: its Lazy Gourmet selection of heat-at-home meals is a superb option for self-caterers. The open-air bar out the back is cool, leafy and has a decent wine and tapas menu.

Mama's Pizza
PIZZA $$

(Map p62; ☏670 0221; Main St; pizzas $10-28; ☺lunch & dinner; ⚹) In Fiji, the word 'pizza' often seems open for interpretation. Not so at Mama's: these prodigious pies could hold their own anywhere in the world. Absolutely loaded with toppings ranging from the traditional to the gourmet, these whoppers are good to the last chomp, with a thick, crunchy American-style crust. There's an equally awesome branch at Port Denarau.

Corner Café
INTERNATIONAL $$

(Map p62; ☏670 3131; Jacks Mall, Sagayam Rd; mains $12-32; ☺8am-5pm; ⚹🛜) Tucked away behind Jack's Handicrafts, the cavernous Corner offers a cool escape from the hot main street. The menu is eclectic, but doesn't suffer from it: big portions and tickled tastebuds are guaranteed whether you choose from Indian, Chinese, Thai, Italian, Fijian or American-style offerings (though it's hard to go past the goat curry).

✗ Martintar

Small Plates
CHINESE $

(Map p64; Queens Rd; dishes from $7; ☺dinner; 🅿) Think Chinese tapas and you've got the measure of this low-key bar/restaurant set in a garden off the main road: you'll know it by the blinking fairy lights. Casual and cool, this one's for those who love to linger: service is as laid-back as Fiji itself, and those not in a rush will enjoy working up an appetite over a cold beer.

★ Taste Fiji
FUSION $$

(Map p64; ☏672 5034; www.tastefiji.com; Lot 1 Cawa Rd; mains $15-25, breakfast $12-22; ☺6.30am-6pm Mon-Thu, to 10pm Fri, to 5pm Sat, 7am-2pm Sun; ⚹❄🛜) Stylish, professionally run and with a cosmopolitan menu featuring stand-out dishes created from local produce, this fabulous restaurant is

not just 'good for Nadi' – it's GOOD. Egg-centric breakfasts are hearty and delicious, and the mains – including the utterly divine caramelised Vuda pork belly – are simple yet sophisticated. The strong coffees and sweets are dangerously addictive. Gluten-free options galore.

Tu's Place
FUSION $$

(Map p64; ☏672 2110; www.tusplace.webs.com; 37 Queens Rd; mains $14-28; ☺7am-10.30pm) Come hungry: the chefs at this popular spot aren't shy when it comes to portion control. Though they do Western-style breakfasts and some tasty Thai meals, the focus here is on Fijian cuisine, especially seafood: this is a great place to try *kokoda* (raw fish marinated in lemon juice and served in coconut milk). Try to squeeze in some *vakalavalava* (baked cassava pudding) for dessert.

Sitar
INDIAN $$

(Map p64; ☏672 7722; cnr Queens Rd & Wailoaloa Rd; mains $10-30; ☺11am-11pm) With a menu boasting flavoursome, flaming hot dishes from India, Fiji and Thailand, Sitar is a standout restaurant, even in a curry-mad town like Nadi. All the universal favourites are on the menu, or give goat or local seafood dishes a try. Good value banquets are available, as is a wide selection of vegetarian options. It's noisy, but in a fun way.

Daikoku
JAPANESE $$$

(Map p64; ☏670 3622; www.daikokufiji.com; cnr Queens Rd & Northern Press Rd; mains $22-55; ☺noon-2pm & 6pm-9.30pm Mon-Sat; 🅿⚹🛜) Tableside chefs slice, dice, flip and serve delicious teppanyaki upstairs at this popular restaurant. Cosier, off-the-menu dining is available downstairs. Its lunchtime specials ($17.50) change daily. Dinner reservations are recommended.

🍷 Drinking & Nightlife

Most of Nadi's beach hostels have sociable watering holes, and are open to nonguests. All of the flashy Denarau resorts have equally swish bars.

Ed's Bar
PUB

(Map p64; ☏672 4650; Lot 51, Queens Rd, Martintar; ☺5pm-late) It doesn't look like much, but this is one of Nadi's best drinking spots. Cheap beer, friendly crew, pool tables and the occasional live band draw locals and visiting social animals. Tables outside fill by early evening.

New Town Beach & Martintar

Nadi Bay

New Town Beach   Wasawasa Rd

Nadi International Airport

MARTINTAR

New Nadi Farmer's Club   BAR
(Map p62; www.nadifarmersclub.com; Ashram Rd;
⊘10am-late Mon-Sat) The cool, inviting beer
garden at this riverside bar/restaurant is a
top spot for a relaxing ale (or a decent feed).
The staff is incredibly attentive, and the atmosphere is such that any ideas of 'just the
one' go immediately out the window. And
why leave? Fire dancing kicks off at 7pm
(Thursday to Saturday), followed by live local
bands (Wednesday to Saturday).

Ice Bar   CLUB
(Map p64; Queens Rd, Martintar; ⊘2pm-5am)
Upstairs at the Jetpoint shopping complex,
Ice Bar is Nadi's most happening nightclub.
Things can get a little crazy (ahem, im-
promptu pole dancing), but staff pride themselves on making sure punters stay safe:
they'll even shuttle you back to your digs at
stumps. For a pre-club puff, hit the **Tantra
Hookah Lounge** (Map p64; www.tantralounge.
com.fj; Jetpoint Complex, Queens Rd, Martinar; ⊘4-
11pm) within the same complex.

🛍 Shopping

Nadi's Main St is largely devoted to souvenir and duty-free shops, but many items are
mass-produced: much of it isn't even particularly Fijian, just vaguely tribal. Your best
bet for locally produced souvenirs include
printed designs on *masi* (bark cloth), *tanoa*
(kava drinking bowls), cannibal forks, war
clubs and wood-turned bowls. The **Handicraft Market** (Map p62; cnr Main St & Koroivolu
Ave; ⊘daily) is your best bet.

ℹ Information

EMERGENCY
Ambulance (☑911)
Fire (☑911)
Police (☑917, 670 0222; Koroivolu Ave)

MEDICAL SERVICES
DSM Centre (Map p62; ☑670 0240; www.
dsmcentrefiji.com; 2 Lodhia St; ⊘8.30am-
4.30pm Mon-Fri, to 1pm Sat) Specialises in travel
medicine; also has radiology and gynaecology
departments.

MONEY
At the airport arrivals concourse there is an ANZ
bank (open for all international flights) with an ATM
just after you exit customs. There's also an ATM in
the domestic terminal. There are ATMs and banks
all over town.

POST
Post Office There are post offices in Nadi's
downtown (Map p62; www.postfiji.com.fj; Sahu
Khan Rd), at Nadi International Airport and at
Port Denarau.

TOURIST INFORMATION
Tourism Fiji (Map p60; ☑672 2433; www.fiji.
travel; Suite 107, Colonial Plaza, Namaka; ⊘8am-

4.30pm Mon-Thu, to 4pm Fri) Crazily, there's no official visitor centre in Nadi (though most hotels have a tours and information desk). Tourism Fiji is more geared towards online info and marketing, but drop in if you're desperate.

TRAVEL AGENCIES & TOUR OPERATORS

Arrivals at Nadi Airport will find scores of operators located on the ground floor. Some well-regarded agencies include:

ATS Pacific (Map p60; ☑672 2811; www.ats pacific.com.fj; Nadi airport concourse) Arranges inbound accommodation, tours and itineraries.

Rosie Holidays (Map p60; ☑672 2755; www. rosiefiji.com; Nadi airport concourse) The largest and best-resourced agency in Fiji. Rosie Holidays manages the tour desks at many resorts and organises trips, treks and transport. It's the agent for Thrifty Car Rental.

Tourist Transport Fiji (Map p60; ☑672 2268; www.touristtransportfiji.com; Nadi airport concourse) This company operates the twice-daily Coral Sun Express Nadi–Suva bus services, and the Feejee Experience hop-on-hop-off transfers and package tours. It also runs the **Great Sights Fiji** (☑672 3311; www.touristtransportfiji.com/ great-sights-fiji; Nadi airport concourse) small-group tours to Viti Levu's interior.

WEBSITES

Lonely Planet (www.lonelyplanet.com/fiji/ viti-levu/nadi)

Tourism Fiji (www.fiji.travel)

ⓘ Getting There & Around

TO/FROM THE AIRPORT

Nadi International Airport is 9km north of downtown Nadi. There are frequent local buses stopping just outside the airport that travel along the Queens Road to town ($0.90). A taxi is about $15: be sure you get your driver to turn on the meter. Most hotels have free transfer vehicles awaiting international flights.

Roadworks affecting the route to and from the airport were underway during research, and weren't expected to be completed any time soon. Allow for delays if catching a flight.

Though Suva is Fiji's capital, all international flights arrive in and depart from Nadi. For a full list of airlines servicing Nadi, see www.airportsfiji. com/international_airline.php.

BOAT

Most boat companies, including Captain Cook Cruises (p116), **Awesome Adventures Fiji** (☑675 0499; www.awesomefiji.com; Port Denarau Marina) and South Sea Cruises (p116), provide free transfers between Nadi hotels and Port Denarau for clients using their island-based boats.

BUS

Local buses depart regularly from New Town Beach for downtown Nadi, stopping all along Queens Road ($0.70, 15 minutes, Monday to Saturday, less frequently on Sunday). **West Bus Transport** (☑675 0777) runs buses regularly from Monday to Saturday (fewer on Sunday) from Nadi bus station and outside Jack's Handicrafts to Denarau island. The first is at 8.30am and the last at 5pm ($1, 20 minutes).

Along the Queen's Road, there are frequent buses from Nadi to Lautoka (30 to 45 minute), Suva (four hours), Pacific Harbour (three hours) and Coral Coast (90 minutes), including all major resorts en route; non-express buses can be caught at stops along the way. The less-developed King's Road runs along the northern coast. Unless otherwise stated, the routes below run on the Queen's Highway.

Coral Sun Express (☑672 3311; www.tourist transportfiji.com) Runs comfortable, air-conditioned coaches between Nadi and Suva ($20, twice daily), plus resorts on the way, including those at Coral Coast ($15) and Pacific Harbour ($18).

Feejee Experience (☑672 5950; www.feejee experience.com) Offers hop-on-hop-off coach transfers (from $458) from Nadi to destinations all over Viti Levu.

Pacific Transport (☑330 4366; www.pacific transport.com.fj) Nine buses run daily to Suva ($15, five hours express or six hours regular) via the Coral Coast ($7.20) and Pacific Harbour ($11). It's $3.50 to Lautoka.

Sunbeam Transport (☑927 2121; www.sun beamfiji.com) Eight daily buses run along the Queen's Road from Nadi to the Coral Coast ($7.75) and Pacific Harbour ($11.60) resorts en route to Suva ($15.70). Frequent services run to Lautoka ($3). Services along the King's Road include Rakiraki ($11.50, 90 minutes) and Suva ($21, six hours).

TAXI

A taxi costs $7, $10 or $15 to the Queens Road junction, downtown or the airport. Insist they turn on the meter.

There are tons of companies offering private drivers for transfers and trips, including the recommended **Fiji Chauffeurs and Transfers** (www.fijichauffeursandtransfers.webs.com).

Denarau Island

This small island (2.55 sq km) is laden with fancy resorts manicured to perfection with heavenly pools and designer suites. Although it's only 6km west of Nadi town, the disparity couldn't be starker: staying here offers little insight into everyday Fijian life. But to splash

Denarau Island

some cash, get spoiled and avoid Nadi, then Denarau is the place to go. Be warned – what the resorts don't advertise is that Denarau is built on reclaimed mangrove mudflats; most of the beach has dark-grey sand and murky water unsuitable for snorkelling.

Yachties are welcome at the busy **Denarau Marina** (☑675 0600; VHF Marine channel 14; www.denaraumarina.com), where moorings are $20 per day, and berths cost from $2.75 per 10m per day. Catamarans and ferries depart to and from here for the offshore islands.

◎ Sights & Activities

All Denarau resorts have kids clubs and also provide varied programs of (mostly free) daily activities for all ages.

Denarau Marina is home to loads of tour and charter desks, most of which – unsurprisingly – proffer day trips and activities in the Mamanuca and Yasawa island groups. One of the most popular is a half-day excursion to South Sea Island, 30 minutes from the marina.

Many tour companies – some based as far away as the Namosi Highlands – will organise pick-up and drop-off from the resorts: ask at your tour desk.

Big Bula Inflatable Waterpark   WATER PARK
(☑776 5049; www.bigbulawaterpark.com.fj; adults/kids/family of 4 $65/55/220; ☺10am-5pm) This year-round waterpark is tons of fun for the kids (or the slightly built adult: weight limit 85kg), with bright, cartoonish inflatable waterslides, jumping castles and obstacle courses. There's also a less full-on gated play area for the very young, and a small cafe for grown-ups needing to match the kids' energy via caffeine. Get there and back on the Bula Bus.

Flavours of Fiji   COOKING COURSE
(☑675 0840; www.flavoursoffiji.com; Lot 5, Denarau Industrial Area; adult/child $150/100;

⊙11am-2pm Mon-Sat) This school holds three-hour *kaiviti magiti* (local feast) classes, teaching guests how to create Fijian and Indian dishes, plus tropical desserts. Menus change with the seasons. Kids aged eight to 16 are welcome to join in. Catch the yellow bus to the Denarau security checkpoint then take the first left; the school is at the end of the cul-de-sac with a lime green door.

Denarau Golf & Racquet Club   GOLF, TENNIS
(☑675 9710; sg_gl2@tappoo.com.fj; ⊙7am-sunset) This club has an immaculate 18-hole golf course with bunkers shaped like sea creatures. Green fees are $130/85 for 18/nine holes (club hire $65/45) and the tennis court is $20 per hour. The breezy bar and cafe overlooks the course.

Adrenalin Fiji   WATER SPORTS
(☑675 0061; www.adrenalinfiji.com; Port Denarau Marina; ⊙8am-8pm) Adrenalin runs the watersports shops at all Denarau resorts and Port Denarau Retail Centre. It specialises in jet-ski safaris ($538/$575 solo/tandem) to select Mamanuca islands and Cloud 9, plus parasailing, game fishing, waterskiing and more. It can also tailor kids' activities based on age (from two years).

☞ Tours

Fiji's Finest Tours   TOUR
(☑675 0046; www.fijisfinesttours.com; Port Denarau Retail Centre; ⊙8am-8pm) This outfit runs zillions of day trips and activities from its base at Denarau, including Sigatoka river safaris and inland cultural jaunts, and can organise water-based trips as well.

Island Hoppers   SCENIC FLIGHTS
(☑672 0410; www.helicopters.com.fj; Port Denarau) For scenic helicopter flights over the Mamanuca islands and Mt Koroyanitu. Ten, 20- and 35-minute flights cost $275, $425 and $540 per person.

⌂ Sleeping

The rates at all of these resorts vary drastically with season and occupancy. They're *very* popular with families during the Australian and New Zealand school holidays. Rooms are tasteful and of a high standard; magnificent pools go a long way towards making up for the lack of good beach.

Hilton Fiji Beach Resort & Spa   RESORT $$$
(☑675 6800; www.hiltonfijibeachresort.com; r from $615; [P❄☎⊠👪]) Seven immaculate pools, a stylish layout and private access to Denarau's best beachfront make this one of the island's most easy-on-the-eye resorts. Rooms and villas (which come with fully equipped kitchens and private barbecue areas) are spacious and modern, many with superb ocean views. The kids club is free for guests aged three to 12; kids up to 10 also eat free.

Radisson Blu Resort Fiji   RESORT $$$
(☑675 6677; www.radissonblu.com/resort-fiji; r from $540; [P❄☎⊠👪]) The Radisson gets top marks from little travellers for its sandy-edged lagoon pools, whitewater tunnel slide and squeal-inducing activities including fish feeding and the nightly torch-lighting run; grown-ups dig the hot tub, day spa, adults-only pool and swim-up bar. And who doesn't love free kayaks, windsurfers and catamarans? There are four good restaurants; the new **Chantra Thai** (mains $32 to $42) gets rave reviews.

Sofitel Fiji Resort & Spa   RESORT $$$
(☑675 1111; www.sofitel.com; r from $550; [P❄☎⊠👪]) Though the adults-only Waitui wing and pool was under construction at the time of research, and the magnificent restaurant **Salt** (mains $36 to $69) does breakfast sans-kids, this resort is beloved by children and their fleeing-reality parents. Family rooms have bunk beds and Playstations, a waterslide splashes down into a free-form pool, and littlies can serve themselves from the kids' height Lagoon buffet.

The Terraces Apartments   APARTMENT $$$
(☑675 0557; www.theterraces.com.fj; 1-/2-/3-bedroom apt $495/655/790; [P❄☎⊠👪]) For families that want easy access to Denarau facilities but prefer to look after themselves, this is a fantastic choice. These gigantic, spotless apartments are great value and completely self-contained; all have a laundry, big fridge, dishwasher and excellent cooking facilities. The poolside cafe is great for light meals. It's a quick stroll to the marina and shopping centre.

Sheraton Fiji Resort   RESORT $$$
(☑675 0777; www.sheratonfiji.com; r from $600; [⊝❄@☎👪]) While this sprawling resort is lovely on its own, the fact that guests can make use of all facilities at sister property **Sheraton Denarau Villas** (www.sheratondenarauvillas.com, r from $865) and the Westin gives it a definite edge: choose from six pools – including its own 1200 sq m lagoon – and 14 restaurants. The kids club (ages four to 12) is free, and children eat for $5.

Westin Denarau Island Resort & Spa RESORT $$$
(☎675 0000; www.westindenarauisland.com; r from $540; P) This is a longtime family fave, though an adults-only lap pool, good gym and the posh Heavenly Spa attract couples by the droves. Free extras like farm tours and local rum and chocolate tastings are fun. Guests have use of the facilities at the Sheraton and Sheraton Denarau Villas, though unlike the Sheraton, there's a one-off $25 fee to join the kids club.

Eating & Drinking

All of the Denarau resorts have restaurants and bars, from gourmet for grown-ups to small-fry smorgasbords. It's easy to sample any of them by jumping on the inter-resort Bula Bus ($8 for unlimited daily travel).

At Port Denarau, there are cafes inside the shopping centre and cosmopolitan restaurants lining the boardwalk – expect to pay upwards from $25 for mains.

If you're looking for lunch, the clubhouse at the Denarau Golf & Racquet Club (p67) also makes a nice change from the resorts: get there between noon and 3pm for all-you-can-eat pizza ($15).

★Nadina Authentic Fijian Restaurant FIJIAN $$$
(☎672 7313; Denarau Marina; mains $30-55; ⊙10am-11pm) This fantastic restaurant specialises in local cuisine, using homegrown and foraged ingredients; it's a great place to try *kokoda*, or opt for the divine fresh prawns with *ota* (a local bush fern) and chef-squeezed coconut cream.

Indigo FUSION $$$
(☎675 0026; www.indigofiji.com; Port Denarau; mains $28-68; ⊙11am-10pm) Indigo dishes up spicy classics from Indian and Southeast Asian cuisines, some with a local twist, including mud crab curry, tandoor-roasted tiger prawns and a very good Singapore curry.

Bonefish SEAFOOD $$$
(☎675 0197; www.bonefishfiji.com; Port Denarau; mains $22-66; ⊙11am-10pm) Lobster, crab and Walu, oh my! This relaxed spot is famous for its sublime seafood and hefty portions. If you have room, be sure to have the ridiculously decadent hot chilli chocolate volcano.

Cardo's Steakhouse INTERNATIONAL $$$
(☎675 0900; www.cardosfiji.com; Port Denarau; mains $24-55, steaks $45-75; ⊙7.30am-late) Carnivores feeling a little fished-out should repair to Cardo's for glorious, sizzling New Zealand steaks. A Denarau institution – it's been going for 25 years – Cardo's also has hearty classics including garlic prawns, chicken schnitzel and pizzas on the menu, plus a decent cocktail list.

Amalfi ITALIAN $$$
(☎675 0200; Port Denarau; mains $22-45; ⊙10am-10pm) Come hungry: Amalfi ladles out gigantic portions of pasta, steak and seafood, plus surprisingly excellent pizzas.

Hard Rock Cafe Fiji INTERNATIONAL $$$
(☎675 0032; www.hardrock.com/cafes/fiji; Port Denarau; mains $26-62; ⊙11am-10pm) Amble on in for classic burgers and the usual Hard Rock favourites, including fajitas, mac and cheese and smokehouse sandwiches. It's a franchise, and there's nothing Fijian about it, but kids and Hard Rock devotees will have a ball.

Lulu Bar and Restaurant INTERNATIONAL $$$
(☎672 5858; www.lulubarfiji.com; Denarau Marina; mains $24-47; ⊙7.30am-late) This fun place offers all the standards – think pastas, curries, steaks, sushi, burgers and belly-busting breakfasts. It's also a top Denarau watering hole, with a decent wine list, lots of tropical cocktails, beers galore and stupendous espresso martinis.

Rhum-Ba BAR
(☎770 7486; www.rhum-ba.com; Port Denarau; ⊙11am-11pm) The brand new – and awfully stylish – Denarau Yacht Club houses the upbeat Rhum-Ba; as the name implies, there are dozens of rums from around the world on offer. It also serves wholesome brunches, lunches and dinners (mains $29 to $45).

Shopping

Port Denarau Retail Centre MALL
(www.portdenarau.com.fj) This schmick mall is worlds away from the strip along Nadi's rough-and-tumble Main St. While there are less hassles and touts here, its homogenous feel can make it hard to remember that you're actually in Fiji. There's a grocery and liquor store, deli, pharmacy, bank, post office and souvenir and clothing shops.

Information

Asia Pacific Superyachts (☎750 5000, 675 0911; www.asia-pacific-superyachts.com; Shop 2, Port Denarau Terminal, VHF Marine channel 16) This group can arrange cruising permits, assemble provision orders, contact tradesmen and much more.

ⓘ Getting There & Away

West Bus Transport operates buses between Nadi and Denarau island ($1). Catch it at the main bus station or outside Jack's Handicrafts.

The inter-resort Bula Bus ($8 for unlimited daily travel) is unmissable: it's the one with the thatched roof. A taxi from Nadi town costs around $14 and from the airport $25. Be wary of the taxis going *from* Denarau: they often charge up to three times the actual fare. Call ☑ 6000 or ☑ 2000 and order a Nadi cab instead.

North of Nadi

Foothills of the Sabeto Mountains

The undulating countryside between Nadi and Lautoka is a lovely area to explore: it's hard to fathom that this peaceful region of farms, villages and sweet scenery is less than 30 minutes from the din of Nadi. If the Sabeto (Sa-*mbeto*) Mountain range is cloud-free, look to its far southeast ridge and you'll see the profile of Mt Batilamu or, in local legend, the Sleeping Giant.

◉ Sights & Activities

These sights are easily accessible from Nadi. A taxi will cost around $50 (return) to either the gardens or hot springs. The Wailoko bus ($1.70) passes both places, leaving Nadi around 9am, 1pm and 4pm and returning around 11am, 2pm and 5pm: allow for Fiji time.

Garden of the Sleeping Giant   GARDENS
(Map p58; ☑ 672 2701; www.gsgfiji.com; Wailoko Rd; adult/child $16/8; ⊙ 9am-5pm Mon-Sat, to noon Sun) More than a garden, this must-see spot is an absolute botanic bonanza. Abloom with more than 2000 varieties of orchids, plus indigenous flora and other tropical beauties, the 20-hectare plantation makes for a gorgeous getaway. Peak flowering seasons are June to July and November to December, but expect a brilliant display year-round. Tours are included in the entrance fee, or go on a solo meander along the jungle boardwalk.

Sabeto Hot Springs   HOT SPRINGS
(Map p58; admission $20; ⊙ 9am-5pm Mon-Sat) Never mind the pricey resort spas: slopping around this natural mud pit and the geothermal hot pools will have you feeling like a million bucks, even if it's just from all the therapeutic giggling you'll be doing. If all the mud-glooping and pool-dipping proves too much of an exertion, local villagers offer soothing massages for about $30.

Sleeping Giant Zipline   ADVENTURE SPORTS
(Map p58; ☑ 666 7935; www.ziplinefiji.com; Holika Rd; adult/child $189/94.50; ⊙ 8am-6pm) This adventure park offers a rush as dramatic as the Sabeto landscape. Ten ziplines loom over jungle and waterfalls at speeds reaching 60km/h; brave kids as young as four can have a go. The price includes unlimited zips, lunch and a tour of the lush surrounds. Free transfers from Nadi and Denarau.

🛏 Sleeping & Eating

⭐**Stoney Creek Resort**   RESORT **$**
(Map p58; ☑ 746 669; www.stoneycreekfiji.net; Sabeto Rd; dm $55, s/d with shared bathroom $65/80, d $135, bungalow from $150; @ 🛋) Minutes from the airport but tucked away in a verdant valley, Stoney Creek is less 'resort' than retreat, with brilliant hosts Michelle and Gary on hand to make your escape as easygoing or energetic as you like: loungers will love the pool, comfy chair-scattered common area and *bure* Jacuzzis, while active types can take advantage of mountain bike hire and organised treks to nearby attractions.

Construction of a mini-golf course was underway at research time; in the meantime, kids will love tearing around the huge grounds and pestering the menagerie of resident cats and dogs. The on-site **restaurant** (mains $18 to $25) dishes up toothsome local fare.

Koroyanitu National Heritage Park

Despite being just half an hour's drive from Nadi airport, Koroyanitu National Heritage Park seems deep within Viti Levu's interior. It's very beautiful, with walks through native *dakua* (a tree of the Kauri family) forests and grasslands, birdwatching, archaeological sites and waterfalls.

There are six small and largely self-sufficient villages within the park that co-operate as part of a conservation project intended to protect Fiji's only unlogged tropical montane forest. The villages are fairly remote; with low visitor numbers, track and lodge maintenance has been an issue.

◉ Sights & Activities

Abaca   VILLAGE
Koroyanitu National Heritage Park is accessed via Abaca (*Am-ba-tha*) village, southeast

of Lautoka, but you can't go alone: trails have been unmaintained for years. Contact **Kalo Baravilala** (☑8077 147, 6253 792; www.exotic holidaysfiji.net), who can arrange everything from guides to accommodation.

From here, it's possible to make a day trek to and from Fiji's sleeping giant, Mt Batilamu. This is a strenuous three-hour hike up, and a knee-wobbling couple of hours down. At the time of research, it was not possible to walk the two-day trek between Abaca and Navilawa villages. You can overnight at Abaca's simple Nase Lodge ($45).

Navilawa   VILLAGE

The rocky 4WD road to Navilawa hugs the Sabeto River, and there are some perfect swimming holes and waterfalls to plunge in: ask permission first from any locals you see. The village is set in an old volcanic crater surrounded by forest and mountains. There's a short rainforest hike to a cave beside a clear-flowing creek; the villagers use the cave during cyclones.

Visitors should take a *sevusevu* (gift) and make themselves known on arrival for a low-key and very authentic kava welcoming ceremony.

There's a simple self-contained lodge ($45) with six beds, or ask around for a homestay. Bring your own food.

At the time of research, there was no access to the national park from here due to a 2011 landslide (though efforts were underway to have the trail re-opened by the end of 2015), but it's a worthwhile visit for those seeking an authentic village atmosphere.

ⓘ Getting There & Away

To get to Abaca, turn right off the Queens Road at Tavakubu Rd – past the first roundabout after entering Lautoka from Nadi. Continue along Tavakubu Rd for about 4.7km, past the police post and the cemetery, then turn right onto the (unsigned) road to Abaca. At the first causeway, fork right and it's another 10km of gravel road up to the village, suitable for 4WDs only. There is no public transport to Abaca; you can charter a carrier from Lautoka.

For Navilawa from Nadi International Airport, follow the Queens Road north for a couple of kilometres then turn right onto Sabeto Rd. Follow this to the (unsigned) turn off to Navilawa village – the turn is on the left, 3.9km after Stoney Creek Resort. Pass through Korobebe village and a gold mining exploration camp, and veer left whenever the road forks. Navilawa village is 13.2km from Stoney Creek. You'll need a 4WD with decent clearance; the road is steep and rocky in places, with creek crossings. Public buses make several trips a day from Lautoka

and Nadi to Korobebe village, from where it's an hour or so hike up to Navilawa. For more transport options, updated conditions information or guided tours, contact Kalo Baravilala (p70).

Viseisei & Vuda Point

According to local lore, Viseisei village (12km north of Nadi) is the oldest settlement in Fiji: the *mataqali* (extended family) here are descendants of the first ocean-going Melanesians who landed 1km north of here around 1500. Fiji's first Methodist missionaries also landed here (1835); the village's Centennial Memorial is the focal point for 10 October (Fiji Day) celebrations. The ceremonial *bure* opposite the memorial is still used on important occasions; Queen Elizabeth II and Prince Charles have been received here. To look around you'll need to pay $5 to the ladies who run the tiny **craft market** (Map p58; ⊗8am-6pm Mon-Sat), remove your hat and wear something that covers your shoulders and knees. A bypass on the Queens Road skips Viseisei; if you're travelling by bus, be sure to check it actually calls by the village.

Beyond Viseisei, **Vuda Point Marina** (Map p58; ☑666 8214; www.vudamarina.com) is a thriving yachties' lure. Facilities include a great cafe and restaurant/bar, free showers, laundry, general store, yacht-repair specialists, a chandlery and the largest travel hoist in Fiji. Berths cost $0.75 per foot per day and electricity costs $4.40 per day. The marina hosts the **Makers and Growers Market** (⊗8am to noon) on the second Saturday of each month.

The beaches around Vuda Point are better than those near Nadi, but still offer little for the avid snorkeller.

🛏 Sleeping & Eating

Viseisei Village Homestays   HOMESTAY $
(Map p58; per person from $60) A number of families offer homestays in Viseisei. Your best bet is to contact **Finau Bavadra** (☑925 5370; dawfinfijitravel@yahoo.com; Viseisei village): she often welcomes couch surfers or will find a bed elsewhere in the village for you.

Anchorage Beach Resort   RESORT $$
(Map p58; ☑666 2099; www.anchoragefiji.com; Vuda Point; mountain/ocean rm from $198/275, villas from $390; P❋🛜🏊) Following massive refurbishments (with additional construction still underway), this resort has gone from tired to terrific. The hilltop wedding *bure* is its centrepiece, with fantastic views

over the bay; most guests gather down the slope, where a buzzing **restaurant** (mains $14 to $45) and bar, ocean-facing lounge beds and massive deck frame the new lagoon pool (with swim-up cocktail bar).

If you don't mind hiking up and down the hill, renovated mountain-view rooms are good value. A boat to sister resort Beachcomber and the Cloud 9 platform leaves every morning at 8.30am for transfers and daytrips; airport pick ups/drop offs also available.

First Landing Resort RESORT $$$

(Map p58; ☑666 6171; www.firstlandingresort.com; Vuda Point; bungalow from $300, apt from $680; P❉☎☒⛵) Vuda Point's most upmarket option, this resort is perched on white(ish) sands among well-manicured gardens.The *bures* and villas are bright and welcoming, with mosquito-screened verandahs; more expensive villas have private pools and kitchens. Like others in the area, the beach isn't great, but there's an artificial, footprint-shaped island and lagoon pool for sunbathers. The beachfront **restaurant** (mains $15 to $50) serves seafood, pasta, curries and wood-fired pizza. Other services include a kids club, daytrips and transfers to nearby islands, and free use of kayaks and snorkelling gear.

Boatshed Café CAFE $

(Map p58; Vuda Point Marina; light meals $3.50-10; ☺7am-4pm; ☎) This boardwalk cafe is a great little hangout, with ambience, views, good coffee and tasty sandwiches on offer.

Boatshed Restaurant
and Sunset Bar INTERNATIONAL $$

(Map p58; www.vudamarina.com.fj; Vuda Point Marina; mains $16-32, pizzas from $24; ☺10am-10pm; ☎) With indoor and outdoor seating, top views and cheery service, this is a very popular spot with visiting yachties and those staying in the area. The varied menu features pizzas, curries, seafood, roasts and lush pastas (hello, lobster ravioli!). Sundays are the best day to visit, with live music and merrymakers aplenty.

SOUTH OF NADI

Naisali

The long, flat island of Naisali (42 hectares) is just 300m off the mainland and about 12km southwest of Nadi. Like Denarau,

Naisali is on the edge of mangroves: the beaches aren't ideal for swimming and the dark sand disappoints some.

Naisali is a 25-minute drive followed by a three-minute boat shuttle (free for resort guests) from Nadi airport. A taxi from the airport costs $32 and the resort shuttle $55.

DoubleTree Resort RESORT $$$

(Map p58; ☑670 6011; www.sonaisali.com; r incl breakfast $500-700; ☀❉@☒⛵) There's plenty of white sand at the DoubleTree Resort, but it's used to create faux beaches and landscape the huge grounds – there's none on the beach. The hub of the resort is a large pool with a swim-up bar and an endless array of activities to keep families happy, including a kids club and watersports.

The resort has had a recent fit-out, and in 2016 is due to come under the Hilton hotel brand. Rooms are either in the main double-storey building (which feels a little tired), or you can go for the semi-detached *bure,* with spa baths built into the verandahs.

Uciwai Landing

Uciwai Landing, used by surfers to access the Mamanuca breaks and island resorts on Namotu and Tavarua, is 25km southwest of Nadi, the last 7km of which is on a slow and pot-holed road. Surfing is really the only reason to head here.

Rendezvous Beach Resort RESORT $

(Map p58; ☑628 1216; www.surfdivefiji.com; dm $28, r with fan $52, r with air-con $74-98; ❉@☒) Rendezvous Beach Resort caters predominantly to surfers on a budget. Quick access to the Mamanuca surf breaks and dive sites are the attraction and the idea is to spend as much time away from the resort as possible. Accommodation is pretty simple, but you're likely to spend most of your time out on the breaks.

There's a guest kitchen, otherwise three meals per day works out to around $75. The staff here are as languid as the seasoned surfers who visit. The daily surf boat goes to where the surf's good and costs $100 to $150 per person (it's cheaper with more than one person) for four hours surfing. Resort transfers are available from Nadi ($40) and the airport ($60), or there are local buses to Uciwai from Nadi bus station ($2.50) departing a couple of times a day Monday through Saturday.

LOOKING UPWARDS...

...as well as outwards. If you're lucky, you'll see the angular silhouette of a frigatebird, one of the ocean's great airborne wanderers and a resident of this coastline. Its almost 2m wingspan is unmistakeable as it rides high and cruises the thermals.

And if you're even luckier, you'll see a frigatebird harassing a gannet in an aerial chase. This results in an exhausted gannet regurgitating its just-caught fish which the frigate then promptly swoops in and swallows. Fast food indeed.

Momi Bay

The first interesting detour off the Queens Road is about 20km south of Nadi, along a sealed road that threads its way between barren hills, pine plantations and sugarcane fields to Momi Bay and the more impressive WWII Momi Guns. From the bunkers, the site of a more recently waged battle – a legal one – is visible. Construction was well underway on the JW Marriott Fiji Resort and Spa, Fiji's second overwater *bure* resort, until work came to a grinding halt in 2006, at which stage Momi Bay briefly became home to a first-class golf course on which no one has ever played. With funding delays now overcome, Marriott expect to open their resort and spa sometime in 2016.

◉ Sights & Activities

Momi Guns   HISTORIC SITE
(Map p58; $5; ⊗9am-5pm) Turn off the sealed road at the signpost to the guns, and onto 4km of rattling gravel road. This leads to two 6in guns that were installed here by the New Zealand 30th Battalion in 1941 to defend Fiji against the Japanese. Fiji was, like most other islands, poorly equipped to take on the might of the Japanese Imperial Army: an army that had already swept through Papua New Guinea, the Solomon Islands and parts of what is now Vanuatu.

A quick scan of the horizon will reveal why this spot was chosen for the battery. The guns (and now tourists) have unobstructed views to Malolo Barrier Reef, the Mamanuca Group and Navula Passage, the only entry into western Fiji for large ships.

The local guides are eager to show off their knowledge (a tip is appreciated).

Scuba Bula   DIVING
(Map p58; ☏628 0190; www.scubabula.com) This excellent, independently owned company is based at the Seashell@Momi resort. It is the only company to dive the outer Navula Reef, and the instructors have a wealth of experience on local reefs. A two-tank dive including equipment costs $240 and a PADI Open Water Course $860. Snorkellers are welcome, and charged $60 for a two-hour outing.

Scuba Bula is proud of its eco-credentials, and works with the Worldwide Fund for Nature on local conservation and monitoring projects on local reefs.

⌬ Sleeping

Seashell@Momi   RESORT $
(Map p58; ☏670 6100; dm/r $32/96, bungalow $160-248, apt $240; ❋❋@❋) The Seashell is 13km from the main road and has an undiscovered air about it. It offers great value if you don't mind the dated decor. Accommodation comes in all shapes and configurations, from self-contained *bure* and apartments to roomy dorms. On-site facilities include a tennis court, a children's playground, two pools, a **restaurant** (mains $15 to $30) and enough palm trees for a whole island.

People don't come here for the beach (although if you walk around the rocky point, there's a larger bay with better sand). Rather, they come to access some of Fiji's hottest dive spots and premier surf breaks – or just to kick back away from the crowds for a few days. A 7am surf trip departs daily for a three- to four-hour session ($65 per person, minimum of two people) to the Mamanuca surf breaks. A meal plan is available for $104.

⊙ Getting There & Away

Airport transfers by resort minibus are $30 per person each way (minimum charge $60) and taxis cost about the same. **Dominion Transport** buses leave Nadi Bus Station for Momi Bay at 8am, 12.30pm, 2.30pm and 4pm and cost $3.50. Buses drop off at the door, but do not operate on Sundays.

Natadola Beach

Gorgeous Natadola Beach is one of Viti Levu's best. Its vast bank of white sand slides into a cobalt sea, which provides good swimming regardless of the tide. Natadola's strong currents often defy the brochures though: instead of glassy, still conditions, you may find sufficient chop for good body surfing – just watch the undertows. And there's serious surfing here, too. **Natadola Inside** break – which is inside the bay (surprise) – is good for beginners, and **Natadola Outside** – at the entrance of the channel – is for experienced surfers.

Local villagers tie up their horses under the trees near the car park and pounce on tourists as soon as they arrive. They are fairly persistent and you'll shock them if you don't want a horse ride – a gentle 45-minutes or so along the beach costs about $30. Graduating from the same school of high-pressure sales tactics are the coconut and seashell sellers. They're great if you want coconuts or shells but tiring if you don't.

🛏️ Sleeping & Eating

Natadola Beach Resort   RESORT $$
(Map p54; ☎672 1001; www.natadola.com; ste $250; ☀) This intimate, adult-only resort has only 11 suites in two blocks. The resort was built in the faux-Spanish colonial style popular a few years back and has a certain *casa del Fiji* charm about it. Each suite has a spacious bathroom and private courtyard. The pool meanders through tropical gardens, with plenty of poolside shade for those wishing to snooze.

When all that R&R gets too much, grab a boogie board and cross the road to the beach. The **restaurant/bar** (mains $28 to $50, lunches $14 to $25) offers tasty food with small, no-frills servings, is open to nonguests and is a popular stop for day trippers. The resort is bang next door to the InterContinental and is perfectly located for strolling over for a sunset cocktail or special dinner.

Yatule Beach Resort   APARTMENT $$
(Map p54; ☎672 8004; reservation@yatule resort.com.fj; villas $420-675; P☉❄☎☀) The thatched roofs of the self-contained *bures* make this small resort look like a Fijian village. Originally built to house the bigwigs involved in the building of the InterContinental, it now offers some excellent chic beachside accommodation. All the villas have mini-kitchens, bedrooms and separate lounges. The family villa has four separate bedrooms and is ideal for teenage kids who need privacy.

Eat in the upscale Na Ua Restaurant, or during the day at the Pool Bar.

Robinson Crusoe Island Resort   RESORT $$
(Map p54; ☎628 1999; www.robinsoncrusoe islandfiji.com; dm $49, bungalow $79-160, lodge $199-249; ☀) The Robinson Crusoe Island Resort covers all of the tiny coral island of Likuri. Once a determined backpacker resort, it's spruced itself in recent years and offers good-quality accommodation, ranging from tidy dorms to some rather charming thatched and airy *bure* tucked away in the greenery. For all this, there's a heavy focus on group activities.

Centrepiece of the action is the Pacific Island Dance Show (including fire-walking), part of a whole day tour (Monday, Wednesday and Saturday, adult/child $199/99) that involves snorkelling and a bush walk. Guests (and especially kids) are as likely to enjoy the free activities from crab-racing and jewellery-making – though parents may want to take care when the little ones want to learn how to climb to the top of the coconut palms. There's snorkelling too, although it's poor compared to further along the coast. Transfers from Nadi cost $100.

Fiji Golf Resort & Spa   RESORT $$$
(Map p54; www.intercontinental.com; r from $684, ste from $1150; ☉❄☎☀) This mammoth Intercontinental-run resort is a conglomeration of slate-grey buildings, somewhat at odds with the tropical land- and seascape, occupying a prime piece of real estate on the beach. The 266 rooms and 91 suites are beautifully appointed and equipped, with spa baths on each balcony. The three indoor/outdoor restaurants all offer sunset views along with an occasional howling trade wind.

The attached 18-hole golf course is spruiked as the finest in the southern hemisphere – a sentiment echoed by golfers we met who'd played it.

ℹ️ Getting There & Away

Natadola Beach is fairly isolated and most people visit as part of a day tour from Nadi or the Coral Coast. The Coral Coast Scenic Railway (p74) is a particularly nice way to arrive. For those with a rental car, turn off the Queens Road onto Maro Rd 36km from Nadi. The road is mostly sealed though the last few kilometres on the old Queens Road are slow and pot-holed – the beach is signposted. For adventurous drivers, a shortcut involves following the main sealed access road into the InterContinental and, about 200m before the lobby entrance, turning right onto a well-defined track that cuts over the hill and down to the beach. (It's not a designated road though, so rental-car drivers beware: insurance won't cover any prangs.)

Those with energy could walk here in about 3½ hours by following the track from Yanuca. Catch the train or bus back.

Paradise Transport buses head to Natadola from Sigatoka ($3, one hour, four daily on weekdays). Otherwise catch any bus, ask to be let off at the Maro Rd junction and catch a taxi from there ($7). A taxi costs $75 each way from Nadi.

Yanuca & Around

Past the turn-off to Natadola, the Queens Road continues southeast, winding through hills and down to the coast at Cuvu Bay and Yanuca, about 50km from Nadi. Yanuca itself is a blink of a village, but it's home to a couple of good attractions.

◉ Sights & Activities

Coral Coast Scenic Railway   SCENIC RAILWAY
(Map p54; ☎652 0434; Queens Rd; adult/child $69/35) The station for the railway is at the causeway entrance to Shangri-La's Fijian Resort. It offers scenic rides along the coast in an old diesel sugar train, past villages, forests and sugar plantations, to beautiful Natadola Beach. The railway was once used for transporting cane and passengers to the Lautoka Mill. The 14km trip takes about 1¼ hours, leaving at 10am on Monday, Wednesday and Friday and returning at 4pm (adult/child $92/46 including barbecue lunch). On Tuesday, Thursday and Saturday, a Sigatoka shopping trip runs east and costs $46/23.

🛏 Sleeping

Namuka Bay Resort   RESORT $$
(Map p54; ☎670 0243; www.namukabaylagoon resort.com; dm incl meals $95, villa $200) These eight, roomy beachfront villas, each comprising two guest rooms with a shared verandah, are tucked 6km down a side road. It's *very* bumpy, but OK for all vehicles in good weather. The resort fronts a lagoon and 2km of beach, with a historic (deserted) village site on the hill behind and a cave walk just along the coast.

It's very secluded and you'd want good weather – or a good supply of books – to fully enjoy it. There's power for a few hours each evening, though there are plans to bring mains electricity the extra mile required. The turn-off is about 5km from the Fijian on the Nadi side.

**Gecko's Resort &
Kalevu Cultural Centre**   RESORT $$
(Map p54; ☎652 0200; www.fijiculturalcentre. com; r/f $130/250; ❂❋@⊠) Directly opposite the scenic railway station, this resort has 35 new, simple-but-nice-and-roomy hotel rooms. Several have interconnecting doors and convert to family rooms. The **restaurant** (mains $25 to $50) is recommended and is often busy with dining escapees from the Shangri-La.

The complimentary South Pacific dance show on Friday and Sunday evenings is popular. In the landscaped grounds is a purpose-built cultural centre showcasing a collection of traditionally built huts and *bures*, pottery, *masi* (bark cloth) and carvings (one-hour guided tour $20 per person between 9.30am and 4pm).

Shangri-La's Fijian Resort   RESORT $$$
(The Fijian; Map p54; ☎652 0155; www.shangri-la. com; r incl breakfast from $490; ❂❋@⊠) Anchored offshore on its own private island, this resort is one of the Coral Coast's premier (and biggest) hotels. Linked to the mainland by a causeway, the 442 rooms come in a variety of configurations and packages. If you like big resorts and armies of squealing kids don't daunt you, you'll enjoy the three swimming pools, excellent restaurants, tennis courts and – possibly – even the lovely wedding chapel.

While mum and dad nip off for a round of golf (nine holes $35) or toddle down to one of the Fijian's swanky day spas or the adult-only pool, they can (lovingly) shunt junior into the child-care centre.

❶ Getting There & Away

The Fijian and surrounds are about a 45-minute drive from Nadi and 11km west of Sigatoka. There are regular express buses, minibuses and carriers travelling along the Queens Road. A taxi to Nadi International Airport is about $75 and the **Coral Sun Fiji** (☎672 3105; www.coralsunfiji.com) coach costs $13.

CORAL COAST

A wide bank of coral offshore gives this stretch of coast between Korotogo and Pacific Harbour its name. Flanked by waves of richly vegetated hills and a fringing reef that drops off dramatically into the deep blue of the South Pacific Ocean, it's the most scenic slice

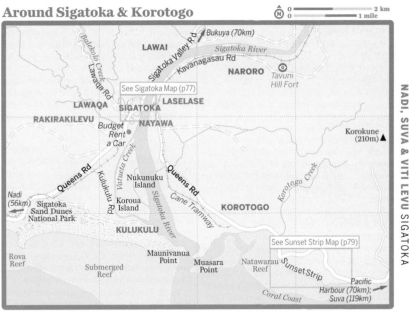

of the Queens Road and resorts of all standards exploit the views. That said, the Coral Coast's beaches are poor cousins to those on Fiji's smaller islands and most swimming is done in hotel pools. Many travellers prefer to focus on inland and other highlights, such as the Sigatoka Sand Dunes, Tavuni Hill Fort, Sigatoka Valley and, near Pacific Harbour, river trips in the Namosi Highlands and diving in the Beqa Lagoon. Lounging in a resort is also a prime pursuit in these parts.

Much of the coast experiences tidal fluctuations that leave a lot of the reef exposed for long lengths of time and (except for some lagoons) it is only possible to swim and snorkel at high tide. Sovi Bay, 2.5km east of Korotogo, is one of the better swimming beaches, but be wary of strong channel currents. The photos you've seen of white, sandy Fijian beaches are unlikely to have been taken along the Coral Coast.

Sigatoka

POP 9500

Sigatoka (sing-a-*to*-ka) is the largest town on the Coral Coast and serves as the commercial hub for the farming communities that grow sugar cane and vegetables upriver in the fertile swathe of the Sigatoka Valley.

Because of its pretty riverside location and accessibility, Sigatoka is a popular day trip from Nadi and the nearby Coral Coast resorts. There is a bustling produce market in the heart of town, a few souvenir shops, a large mosque and a fantasy-style, privately owned mansion overlooking the lot. The Sigatoka River, the second largest in Fiji, flows along the eastern edge of town. If you find your enthusiasm for souvenirs exhausted, stroll across the smaller of the two bridges (the one damaged in a 1994 hurricane) to see if you can spot the shark god, Dakuwaqa, swimming in the murky waters beneath.

Sigatoka's major draws – the sand dunes, surfing and the Tavuni Hill Fort – are all a few kilometres out of town, but are easily reached by a short taxi ride.

Sigatoka doesn't offer any outstanding accommodation options, though a few basic hotel rooms can be found if you go looking. You're better off heading to nearby Korotogo for a bed.

Sights

Sigatoka Sand Dunes NATIONAL PARK
(adult/child/family $10/5/25, child under 6yr free; ⊙8am-5pm) One of Fiji's natural highlights, these impressive dunes are a ripple of peppery monoliths skirting the shoreline near

the mouth of the Sigatoka River. Windblown and rugged, they stand around 5km long, up to 1km wide and on average about 20m high, rising to about 60m at the western end. They were made a national park in 1989.

Don't expect golden Sahara-like dunes: the fine sand is a grey-brown colour and largely covered with vines and shrubs. The dunes have been forming over millions of years as sediments brought down by the Sigatoka River are washed ashore by the surf and blown into dunes by the prevailing winds. Walking trails take you down to the coast across open rolling grassland. A mahogany forest was planted in the 1960s to halt the dunes' expedition onto the Queens Road,

Since the coastal margin of the dunes is largely unstable, human bones and early pottery are sometimes exposed. Archaeological excavations here have uncovered pottery more than 2600 years old and one of the largest burial sites in the Pacific. The visitor centre houses a few pottery shards and ceramic pots from some of these excavations, along with helpful staff.

Park access is 4.5km southwest of Sigatoka on the Queens Road. Stick to the designated trails and allow one or two hours for the short or long self-guided walking tours respectively. And if by chance you do come across a thighbone jutting from the sand, know that you'll be cursed forever if you attempt to remove it.

Most buses (excluding express services) travelling between Nadi and Sigatoka can drop you right outside the visitors centre on the main highway. A taxi from Sigatoka town costs $6.

Tavuni Hill Fort HISTORIC SITE
(adult/child $12/6; ⏱8am-5pm Mon-Sat) Although there are many forts like it scattered all over Fiji, Tavuni Hill Fort is the most accessible for visitors. Built in the 18th century by Tongan chief Maile Latumai, this fort was a defensive site used in times of war and is one of Fiji's most interesting historical sights.

The steep 90m-high limestone ridge at the edge of a bend in the Sigatoka River is an obvious strategic location for a fortification. The views over the valley are tremendous.

From this position, the surrounding area could easily be surveyed, both upstream and downstream, and the views are spectacular. Substantial earthworks were carried out to form *yavu* (bases for houses) and terraces

CANNIBALISM

Archaeological evidence from food-waste middens shows that cannibalism was practised in Viti Levu from around 500 BC until the mid- to late 19th century, during which time it had become an ordinary, ritualised part of life. In a society founded on ancestor worship and belief in the afterlife, cannibalising an enemy was considered the ultimate revenge. A disrespectful death was a lasting insult to the enemy's family.

Bodies were consumed either on the battlefield or brought back to the village spirit house and offered to the local war god. They were then butchered, baked and eaten on the god's behalf. The triumph was celebrated with music and dance. Men performed the *cibi* (death dance) and women the *dele* or *wate* (an obscene dance in which they sexually humiliated corpses and captives).

Mementoes of the kill were kept to prolong the victor's sense of vengeance. Necklaces, hairpins or ear-lobe ornaments were made from human bones, and the skull of a hated enemy was sometimes made into a kava drinking bowl. To record a triumph in war, the highlanders of Viti Levu placed the bones of victims in branches of trees outside their spirit houses and men's houses as trophies. The coastal dwellers had a practical use for the bones: leg bones were used to make sail needles and thatching knives. Rows of stones were also used to tally the number of bodies eaten by the chief.

The growing influence of Christianity had a great impact on cannibalism and the practice began to wane in the mid-1800s. By all accounts, it had ended by the turn of the century. Western fascination with the gruesome practice has remained alive and well, however. Original artefacts can be seen in the Fiji Museum (p88) in Suva, and souvenir cannibal forks are sold in abundant quantities everywhere. Traditionally, chiefs used these because it was forbidden for human flesh to touch their lips. Considered sacred relics, these forks were kept in the spirit house and were not to be touched by women or children. Today, it would appear, they make interesting wall features.

Sigatoka

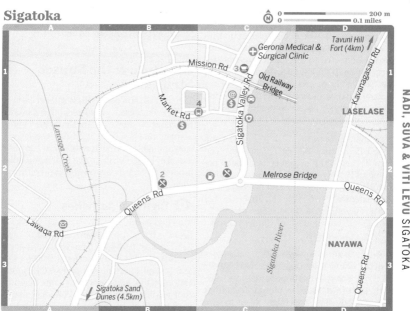

for barricade fencing. There are also a number of grave sites, a *rara* (ceremonial ground) and a *vatu ni bokola* (head-chopping stone), as well as some beautiful curtain figs and an *ivi* (Polynesian chestnut tree) on the site.

The fort is about 4km northeast of Sigatoka on the eastern side of the river, above Naroro village. Occasional local carriers make the trip past the entrance gate. A taxi costs $5.

👉 Tours

Adventures in Paradise   TOUR
(✆652 0833; www.adventuresinparadisefiji. com; tours per person incl Coral Coast/Nadi hotel transfers $99/119, child 5-12yr half-price) Offers day trips to the Naihehe Cave on Tuesdays, Thursdays and Saturdays. Lunch and a *bilibili* (bamboo raft) ride downstream are included – children love it. The Savu Na Mate Laya Waterfall tour leaves Mondays, Wednesdays and Fridays and involves non-strenuous walking to a waterfall-fed swimming hole.

Coastal Inland Tours   TOUR
(✆650 1161, 70778 380; www.coastalinlandtours. com; tours from $120) A smaller-scale local tour operator, which offers a variety of half-day trips based around the Sigatoka River.

They visit Biausevu village, which has a nearby waterfall where you can swim, and travel by boat upstream to Nahigatoka.

Sigatoka River Safari   TOUR
(✆650 1721; www.sigatokariver.com; jet-boat tours per person incl Sigatoka/Coral Coast hotel transfers $249/289, child 4-15yr $125/145) These popular half-day jet-boating trips include a 45km whirl up the Sigatoka River, a village visit and lunch.

🍴 Eating & Drinking

Self-caterers can stock up at the market and at Morris Hedstrom Supermarket or one of the other many supermarkets in town.

Raj's Curry House INDIAN $

(Map p77; ☑650 1470; Queens Rd; curries from $13; ☺8am-9pm) Ask a Sigatoka taxi driver where to eat and there's a good chance you'll be directed to this small canteen-style curry house. It's a long way from flashy, but the food is cheap and cheerful, with plates of tasty curry with rice and roti (plus some Western dishes), all accompanied by a TV trilling Indian soap operas in the corner.

True Blue Restaurant INDO-FIJIAN $

(☑650 1530; mains $15-45; ☺7am-11pm) The draw at this local hangout is its elevated position and lovely views from the cavernous, dancehall-like restaurant and balcony along the mangrove-lined Sigatoka River. It's all pretty informal. The food leans heavily to Indo-Fijian, with a dash of Chinese thrown in for good measure.

Vilisite's Seafood Restaurant SEAFOOD $$

(Map p77; ☑650 1030; Queens Rd; mains $18-35; ☺lunch & dinner) First impressions can mislead: picture a tatty tropicana restaurant from the late '70s. You might want to give perennial favourite Vilisite's a miss. Don't. While there are Chinese and curry options on the menu, everyone goes for the seafood (three-course set menus from $30, or blow out on the $60 lobster), followed by an ice-cream cone from the shack outside.

Cuppa Bula COFFEE

(Map p77; ☺7.30am-5pm) Coffee fiends will find that Cuppa Bula makes a decent flat white. It's tucked inside the Tappoo shopping centre, but also has an open front to watch the world go by from. If you're after a bite to accompany your drink, the sandwiches are pretty good, and there's often one or two hot plate options on the go as well.

ℹ Information

Westpac and ANZ have banks in town.

Gerona Medical & Surgical Clinic (Map p77; ☑652 0128; Sigatoka Valley Rd; ☺8.30am-1pm, 2-4pm & 7-8pm Mon-Fri, 8.30am-1pm Sat)

Super Nadro computers (Map p77; Sigatoke Valley Rd; per 20 min $1; ☺8am-5.30pm) Get online at this internet cafe.

ℹ Getting There & Around

Pacific Transport (Map p77; ☑650 0088; www.pacifictransport.com.fj) and **Sunbeam Transport** (Map p77; www.sunbeamfiji.com) run several express buses a day between Nadi and Sigatoka ($5.50, 1¼ hours) and between Siga-

toka and Suva ($10.25, three hours) via Pacific Harbour ($6, two hours). A taxi to the Sunset Strip resorts will cost around $8.

Korotogo & the Sunset Strip

The start of the Coral Coast begins in earnest at this condensed group of hotels flanking the water on Sunset Strip. Korotogo itself is a small village, but at high tide the lagoon is swimmable and at low tide you can take a decent-length walk on the beach and poke around in rock pools on the exposed coral shelf.

◉ Sights & Activities

Kula Eco Park WILDLIFE RESERVE

(☑650 0505; www.fijiwild.com; adult/child $25/12.50; ☺10am-4pm) This wildlife sanctuary is supported by the National Trust for Fiji and several international parks and conservation bodies, and showcases some magnificent wildlife. This includes Fiji's only native land mammal, the Fijian flying fox; and an aviary full of quarrelsome kula parrots, Fiji's national bird and the park's namesake. The park runs invaluable breeding programs, with success stories for the Pacific black duck (Fiji's only remaining duck species) and the crested and banded iguana.

Kula Eco Park is set in rambling forested grounds. Ambling down the wooden walkways, reading the labels on the native plants and poking in and out of the walk-through aviaries is a lot of fun (and less confronting than viewing the owls and raptors in their small individual cages). The park is 100% funded by gate receipts and donations. There's also decent wheelchair access.

Hot Glass Fiji GLASS

(☑909 3200; www.hotglassfiji.com; ☺Tue-Fri 10am-3pm) If you're looking for something a little different on the Coral Coast, pay a visit to Fiji's only glass-blowing studio. It's run by an English artist, who doesn't just sell her creations in the studio, but offers you the chance for a hands-on experience as well. Try the 'Quick slick glass trick' for $175, where you can blow your own unique glass souvenir of Fiji (children over seven are welcome), or sandcast your own creation with molten glass.

If you want to get really stuck in, a half day glass-blowing class costs from $350, with private tuition also available.

Sunset Strip

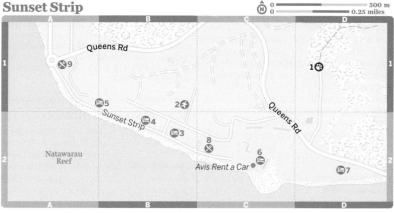

🛏 Sleeping

Crow's Nest Resort RESORT **$**
(☑650 0230; www.crowsnestresortfiji.com; Sunset Strip; villa $199-239; ✿❄@🏊) Nautical terms abound at these smart, grey, split-level timber bungalows. Each has a lovely balcony and ocean views, and they're in good nick and are good value. The slightly more expensive rooms are self-contained, but all can accommodate a family of four. The **restaurant** (mains $17 to $25) faces the hillside pool and has a cosmopolitan menu (we enjoyed the pastas with various shellfish).

Tubakula Beach Bungalows RESORT **$**
(☑650 0097; www.fiji4less.com/tuba.html; dm $30, s/tw $70/77, chalet $140-198; ✿🏊) If it weren't for the palm trees, pool and waterfront setting, this low-key resort would be right at home in the mountains. Simple dorms, singles and twins have shared facilities. The A-frame chalets have strapping timber frames, modern kitchens and verandahs with slouchy wooden seats. It's ideal for self-driving, self-catering, self-sufficient types wishing to escape the crowds.

It's right on the beach and free snorkel equipment is available. Though the menu is limited – there's a lot of pizza – the **restaurant** (pizzas from $15; ⊙breakfast & dinner) is fair value (but closed on Tuesday).

Casablanca Hotel APARTMENT **$**
(☑652 0600; casablanca@connect.com.fj; Sunset Strip; s/d $65/74; 🏊) This mock-Spanish mansion offers eight self-contained rooms that are cheap, cheerful and look like they were decorated with furniture picked up at a garage sale. They're a bit worn, but

Sunset Strip

all have fantastic balcony views. Although there's a restaurant/bar, breakfast isn't on offer, but rooms have simple stoves if you want to self-cater.

Bedarra Beach Inn INN **$$**
(☑650 0476; www.bedarrafiji.com; Sunset Strip; r $180-260; ❄🛜🏊) This modern hotel is a gem. It offers spacious, spotlessly clean rooms with tiled floors and plenty of natural light, most of which have ocean views. There's a good balance between resort-style comfort and do-it-yourself practicality. The open bar area is designed for maximum sociability.

All guests are offered a free Fijian foot ritual spa on arrival to get you in a suitably relaxing holiday mood.

★**Outrigger Fiji Beach Resort** RESORT **$$$**
(☑650 0044; www.outrigger.com/fiji; r from $639, bungalow from $1069; ✿❄@🛜🏊♿) The 7m outrigger canoe suspended from the ceiling

in the main lobby and the stunning balcony views create a powerful first impression at this much-touted resort. From the main building, an artificial stream meanders through lush gardens to a huge, lagoon-style pool. It can get noisy with excited kids, but there's an adult-only pool for others to retreat to if needed.

The *bures*, with their high, hand-painted *masi* ceilings, are fabulous, as is the day spa with its superb hilltop location. There's a kids club and children eat for free (depending on which package you have). Dive Away Fiji runs the dive shop here.

✖ Eating

★ **Beach Bar & Grill**   BISTRO $$
(☑652 0877; Sunset Strip; mains $15-38; ☺5.30-9.30pm) Formerly Le Café, the Beach Bar & Grill is deservedly popular with those wanting to eat outside their resorts. It's a simple thatched outfit, but has an impressive menu, with lots of excellent local seafood and an interesting blend of Fijian, Thai and French flavours in the offerings (if that sounds odd, we can attest that it works).

If you just want a drink, you're also welcome to prop up the bar.

Koko's Bar   INTERNATIONAL $$
(Sunset Strip; mains $14-29; ☺12-2pm & 5pm-late) This diner-style restaurant facing the sea is a good place to refuel. A smart, open-fronted wooden building with a sports bar at the back, it has a decent line in Fijian dishes like Ika Vakalolo (fish cooked in coconut), Indo-Fijian curries, plus some good pizzas and burgers and great service. The cocktails are great, and there's a kid's menu for $12.

Ocean Terrace Restaurant   INTERNATIONAL $$$
(☑650 0476; Sunset Strip; mains $25-35; ☺breakfast, lunch & dinner) Slightly pricier than its neighbours and boasting a breezy dining area overlooking the ocean, the food outlets at the Bedarra Inn often lure guests from the Outrigger. It's a great place to try some creative Fijian fusion dishes, but for the less adventurous there's steak, pizza and curries. A smart casual dress code is requested. Happy hour runs from 5pm to 6pm.

❶ Getting There & Around

Pacific Transport (p78) and **Sunbeam Transport** (www.sunbeamfiji.com) run regular buses along the Queens Road, stopping at resorts along the way ($7.55 from Nadi, 1½ hours, or $10.25 from Suva, three hours). **Coral Sun Fiji** (www.coralsunfiji.com) has air-conditioned coaches that also stop outside resorts ($15/17 from Nadi/Suva). The cheapest way from Korotogo to Sigatoka is to walk to the roundabout and catch one of the local buses ($1) which run throughout the day. A taxi is $6 to Sigatoka and around $70 to Nadi.

Korolevu & Around

Further east, the section of the Queens Road between Korotogo and Korolevu is the most beautiful. The road winds along the shore, affording views of scenic bays, beaches, coral reefs and mountains. Photo opportunities beg around every bend: it's an especially spectacular trip at sunrise or sunset. A good range of accommodation peppers the coast, each pocketed within its own private cove.

East of Korolevu, the Queens Road turns away from the shore and climbs over the southern end of Viti Levu's dividing mountain range. To the east of this range the road improves and the scenery changes to lush rainforest as the road winds its way past wider bays.

🏃 Activities

Besides slumming it at the beach, the most popular activities are snorkelling and diving. Resorts ferry guests to and from the outer reefs daily for close encounters of the marine kind.

This area is also well served by the tour companies at Sigatoka and Pacific Harbour, which all pick up from the hotels. Savu Na Mate Laya Waterfall is 2.5km inland from the turn-off to Biausevu village, a 15-minute drive east of Hideaway Resort. The waterfall is an easy 30-minute walk from the village. Make sure you read about village etiquette before arriving.

The Korolevu stretch of coast offers some spectacular diving within close distance of the shore. Some notable sites include **Wonderwall**, with its 'snowdrift' of white soft corals, and, for the experienced, the **Gunbarrel**, an adrenalin-laced dive riding a strong current through a narrow gorge amid schools of snapper and surgeonfish. Most dives are conveniently close to shore.

Dive Away Fiji   DIVING
(☑926 3112; www.diveawayfiji.com) Runs the dive shops at the Outrigger (on the Sunset Strip) and Fiji Hideaway resorts. Most guests are ferried to Hideaway or Mango Bay from

where the dive boats depart. A two-tank dive costs $160 and the PADI Open Water Course costs $920.

South Pacific Adventure Divers   DIVING

(☑653 0555; www.spadfiji.com) Dive operators for the Warwick and Naviti resorts but, like Dive Away, they'll collect from other nearby hotels. A two-tank dive costs $145, and the PADI open water course costs $980. They also offer shark diving at Beqa Lagoon on Mondays and Saturdays ($360).

🛏 Sleeping

Most accommodation options are along the 20km or so stretch of coast around Korolevu.

Beachhouse   HOSTEL $

(☑653 0500; www.fijibeachhouse.com; dm $45, d $140-180, incl breakfast; ⊖🛜🗷) Aimed squarely at backpackers, this long-time favourite combines simple digs with heady social activities in a consistently winning formula. The dorms (including a women-only dorm) are in two-storey houses and the doubles are in colourful duplex bungalows. Buses will stop right outside and there's a pretty pool, a cheap cafe and on-site cooking facilities. A great place to meet travellers.

Mango Bay Resort   HOSTEL $

(☑653 0069; www.mangobayresortfiji.com; dm/d/ bungalow incl breakfast $40/200/280; ⊖@🛜🗷) The dorm, cabins and *bures* are scattered through 6 hectares of parklike grounds. Facilities are excellent for the budget – the dorms are modern, the *bures* have atrium showers and the beach is one of the best on the Coral Coast. Mango mainly targets a younger crowd with plenty of activities of the full-moon-party, crab racing and sunset-bonfire variety. Snorkelling is available.

★ Waidroka Surf & Dive Resort   RESORT $$

(☑330 4605; www.waidroka.com; r $275, bungalow $375-425; @🗷) Over a hilly 4.5km of dirt road, Waidroka caters to serious surfers and divers looking for an upmarket alternative to the Yanuca island surf camps. Check out the variety of combined packages on their website. There's a small flotilla of boats on hand to take guests to local breaks and Frigate Passage.

The resort crew are skilled at finding the best waves and run a dive operation that includes shark diving off Beqa. Non-surfing/ diving partners are also well catered for with free snorkelling and kayaking, beachside massages and an excellent **restaurant**

(meal packages $110). Guests stay in either bright-orange *bures* or the adjoining terrace rooms – both are very smart.

Tambua Sands Beach Resort   RESORT $$

(☑650 0399; http://warwickhotels.com/tambuasands; r $172-249; 🗷) Tambua Sands is smeared across a pretty slice of coast and keeps its guests busy with village tours, reef-walking excursions and a tour desk. The manicured lawns are littered with sun loungers. Individual high-ceilinged *bures* feature a smart mix of dark woods and bright tropical paintings, set either amid the gardens or directly facing the ocean.

Crusoe's Retreat   RESORT $$

(☑650 0185; www.crusoesretreat.com; r incl breakfast from $235; 🛜🗷) Driving down the long dirt track to Crusoe's Retreat off the Queens Road, you'd be forgiven for thinking you were heading to the middle of nowhere, but there's a real gem at the end of the road. Many of the 28 spacious and fan-cooled *bures* are located on a hillside and the stairs are not ideal for older guests, but it's a truly tranquil retreat for others.

The pool is small but the **restaurant** (mains $15 to $25) serves classy fare, and you can also walk along the beach to the Wellesley for a change of scene. The inhouse Dive Crusoes (www.divecrusoes.com) dive shop offers everything for both scuba fiends and first-timers alike.

Wellesley Resort   RESORT $$

(☑603 0664; www.wellesleyresort.com.fj; Man Fri Rd; d from $249, ste incl breakfast $349-559; ⊖✳@🗷) This top-end, adults-only resort oozes comfort, style and tranquility. The 15 suites saddle a small valley that leads to a pretty coves and even the most ardent adrenalin junkies will soon rediscover their inner sloth. The restaurant (anyone for 'Fijian tapas' meets contemporary Pacific?) is excellent, and you can ease off the calories in the indulgent spa. The resort is nearly 5km off the Queens Road.

Hideaway Resort   RESORT $$$

(☑650 0177; www.hideawayfiji.com; r $375-564; ⊖✳@🗷🛶) This enormous resort has 116 *bures* of varying shapes and sizes spread out amid some lush gardens and along calm sandy beach and neatly manicured lawn, but impressively its size never feels overwhelming. It's had a serious spruce-up since our last visit, and accommodation is smart and airy (with fresh cream-and-white walls), and generously-sized. There's a pool-side lagoon bar, waterslide for the kids (it's a popular place with families, who also enjoy the kids club) and a decent restaurant. Dive Away Fiji is based here.

Naviti Resort RESORT $$$
(☑653 0444; www.navitiresort.com.fj; r incl breakfast $285-799; ☯☀@☒🏊) Heavy on the greenery and light on the concrete, the Naviti's 220 rooms have access to all the goodies – four restaurants, five bars, a nine-hole golf course, a swim-up bar, a health spa and a kids club. Unlike most resorts, all-inclusive packages include beer, wine, Sigatoka shopping excursions, a sunset cruise and a choice between à la carte or buffet dining. The two tiny islands offshore are used for weddings and there's an all-tide swimming lagoon to compensate for the poor beach.

Warwick Fiji Resort & Spa RESORT $$$
(☑653 0555; www.warwickfiji.com; r incl breakfast $554, ste incl breakfast $745; ☯☀@☒) Owned by the same crowd that own Naviti (there's a free shuttle between the two and guests can use both resorts' facilities), the Warwick is another feature-laden, activity-rich resort. The public areas feature tiles, wooden floors, cane furniture and soft brown furnishings. There are five restaurants, seven bars (one of which has Middle Eastern water pipes) and lagoons with all-tide swimming areas.

South Pacific Adventure Divers (p81) is based here and at Naviti resort.

✖ Eating

★ Eco Café ITALIAN $$
(☑653 0064; Votua village; pizza $25-38, pasta $25; ☻2-9pm Fri-Tue) This joint Italian-Fijian enterprise doesn't disappoint. It's a charming open-fronted, wood-and-bamboo place facing directly onto the sea with a mellow beach bar vibe. Pizzas are cooked in a wood-fired oven, and the focaccia is excellent. There's also some great Fijian food (with a strong emphasis on fresh veggies), but you'll need to call a day in advance to order.

Eco Café doesn't have an alcohol license, but welcomes BYO (a small corkage fee applies). Otherwise, enjoy the excellent Italian coffee or the refreshing homemade lemonade. The restaurant is on the Queens Road between the Naviti and Warwick resorts.

Vilisite's Restaurant FISH & CHIPS $$
(☑650 1030; Queens Rd; mains $15-40; ☻breakfast, lunch & dinner) If you're wearing your *bula* shirt, you'll feel right at home as this place drips tropical garb. It's a couple of kilometres beyond the Naviti and has sweeping sea views. There's Chinese, seafood curries and lobster on offer, but everyone seems to order the fish and chips.

❶ Getting There & Around

There are plenty of buses shuttling along the Queens Road (getting to Suva or Nadi costs about $7 to $9 depending on where you start from) and drivers will pick up and drop off at resort gates. The Warwick and the Naviti have a free shuttle bus for guests to Nadi International Airport. A taxi to Sigatoka takes 20 minutes and costs around $15 to $20.

Pacific Harbour

Leaving the glorious vegetation and hilly passes of Korolevu in its wake, the Queens Road sweeps across a small bridge into Pacific Harbour, the self-labelled 'Adventure Capital of Fiji'. A range of activities, guaranteed to have hearts racing and knees knocking, backs up the claim.

Pacific Harbour itself looks anything but adventurous. It began in the 1970s as a canal development, then evolved into a place for holiday homes. The resulting wide culs-de-sac, manicured lawns and orderly river settings are more 'soccer dad and bridge parties' than Fijian. The current big development is the Pacific Palm Marina, the first stage of which was due to open in early 2016 at the mouth of the river, next to the Pearl South Pacific resort. A large marina is planned, plus restaurants, spa, a golf course and residential units.

🏃 Activities

Arts Village CULTURAL TOUR
(Map p83; ☑345 0065; www.artsvillage.com.fj; day pass per adult/child from $60/30; ☻9am-4pm Wed-Sat) This faux village is unashamedly 'Fiji in a theme park', and within its Disneylike confines are a temple, chiefly *bure*, cooking area with utensils and weaving hut. Fijian actors dressed in traditional costumes carry out mock battles, preach pagan religion and demonstrate traditional arts. Tours include a canoe tour (for the kids), Island Temple Tour and Arts Village Show, and fire-walking (11am). It's fun for families, but not much to do with authentic village life.

Attached to the Arts Village, the Marketplace is a congregation of eateries, supermar-

Pacific Harbour

N | 0 ——— 500 m
0 ——— 0.25 miles

Zip Fiji (20km);
Suva (52km)

Sigatoka (79km)
Deuba Beach

Beqa Passage

Pacific Harbour

Activities, Courses & Tours
1 Aqua-Trek Beqa B3
2 Arts Village... C2
3 Jetski Tours.. B3
4 Rivers Fiji... B3

Sleeping
5 Club Oceanus B3
6 Lagoon Resort..C1
7 Pearl South Pacific C3

8 Tsulu Backpackers....................................D2
9 Uprising Beach Resort...........................D2

Eating
10 Baka Blues Cafe.......................................C2
Mantarae Restaurant.................... (see 7)
11 Oasis Restaurant.....................................C2
12 Sakura House B2
13 Tiki Bar & Melting Pot Restaurant.........C2
14 Water's Edge..C2

---

kets and souvenir shops, and is a pleasant spot in which to kill an hour or so.

Diving

There are more than 20 dive sites near Pacific Harbour, mostly within Beqa Lagoon and its fantastic soft coral sites. These include **ET**, which features a vast tunnel more than 30m long, densely blanketed with sea fans and soft corals. But the main attraction here are the sharks – and we're not talking wimpy white-tips. **Beqa Lagoon** is one of the few places where it's possible to dive with massive, barrel-chested bull and tiger sharks without being caged or sedated (that's either the sharks or the divers).

Other impressive dives include **Side Streets** (soft corals, coral heads and gorgoni-an fans), **Frigate Walls** (a 48m wall in Frigate Pass, with large pelagic fish), and **Caesar's Rocks** (coral heads and swim-throughs).

Aqua-Trek Beqa   DIVING
(Map p83; ☎345 0324; www.aquatrek.com; Club Oceanus) Pacific Harbour's dive operator makes big thing of their shark encounter dives at Beqa ($345 plus $15 marine reserve fee, compared to their regular $280 two-tank dive). For newbies, an introductory dive costs $280, or you can sign up for the PADI Open Water Course ($1018). The shark-feeding dives are available Mondays, Wednesdays, Fridays and Saturdays.

Fishing & Boating

Pacific Harbour's reefs, shoals, bait schools, current lines and drop-offs are ideal for both and popping. Wahu, mahi mahi, and yellowfin tuna are all regularly

Xtasea Charters FISHING

(☑345 0280; http://xtaseacharters.com; full boat charters per day around $1800) Game fishing charter boat serving those who want to troll for light fish or wrestle their strength against the bigger game fish. Knowledgeable crew will set a course for the best local fishing between Pacific Harbour, Beqa and further afield.

Freedive Fiji FISHING

(☑973 0687; www.freedivefiji.com; half day per person $240) If spear- or game-fishing is your thing, this is the outfit for you. There are set departures each day, but you can organise whole boat charters too.

Ziplining

Zip Fiji ADVENTURE SPORTS

(Map p54; ☑672 6045; www.zip-fiji.com; zip line $225; ☺8am-8pm) This outfit lets squealing thrill-seekers whoosh from one platform to another through dense forest canopy in a series of eight aerial zip lines that stretch 2km – the longest zip is a dizzying 210m. The zipline is 25 minutes' drive from Pacific Harbour, but the cost includes transfers.

Kila Eco Adventure Park ADVENTURE SPORTS

(Map p54; ☑331 7454; www.kilaworld.com; half/full day adult $122/170, child $97/142, nature walk only $15; ☺10am-4.30pm) This adventure park is aimed at the whole family. There are high and low rope walks, a zip line, abseiling and what bills itself as Fiji's biggest swing – at 12m high, it almost feels like a bungee jump. For those who prefer a little less adrenaline, there are also 10km of nature walks, with picnic *bures* along the way, and waterfalls where you can take a dip. Individual activities cost $60 if you don't want to buy a whole tour. The park is near Navua.

👉 Tours

Based just out of town in Navua, but also working the Pacific Harbour hotels, are Discover Fiji Tours (p86) and **Namuamua Inland Tour** (☑672 2074; www.touristtransport fiji.com/great-sights-fiji), both of which offer tours into the Navua River area.

Rivers Fiji ADVENTURE TOUR

(Map p83; ☑345 0147; www.riversfiji.com; Pearl South Pacific) Rivers offers excellent kayaking and white-water rafting trips into the Na-

mosi Highlands north of Pacific Harbour. The day trip ($310 per person including lunch) to Wainikoroiluva (Luva Gorge) is highly recommended and the scenery alone is worth the bumpy two-hour carrier trip up to Nakavika village. After the obligatory kava session with the chief, you paddle downstream (four hours) by inflatable kayak over stretches of gentle rapids and past waterfalls to Namuamua village. Here, where the Wainikoroiluva River joins the Upper Navua River, the tour is completed with a motorised longboat ride. For spectacular gorges and grade two/three rapids, try the day trip to the Upper Navua River ($460 per person). It is more physically demanding and involves about five hours on the water. The one-hour road trip to Nabukelevu village is very scenic.

Jetski Tours ADVENTURE TOUR

(Map p83; ☑345 0933; www.jetski-safari.com; 158 Kaka Pl) Jetski Tours takes travellers on a four-hour, full-throttle, 65km jet-ski tour (solo rider $530, twin share $290 per person) around Beqa Lagoon. Lunch, snorkelling gear, wetsuits and life jackets are included. Book at least a day in advance.

🛌 Sleeping

Tsulu Backpackers HOSTEL $

(Map p83; ☑345 0065; dm $35, d 70-90, apt $150; ❄@❄) Attached to the Arts Village, the Tsulu has picked up the artistic gauntlet and run with it. The walls of the dorms and double rooms are painted in vibrant murals. It's super cheap, but has something of a school dormitory feeling to it that even the cheery walls can't overcome. All bathroom facilities are shared.

Club Oceanus MOTEL $

(Map p83; ☑345 0498; www.cluboceanus.com; 1 Atoll Pl; dm $30, r $150-190; ☺❄☎❄) This waterside resort (all rooms face the river) has a selection of clean and comfortable rooms in a long, compact block. The cosy 'loft' sleeps four, and there are kitchen facilities in the 12-bed dorm. It's good value, located in a convenient spot on the canal close to the Arts Village complex and has Brizo's Grill bar-restaurant on site.

Lagoon Resort RESORT $

(Lagoon Resort; Map p83; ☑345 2096; Fairway Pl; r $100-130; ☺❄❄) This grandiose colonial hotel was built in the '80s as a bordello, was painted pink by Korean owners in 1995 and has undergone several changes of fortune since. It has hosted the cast of *Anaconda 2* – the boat from the movie lies in a dilapidated state outside the bar: a good metaphor for the current poor state of the hotel's offerings.

Uprising Beach Resort RESORT **$$**

(Map p83; ☑345 2200; www.uprisingbeach resort.com; dm incl breakfast $60, bungalow incl breakfast $255-300, villa from $355; ❄🤝🏊) The Uprising continues to give other resorts a run for their money, recently raising the bar with 12 very swish villas to add to the 12 spacious *bures*. There are nifty outdoor showers and bifolding doors to catch the ocean breeze. The 'treehouse' dorm is spotlessly clean and although it isn't in a tree, it does afford beautiful views from the verandah.

The restaurant serves global cuisine and there are usually enough barflies buzzing around to give the bar a cheery vibe, especially on weekends when people come up from Suva.

Pearl South Pacific RESORT **$$$**

(Map p83; ☑345 0022; www.thepearlsouth pacific.com; Queens Rd; r $485, ste from $550; ➡❄@🏊) This resort was undergoing a massive extension program when we visited to almost double its size. It's high-end stuff – Fijian-Asian fusion rooms that come themed in six flavours including Red Passion and Moody Blues. Style gurus will overdose on the marble bathrooms, low-slung beds and private decks with cushioned sun loungers – even if some of the final finish is a bit lacking.

There's no kids club here but there are plenty of activities to keep adults happy: a day spa, Sunday BBQ with live music, the stylish Seduce restaurant on the waterfront, discounted fees at the affiliated golf course and two boats available for fishing and charters. When the new marina opens, this place will be jumping even more.

🍴 Eating

⭐**Baka Blues Cafe** FUSION **$$**

(Map p83; Arts Village Marketplace; mains $20-30; ⏱11am-10pm Tue-Sun) New Orleans blues accompanies the Cajun-influenced menu at this restaurant, which is the marketplace's standout offering. There's live music on Wednesday, Friday and Sunday evenings.

Tiki Bar & Melting Pot Restaurant INTERNATIONAL **$$**

(Map p83; Arts Village Marketplace; mains $8-30; ⏱lunch & dinner) In keeping with the faux-Fijian theme of the Arts Village, this open-air eatery is on the sand banks of a swimming pool. Overlooked by an 18m-tall, Aztec-like tiki head, this place is great for kids, who can swim in the pool or pickle themselves in the cannibals' 'hot pot' spa. Oh...and the food's not bad either. Day visitors can swim too (adult/child $5/2.50).

Water's Edge PIZZA **$$**

(Map p83; Arts Village Marketplace; mains $8-28; ⏱lunch & dinner) The deckside dining at Water's Edge is surrounded by the water-lily pond and makes a scenic lunch stop. The menu is strong on pizza and Indian (tandoori chicken pizza $20).

Oasis Restaurant INTERNATIONAL **$$**

(Map p83; Arts Village Marketplace; mains $16-36; ⏱breakfast, lunch & dinner; ❄) Burgers, sandwiches, tortillas, curries and a whole lotta seafood is served at this long-time local favourite. The secondhand books for sale may not be great literature but go really well on a sun lounger.

Mantarae Restaurant FUSION **$$$**

(Map p83; ☑345 0022; Pearl South Pacific; mains $28-40; ⏱dinner Tue-Sat) This place offers interesting contemporary, fusion-style cuisine that has diners licking their lips from entrée to dessert. The Thai night when we visited was delicious. Sprawled out on a day bed, or sequestered behind the bar with its mirror-backed water feature, it's fine dining all the way – with a wine list to match.

Sakura House JAPANESE **$$$**

(Map p83; ☑345 0256; River Dr; mains $25-40; ⏱dinner) Although it features other Asian dishes, the Japanese tempura, sashimi, *shabu-shabu* (thinly sliced meat and vegetables cooked tableside in a pot of boiling water) and teriyaki are Sakura's speciality.

🛍 Shopping

Attached to the Arts Village is the Arts Village Marketplace, an open-air shopping mall of mock-colonial buildings. It has a supermarket, several cafes (try fresh juices and smoothies at Mai Juice) and several souvenir shops selling Fiji-style resort wear and some good but pricey handicrafts.

ℹ Information

Rosie's Tours (Map p83; ☑345 0655) has a tour desk at Arts Village Marketplace and can book all of the activities within the area. There's also an ATM in the shopping mall and internet can be found at Oasis Restaurant and the Tsulu Backpackers & Apartments arcade.

❶ Getting There & Around

There are frequent **Pacific Transport** (☑ 330 4366; www.pacifictransport.com.fj) and **Sunbeam Transport** (www.sunbeamfiji.com) buses travelling the Queens Road between Lautoka and Suva, as well as vans and carriers. They all call in at Pacific Harbour.

The first bus from Pacific Harbour to Nadi ($15, 3½ hours) leaves at about 7.50am and the last at around 7pm. The first bus to Suva ($4.15, one hour) leaves at 10.15am and the last at 9.40pm. Coral Sun Fiji (www.coralsunexpress.com) buses stop opposite Rosie's Tours at 8.20am and 4.45pm for Nadi ($18) and at 10.50am and 4.15pm for Suva ($10). A taxi costs about $40 to Suva and about $145 to Nadi.

Around Pacific Harbour

Navua & The Namosi Highlands

The steamy Namosi Highlands north of Pacific Harbour have some of Fiji's most spectacular mountain scenery, including dense lush rainforests, steep ranges, deep river canyons and tall waterfalls. If you have your own wheels (preferably 4WD and in dry weather), take a detour as far inland as you can from Nabukavesi, east of Navua. Or drive the back road to Suva if you're heading that way. If you intend to visit a village, take along some kava. Sunday is observed as a day of rest. Navua itself isn't much of a draw, but it is the launchpad for trips into the interior. The agricultural town is a base for dairy farming, rice and other crops.

☞ Tours

Discover Fiji Tours   ADVENTURE TOUR
(Map p54; ☑ 345 0180; www.discoverfijitours.com) Discover runs several tours to the Navua River area. Tours include waterfall visits, 4WD trips, trekking, kayaking and white-water rafting – there seem to be a dizzying number of permutations on offer – and cost between $225 and $469. Prices vary according to transfers: they'll pick you up anywhere between Nadi and Suva. All day tours last about six hours and include lunch.

Rivers Fiji   ADVENTURE TOUR
(☑ 345 0147; www.riversfiji.com) Rivers Fiji, based in Pacific Harbour, also offers longer trips deeper inland into this beautiful wilderness area that travellers otherwise rarely see.

🛏 Sleeping

Navua Upriver Lodge   LODGE **$**
(Map p54; ☑ 933 7157, 336 2589; navuaupriver lodge.com; Nuku Village; dm/d $30/90) Situated about 25km north of Navua town, this Fijian-run lodge offers travellers a genuine river-village experience. Accommodation is in three basic buildings surrounded by stunning green scenery. You can trek into the highlands or just watch the locals pass by on their *bilibilis* (bamboo rafts). In the evenings, villagers will often join you for a kava session.

The food is pretty simple, and you might want to take extra for self-catering or just snacking. The lodge is a two-hour boat ride from Navua, passing more than a dozen waterfalls – the perfect way to ease yourself into a visit. Call the lodge well in advance and they'll arrange a boat transfer for you.

❶ Getting There & Away

The regular express buses along the Queens Road stop at Navua – it's just 30 minutes from Suva ($3.50).

There are boats to and from Namuamua and Nukusere villages, about 20km up the Navua River. The trip can take up to two hours ($15 each way), depending on the river's water level and general conditions. The boats leave any time between 10am and noon, but do not always return before the next morning (sometime between 6am and 7am).

Offshore Islands

World-class diving and snorkelling can be had in the waters that surround the islands off southern Viti Levu and are the principal reason for visiting this area. The easiest way to dive or snorkel on the surrounding coral reefs is with one of the dive-shop operators based in the Pacific Harbour resorts.

Beqa

The high island of Beqa (be-*ng*a), about 7.5km south of Pacific Harbour is visible from the Queens Road and even from Suva on a clear day. The island is about 7km in diameter, with a deeply indented coastline and rugged interior that slopes steeply down to the coast. The villagers of Rukua, Naceva and Dakuibeqa are known for their tradition of fire-walking. It's now performed chiefly for tourists at the Coral Coast resorts. Beqa is also known for the **Shark Reef Marine Reserve**, established

SOME LIKE IT HOT

Of all Fiji's cultural rituals, the extraordinary art of fire-walking is perhaps the most impressive. Watching men display the poise of a lead ballerina while they traverse a pit of blazing embers without combusting is truly baffling. Even more mystifying is the fact that, originally, this ritual was practised in Fiji only on the tiny island of Beqa. Indigenous Fijian fire-walking is known as *vilavilairevo* (literally 'jumping into the oven'). The ability to walk barefoot on white-hot stones without being burned was, according to local legend, granted to a local chief by the leader of the *veli*, a group of little gods. Now the direct descendants of the chief serve as the *bete* (priests) who instruct in the ritual of fire-walking.

Preparations for fire-walking used to occupy a whole village for nearly a month. Firewood and appropriate stones had to be selected, costumes made and various ceremonies performed. Fire-walkers had to abstain from sex and refrain from eating any coconut for up to a month before the ritual. None of the fire-walkers' wives could be pregnant, or it was believed the whole group would receive burns.

Traditionally, *vilavilairevo* was only performed on special occasions in the village of Navakaisese. Today, though, it's performed only for commercial purposes and has little religious meaning. There are regular performances at the Pacific Harbour Arts Village, at the larger resort hotels and at Suva's annual Hibiscus Festival.

---

in 2004. Eight species of shark are found on the reef, and local villages provide wardens to prevent illegal fishing. All dives that visit the reef include a fee that goes towards the reef community fund.

🛏 Sleeping

Lawaki Beach House LODGE $
(Map p54; ☑992 1621, 368 4088; www.lawaki beachhousefiji.com; sites per tent incl meals $93, dm/s/d $139/159/198) 🍃 This small resort sits in front of an isolated beach on the southwestern side of Beqa. The place comprises two double *bures* with en suites and verandahs, and a six-bed dorm. The unobtrusive and cosy set-up blends well with the surrounding environment as do the solar, recycling and water-use practices. Guests mingle together in the communal lounge, soaking up the relaxed mood.

There is good snorkelling off the secluded, pristine white-sand beach, as well as diving, surfing, and visits to the nearby village. Transfers from Pacific Harbour cost $220 one way (one or two guests). Alternatively, you catch the small public ferry from the Navua Jetty. The ferry usually leaves between noon and 2.30pm Monday through Saturday, and costs $40 per person one way. It returns to Navua at 7am every day but Sunday.

Beqa Lagoon Resort RESORT $$$
(Map p54; ☑330 4042; www.beqalagoon resort.com; 3-night stay with meal plan from $845; ❋@⚊) The 25 stylish and well-maintained

bures here come with opulent bathrooms and traditional interiors, and some with plunge pools. The surrounding landscape and calm bay in front lends itself to excellent snorkelling and kayaking. There's a restaurant-lounge serving fabulous food, and a spa and a pool beside a coconut tree–fringed beach. It's a dive resort fair and square, offering all-inclusive packages.

Yanuca

Tiny Yanuca island is a hilly speck inside Beqa Lagoon, about 9km west of Beqa. It has comely beaches, good snorkelling and is close to the humbling breaks of Frigate Passage. Unsurprisingly, it lures avid surfers, many of whom come for a week, slip into the lifestyle and stay for a month. If living in your swimmers 24/7 is your idea of bliss, then you've found utopia.

Batiluva Beach Resort RESORT $$
(Map p54; ☑345 0384, 992 0021; www.batiluva. com; all inclusive $175, transfer from Pacific Harbour $50) The sturdy accommodation houses three spotless and airy dorms, and two double rooms. The per-person price is the same for each, but couples get first dibs on the doubles (there's not much privacy though as the internal dividing wall doesn't reach the ceiling). The all-inclusive rate includes the daily boat out to the reef for the surf-till-you-drop clientele. The beach here is quite pretty with plenty of fish, but for good snorkelling over coral you need to go on a short boat trip (free of charge).

SUVA

POP 167,975

Suva (soo-va) is the heart of Fiji, home to half of the country's urban population and the largest city in the South Pacific. It's a lush green city on a hilly peninsula, that gets more than its fair share of rain, and has a vibrant cultural scene.

Downtown is as diverse architecturally as the populace is culturally. A jigsaw of colonial buildings, modern shopping plazas, abundant eateries and a breezy esplanade all form the compact central business district. Small passages are lined with curry houses, sari shops and bric-a-brac traders. Bollywood and Hollywood square off at the local cinema and within the same hour you're likely to see businessmen in traditional sulu (sarong) and student hipsters from across the Pacific region rocking the latest styles.

History

Suva was something of a village backwater until the 19th-century reign of Chief Cakobau (pronounced tha-com-bau). A raid on the village by his rivals from Rewa helped spark an 11-year war that eventually saw Cakobau become the most powerful ruler in the islands. In the late 1860s, the perennially indebted chief leased the land round Suva to the Australian Polynesia Company in return for having his balance of payments cleared.

The incoming Australians cleared the land and drained its swamps, in an unsuccessful attempt to grow cotton and sugar cane. However, things didn't take off until the colonial capital at Levuka began to run out of land to expand. Two Melbourne merchants, Thomson and Renwick, encouraged the government to relocate the capital to Suva with incentives in the form of land grants. The government officially moved to Suva in 1882, when it was a township of about a dozen buildings. By the 1920s it was a flourishing colonial centre, and was officially declared a city.

Suva's recent history is inevitably linked to the coups. The 1987 coup threw the city into chaos, and in May 2000 its parliament buildings became the site of a hostage drama when George Speight and his militia held 36 government officials captive for almost two months.

◉ Sights

As well as living a cosmopolitan lifestyle, the majority of Suva's residents are very religious, and dash off to temple or church on a regular basis. Chatty and welcoming custodians at most of the city's churches, mosques and temples are happy to talk to visitors.

★ Fiji Museum
MUSEUM

(Map p90; ☎331 5944; www.fijimuseum.org. fj; Ratu Cakobau Rd; adult/child $7/5; ⊙9am-4.30pm Mon-Sat) This museum offers a great journey into Fiji's historical and cultural and evolution. To enjoy the exhibits in chronological order, start with the displays behind the ticket counter and work your way around clockwise. The centre piece is the massive Ratu Finau (1913), Fiji's last waqa tabus (double-hulled canoe), over 13m long and with an enclosed deck for rough weather. Other attractions in the main hall include war clubs, a gruesome display about cannibalism and the rudder from The Bounty (of Mutiny fame).

The growing influence of other South Pacific and European cultures is documented in a hall on the other side of the museum shop. It is here that you'll find the well-chewed, but ultimately inedible, shoe of Thomas Baker, a Christian missionary eaten for his indiscretions in 1867. Upstairs, a small Indo-Fijian hall chronicles some of the contributions made by the Indian workers and their descendants who were brought to Fiji in the 1870s as indentured labourers. Also on the same floor is a gallery of beautiful masi by some of Fiji's finest contemporary artists.

The museum continually undertakes archaeological research and collects and preserves oral traditions. Many of these are published in Domodomo, a quarterly journal on history, language, culture, art and natural history that is available in the museum's gift shop. The museum has excellent open days on the last Saturday of every month, with live music, traditional dance (and sometime firewalkers), poetry, food and craft stalls.

After visiting the museum, ponder your new-found knowledge with a wander through the compact but beautiful Thurston Gardens. The dense conglomeration of native flora and surrounding lawns are less manicured and growing more haphazard with every coup, but it was here that the original village of Suva once stood. It's a

Suva

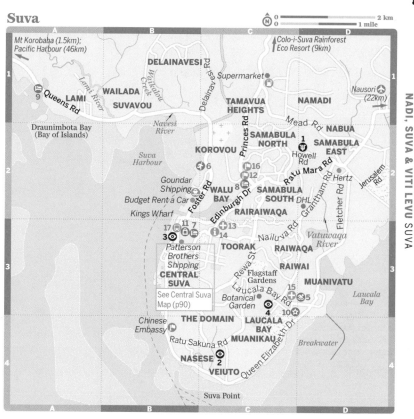

Suva

◎ Sights
1 Mariamma Temple	D2
Oceania Centre for Arts & Culture	(see 4)
2 Parliament of Fiji	C4
3 Suva Municipal Market	B3
4 University of the South Pacific	C3

✪ Activities, Courses & Tours
5 National Aquatic Centre	D3
6 Royal Suva Yacht Club	C2

🛏 Sleeping
7 Colonial Lodge	B3
8 Five Princes Hotel	C2
9 Novotel Suva Lami Bay	A1

✪ Entertainment
10 National Stadium	C3

🛍 Shopping
11 Suva Flea Market	B3
USP Book Centre	(see 4)

ℹ Information
12 Australian High Commission	C2
13 Colonial War Memorial Hospital	C3
14 Fiji Disabled People's Association	C3
15 Maharaj Medical Centre	C3
16 US Embassy	C2

ℹ Transport
17 Bus Station	B3
Taxi Stand	(see 17)

lovely spot for a picnic – particularly if you camp yourself under one of the grand and stately fig trees.

The Triangle MONUMENT
(Map p90) This intersection is the symbolic centre of Suva. A whitewashed marker com-

Central Suva

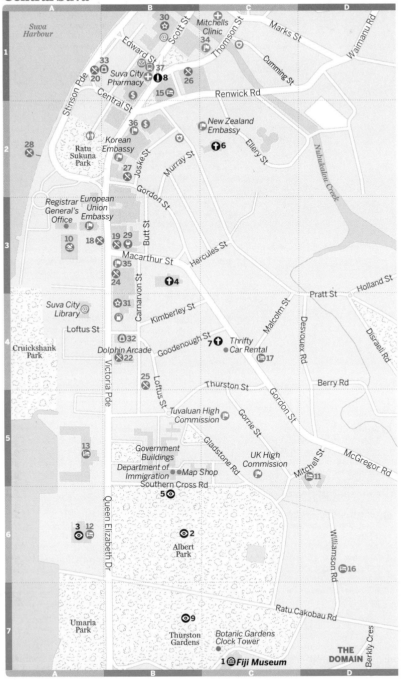

memorates the dates of the first missionaries arriving in Fiji, the establishment of the capital and the first public land sales in the country. It's a useful place for getting your bearings downtown.

Suva Municipal Market MARKET
(Map p89; Usher St; ⊗6am-6pm Mon-Fri, to 4.30pm Sat) It's the beating heart of Suva and a great place to spend an hour or so poking around with a camera. The boys with barrows own the lanes and they aren't afraid to mow down a few tourists to deliver their cassava on time. Besides the recognisable tomatoes, cabbages and chillies, look out for bitter gourds, jackfruit, *dalo* (taro), cassava and yams. Produce is cheaper than in supermarkets and there's no need to haggle – prices are clearly marked.

If you need refreshment, try the fresh pineapple juice stands. Head upstairs to buy your *sevusevu*. *Yaqona* (kava) root costs anything from $25 to $40 a kilo and a gift of these guarantees 100-watt smiles. Only cheapskates opt for the powdered, less potent, stems.

★**Colo-i-Suva Forest Park** FOREST
(Map p54; ☑332 0211; adult/child $5/1; ⊗8am-4pm) Colo-i-Suva (pronounced tholo-ee-s*oo*-va) is a 2.5-sq-km oasis of lush rainforest teeming with tropical plants and vivid and melodic bird life. The 6.5km of walking trails navigate clear natural pools and gorgeous vistas. Sitting at an altitude of 120m to 180m, it's a cool and peaceful respite from Suva's urban hubbub.

Slipping and sliding through the forest over water-worn rocks is the Waisila Creek, which makes its way down to Waimanu River and forms the water swimming holes along the way.

The mahogany and pines were planted after a period of aggressive logging in the 1940s and '50s to stabilise the topsoil without impinging on the indigenous vegetation. Among the wildlife are 14 different bird species, including scarlet robins, spotted fantails, Fiji goshawks, sulphur-breasted musk parrots, Fiji warblers, golden doves and barking pigeons.

The visitor information centre is on the leftside of the road as you approach from Suva. Buy your ticket here, check the state of the trails and any current security warnings, then head to the entrance booth on the other side of the road. The recommended route is to follow Kalabu Rd as it skirts the park,

Central Suva

turning up Pool Rd to the car park. From here, you take the Nature Trail to the Lower Pools for swimming, the aforementioned rope swinging and, if you remembered to bring it, lunch. It's a sweaty, uphill walk back to the main road via the Falls Trail. Without stopping this loop takes about 1½ hours to complete.

There have been very occasional incidents of muggings in the park and thefts from parked vehicles. Use your judgement. Rangers will lead guided two-hour walks ($30). The park receives an annual rainfall of 420cm and the trails can be extremely slippery, so sturdy footwear is essential.

The Sawani bus leaves Suva bus station every half hour ($2, 30 minutes) and will drop you at the gate. A taxi costs $15. If driving, follow Princes Rd out of Suva through Tamavua and Tacirua village.

University of the South Pacific UNIVERSITY
(USP; Map p89; ☎331 3900; www.usp.ac.fj; Laucala Bay Rd) While not necessarily a must-see from a tourist's perspective, this is the foremost provider of tertiary education to the island nations of the Pacific region. The USP's main Laucala Campus offers some fascinating people-watching and picturesque strolling through a small botanical garden where you can see temporary exhibits of paintings and carvings at the **Oceania Centre for Arts & Culture** (Map p89). The USP Bookshop nearby is particularly well-stocked.

The governments of 12 Pacific countries jointly own the university and mingling among the Fijian students you're likely to see young academics from the Cook Islands, Kiribati, Tonga, Vanuatu and Western Samoa. As this is a fee-paying institution, many of the 11,000 or so students rely on scholarships, and the competition for them is fierce.

Parliament of Fiji LANDMARK
(Map p89; www.parliament.gov.fj; Battery Rd; admission free) FREE Opened in June 1992, the parliament complex must be one of the world's most striking political hubs. It was

designed in the post-1987 atmosphere. The aim of maintaining indigenous Fijian values is apparent through the open-air corridors, traditional arts and structures, and *masi* cloths throughout. The main building, *vale ne bose lawa* (parliament house), takes its form from the traditional *vale* (family house) and has ceremonial access from Ratu Sukuna Rd.

The complex is 5km south of the city centre. Free tours are offered, but you need to email in advance to arrange the visit. It's also possible to watch debates when parliament is in session – a calendar of sitting days is available on the website.

It's easiest to reach by taxi, but you can hop on a bus along Queen Elizabeth Dr and walk along Ratu Sukuna Rd for 1km.

Holy Trinity Cathedral CHURCH
(Map p90; cnr Macarthur & Gordon Sts) This cathedral, with its unique boat-shaped interior, interesting Fijian tapestries and wood-beamed ceiling, is a peaceful retreat. The gigantic tree in front of the church is a showcase of Pacific plants, with cacti and ferns making themselves at home in its branches.

Roman Catholic Cathedral CHURCH
(Map p90; cnr Murray & Pratt Sts) This 1902 cathedral is built from sandstone imported from Sydney and is one of Suva's most prominent landmarks.

🏃 Activities

Suva all but closes down on a Sunday, so try to organise activities in advance or attend a Fijian church service to hear some uplifting, boisterous singing. Many of the tour companies based in Pacific Harbour and Navua also pick up from Suva hotels.

Trekking

Colo-i-Suva Forest Park is an easy place for bushwalking close to Suva. You can also hike to Mt Korobaba, about a two-hour walk from the cement factory near Lami. Joske's Thumb is an enticing spectacle for serious climbers. A climb to this peak was featured in the film Journey to the Dawning of the Day.

Keen trekkers should contact Suva-based **Talanoa Treks** (📞947 2732; www.talanoa-treks-fiji.com), Fiji's only dedicated trekking company, for details on their regular hiking departures or tailored trips, which can include Joske's Thumb. If you're in the area for an extended period consider signing up to the **Rucksack Club** (www.facebook.com/FijiRucksackClub), an expat group who organises regular hikes and other trips around the island. New members are always welcome.

A gentler but very popular walk (or jog or cycle or skateboard) is the several-kilometre stretch of Suva waterfront, on a well-used path that follows the sea wall along the length of Queen Elizabeth Dr. It's busy with Suvans exercising at dawn and dusk (but is not a place to exercise after dark).

Sailing

Royal Suva Yacht Club SAILING
(Map p89; 📞331 2921; www.rsyc.org.fj; ⏰office 8am-5pm Mon-Sat, 9am-4pm Sun) The Royal Suva Yacht Club is a popular watering hole for yachties and locals alike. It has great sunset views of the Bay of Islands, though the food can be hit and miss. Even without a yacht, overseas visitors are welcome and the atmosphere at the bar can be lively and salty; everyone has a story to tell.

The noticeboard is a good place to find crewing positions and the marina has dockside fuel and water. The Yacht Shop handles

---

GRAND DESIGNS

A short stroll along Suva's foreshore towards Albert Park brings you to one of Fiji's most dignified, and yet most neglected, buildings, the Grand Pacific Hotel (p97). In his book *The World is My Home*, James A Michener describes it as having '...a huge central dining area filled with small tables, each meticulously fitted with fine silver and china...and the barefoot Indians who served the meals [here] had a grace that few hotels in the world could offer and none surpass'.

Built in 1914 by the Union Steamship Company, the splendid white facade still hints at the hotel's former glory, also described by Somerset Maugham when he stayed here in 1916. It closed in 1992 and for a long time remained abandoned and in a continuing state of decay: floorboards upstairs rotted, shutters hung from glassless windows, wallpaper peeled from decaying walls and the army moved in to camp. In 2011, restoration finally began, and the hotel reopened with great ceremony in late 2014. Nonguests are welcome to visit the bar and restaurant (and goggle at the fabulous reception hall too, no doubt).

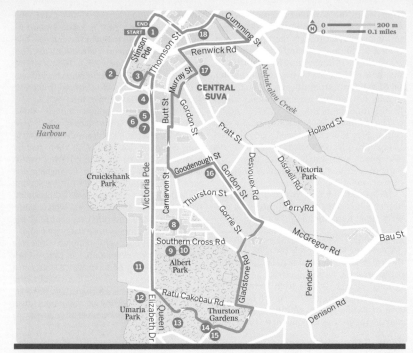

City Walk
Downtown Suva

START STINSON PDE
END STINSON PDE
LENGTH 3.5KM; TWO TO FOUR HOURS

Downtown Suva has a scattering of colonial buildings and places of interest, making it a pleasant place to wander around.

Start on Stinson Pde at the **1** **Suva Curio & Handicraft Market** (p99). Cross the street and follow the esplanade south, enjoying the views of Suva Harbour. Once you reach **2** **Tiko's Floating Restaurant** (p98), cross the road and amble through the tree-lined **3** **Ratu Sukuna Park**.

Continue south down Victoria Pde, past the 1926 **4** **Fintel building** and the 1904 **5** **old town hall**. The **6** **Suva Olympic Swimming Pool** (p95) is set back between this building and the 1909 **7** **Suva City Library** (p100).

Continue down Victoria Pde. On your left are the stately **8** **government buildings**. Just south is **9** **Albert Park**, a large sporting field. The **10** **Kingsford Smith Pavilion**, named after the famous aviator who landed here, is on Southern Cross Rd. Opposite the park is the glorious **11** **Grand Pacific Hotel** (p93). Just past Ratu Cakobau Rd is **12** **Umaria Park & Suva Bowls Club**, where you can take a breather with a cold drink.

Cross the road at Queen Elizabeth Dr and enter **13** **Thurston Gardens**. Meander through this colourful park, stopping at the **14** **Botanic Gardens Clock Tower** and the **15** **Fiji Museum** (p88). Turn left and walk along the edge of Albert Park along Gladstone Rd, before cutting up the pedestrian path to McGregor Rd. Head downhill and turn left at **16** **St Andrew's Church**, follow Goodenough St and dog-leg onto Carnarvon St. Stroll north past the bars and clubs to the **17** **Roman Catholic Cathedral** (p93), one of Suva's most prominent landmarks.

Turn left, then right and window-shop your way to Cumming St, then turn left to immerse yourself in Suva's little India – streets lined with Indian-run shops.

Make your way past the stately old **18** **Garrick Hotel**, then head back to the Curio & Handicraft Market. If you've got any energy left, spend it on a bout of souvenir shopping.

parts and repairs. Anchorage fees are $5 per day, or $50 if you prefer to overnight in one of the marina berths. There are laundry and shower facilities for those who have just arrived, and the office advises on customs and immigration procedures. Yachties use channel 16 to call ahead of arrival.

Sports

Suva has three off-shore breaks for surfers – a left-hand break at Sandbar and two right-handers at Lighthouse and Rat's Tail. You'll need to ask around locally to access them, though. Try the noticeboard at the Yacht Club.

Suva doesn't have a beach. The best places for a swim are the National Aquatic Centre and Suva Olympic Swimming Pool.

National Aquatic Centre SWIMMING
(Map p89; 679 3312177; Laucala Bay Rd; adult/child $5/3; 5am-7pm) Built for the 2003 South Pacific Games. Enter by the open side gate before 7am.

Suva Olympic Swimming Pool SWIMMING
(Map p90; 224 Victoria Pde; adult/child $3/1.50; 10am-6pm Mon-Fri, 8am-6pm Sat) Absolutely central.

Festivals & Events

Hibiscus Festival BEAUTY PAGEANT
(www.hibiscusfiji.com) Since its inception in 1956, the Hibiscus Festival has grown into a nine-day event, drawing large crowds from around Viti Levu. It is held every August to coincide with the second-term school break. The annual beauty pageant and the crowning of the 'Hibiscus Queen' are the chief draws, but families also flock to the live music and the amusement park, browse stalls and enjoy other free entertainment.

The festival has always been held in Albert Park, but it's been rumoured that it may swap locations in future – check the website for details in advance.

South Indian
Fire-Walking Festival RELIGIOUS
The extraordinary South Indian fire-walking festival is held at the Mariamma Temple (Map p89; 337 2773, 338 2357; Howell Rd, Samabula) annually in either July or August. On the day of the ritual, yellow-clad devotees gather at Suva Point, near the National Stadium, to bathe in the sea and make their final preparations for the fire-walking ahead. Temple pundits (Hindu priests) pierce the tongues, cheeks and bodies of the devotees with three-pronged skewers and smear their faces with yellow turmeric, a symbol of prosperity and a powerful totem over disease.

At around 2pm, the participants dance the 3km to the Mariamma Temple (arriving around 4pm) where a large crowd waits. Fire-walking over a bed of hot ash and coals is seen as a sign of devotion and self-sacrifice, the culmination of a 10-day ascetic period during which devotees rely solely on the offerings from the local Hindu community, abstain from sex and eating meat, and meditate to worship the goddess Maha Devi. It is believed that if the fire-walkers are cleansed of physical and spiritual impurities and thus focused on the divine Mother, they will feel no pain.

Sleeping

Accommodation options in the capital aren't as modish as those found in the more tourist-oriented towns elsewhere on the island. Most places cater to business travellers rather than tourists or backpackers, so the range of hotels is more restricted than elsewhere.As a rule, where wi-fi is available it's not included in the rate.

★ **Colo-i-Suva**
Rainforest Eco Resort LODGE $
(332 0113; www.raintreelodge.com; Princes Rd, Colo-i-Suva; dm/d $35/80, bungalow $185-255; @) It is hard to believe that the tranquil, rainforest-fringed lake that provides such a lush backdrop here was once a rock quarry. The three dormitories, communal kitchen, and double and twin rooms with shared bathrooms are clean and comfortable. There are also five *bures* set among the trees and these offer excellent value with plump beds and private decks. The lakeside bar/restaurant (mains $15 to $35) is a gorgeous place to hang out.

It's 11km from Suva centre – buses cost $2 and take 30 minutes and will drop you at the gate. A taxi costs $15.

South Seas Private Hotel HOSTEL $
(Map p90; 331 2296; www.fiji4less.com/south.html; 6 Williamson Rd; dm $25, s/d without bathroom $47/60, r with bathroom $77;) Set on a quiet street just a step away from the museum and botanic gardens, this is one of the few truly budget places in Suva. The sweeping interior verandah, classic white exterior, high ceilings and wide halls speak of the romance of a bygone era. This large colonial house has simple, clean rooms,

comfortably ageing lounge furniture and a shared kitchen.

Peninsula International Hotel
HOTEL $

(Map p90; ☏331 3711; www.peninsula.com.fj; cnr McGregor Rd & Pender St; s/d from $125/140; ⊛☀❋) Pleasantly situated in a leafy residential area, the Peninsula provides pretty good value. From the outside it looks like an apartment block and is recognisable by the overhanging window canopies (which get in the way of what would have been excellent views). There is a small pool, restaurant and bar on site. If you plan to stay here, aim high – the rooms and views get better the higher you go.

Colonial Lodge
GUESTHOUSE $

(Map p89; ☏330 0655; www.facebook.com/coloniallodge; 19 Anand St; dm $35, r $75, treehouse $140) This home-cum-hostel caters to backpackers and volunteers. It operates a lot like a homestay (and you'll get to know the owner's cats and dogs), but with simple dorm accommodation through the main house. There's a cute if rustic 'treehouse' extension annexe at the rear, with its own kitchen facilities. Basic but friendly.

Five Princes Hotel
BOUTIQUE HOTEL $$

(Map p89; ☏338 1575; www.fiveprinceshotel.com; 5 Princes Rd; d/bungalow/villa $240/280/400; ❋@☆❋) This one-time colonial villa is a great retreat away from the centre of Suva. Solid teak furniture, polished timber floors, power showers, satellite TV and wi-fi connections are all to be had in beautifully appointed rooms. Set in landscaped gardens, the stand-alone villas are similarly decorated and also include kitchenettes and private verandahs.

Quest Serviced Apartments
APARTMENT $$

(Map p90; ☏331 9117; www.questsuva.com; Thomson St; studio/1-bed apt $260/296) You'd never know these gems of apartments were here, tucked away on the 6th and 7th floor of the Suva Central building. Central, quiet, well-maintained and secure, they are popular with the long-stay embassy and development agency crowd, but there are always a few units available – there's a two-night minimum stay. There's an air-conditioned gym on-site too.

Best Western Suva Motor Inn
HOTEL $$

(Map p90; ☏331 3973; www.hexagonfiji.com; cnr Mitchell & Gorrie Sts; studio/2-bed apt $165/240; ❋@❋) The four-storey Best Western (no lift) is shaped like a 'U' around a richly planted courtyard with a small pool into which snakes a water slide. All rooms have balconies (the best with views to Albert Park) and the larger two-bedroom apartments sleep four and have kitchens. It's a good,

MOVING TO THE BEAT OF A DIFFERENT DRUM

Dancers pay homage to the steady beat of the drums, seemingly oblivious to the spectators. The poorly lit room is crowded with both tourists and locals yelling 'bula' to one another over the din. As a big, indigenous Fijian man – who better meets the image you may have of a traditional Fijian chief – approaches with a flower behind his ear and a pitcher of beer on his tray, you don't need any reminding that this is no meke (dance performance that enacts stories and legends). This is Saturday night in Suva, when the country's urban youth let down their hair and pole dance to pop music.

Fiji's urban youth face many of the same difficulties as young people around the globe: teenage parenting, crime, drugs and skyrocketing unemployment. However, these youths also find themselves straddling two opposing worlds: the traditional, conservative society of the villages many have left behind, where life was filled with cultural protocols, and the liberal, individualistic lifestyle of the modern and increasingly Westernised city. With 90% of television airtime devoted to Western sitcoms, young people watch a TV screen filled with an irrelevant and often unattainable world. On the positive side, the rising club and cafe culture is bringing together youths from indigenous and Indo-Fijian backgrounds, in the midst of a city filled with ethnic tension. On the negative side, many have difficulty finding a job and returning 'home' to a village sporting dreadlocks and skin-tight jeans isn't much easier. Youth have little room to voice their own opinions and it's not entirely surprising that many look for routes out of the country.

This is not the Fiji of postcards, of grass skirts and beachside lovo (Fijian feast cooked in a pit oven). However, it's well worth grabbing a cappuccino or putting on your dancing shoes to check out Fiji's rising urban youth culture. It's an unexpected eye-opener.

solid midrange choice. Wifi costs $30 a day. Road access is via Gladstone St, rather than McGregor Rd.

Holiday Inn
HOTEL $$

(Map p90; ☏330 1600; reservations@holidayinn suva.com.fj; Victoria Pde; r $272-497; ➌✳@☎☄) This inn occupies a great location on the harbour shore, across from the government buildings and near the museum. Rooms are generically spacious, cool and comfortable and will please picky travellers. The inn appeals to business travellers and those on coach tours, and it has the facilities, including wi-fi throughout, to match.

De Vos Hotel
HOTEL $$

(Central St; r $118-208; ☎) This hotel has a great location, opening straight onto Ratu Sukuna Park. It's all 1970s concrete and undeniably a little tatty around the edges, but the rooms are generously sized for the price (get one with a park view), the service is friendly, and there's a reasonable restaurant on the ground floor. As the sign on the elevator seemed to sum it up for us: 'Our lift is old and quirky – but well-maintained.'

Tanoa Plaza Hotel
HOTEL $$

(Map p90; ☏331 2300; www.tanoahotels.com; cnr Gordon & Malcolm Sts; s/d $290/300; ➌✳@ ☎☄) Functional and forgettable might be the byword for the rooms at the Tanoa. It's sleek and sophisticated in a minibar and pamper-products-in-the-bathroom kind of way, but what really sticks in the mind are the great views of Suva and the prompt and professional service. The Tanoa attracts a stream of visiting politicians and professionals.

★ Grand Pacific Hotel
HERITAGE HOTEL $$$

(Map p90; ☏322 2000; www.grandpacifichotel. com.fj; Victoria Pde; r $490-550, ste $650-1200; ✳☎☄) The GPH, as it's locally known, is one of Suva's jewels. This iconic 1914 building facing Albert Park has undergone extensive renovation to return it to its former glory. The original white porticoed building holds sumptuous suites, while the majority of rooms are in a sensitively designed new annexe at the rear. All rooms have pool or ocean views. The restaurant is well-priced for the venue, and one of the few places in Suva where you can sit outside next to the sea. There's a Swiss coffee shop out front, as well as a gym and spa for less calorifically indulgent moments.

Novotel Suva Lami Bay
HOTEL $$$

(Map p89; ☏336 2450; www.novotel.com; Queens Rd, Lami; r from $190-300; ☐✳☎☄) The low-slung Novotel offers no-nonsense business-style accommodation, but it has a great waterfront location and a pleasantly fresh and open restaurant with views across Draunimbota Bay. The only drawback is the location – Lami is a 10-minute drive from central Suva.

✖ Eating

For a compact city, Suva offers a relatively diverse and multicultural array of eateries. It's the best place in Fiji to try authentic Fijian and Indo-Fijian food, but there are plenty of Western-style options on offer as well.

Cafe Thirty
BISTRO $

(Map p90; 30 MacGregor Rd; mains $18-30, sandwiches $6-16; ☺8am-10pm Mon-Fri, to 3pm Sat) A cheery and unpretentious place to grab a bite, particularly at lunchtime when the sandwiches and wraps are on offer. All the servings are generous, from salads to *kokoda*. The fish and chips (get a plate to share) coat your mouth in an oily snuggle. There's no alcohol served, but you won't miss it with the array of refreshing fruit juices.

Old Mill Cottage
FIJIAN $

(Map p90; ☏331 2134; 49 Carnarvon St; dishes $5-12; ☺breakfast & lunch Mon-Sat) Officials and government aides from the nearby embassies cram the front verandah of this cheap and cheerful Suva institution to indulge in authentic Fijian fare. Dishes, including *palusami* (meat, onion and *lolo* – coconut cream – wrapped in *dalo* leaves), are displayed under the front counter alongside Indian curries and vegetarian dishes.

Bad Dog Cafe
BISTRO $

(Map p90; ☏331 2322; cnr Macarthur St & Victoria Pde; mains from $15; ☺11am-11pm Mon-Sat, 5-11pm Sun) Straddling the divide between cafe, bar and restaurant, Bad Dog offers up an Western-style mix of steaks, burgers, salads and seafood. Pizza night is on Tuesday, with two-for-one pizzas. There's a reasonable wine list and better-than-average selection of imported beers.

Singh's Curry House
SOUTH INDIAN $

(Map p90; ☏359 1019; Gordon St; mains around $12; ☺10am-5pm) Owner Mamaji runs a tight ship at this great little curry joint, where a delectable array of mostly South Indian curries tempts diners from the front counter. Seating is at booths or you can take away. It's one of the few places open on a Sunday and a great option for vegetarians.

Barbecue Stands BARBECUE $

(Map p90; beside the handicraft market; meal boxes $6; ☉5pm-4am Tue-Sat) The teams of cooks here serve Suva's best-value meals into the wee hours of the night. Styrofoam boxes are crammed with enough carbs and cholesterol (*dalo*, sausage, chops, cassava, lamb steak, eggs with a token serve of coleslaw) to arrest the heart of a marathon runner.

Republic of Cappucino CAFE $

(Map p90; Dolphin Plaza, Victoria Pde; coffee $4-5.40, sandwiches $3-9) Popular for informal work meetings, this air-con cafe serves good coffee and ordinary cakes and sandwiches. Regular clientele include government and international workers from the offices opposite.

Maya Dhaba INDIAN $$

(Map p90; ☎331 0045; 281 Victoria Pde; mains $15-25; ☉11am-2.30pm & 6pm-10.30pm; ❄) Maya Dhaba is one of Suva's most urbane restaurants, serving up Indian dishes in bright, modern surroundings. The meals are excellent: wrap your naan around any number of familiar and not so familiar North and South Indian classics. Takeaway options are also available.

★ Governors INTERNATIONAL $$

(Map p90; Knolly St; mains from $20; ☉9am-3pm Mon-Wed, 9am-3pm & 6-10pm Thu-Fri, 8am-4pm Sat, to 2.30pm Sun) Housed in a converted colonial bungalow that was once home to Ratu Sir Laulu Sukuna, Governors is the newest fashionable eating place on the block. You can see why: great food (Italian and Thai notes on a Fijian base) plus great decor, with vintage travel posters and luggage, as is the live weekend evening music. Weekend brunch is incredibly popular, as is the live weekend evening music.

If you've got space for dessert, we counted six (!) different types of cheesecake, so plan for a return visit.

Ashiyana INDIAN $$

(Map p90; ☎331 3000; Old Town Hall Bldg, Victoria Pde; mains $10-20; ☉11.30am-2.30pm & 6-10pm Tue-Sat, 6-10pm Sun) This pint-sized restaurant is a long-standing Indian favourite with some of the best butter chicken in town and curries so spicy even the taxi drivers consider them hot. It has something

of a downtown English curry house feel to it, but is always packed (not that it takes much), so call ahead for a table.

Shanghai Seafood House CHINESE $$

(Map p90; ☎331 4865; 6 Thomson St; mains $13-20; ☉lunch & dinner) In the heart of the shopping district, this 1st-floor restaurant is plush in a kitschy, fake-flower kind of way. The encyclopaedic menu and al fresco seating on the 1914 building's balcony induce long and lazy lunches.

Daikoku JAPANESE $$$

(Map p90; ☎330 8968; Victoria Pde; mains $25-40; ☉noon-2pm & 6-10pm Mon-Sat) Upstairs past the closet-sized bar, the acrobatic culinary skills of Daikoku's teppanyaki chefs are reason enough to spend an evening here. The seafood, chicken and beef seared on sizzling teppanyaki plates would hold up in any Tokyo restaurant; the sushi is nearly is good. The lunch specials are popular with the international crowd, and tables fill up fast.

Tiko's Floating
Restaurant INTERNATIONAL $$$

(Map p90; ☎331 3626; Stinson Pde; mains $19-55; ☉noon-2pm & 5.30-10.30pm Mon-Fri, 5.30-11pm Sat; ❄) The only way you could be any more harbourside would be if you were standing in the water. This permanently moored former Blue Lagoon cruise ship has excellent surf-and-turf fare including good steaks, fresh local fish (*walu* and *pakapaka*) and an extensive wine list. Everything is served on white linen and in fine china and glassware.

🍷 Drinking & Nightlife

Suva has a good mix of drinking and dancing dens. The place to be on Thursday, Friday and Saturday nights is at the bars around Victoria Pde and Macarthur St. Generally, dress standards are very relaxed and although some of the bars may seem rough, the ones we recommend are all fairly safe. If a band is playing or the hour late, expect to pay a small cover charge (usually no more than $10). On the other hand, if you arrive early, entry is free and drinks are discounted between the happy hours of 6pm and 8pm.

Be cautious around other nightclubs. They tend to become dodgier as the night progresses and most locals attend them only with a group of friends – you should do the same. Watch out for pickpockets on the dance floor and always take a taxi after dark, even if you're in a group. The *Fiji*

Times' entertainment section lists upcoming events and what's on at the clubs.

O'Reilly's
PUB

(Map p90; ☑331 2322; cnr Macarthur St & Victoria Pde) O'Reilly's kicks the evening off in relatively subdued fashion with relaxed punters eating, playing pool or watching sport on the numerous TVs. But it brews quite a party as the hours tick by and come 11pm-ish the place is generally throbbing with a diverse crowd shaking their bits to anything that keeps the crowd moving.

O'Reilly's is popular with expats and professional Fijians, and is one of the few pubs where a reasonably smart dress code prevails

☆ Entertainment

Fijians are fanatical about their rugby and, even if you aren't that keen on the game, it's worth going to a match. The season lasts from April to September.

National Stadium
STADIUM

(Map p89; Laucala Bay Rd) Rugby teams tough it out here and the match atmosphere is huge. You can also catch players training hard at Albert Park during the week.

Traps Bar
LIVE MUSIC

(Map p90; ☑331 2922; Victoria Pde) Something of a subterranean saloon bar with a series of cavelike, dimly lit rooms. Take a seat in the pool room with wide-screen TV (yes, with sports) or join the happy din at the main bar. The crowd is generally young, trendy, relatively affluent and dancing by 11pm. There's live music (usually on Thursdays).

Damodar Village Cinema
CINEMA

(Map p90; www.damodarvillage.com.fj; Scott St; adult/child $6/5) Recently released Hollywood and Bollywood films battle it out at Suva's six-screen cinema complex.

🛍 Shopping

Your best chance of finding something truly unique is to skip the mass-produced stuff found in the chain tourist stores (which are carbon copies of their Nadi parents) and head straight to the markets.

Suva Curio & Handicraft Market
HANDICRAFTS

(Map p90; Stinson Pde) Strap on your barter boots: this market has endless craft stalls and, if you know your stuff, can offer some fantastic deals. Just be aware that not many of the artefacts are as genuine as the vendor would like you to believe. Only pay what the object is worth to you. A 2.1m by 1.2m *ibe* (mat) goes for between $45 and $75 (depending on how fine the weaving is) and a completely plain white *tapa* cloth costs around $45 for a 3.6m by 0.6m length.

Suva Flea Market
HANDICRAFTS

(Map p89; Rodwell Rd) Less touristy than the handicraft market previously mentioned, this is another great place to buy *masi* and traditional crafts, but you might have to sort through the Hawaiian shirts to find them. There's a great secondhand bookshop out the back.

ROC Market
CRAFTS

(Map p90; Dolphin Plaza, Victoria Pde) It's worth heading to Dolphin Plaza on the third Sunday of every month, when it hosts a small but eclectic market. Stalls feature homemade food and arts and crafts at reasonable prices, and there's usually some live music or other entertainment.

USP Book Centre
BOOKS

(University of the South Pacific; Map p89; ☑323 2500; www.uspbookcentre.com) The bookshop at the University of the South Pacific campus is probably the best bookshop in the country. It has an excellent selection of local and international novels, travel guides and books about the region.

Fiji Museum
BOOKS

(Map p90; ☑331 5944; www.fijimuseum.org.fj; Thurston Gardens; ☺9.30am-4.30pm Mon-Sat) The gift shop stocks a good selection of Fijian books on history, cooking and birds.

ℹ Information

DANGERS & ANNOYANCES

Suva suffers many of the same dangers as most urbanised centres. Walking around during daylight hours is perfectly safe, but as night descends, follow the example of locals and catch a taxi. They are metered, cheap and safe.

EMERGENCY

Ambulance (☑911, 330 2584)
Fire (☑911, 331 2877)
Police (Map p90; ☑331 1222, 911; Pratt St) There is also a police post on Cumming St (Map p90; ☑911; Cumming St)

INTERNET ACCESS

Internet access is cheap and abundant in Suva. Convenient places include **Connect Internet Café** (Map p90; Scott St; per hr $3; ☺8am-10pm Mon-Fri, 9am-10pm Sat, 9am-8pm Sun) and

Suva City Library (Map p90; Victoria Pde; per hr $3; ⊙9.30am-5.30pm Mon-Fri, to noon Sat).

MEDICAL SERVICES

Visits to general practitioners are usually between $20 and $30.

Colonial War Memorial Hospital (Map p89; ☑331 3444; Waimanu Rd) Fiji's **Recompression Chamber Facility** (☑321 5525; ⊙7am-5pm Mon-Fri) is located here. It's on-call 24 hours a day.

Maharaj Medical Centre (Map p89; ☑327 0164; Sports City Centre, Laucala Bay Rd, Laucala Bay; ⊙9am-1pm & 2-6pm Mon-Fri, 9am-1pm Sat & Sun) Private medical centre.

Mitchells Clinic (Map p90; ☑337 1133; mitchellclinic@connect.com.fj; 4th fl, Tappoo City) Consulations cost $30. GP surgery recommended by expats and UN staff.

Suva City Pharmacy (Map p90; Thomson St) Large and well-stocked pharmacy. There are many in town.

MONEY

There are plenty of ATMs and Western Union–affiliated currency exchange shops scattered along Victoria Pde. Both ANZ Bank and Westpac Bank have ATMs and foreign-exchange counters.

ANZ Bank (Map p90; ☑132 411; 25 Victoria Pde) ATM and foreign exchange.

Westpac Bank (Map p90; ☑132 032; 1 Thomson St) ATM and foreign exchange.

POST

Post Fiji (Map p90; Edward St) For parcels as well as regular post.

TOURIST INFORMATION

There is no longer a visitor centre in Suva. The information desks at the Grand Pacific Hotel (p97), Holiday Inn (p97) and Novotel (p97) are all helpful and can arrange tours.

❶ Getting There & Away

Suva is well connected to the rest of the country by air and inter-island ferries, and to Viti Levu by buses and carriers. Most international flights, however, arrive at Nadi International Airport.

AIR

Nausori International Airport (Map p54) is around 23km northeast of central Suva. A taxi from the airport to or from Suva costs $30.

Airline offices in Suva include the following:

Air New Zealand (Map p90; ☑331 3100; www.airnewzealand.com; Queensland Insurance Bldg, Victoria Pde)

Fiji Airways (Fiji Air; www.fijiairways.com; Colonial Bldg, Victoria Pde)

Qantas (Map p90; ☑331 1833; www.qantas.com; Colonial Bldg, Victoria Pde)

BOAT

Ferries leave from the ferry quay at Walu Bay, on the northern edge of Suva. Weekly ferries include services to Vanua Levu (Savusavu), Taveuni and Kadavu. There are also less frequent ferries to the Lau and Moala island groups.

Patterson Brothers (Map p89; ☑331 5644; 1st fl, Epworth Arcade, Nina St) run a combined bus-ferry service to Levuka ($35, four to six hours), leaving from the bus station at 1.30pm every day except Sunday.

BUS

There are frequent local buses operating along the Queens Road and Kings Road from Suva's main **bus station** (Map p89; Rodwell Rd). They all stop at resorts along the way upon request. Recommended companies are listed below. Try to catch a faster express service instead of those that stop at every homestead between Suva and Nadi.

Sample times and fares include: Pacific Harbour ($4.40, one hour), Sigatoka ($10.25, three hours), Nadi ($17.80, four hours), and Rakiraki ($14, 4½ hours). If you're going to Lautoka, it's faster via the Queens Road ($17.80, 4½ hours).

Coral Sun Fiji (☑620 3086; www.coralsunexpress.com) Runs a twice-daily service between Suva and Nadi International Airport, stopping at the main resorts on the Queens

---

WINGING IT

Charles Kingsford Smith was the first aviator to cross the Pacific, flying in his little Fokker trimotor, *The Southern Cross*, from California to Australia. The longest leg of the flight was the 34-hour trip from Hawaii to Fiji. Suva's Albert Park, with its hill at one end and the Grand Pacific Hotel at the other, was made into a makeshift landing strip for his arrival. Trees were still being cleared after Kingsford Smith had already left Hawaii. Kingsford Smith and his crew arrived on 6 June 1928 and were welcomed by a crowd of thousands, including colonial dignitaries who had gathered at the Grand Pacific Hotel to witness and celebrate this major event. Because the park was too short to take off with a heavy load of fuel, Kingsford Smith had to unload, fly to Nasilai Beach and reload for take off to Brisbane and Sydney. Kingsford Smith and his crew were presented with a ceremonial *tabua* (whale's tooth) as a token of great respect.

Road along the way. Pick up is at the Holiday Inn on Victoria Parade. Slightly more expensive that its competitors, but with a comfier coach.

Pacific Transport (☑330 4366; www.pacific transport.com.fj) Runs several daily express buses to Lautoka via the Queens Road, with stops at Pacific Harbour, Korolevu, Sigatoka and Nadi.

Sunbeam Transport (☑338 2122, 338 2704; www.sunbeamfiji.com) Runs several express buses daily to Lautoka via both the southern (Queens Road) and northern (Kings Road) routes.

ⓘ Getting Around

Taxis are cheap for short trips ($3 to $5) and metered. The city's one-way looping streets may make you think the taxi driver is taking you for a ride, but along Victoria Pde it's easy to get caught on a long run around the market and wharf area. Two 24-hour services are **Matua Taxis** (☑5115) and **Piccadilly Taxis** (☑330 4302).

Local buses are cheap and plentiful, and depart from the main bus station. There are relatively few buses in the evening and barely any on Sundays. Tickets are $1 or less.

EASTERN VITI LEVU

Carving a scenic route between Suva and Lautoka, the Kings Road is every bit as spectacular as the faster and more popular Queens Road route. It takes you through a lush interior with gorgeous views over the Wainibuka River, with the occasional village meandering its way along the road and river, plus some wonderful rugged country around Rakiraki, where the nearby island of Nananu-i-Ra offers the perfect place to get away from it all.

Sunbeam Transport and Pacific Transport run express buses throughout the day between Suva and Lautoka along the Kings Road ($21, six hours), stopping en route at Nausori, Ellington Wharf, Rakiraki, Tavua and Ba.

Nausori & the Rewa Delta

Nausori

POP 47,600

The township of Nausori is on the eastern bank of the Rewa River, about 19km northeast of downtown Suva, with the country's second-largest airport on its outskirts. Nausori is a bustling service centre and transport hub for the largely agricultural- and manufacturing-industry workers.

The town developed around the CSR sugar mill that operated here for eight decades between 1881 and 1959, when everyone realised that the canes actually grew better on the drier western side. Recent experiments to grow and mill rice on a large scale also proved futile, though a new rice mill was opened in 2011 for local use.

There are many eroded 18th-century and earlier ring-ditch fortifications in the Rewa Delta. About 10m wide with steep, battered sides and a strong fence on the inner bank, they were necessary for the survival of a village in times of war, protecting it against a surprise attack.

ⓘ Getting There & Away

The Kings Road from Suva to Nausori is the country's busiest stretch of highway, although expansion work in 2015 should ease congestion. Buses ($3, 30 to 45 minutes) travel this route throughout the day, from Nausori's new bus station on the main street, and stopping at destinations along the way to Lautoka ($19, 5½ hours).

Regular buses run from Nausori to nearby boat landings: Natovia Landing (for Ovalau), Wainibokasi Landing (for Nasilai village) and Nakelo Landing (for Toberua).

Nasilai Village & Naililili Catholic Mission

Nasilai village is well-known for its pottery, and is the home village of master Fijian potter Taraivini Wati. Pottery is a major source of income for the village and when large orders are placed everyone participates in the process – helping to collect and prepare the clay and make the pots. When a baby girl is born in the village, a lump of clay is placed on her forehead. It's believed she will then automatically know how to carry on the pottery-making tradition.

Near the village is the Naililili Catholic Mission (Map p54), built by French missionaries at the turn of the 20th century. The stained-glass windows were imported from Europe and incorporate Fijian writing and imagery.

There are regular buses to Wainibokasi Landing from Nausori bus station ($1.50, 20 minutes). There you can catch a boat to the Naililili Catholic Mission, which is almost opposite the landing, or take a short trip downriver to Nasilai village. Ask a local for permission to visit the village and take along some kava for a *sevusevu*.

If driving from Nausori, head southeast for 6km on the road that runs parallel to the Rewa River. Pass the airport entrance and turn right at the T-junction. The landing is a further 5km from here, well past the bridge across the Wainibokasi River – follow the sealed road.

Bau

In the 19th century this tiny island was the power base of Cakobau and his father Tanoa. In the 1780s, there were 30 *bure kalou* (ancient temples) on the small chiefly island, including the famous Na Vata ni Tawake, which stood on a huge *yavu* faced with large panels of flat rock. Also of interest are its chiefly cemetery, Methodist church and a sacrificial killing stone on which enemies were slaughtered before being cooked and consumed, prior to Cakobau's conversion to Christianity.

To visit Bau you must be invited by someone who lives there. If you dress conservatively, show polite and genuine interest, take a large *waka* (bunch of kava roots) for presentation to the *turaga-ni-koro* (village headman) and ask around at Bau Landing, you'll probably be invited to visit.

There are regular buses from Nausori bus station to Bau Landing, which is northeast of Nausori International Airport. If you are driving from Nausori, turn left onto Bau Rd about 1km before the airport and follow the road to its end. Small boats cross to nearby Bau ($6).

Toberua

This small island (2 hectares) is just off Kaba Point, the easternmost point of Viti Levu, about 30km from Suva.

All the island's tiny landmass is taken up by low-key Toberua Island Resort. The

MONEY MATTERS

Take plenty of *really* small change with you when you're on the road in a rental car and make time to stop at remote roadside stalls along the way. You'll be able both to boost the income of villagers and eat some of the freshest fruit you could wish for, not to mention the possibility of having surprising and memorable encounters with locals at the same time.

transfer from Nakelo Landing involves a lovely 40-minute boat trip along a stretch of the Rewa River delta and coast.

Toberua Island Resort RESORT **$$**
(Map p54; ☑347 2777; www.toberua.com; bungalow $440-645; ✳🤖🏊) The 15 waterfront *bure* here scattered along the beach have gloriously high roofs, minibars, sun decks and stylish bathrooms. The sunset-facing bar and restaurant serves delicious fresh food, with homemade snacks at cocktail hour and afternoon tea. At low tide the beach is used for golf and there is snorkelling, paddle boating, and tours to the nearby bird sanctuary and mangroves.

Toberua only receives about one-third of Suva's annual rainfall so the climate is balmy for most of the year, making it a popular weekend destination from Suva. Meal plans cost $160/88 (adult/children). Toberua has a PADI dive shop, and can offer certification. There are around 20 dive sites in the nearby Toberua Passage, with several reefs and coral gardens.

Korovou to Rakiraki via Kings Road

The Kings Road from Korovou to Rakiraki is one of the prettiest road trips in the country, and thanks to the recent paving of the highway, one of the smoothest. It passes through rich dairy-farming country, winds through hills and along the Wainibuka River, and passes many villages, before hugging the coast along the stretch to Ellington Wharf.

Korovou is not much more than a transport intersection, about 50km north of Suva. From here, the Kings Road continues to the northwest and over the hills. About 14km from Korovou on the Kings Road, you'll pass the beautiful Uru's Waterfall, which descends over a rocky slope on the northern side of the road and ends its journey in a serene pool surrounded by colourful foliage. It's possible to swim here – just ask one of the villagers for permission.

⦿ Sights

Snake God Cave CAVE
(Map p54; Wailotua; $15) At Wailotua village, 23km west of Korovou, the Snake God Cave is one of the largest caves in Fiji. The name is derived from six glittering stalactites in the shape of snakes' heads. During times of tribal war, the village would pack up en

FIJI'S BEST WATERFALL?

Fiji is a land blessed with beautiful waterfalls, but the remote Nabalasere village might just be home to the most spectacular. It's a long day-trip from Suva, turning off the Kings Road at Nalawa (just after Korovou), and you'll need a 4WD for the rough, unmade road. Nabalasere is at the end of the road, and is a pretty place, with neatly tended gardens and all the houses painted in the same mint green shade. It's no surprise that it once won a prize as Fiji's best-kept village.

Villager guides will accompany you on the 1km walk to Savulelele waterfall (it can be a muddy, slippery walk in places). You'll hear the falls before you reach them, and then come across the curtain raiser where the jungle parts to reveal a smooth, deep swimming hole scalloped out of the rock by the water. As you climb a little higher around the corner, the massive falls are revealed, tumbling down nearly 70m into a huge pool. It's an extraordinary site, and you're free to jump in, or if you're feeling brave, walk along the bottom of the cliff to stand behind the thundering curtain of water. When you're done, your guides refresh you with a steaming mug of freshly brewed draunimoli (lemon-leaf tea), then it's back to the village for kava and lunch.

Nabalasere has only recently opened up to tourism, and has partnered with **Talanoa Treks** (☎ 947 2732; www.talanoa-treks-fiji.com) to organise trips to the village and control visitor numbers. As well as providing transport, Talanoa Treks arrange the *sevusevu* (gift presentation). Bring a *sulu* to wear in the village, and a change of clothes if you intend to swim.

masse and seek shelter in the cave's pitch-black labyrinth.

Certain places in the cave complex were used for human sacrifice, others to test a partner's fidelity (the two are not related). The cavern culminates in a huge chamber inhabited by a colony of rare blossom bats.

To get here, take any Suva–Lautoka bus and ask the driver to let you off at the village. Ask the first person you approach if you can visit the cave – they'll organise a guide, who will provide a surprisingly detailed commentary on the cave. Wear a *sulu* and don't forget the torch.

Korovou to Rakiraki via the East Coast

The sealed Tailevu Coast Rd leaves the Kings Highway at Korovou to head towards Natovi Landing. This is the ferry point for the ferry to Ovalau or Savusavu, but when the boat is out there's little here but a jetty with a few people hand-fishing.

Beyond Natovi, the gravel road continues north along the coast before curving inland to meet the Kings Road about 30km south of Rakiraki. A 4WD is preferable if you're driving yourself. It feels remote, but is worth the trip for the two small resorts at Nataleira village, and the opportunity to go dolphin watching on nearby Moon Reef.

Nataleira also has a gorgeous waterfall, where you can swim, and the opportunity to hike nearby Mt Tova. Both resorts can organise all activities.

The Suva–Burewai bus ($5.80, three hours) departs at 7am, 8am and 2pm and drops off about 300m from Natalei Eco Lodge.

🏃 Activities

Dolphin Watch Fiji WILDLIFE WATCHING
(☎ 991 6338; takalana@gmail.com; $55) A 25-minute boat ride from Nataleira is where you'll find Moon Reef, which has a resident pod of spinner dolphins. Boat trips visit the reef in the morning, and as well as seeing the dolphins play around the boat, the reef also offers some great snorkelling. Lunch and snorkel gear is provided.

🛏 Sleeping

Natalei Eco Lodge LODGE $
(Map p54; ☎ 949 7460; nataleiecolodge@gmail.com; dm/r incl meals $80/150) At Natalei is this low-key, village-based tourism project, about half an hour's drive beyond Natovi, which provides a great opportunity to swerve right off the beaten track and into a cultural adventure. The double and dorm *bure* are frugal (as are the meals – take some snacks), but exploring the surrounding sea and landscape is the real appeal here.

Takalana Bay Retreat　BUNGALOW **$$**
(Map p54;　☑991 6338;　http://takalana.blog
spot.co.uk; d $250, s/d incl with shared bathroom
$115/220, bungalow $285) High on a breezy
rise above the bay is a two-room *bure,* just
along the road from Nataleira and run by
a family from the same village. While it's
more comfortable and private, it's further
from the beach. Rates include all meals.

Rakiraki & Around

The scenery continues to be stunning along
the Kings Road, winding past Viti Levu Bay
and into the beautiful region of Rakiraki,
Viti Levu's northernmost tip. The climate
on the northern side of the Nakauvadra
Range is similar to that of western Viti Levu
– drier and suited to growing sugarcane –
but far windier. According to local legend,
the imposing mountains are the home of
the great snake-god Degei, creator of all the
islands. The opening and closing of his eyes
prompt night and day, and thunder is said
to be Degei turning in his sleep.

The (well-signed) turn-off to Ellington
Wharf is about 5km east of Rakiraki junc-
tion and it is here that resorts collect their

Rakiraki & Nananu-i-Ra

guests for the 15-minute boat ride across to Nananu-i-Ra. A small shop sells hot and cold drinks, plus the odd snack, for those waiting for their boat. Tickets to Suva from Ellington Wharf cost $13.25; buses drop off/pick up at a covered stand by the turn-off.

Rakiraki is the more commonly used name for the town of Vaileka. It's a reasonable place to stock up on provisions before heading offshore. Besides the bus station itself, town amenities include a New World supermarket, taxi rank, produce market, several ATMs (including Westpac) and several fast-food restaurants.

◉ Sights

Naiserelagi Catholic Mission   CHURCH
(Map p54) About 25km southeast of Rakiraki, overlooking Viti Levu Bay, this 1917 church is famous for its mural depicting a black Christ, painted in 1962 by Jean Charlot. The three panels of biblical scenes depict Christ on the cross in a printed bark-cloth *sulu* with a *tanoa* at his feet. Indigenous Fijians are shown offering mats and *tabua* (whale's tooth), and Indo-Fijians presenting flowers and oxen. Visitors are welcome and a small donation is appreciated.

Any local bus heading south from Rakiraki will take you past Naiseralagi ($2, 25 minutes). A taxi will cost about $40 return. Naiserelagi is just south of Nanukuloa village, on the right past the school. The mission is on the hill, about 500m up a winding track.

Udreudre's Tomb   HISTORIC SITE
(Map p104) If you have commandeered your own taxi, ask the driver to show you the resting place of Fiji's most notorious cannibal. The tomb isn't very impressive, just a rectan-

gular block of concrete often overgrown with weeds, but it's just by the roadside, on the left about 100m west of the Vaileka/Kings Road intersection.

Navatu Rock   LANDMARK
(Map p54) About 10km west of Rakiraki, near Vitawa, is a large outcrop known as Navatu Rock. There was once a fortified village on top of the rock and it was believed that from here spirits would depart for the afterlife.

🏃 Activities

One of the principal reasons to visit the Rakiraki area is the excellent scuba diving to be had on the nearby Cakau Vatu Lacca and Cakau Tanau Reefs, where notable dive sites include **Dream Maker**'s large coral heads, **Breath Taker**'s concentration of fish, **Spud Dome**'s dramatic scenery and the possibility of pelagics at **Heartbreak Ridge**. The mainland resorts and those on Nananu-i-Ra island all use the same dive spots and will happily collect divers from anywhere in the area (usually for around $40, depending on how far they have to come).

Offshore, Nananu-i-Ra is renowned for windsurfing and kiteboarding.

🛏 Sleeping

Tanoa Rakiraki Hotel   HOTEL $
(📞669 4101; www.tanoarakiraki.com; Kings Rd; dm/r $50/150; P✳️🖥️🍴) If you have a need to stay in Rakiraki, this is an unexpectedly good option located 1.8km east of the Vaileka turn-off. The rooms in the lodge at the back have smart comfortable rooms, plus a small pool, billiards table and bowling green. The food in the restaurant is good, but breakfast isn't included in the price. Suva–Lautoka buses pick up and drop off at the door.

Volivoli Beach Resort   RESORT $$
(📞669 4511; www.volivoli.com; Volivoli Rd; bungalow $330-485; ✳️🖥️🍴) Located on the northernmost point of Viti Levu, Volivoli has a variety of modern, crisp *bure* that wrap themselves around a curved spit of land, all with decks and views out to sea. The rooms are in a modern and spotlessly clean hillside lodge, sharing a huge deck. There's a great semi-open **restaurant** (mains $20 to $35) and bar, and a small beach with snorkelling.

Ra Divers (www.radivers.com) operates out of Volivoli, and can also organise sport fishing and scenic tours – or just collapse into a pampered heap in the resort's spa.

Wananavu Beach Resort　　　RESORT **$$$**
(☑669 4433; www.wananavu.com; bungalow incl breakfast $495-845, honeymoon bungalow $1185-1280; ✳@☀) Wananavu has an indoor and outdoor **restaurant** (mains $16 to $40) with views out over the beautiful pool area and across to Nananu-i-Ra island. All *bure* have timber floors, panelled walls, air-con and their own small decks. They are surrounded by pretty palm- and bougainvillea-filled gardens. Garden *bure* prices rise as you head down the hill towards the water and, towards the romantic honeymoon accommodation.

The beach here is entirely artificially created and although the landscapers have done an excellent job, with strategically placed palm trees perfect for slinging a hammock between, most guests end up swimming in the pool. The resort holds regular and fascinating talks to introduce guests to the region's plants and wildlife. **Dive Wananavu** (☑990 5568; www.divewananavufiji.com) is based at the resort, and is one of only two dive operators on Viti Levu with nitrox facilities.

🛈 Getting There & Around

If you're not driving yourself, the best way to reach the resorts of Rakiraki and Nananu-i-Ra island is to catch a **Sunbeam Transport** (www.sunbeamfiji.com) express bus along the Kings Road from either Suva ($14, 4½ hours) or Nadi ($12.50, 2¼ hours) and get off at Vaileka, Rakiraki's main town, or Ellington Wharf. Keep hold of your bus ticket because the conductors on this route are tirelessly dedicated to checking them. From Vaileka, a taxi costs around $15 to Volivoli Beach Resort, Wananavu Beach Resort or Ellington Wharf.

Nananu-i-Ra

This pocket-sized island is on the itinerary for most travellers to northern Viti Levu. The 3.5-sq-km island is beautifully hilly, and is surrounded by scalloped bays, whitesand beaches and mangroves. There are, however, neither roads nor villages, and accommodation is simple. Former cattle grazing cleared much of the dense vegetation and today rolling hills of grass inhabit the interior. It's only 3km north of Ellington Wharf, but the atypical landscape and small enclave of wealthy holiday homes exaggerate the distance. Nananu-i-Ra's original inhabitants were wiped out by disease and tribal war, and their land was sold by their surviving heirs, mostly to Fijians of European descent.

Nananu-i-Ra is renowned for its offshore reefs and for windsurfing and kiteboarding. It can get very windy on the east side of the island from May through to July and again from late October to December during the cyclone season. The narrow strip of land that separates the west (Front Beach) from the east (Back Beach) is only 200m wide and no matter which way the wind blows, it's only a short walk to the calmer side. Walking tracks across the inland hills offer a good chance to stretch your legs.

🏃 Activities

Trekking
The island is good for trekking, with tracks across the top and wonderful views to the mainland. A common sight from the southern side of the island is billowing white clouds swallowing the volcanic Nakauvadra mountain range. The grassy hilltops also provide bird's-eye views of the surrounding turquoise reefs and the aptly named Sunset Point, where Ed Morris, a past president of the International Brotherhood of Magicians, has constructed a (small) labyrinth. If you are lucky, Ed will be around to explain what it all means.

If you time it right with the tides, you can walk around the island in about four to five hours (passing the mangroves at low tide). Part of the island is rocky so shoes are recommended.

Diving & Snorkelling
Snorkelling offshore you can expect to see some coral, abundant fish and, on the north side of the island, many sea snakes. The surrounding reefs and especially the **Vatu-i-Ra Passage** (also known as Blight Passge) to the north have some amazing dive sites.

The only PADI dive operation on the island is run by **Safari Lodge** (☑628 3332, 948 8888; www.safarilodge.com.fj; 2-tank dive $250, PADI Open Water Course $890).

Windsurfing, Kiteboarding & Paddleboarding
The climate here is relatively dry and the island's exposure to the southeast trade winds make it especially suited for windsurfing. Many windsurfers come here between May and July when winds are generally 10 knots or more on most days. Safari Lodge has both kiteboarding ($220/580 per two/six hours) and wind-

surfing gear for hire (beginner/advanced equipment $50/85 per hour), together with an experienced instructor. Because of the reef, and the possibility of torn sails, a first-time, one-off lesson ($85) is advisable to access your coral-avoiding skills.

Safari Lodge also has paddleboards for hire ($45/65 two-/four-hour paddles), or go on a two-hour guided paddle for $75.

🛏 Sleeping & Eating

Most places accept credit cards – check before you go – and are well set up for self-caterers. Safari Lodge, Betham's and McDonald's Beach Cottages have indoor/outdoor cafes with limited menus and small stores selling the basics. Vegetarians might want to bring their own fruit and vegetables from the mainland to ensure supply.

Expect cold-water showers and for the generator to be switched off around 10pm at most places.

★**Safari Lodge**   LODGE $
(☑628 3332, 948 8888; www.safarilodge.com.fj; dm/d/q $30/110/150, r $150, bungalow $295) 🏄
With the great range of outdoor activities available, Safari Lodge is the place to stay for the wind- and water-sports inclined. It's run with a windsurfer's chilled-out attitude. Simple, comfortable rooms and balconies peep through foliage to the ocean and creep up the hillside towards wide views and breezes.

Safari Lodge is heavy on sustainability and light on the environment: wind turbines provide 24-hour power (the only round-the-clock electricity on the island) and solar panels provide hot water. The owner operates Ellington Wharf, and boat transfers cost $50 return.

AN UNEARTHLY APPETITE

In 1849, some time after the death of Ratu Udreudre, the Reverend Richard Lyth asked Udreudre's son, Ratavu, about the significance of a long line of stones. Each stone, he was told, represented one of the chief's victims and amounted to a personal tally of at least 872 corpses. Ratavu went on to explain that his father consumed every piece of his victims of war, sharing none. He ate little else, and had an enormous appetite.

Betham's Beach Cottages   CABIN $
(☑992 7132; www.bethams.com.fj; dm/tw/cottage $35/110/160) Betham's has some sound, old-fashioned beach-house accommodation options. The duplex beachfront cottages have large kitchens, tiled floors and can sleep up to five people. The double rooms are good value and there is a large communal kitchen that is shared by those in the spacious eight-bed dorm. The open-air restaurant (mains $25 to $35) here serves hearty meals if you place your order by 1pm.

Boat transfers cost $50 return.

McDonald's Beach Cottages   CABIN $
(☑628 3118; www.macsnananu.com; dm/tw $30/95, cottage $150) McDonald's offers a scattering of supertidy self-contained cabins on a nicely landscaped property right in front of the jetty. The cute blue-and-yellow cottages are self-contained and it's popular with do-it-yourself types. The restaurant specialises in pizzas.

Charlie's Beach Cottages   CABIN $
(☑628 3268; www.charliescottages.com; dm/d $30/125) Charlie's has a large beach cottage made of concrete blocks and is fairly basic. There's a double bed in the bedroom and the lounge can take a further four single beds if required. There is also a seven-bed dorm in a similar but smaller cottage. Meals are available on request. Boat transfers cost $45 return.

❶ Getting There & Around

Nananu-i-Ra is just a 15-minute boat ride from Ellington Wharf. All the resorts on Nananu-i-Ra have their own boat transfers but you need to arrange your pick-up in advance – as well as onward transport when you leave. If you have your own vehicle, there's secure parking at the wharf.

The Suva-Lautoka buses pick up and drop off at the junction for Ellington Wharf – without transport it's a further 20-minute walk to the wharf.

LAUTOKA

POP 52,900

According to legend, Fiji's second-largest city derives its name from a battle cry that means 'spear-hit'. The story goes that when an argument erupted between two local chiefs, one cried out the words *lau toka* as he killed the other by spearing him through the chest, simultaneously stating the obvious and naming the location.

Lautoka

Lautoka

◉ Sights
1 Sri Krishna Kaliya Temple B3

🛏 Sleeping
2 Cathay Hotel.. B2
3 Northern Club... B2
4 Sea Breeze Hotel C1
5 Tanoa Waterfront Hotel.......................... A1

✕ Eating
6 Blue Ginger Café & Deli.......................... B2
7 Chilli Bites C2
8 Chilli Tree Café B1

Fins Restaurant .... (see 5)
9 MH Supermarket...................................... C1
10 Nang Ying B1
11 Town Market C2

✪ Entertainment
12 A-SK Pasifika.. B2
13 Damodar Village Cinema......................D2

ℹ Transport
Pacific Transport............................(see 14)
14 Sunbeam Transport............................... C1

Lautoka's recent history is entwined with the fortunes of sugar, which gives rise to its other name, Sugar City.

Lautoka doesn't have much to detain travellers, but it is a pleasant enough spot with wide streets steeped in foliage, a picturesque esplanade, a couple of decent cafes and the backdrop of Mt Koroyanitu (Mt Evans) to remind everyone that the urban reaches are well and truly finite.

◉ Sights & Activities

In lieu of beach sports, join the locals who walk, jog, promenade and picnic along Lautoka's landscaped waterfront at dawn,

dusk and the weekend. The nearest stretch of sand is the unappealing but popular Saweni Beach, 8km out of town.

Sri Krishna Kaliya Temple   HINDU
(☏666 4112; 5 Tavewa Ave; ⊗8am-6pm) Fiji has the highest percentage of Hare Krishnas per capita in the world and this temple is the foremost International Society for Krishna Consciousness (ISKCON) temple in the South Pacific. Visitors are welcome anytime, but an interesting time to visit is during the noon *puja* (prayer) on Sunday. Sit according to your gender and expect a whole lot of drum beating, bell ringing, conch blowing and chanting, which is the

way Krishnas approach God and achieve transcendental bliss.

Keep a donation handy for the tray that a child circulates at the end of the service. Everyone, whether giving money or not, is invited to the 1pm vegetarian lunch that follows.

Lautoka Sugar Mill HISTORIC BUILDING
(Nadovu Rd) From Marine Dr it is possible to walk to this mill, the backbone of the local economy. The mill opened in 1903 and is still by all accounts the largest sugar mill in the southern hemisphere. There are no tours, but you should be able to see the conveyors and pipeline for loading sugar, woodchips and molasses into the waiting cargo boats.

🛏 Sleeping

Northern Club APARTMENT $
(☑992 6469, 666 2469; northernaccom@yahoo. com.au; Tavewa Ave; apt $120; ❄❅) While you don't have to be a club member to stay here, a member will have to sign you in to the comfortable and relaxed facilities in the main club building. The six self-contained, one-bedroom apartments in the landscaped grounds provide everything else you need. They're great value, comfortable and clean as a whistle and just a few minutes' walk into town.

Sea Breeze Hotel HOTEL $
(☑666 0717; seabreezefiji@connect.com.fj; Bekana Lane; s $54-70, d $60-76; ❄❅❆) From the outside, the Sea Breeze resembles a jaunty blue-and-white apartment building. Inside, the austere rooms are a clean and tranquil sanctuary for noise-weary travellers. The fan-cooled digs are the cheapest, but the sea-view rooms with air-con are the nicest. The well-maintained pool looks over the water, as does the TV lounge where breakfast ($10) is served.

Cathay Hotel HOTEL $
(☑666 0205; www.fiji4less.com; Tavewa Ave; dm $24-26, r $66-88; ❄❅) This low-key, budget hotel is the choice of travelling government and NGO workers. Dorms here are good value: they have a maximum of four people to a room and each has its own bathroom. Otherwise, choose between spacious rooms with air-con and simpler but still roomy, fan-cooled rooms with shared bathrooms.

It's quiet – as long as you get a room off the main road, and avoid the weekends

when there's a nearby nightclub – and the pool area is pleasant.

Tanoa Waterfront Hotel HOTEL $$
(☑666 4777; www.tanoawaterfront.com; Marine Dr; r $250; ❄❅@❆) Lautoka's top-end hotel has a great waterfront location. The cheapest rooms are spotless and have the ambience and trimmings of a midrange US hotel chain. The more expensive rooms have contemporary interiors, flat-screen TVs and small balconies overlooking two pools. There is a gym, a small children's playground, a bar and restaurant on site. Prices tumble if you book online.

🍴 Eating

Lautoka has fewer restaurants than Nadi or Suva, but there are lots of inexpensive lunchtime eateries frequented by locals.

Self-caterers can stock up at any one of several supermarkets, including **MH Supermarket** (cnr Naviti & Vidolo St) and at the produce market, which is part of the larger, **town market** (⏰7am-5pm Mon-Fri, to 3pm Sat).

★ **Blue Ginger Café & Deli** CAFE $
(Post Office Roundabout; meals from $6; ⏰7.30am-5pm Mon-Sat; ❄) Delicious breakfasts (the menu includes homemade yoghurt, fruit and poached eggs) and lunches of wholemeal sandwiches, interesting wraps, fresh salads and lovely cakes and biscuits. Blue Ginger is run by a Swiss–Filipina couple and also serves truly good coffee (and/or a decent glass of wine) to go with the food.

Chilli Bites INDIAN $
(Yasawa St; meals $10-15; ⏰breakfast, lunch & dinner Mon-Sat, lunch & dinner Sun; ❄) Ignore the scratched formica tables and enjoy this authentic north Indian food made by authentic north Indian Indians. The tandoor breads, rich and flavoursome curries, and sweet or salt yoghurt lassis are cheap and delicious.

Chilli Tree Café CAFE $
(☑665 1824; 3 Tukani St; meals $8-15; ⏰7.30am-5pm Mon-Sat; ❄) This corner cafe is a good place to grab a paper and coffee, build a sandwich, wrap or slice of cake and settle into a chair for some serious people watching behind the plate-glass windows.

Nang Ying CHINESE $$
(☑665 2668; Nede St; mains $15-35; ⏰lunch & dinner Mon-Sat, dinner Sun) Twinkly lights, backlit pictures and fake flowers give this

place an air of Chinatown authenticity that would do San Francisco proud. Fragrant poultry and noodle dishes, sizzling seafood hotplates and fried-rice specials demonstrate that these cooks know their way around their chopsticks.

Fins Restaurant INTERNATIONAL $$
(☑666 4777; Marine Dr; mains $25-45; ⊘6.30am-9.30am, 11.30am-2.30pm & 6pm-10.30pm; ❋) This restaurant attached to the Tanoa Waterfront Hotel is Lautoka's fanciest dining option, and has a scenic outlook onto the waterfront. The menu has lots of seafood, steaks, pizza and regular barbecues.

🍷 Drinking & Nightlife

Lautoka lacks the sophistication of Suva and the small number of pubs and clubs are generally on the seedy side.

Fighting and drinking are a popular pastime for some and, if you haven't noticed, Fijian men aren't exactly petite; we don't recommend nightclubbing for solo travellers.

A-SK Pasifika LIVE MUSIC
(☑666 8989; 151 Vitogo Pde; ⊘5pm-1am Mon-Sat) Popular with Fijians who flock here on 'sponsored nights' when the beer is cheaper. A $5 cover charge applies on Friday and Saturday when a band or DJ plays.

☆ Entertainment

Damodar Village Cinema CINEMA
(Namoli Ave) Hollywood and Bollywood hits.

❶ Information

Internet access is cheap and plentiful in Lautoka. Check out the line of shops opposite the mosque and around the market.

There are several banks downtown that will change money and travellers cheques. There are ANZ bank ATMs on Vitogo Pde, on Yasawa St and near the cinema on Namoli Ave.

Ambulance (☑911)
Police (☑666 0222, 911; Drasa Ave) There is also a police post on Tui St.
Post Office (cnr Vitogo Pde & Tavewa Ave)

❶ Getting There & Around

Local buses depart for Nadi ($2.50, one hour, 33km) via the airport every 15 minutes.

Sunbeam Transport (☑666 2822; www.sunbeamfiji.com; Yasawa St) and **Pacific Transport** (☑666 0499; Yasawa St) have offices in Yasawa St opposite the market, and both have frequent services to and from Suva ($17.80, five hours)

via the Queens Road. Sunbeam also has seven daily departures to Suva via the Kings Road ($18, six hours).

Local buses connect Lautoka with Saweni Beach ($1.50, 45 minutes, six daily). Alternatively, any local bus to Nadi will drop you at the turn-off, from where it is an easy walk along 2km of unsealed road. A taxi from Saweni will cost approximately $10 to Lautoka, or $35 to Nadi International Airport.

Arriving yachts wishing to clear customs and immigration at **Lautoka Port** (VHF Marine channel 16; ⊘8am-1pm & 2-4.30pm Mon-Fri) will need to announce their arrival to port authorities and get instructions on where to moor.

LAUTOKA TO RAKIRAKI

Ba

POP 15,800

Although few find reason to visit Ba, it is Fiji's fifth largest town and characterised by its sizeable Indo-Fijian and Muslim population – most of whom are soccer-mad. Ba boasts Fiji's best racecourse and the town's horse-racing and bougainvillea festivals are in September. However, you're most likely to be in Ba to change buses and catch onward transport into the Nausori Highlands. Unless for some reason you have to overnight at the **Ba Hotel** (Map p54; 110 Bank St; s & d $80-85; ❋☀), head for the more salubrious options on offer in Tavua or Lautoka.

❶ Getting There & Away

Pacific Transport buses travelling between Lautoka ($3.10, one hour) and Suva ($20.25, six hours) call in at Ba bus station throughout the day.

Nadarivatu, Navai & Koro-Ni-O

In the dry season you can head up to the forestry settlement of Nadarivatu (30km southeast of Tavua). From here you can hike to Fiji's highest peak, Tomanivi (1323m, also known as Mt Victoria) or to Mt Lomalagi ('sky' or 'heaven' in Fijian). The Mt Lomalagi hike takes about three hours return and has great views. The **District Officer** (☑620 9645) will put you in touch with the Forestry Department in Nadarivatu. Its office is on the side of the road in the village and can arrange camping or a homestay with a local family. Bring provisions and give money or groceries to your hosts to cover costs.

You can also walk from Navai, which is 8km southeast of Nadarivatu, to Tomanivi's peak. Allow at least five hours (return) to hike from the village. Guides can be hired for $20. The last half of the climb is practically rock climbing and can be very slippery.

The Wainibuka and Wainimala Rivers (eventually merging to form the Rewa River) originate around here, as does the Sigatoka River. Past Navai, the road deteriorates and a 4WD is needed. Koro-ni-O ('village of the clouds' in Fijian) and the Monasavu Dam are about 25km to the southeast. The Wailoa/Monasavu Hydroelectric Scheme here provides about 93% of Viti Levu's power needs.

❶ Getting There & Away

The turn-off to the hills, crossing Fiji's highest mountain range and eventually ending up in Suva, is about 3km east of Tavua. The windy, rough gravel road climbs sharply, affording spectacular vistas of the coast and it takes about 1½ hours by 4WD to Nadarivatu. Nandan local bus service runs between Tavua and Nadarivatu ($4) a couple of times a day. Beyond there you may be able to negotiate a lift in a carrier as far as Koro-ni-O. Otherwise you'll need a 4WD to get to Suva.

NAUSORI HIGHLANDS

In stark contrast to the dense rainforests of the eastern highlands, the Nausori Highlands ascend into the interior in a panorama of grassy moguls. Massive folds of pale green tussle and tumble into the background as the coastline diminishes along the horizon. Patchy areas of forest and small villages are scattered in the hills. The more remote the village, the more traditional the villagers are in their ways. Sunday is a day of rest and worship, so visits to the two main villages of Navala and Bukuya on this day may be disruptive and unappreciated. The villagers in Navala are Catholic and the villagers in Bukuya are Methodist.

If you have your own transport, the loop from Nadi or Lautoka to Ba, then via Navala to Bukuya, and then back down to Nadi – or down to the Coral Coast via the Sigatoka Valley – is a scenic, fun and usually easy, though long, day trip. You'll need decent weather, a 4WD and a picnic. Check road conditions before heading for the hills.

☞ Tours

Nadi-based tour operators **Great Sights Fiji** (✆672 2074; www.touristtransportfiji.com) and **Rosie Holidays** (✆672 2755; www.rosie fiji.com) arrange tours in the Nausori Highlands, including day trips to Navala.

Navala

POP 800

Nestled in rugged, grassy mountains, Navala is by far Fiji's most picturesque village. Navala's chief enforces strict town-planning rules: the dozens of traditional thatched *bure* are laid out neatly in avenues, with a central promenade sloping down to the banks of the Ba River. All of the houses here are built with local materials; the only concrete block and corrugated iron in sight is for the school, Catholic church and radio shed (which houses the village's emergency radio telephone). The rectangular-plan houses have a timber-pole structure, sloping stone plinths, woven split-bamboo walls and thatched roofs. Kitchens are in separate *bure,* and toilets in *bure lailai* (little houses).

Navala is a photographer's delight, but you need to get permission and pay the $15 entrance fee before wandering around. If arriving independently, ask the first person you meet to take you to the *turaga-ni-koro* (the chief-appointed headman who collects the entrance fee). As the village charges a fee to enter, a traditional *sevusevu* is not required although all other village etiquette rules apply. If you arrive with Tui from Bulou's Eco Lodge, he will take care of protocol.

☐ Sleeping

Bulou's Eco Lodge   LODGE $

(Map p54; ✆628 1224; sipirianotui@gmail.com; dm/bungalow per person incl meals $75/180) To experience Fijian hospitality at its finest, a night (or two) spent with Bulou and her son (and hereditary chief) Tui is highly recommended. Their home and ecolodge is 1km past Navala village; phone ahead and they'll meet you at the bus stop. Tui is an excellent guide and accompanies all guests around the village introducing them to his relatives and friends (tours for nonguests $20 per group of four).

Tui can also arrange horse riding ($25) and trekking ($20) in the surrounding hills.

Guests can choose between two simple traditional *bure* in the garden and a 10-bed dorm attached to the house. There are cold-water showers, flush toilets and a limited electricity supply.

It is polite to bring a small *sevusevu* (a $5 pack of ground kava is enough) to present to the hosts during the welcoming ceremony (though they will neither ask for nor expect it).

❶ Getting There & Away

The local buses from Ba to Navala ($3, 90 minutes) leave Ba bus station at 12.30pm, 4.30pm and 5.15pm Monday to Saturday. Buses return to Ba at 6am, 7.30am and 1.45pm Monday to Friday. Locals pay $45 one way to charter a carrier but it is unlikely that you will be able to get it for this price. The rough gravel road has a few patches of bitumen on the really steep bits. While only 26km away, Navala is about a 1¼-hour drive from Ba, past the Rarawai Sugar Mill, through beautiful rugged scenery.

If driving from Ba, there are a couple of turns to watch out for. At the police post, take the right turn passing a shop on your right and at the next fork in the road, keep left. The road is rough and rocky, but usually passable as long as the car has high clearance. The Ba River can flood (and does, quite regularly, actually) for a few hours in the evening after heavy afternoon rains. Then the concrete bridge just before the village becomes impassable, so be prepared to sit it out.

Bukuya

POP 700

Bukuya is a little more commercial than Navala and not as picturesque, but it is still a worthy cultural experience. It's at the intersection of the gravel roads from Sigatoka (66km), Nadi (48km) and Navala (20km). The drive from Sigatoka up the Sigatoka Valley is a stunning two hours or so, as is the journey from Ba via Navala. The journey from Nadi along the Nausori Highlands Rd can take up to three hours.

TAVUA HOTEL

Tavua's **historic hotel** (Map p54; ☑ 668 0522; tavuahotel@connect.com.fj; Vatia St; r $50; ❋ ❇) is the only place to stay in town, and it's an unexpected gem. Built in the 1930s heyday of the gold boom, it's all polished wood, high breezy rooms and open public spaces. In the original building, the eight bedrooms – all with private bathrooms – have an attractive air of faded elegance. A few newer rooms are laid out in the landscaped grounds. Drop in for a drink or meal at least, and enjoy the old photos on the downstairs walls.

All roads to Bukuya are rough and unsealed, and no public transport runs this far. It's a bone-crunching ride in the back of a carrier, which will cost around $60 to/from Ba or $18 to/from Navala.

Tavua

POP 2400

Tavua is a small, quiet agricultural town with lots of temples, churches and mosques. There are plenty of old houses and an air of faded glory – the town's fortunes have risen and fallen with the Emperor Gold Mining Company which mined here from the 1930s until 2006 when the mine was closed. Until then, most of the mine's 1800 workers lived in Vatukoula, a purpose-built town 9km south of Tavua. The mine reopened on a much-reduced scale in 2008, but the town continues to struggle with the resulting economic hardships.

Mamanuca & Yasawa Groups

Best Places to Eat

➡ Navutu Stars (p133)

➡ Mantaray Island Resort (p132)

➡ Botaira Beach Resort (p133)

➡ Travellers Tea House (p136)

Best Places to Stay

➡ Coconut Beach Resort (p135)

➡ Beachcomber Island Resort (p119)

➡ Blue Lagoon Beach Resort (p136)

➡ Navini Island Resort (p120)

➡ Castaway Island Resort (p123)

Why Go?

They're but a streak on the map, the 50-odd islands that make up the Mamanuca and Yasawa groups are a behemoth of beauty that pack a powerful – and paradisiacal – punch. Though they're easily accessible from Nadi, the region is home to everything far-flung-tropical-island daydreams are made of: rustling palms, obscenely blue waters, blinding white sands and local smiles just as bright. Incredibly, this eden is open to all; no matter your budget, you'll find quality accommodation and million-dollar views.

The 20 or so picture-perfect coral atolls and islands of the Mamanucas arc west through the large lagoon formed by the Malolo Barrier Reef and Viti Levu. It's a treasure trove of surf breaks, sea turtles, reef sharks and vast schools of multicoloured tropical fish.

To the north, the volcanic islands of the Yasawas reward visitors with blue lagoons, exquisite beaches, technicolour coral gardens and craggy landscapes aching to be explored.

When to Go

Mamanuca & Yasawa Groups

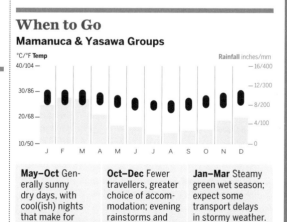

May–Oct Generally sunny dry days, with cool(ish) nights that make for good sleeping.

Oct–Dec Fewer travellers, greater choice of accommodation; evening rainstorms and humidity increase.

Jan–Mar Steamy green wet season; expect some transport delays in stormy weather.

MAMANUCA GROUP

'Tropical paradise' might be the most hackneyed cliché in the travel-writing world, but there's no getting away from it here: the Mamanuca islands tick every box, with brochure-blue seas and beaches so brilliant they're Hollywood celebrities unto themselves. With romance, relaxation and a disproportional number of fantastic resorts on offer, the Mamanuca group is unsurprisingly one of Fiji's most popular destinations.

Though they're valued more for their natural attributes than any contribution they make to the national culture, nobody could accuse the Mamanucas' beauty of being shallow: kaleidoscopic coral reefs and masses of marine life await those who take the plunge into their crystal-clear waters. Despite the subsurface calm, the Mamanucas are also home to a collection of world-class surf breaks.

Back on sand, the islands have enough facilities, activities and adventure opportunities to satisfy every day-tripper (and there are a lot of them). Those who come to stay are welcomed with a bellowing *bula!* and sunny hospitality, whether they choose family-friendly, couples-only or budget accommodation.

Life here bears little resemblance to the realities experienced by most Fijians. Only two resort islands, Mana and Malolo, support Fijian villages, though tourists outnumber locals. Not that they mind – almost all resorts lease their land from local communities and so, while heavy physical and metaphorical rain clouds may hang over the mainland, the sun always shines on the magical Mamanucas.

🏃 Activities

The Mamanucas are all about water sports and extreme relaxation. Whether you are staying for a week or visiting for a day, non-motorised water sports (like snorkelling, windsurfing, kayaking and sailing in catamarans) are nearly always provided free of charge. However, the moment an engine is fired you can expect to be billed. Village trips or snorkelling on the outer reef cost between $25 and $50 per person, and reef-fishing trips average around $150 to $170 per hour for four people. Island-hopping tours cost anywhere between $80 and $200 per person, depending on how many islands are visited and whether lunch is included.

Mamanuca & Yasawa Groups Highlights

❶ Waxing up your board – the mighty surf breaks of **Cloudbreak** (p115) and **Restaurants** (p115) await.

❷ Re-enacting your favourite scene from Tom Hanks' *Cast Away* on **Modriki** (p122), where the film was shot.

❸ Treating the kids to a holiday they'll never forget at **Treasure Island** (p120) or **Castaway Island** (p123).

❹ Frolicking in the fluorescent waters of the **Blue Lagoon** (p135).

❺ Catching a water taxi (or joining a tour) to the magical, mystical **Sawa-i-Lau Cave** (p137).

❻ Living like a local at a **Waya village homestay** (p130).

❼ Island-hopping on the *Yasawa Flyer* (p127) to see if the sand is any whiter at the other end of the island chain.

❽ Diving off a boat and doing your best to keep up with the giant **manta rays** (p131).

THE SACRED ISLANDS

The gorgeousness of the Mamanucas has invoked many an 'Oh my god!' from gob-smacked visitors. But to their remote northwest lies an island group that truly is divine: the Sacred Islands. These four islands – Eori, Navadra, Kadomo and Vanua Levu (not to be confused with Fiji's second-largest island to the east) – are held holy in Fijian myth and legend: many consider them to be the birthplace of Fijian culture, and believe the first footstep on Fiji fell here more than 2500 years ago. Today, visitors can leave an offering to the gods of the islands at a shrine on Navadra. Villagers on the tiny island of Tavua consider themselves to be the group's guardians.

While no humans live on the Sacred Islands, they are home to wild goats and a wealth of bird species, including the rare White Kern, burrowing Shearwaters and large Pacific Harriers, birds of prey which hunt resident flying foxes.

There is fantastic snorkelling to be had at the islands, particularly at high tide. The nearby Dunk's Canyon is known for its high-visibility drop-off dives (30m).

Various cruisers – including Blue Lagoon Cruises (p127) and Captain Cook Cruises (p116) – drop into the Sacred Islands, and many resorts in the northern Mamanucas offer tours: ask at your accommodation if a trip can be arranged.

Whatever you do, don't forget your book – hammocks just aren't the same without one.

Diving

Mamanuca dive sites teem with fantastically gaudy fish circling psychedelic corals. The visibility here astounds first-time divers and you can see for up to 40m through the water much of the year. Notable sites include **Bird Rock**, a 40m-wall with caves and swim-through passages, **Fish Market** (self-explanatory) and **Sherwood Forest** with its waving gorgonian sea fans. Also look out for **Gotham City**'s batfish, the big fish at the **Big W**s and the artificial reef at the wreck of the **Salamanda**.

The following are the big fish in the pond, with dive shops on multiple islands; other resorts have their own dive operators, detailed in resort descriptions.

Subsurface Fiji   DIVING
(☑999 6371; www.fijidiving.com) Subsurface runs dive shops at resorts including Plantation Island, Lomani, Musket Cove and Malolo Island Resort. A two-tank dive costs $295, and a three-day PADI Open Water Course is $975 ($860 if online course completed). It also offers child-friendly dives for kids aged eight and up (from $100).

Tropical Watersports   DIVING
(☑995 9810; www.fijitropicalwatersports.com) This outfit services Treasure, Bounty, Beachcomber and Navini resorts. A two-tank dive is $289, a PADI Open Water Course is $850.

It also offers flyboarding ($229), an extreme sport that lets thrillseekers 'surf the sky' attached to a water jetpack.

Surfing

The reefs off the southern Mamanuca islands have some of the world's most formidable breaks including Cloudbreak and Restaurants. You've gotta be stoked with breaks like this:

Cloudbreak World famous and for experienced riders only. Hollow left breaking on a reef. Best swell angle is with south-southwest winds, when tubes of up to 250m form.

Restaurants A powerful, superfast left-hander over shallow coral. Up to 200m long for advanced surfers. Beginners can test their skills at nearby **Kiddieland**.

Namotu Left A cruising, fun, longboard-type left-hander up to 150m long.

Swimming Pools A fun, easy right. Good for longboarders.

Wilkes Passage Long, fast, down-the-line right. A swell magnet, it can get as mean as Cloudbreak on some days.

Mini Clouds High-tide break. Best on a south to southwest swell; a quick, short, punchy wave.

Desperations Ideal in southeast swell conditions. Right and left.

Tours & Cruises

Many, though not all, of the island resorts accept day trippers and every morning

Mamanuca Group

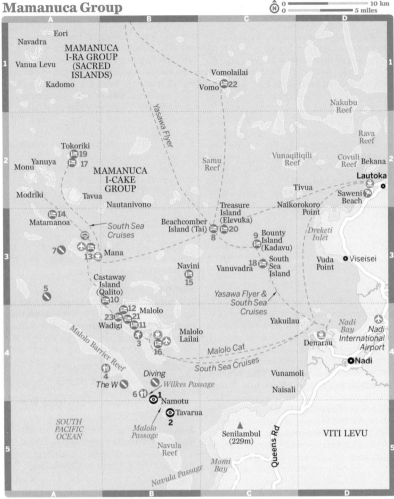

a whole armada of launches and yachts leaves Port Denarau with boatloads of people keen to spread their beach towels on some of that glorious white sand.

South Sea Cruises   CRUISE
(Map p66; ☑675 0500; www.ssc.com.fj; Port Denarau Marina) This shipshape outfit runs tons of tours, trips and cruises from its base at Denarau to islands and resorts across the Mamanucas. Three-hour catamaran sightseeing cruises (adult/child $66/33) follow their resort-transfer routes; if you'd prefer to get your feet sandy, hop aboard a day cruise to islands including South Sea (adult/child $113/56), Treasure ($132/66), Mana ($129/69), Castaway ($138/101) and Malolo ($132/69).

Day cruises include lunch, the use of the resort facilities and pick-up and drop-off from Nadi. Half-day options also available.

Captain Cook Cruises   CRUISE
(Map p66; ☑670 1823; www.captaincookcruises fiji.com) Offers a day cruise (adult/child $193/129) from Denarau to Tivua, a tiny coral island, on the *Ra Marama*, a 33m former governor's brigantine; overnight stays from

Mamanuca Group

$350. Its sunset dinner cruise (adult/child $149/95, three hours) includes a buffet barbecue meal and lobster tails. Captain Cook Cruises also has popular three-night cruises to the Mamanucas and southern Yasawas.

**PJ's Sailing, Snorkelling
& Fishing** CRUISE, FISHING
(Sailing Adventures Fiji; Map p66; ☑672 5022; www.pjfishsailfiji.com) This lively outfit offers private fishing charters (half/full day $800-1350), as well as shared fishing trips ($250 per person). It also does popular day sails to Bounty Island (adult/child/family $185/95/510); the trips include lunch, guided snorkelling and use of Bounty's facilities.

Seaspray CRUISE
(Map p66; ☑675 0500; www.ssc.com.fj; cruise per adult/child $135/79) This cruise aboard the two-masted schooner *Seaspray* is run by South Sea Cruises. The highlights of the nine-hour expedition are anchoring off, snorkelling and exploring the deserted Modriki Island (where the Tom Hanks film *Cast Away* was filmed), and a village visit on Yanuya Island. Travel is by catamaran from Denarau to Mana Island, and onwards on the *Seaspray*.

Schooner Whale's Tale CRUISE
(☑670 2443; www.whalestale.com.fj; adult/child $199/99) Intimate seven-hour cruises on this 100ft schooner wind their way through the Mamanucas before settling down for the day on the small, privately owned Schooner Island. Snorkelling gear, a kava ceremony, bar-

becue lunch and champagne breakfast are all included in the price.

Jet Ski Island Adventures ADVENTURE TOUR
(☑999 3454; www.jetski-islandadventuresfiji.com) If sailing doesn't fulfil your need for speed, give these zippy jetski tours a go. There are three-hour jaunts to Modriki Island (where *Cast Away* was shot, $595) and the Cloud 9 platform ($595), plus 30-minute/one-hour ($250/400) guided tours that bucket along past islands and reefs. It's based on Castaway and Malolo islands; free boat transfers are available from most Mamanuca resorts.

⊙ Getting There & Around

Thanks to their proximity to Port Denarau and Nadi airport, the Mamanuca islands are easily reached by catamaran, speedboat, water taxi or charter.

Alternatively, flying over tropical islands and reefs is more scenic and much quicker (no more than 15 minutes). **Turtle Airways** (☑672 1888; www.turtleairways.com; from $275) and **Pacific Island Air** (☑672 5644; www.pacificislandair.com; seaplanes from $340) offer seaplane charters to the Mamanuca resorts, as does helicopter outfit **Island Hoppers** (☑672 0410; www.helicopters.com.fj).

Awesome Adventures Fiji (☑675 0499; www.awesomefiji.com) Runs the *Yasawa Flyer* (also known as the 'Yellow Boat'), which connects with South Sea Island ($80), Bounty Island ($90), Beachcomber and Treasure islands ($105) and Vomo ($165) on its way north to the Yasawas.

Malolo Cat (Map p66; ☑675 0205; www.malolocatfiji.com; $70) Runs daily transfers between Port Denarau and Plantation, Musket Bay and

ℹ KEEP YOUR COOL

While most of the country runs on 'Fiji time', it's in the islands where this mellow, unhurried way of doing things really comes into its own. Despite activity schedules, set meal times and promises to 'be there in five minutes', things don't always go the way those from clock-watching cultures may be accustomed to. While this can jar, keep in mind the reasons most people come out here: to slow down, decompress and escape the hectic schedules of 'the real world'. Before blowing your top (we've seen it happen), take a deep breath of that salty island air, sink a little deeper into your hammock, and relax. It'll get done. Eventually.

Note: Boats, though they do their best to adhere to route schedules, are at the mercy of the tides (and winds). Be sure to allow yourself plenty of time if you have other connections to make.

Lomani resorts on Malolo Lailai Island. A boat leaves Port Denarau at 7.30am, 10.30am, 2pm and 5.30pm; from the island, it leaves at 5.45am, 8.45am, 12.15pm and 4pm. The trip takes 50 minutes.

Mamanuca Express (☑675 0151; www.mamanucaexpress.com) This 24-hour water taxi operates between Denarau and all Mamanuca resorts. Fares vary by destination.

Mana Flyer (☑625 3573; www.manaflyerfiji.com; $75) This tiny speedboat runs between the budget resorts at New Town Beach to Bounty, Beachcomber, Treasure, Mana and Malolo islands.

Marama Jaz Water Taxi (☑996 4267) This 100% local, female-owned water taxi does pickups and transfers from Wailoaloa Beach and Denarau across the Mamanucas.

Sea Fiji (☑675 0611; www.seafiji.net) For 24-hour transfers to the Mamanucas and southern Yasawas. Contact them for specific rates. It has bases at Denarau and Mana Island.

South Sea Island

South Sea is the smallest of the island resorts and little more than a bump of sand – albeit a beautiful bump – with some trees growing on top. You can walk around the whole island in three minutes. Being so small – and only 30 minutes from Denarau – it can feel a little overrun with day trippers. That said, it's a popular destination for those on limited time but keen to sample the Mamanucas. Kids are well-catered for, with free fun stuff like palm-frond weaving, face painting, use of kayaks and squealing at the sight of sharks and starfish from a semi-submersible.

The beach is good for swimming and not bad for snorkelling; there's also small freshwater swimming pool. Reef Safari runs the dive shop here. Transfers are by South Sea Cruises or the *Yasawa Flyer*.

South Sea Island Hostel　　　HOSTEL $
(☑675 0500; www.ssc.com.fj; dm $120; 🛜🖭)
Many backpackers spend a night on South Sea on their way to or from the Yasawas. Accommodation is in a breezy 32-bed upstairs dorm. Night-time crowds are limited: dinner is a pleasant low-key event on the beach, and the cute bar never gets too crazy. The price includes all meals and the use of all nonmotorised water-sport equipment.

Bounty Island

Bounty Island (Kadavu), is a 20-hectare coral island just 45 minutes from the mainland. It's bigger than its immediate neighbours but it still only takes 30 minutes to walk around or, if you don't stop to tease the clown fish, 1½ hours to snorkel. The white-sand beach attracts both endangered hawksbill turtles and day trippers.

In addition to water sports (diving and flyboarding with Tropical Water Sports), there's a forest to trek, beach crabs to chase and a baby turtle sanctuary to coo over. The bar, overlooking a small freshwater pool, has ping-pong and a pool table.

Transfers are with South Sea Cruises or the *Yasawa Flyer*.

Bounty Island Resort　　　RESORT $$
(☑776 3391; www.fiji-bounty.com; dm $45, bungalow $145-175; ❉🛜🖭) This friendly, low-key resort is an excellent choice for families on a budget and backpackers. The air-conditioned 20- and 14-bed dorms have comfy, oversized bunks, though island *bures* are a good value step-up if you're after privacy. The beachfront *bures,* a short, sandy hike from the bar/restaurant, have verandahs and hammocks. Bonus points for hot showers, 24-hour electricity and potable water.

The compulsory meal plan ($85) is fantastic value, with delicious three-course dinners and – a rarity – gigantic cooked breakfasts.

Beachcomber Island

Pretty little Beachcomber Island is circled by a comely coconut palm–studded beach. Its quintessential cuteness belies its reputation as being *the* party island in the Mamanucas: tales of drunken debauchery are slurred far and wide. True this may be, but Beachcomber's white sands, water sports options and turtle sanctuary also attract flocks of families on both daytrips and overnight stays: somehow the debauched and the (slightly more) decorous manage to co-exist quite nicely.

Beachcomber is 45 minutes from the mainland on either the *Yasawa Flyer* or a South Sea Cruises catamaran.

★**Beachcomber Island Resort** RESORT **$$**
(✆666 1500; www.beachcomberfiji.com; dm/rm/bungalow from $39/249/400; ❄️🌐🏊) This resort is a wonderful oddity: beloved by backpackers for its anything-goes atmosphere, sand-bar and huge, somehow airy – even with 84 beds! – dorm, the sprawling Beachcomber also welcomes equal numbers of families, who keep to *bures* and (very) beachfront rooms far from the nighttime revelry. Surprisingly, there aren't any young vs younger battles over the water trampoline and putt-putt course.

Snorkelling equipment is free, as are other activities including crab and broom racing, cultural lessons and coral viewing; diving and other water sports are provided by Tropical Watersports (p115).

The compulsory meal plan is $79: the all-you-can-eat meals here are very good.

Treasure Island

Like nearby Bounty and Beachcomber, Treasure Island (Elevuka) is a sweet little speck that takes mere minutes to walk around. But as everyone knows, size doesn't

ISLAND-HOPPING TIPS FOR BUDGET TRAVELLERS

➡ The quality of accommodation rises and falls like the tide. Work the grapevine on the boats and at each island to see which places are currently good value.

➡ Some accommodation is still little more than simple, thatched *bures* with concrete bathrooms or bunk dorms with shared bathrooms. Mosquito nets should be offered, but may not be – arm yourself with a pack of mozzie coils.

➡ Double rooms are popular; if you want some time to yourself, consider prebooking these to avoid ending up in a dorm.

➡ Bed bugs make their way up and down the islands along with whichever traveller is unknowingly carrying them at the time; a dorm that's clear one week may be temporarily infested the next. Most resorts are rigorous about airing mattresses and keeping rooms clean but, if you're worried, having your own bed sheet will offer some protection.

➡ Bring a padlock; security is often relaxed and few resorts have safe-deposit boxes so locking your bags may be your best security option.

➡ Meals are included but can be fairly basic – bring snacks if you are a big eater. Be careful where you store these if they'll attract rats and ants.

➡ Expect intermittent electricity in much of the Yasawas. The generator is usually off for a few hours during the day, on for a few hours after dusk, and then off again when the last bar-fly heads to bed.

➡ Carrying a tent will save you a little money, but very few places offer camp sites.

➡ The resorts appreciate it if you make bookings directly with them, as they then don't have to pay commissions.

➡ In low season it's not unusual to be the only guest at some of the smaller, more isolated Yasawa resorts – be prepared to enjoy the solitude or to move on.

➡ Snorkelling equipment costs about $10 per day to hire at some resorts. Avid snorkellers may want to bring their own.

➡ Sundays are quiet on the islands but the church services go off.

matter: this place is supremely popular with holidaymakers – half of them repeat guests – blissing out at the resort, and daytrippers taking advantage of the many facilities and activities on offer.

The island is serviced by the *Yasawa Flyer* and South Sea Cruises' catamarans.

Treasure Island Resort   RESORT **$$$**
(☑666 0380; www.treasureisland-fiji.com; bungalow $845-1173; ✳🛜🏊🛖) Opened in 1972, this is one of the Mamanucas' oldest resorts and a long-time family favourite (though the 120 weddings held annually in its sleek chapel point at another popular market). There's a fantastic kids club, plus a baby turtle sanctuary, mini-golf, a toddler pool and the Kidzspa. Adults dig the spa, tennis court and infinity pool. The on-site medical centre is a major plus.

Treasure's 68 refurbished, air-conditioned units are housed in witch-hatted *bures;* space varies, but all are well-appointed and comfortable and none are further than 30m from the water. Optional full/half meal packages are $150/115 for adults and $60/35 for kids (under fives eat free): the 5.30pm kids' buffet dinner is a sanity saver. Diving and more is possible with Tropical Water Sports.

Treasure is serviced by the *Yasawa Flyer* and South Sea Cruises' catamarans; the resort also provides after-hours transfers for guests to/from Nadi Airport ($312) and Vuda Point Marina ($216).

Vomo

This wedge-shaped, 90-hectare private island rises to a magnificent high ridge, and has two lovely beaches and some of the best snorkelling in the Mamanucas. It's large enough to be interesting – it takes an hour to walk around – but small enough to be intimate. It's home to the Vomo Island Resort.

Guests arrive by helicopter, seaplane, South Sea Cruises cats or the *Yasawa Flyer*.

Navini

This itty bitty islet is ringed by a glowing white beach and vibrant reef just snorkelling distance offshore. It's owned by the people of Solevu on Malolo, who once held chiefly meetings and fished here. That was until fishing was banned many years ago and a marine sanctuary established. Beware of friendly fish!

Get there via 24-hour transfers from Nadi by resort speedboat (one way $160/82/480 per adult/child/family).

⭐**Navini Island Resort**   RESORT **$$$**
(☑666 2188; www.navinifiji.com.fj; bungalow $645-860, villa $960; 🛜) This boutique resort gets top marks, not only for its stunning surrounds and tasteful, airy accommodation, but for possibly having the most hospitable staff in the Mamanucas. With only 10 *bures* and no distracting daytrippers, staff actually outnumber holidaymakers: it's a rare guest that leaves without feeling like a family member. All rooms have their own slice of beachfront and private courtyards.

Guests eat at the same long table and meals are a social occasion – if this isn't your thing, more intimate beachside dining can be arranged. The compulsory meal package ($132/119 for three/two meals daily for adults; child rates available) still allows guests to choose from a daily menu.

There are cultural and sporty activities galore: diving is with Tropical Watersports (p115).

Mana

The beautiful but literally divided island of Mana is about 90 minutes northwest of Denarau. It's home to two upmarket resorts – Mana Island Resort and Tadrai – and a couple of hostels next to the village on the southeastern end. A fence, and occasionally

EPICUREAN ESCAPES

The islands of the Mamanucas and Yasawas are a paradise whatever your budget. But if you've got cash to splash, these elite resorts offer a rung up on the stairway to holiday heaven. All offer impeccable service, gourmet meals, gorgeous beaches, top-notch activities and an exclusive, far-from-the-madding crowd feel; some have butler service and personal chefs. None are less than $1600 per night.

In the Mamanucas, **Vomo Island Resort** (✆ 666 7955; www.vomofiji.com; $2280-9550; ✳ @ ✖) and **Wadigi Island Lodge** (✆ 672 0901; www.wadigi.com; from $4435; ✳ ⛶ ✖) are the only five-star resorts allowing children. But they, like the adults-only **Tadrai** (✆ 910 3333; www.tadrai.com; $3000; ✳ ⛶ ✖) and the islands' only overwater *bure* resort, **Likuliku Lagoon** (✆ 666 3344; www.likulikulagoon.com; overwater bungalow $2990, other bungalows $1790-2590, all meals included; ✳ ⛶ ✖), offer enough space and serenity to satisfy the seclusion-seeking sybarite.

Right up north at the top of the Yasawas, **Turtle Island Resort** (✆ 672 2921; www.turtlefiji.com; from $4420; ✳ ⛶) and **Yasawa Island Resort** (✆ 672 2266; www.yasawa.com; from $1665-3500; ✳ ⛶ ✖) are oases of opulence: guests at the former even get their own 'bure mama' to take care of every conceivable need. Both of these are adult-only, apart from scheduled 'family weeks'.

a guard, separates the Mana Island Resort *bure*-bunnies from the dorm-dwellers, and signs throughout the resort warn 'nonguests' that they are not welcome. For their part, the budget spots and their restaurants welcome everyone.

Fence or no fence, the beaches are (mostly) open to all. Walking around the island isn't really an option because of rocky points on the coast, but there are a couple of 20-minute hikes to Sunset Beach and to a lookout. There's plenty of fish-gawking to be had anywhere off the beach, and decent coral off Sunset. Check out the south-beach pier for a night snorkel; the fish go into a frenzy under the wharf lights.

🛏 Sleeping & Eating

The backpacker resorts are sewn into a Fijian village along the waterfront. If you prebook, beware of paying midrange prices for *very* budget rooms; unless it's peak season, you're better off arriving and then booking a bed after shopping around. Activities on offer at the budget resorts include snorkelling trips, kayaking, hand-line fishing trips and island-hopping (half/full day $70/90). Nightly activities are as much about beer consumption as they are about entertainment, though sunset on the deck or the beach is a must for all.

Looking landwards from the ferry wharf, the hostels are a few minutes' walk to the right. The only eating options are at the accommodation places.

Mana Lagoon Backpackers   HOSTEL $
(✆ 924 6573; www.manalagoonbackpackers.com; tent site/dm/r incl meals $60/85/210) Owned and run by locals, this endearingly ramshackle place feels more like a village homestay than a typical backpackers. Unlike the larger resorts, there's a charming family feel here, and the thatched-roof beach shelters and sandy-floored restaurant/bar define 'mellow island holiday'. Rooms are basic and electricity is sporadic; you'll be too busy snorkelling (free) and taking part in organised activities to notice.

Ratu Kini Backpackers and Dive Resort   HOSTEL $$
(✆ 628 2375; www.ratukinidiveresort.com.fj; camping $35, dm $39-65, r $180-230, bungalow $200-250, incl breakfast; ✳ ⛶) This fun and friendly stripside spot is a longtime Mamanucas drawcard: it even attracts guests from the fancier resorts to its social sunset bar and excellent seafood restaurant. No-fuss, no-frills, decent-sized dorms share cold-water showers; quieter rooms and *bures* have private facilities and loads of space.

As evident by its name, the resort is big on diving, and is close to top underwater spots including Supermarket and Gotham City. The PADI Open Water Diver Course is $825, two-tank dives $230.

Mana Island Resort   RESORT $$$
(✆ 665 0423; www.manafiji.com; bungalow $380-900, rm $470, ste $840, honeymoon bungalow $1080; ✳ ⛶ ✖ ⛲) One of the oldest and

largest (at 121 hectares) island resorts in Fiji, the 152 rooms, suites and *bures* span the spacious, beautifully landscaped low-lying grounds between the north and south beaches. Mana caters for everyone – couples, honeymooners and families – the latter dominating during Australian and New Zealand school holidays. Extensive renovation work in mid-2015 hadn't stopped a near-constant flow of guests.

Celebrity chef Lance Seeto is in charge of the two beautiful indoor/outdoor restaurants, though some guests amble down the beach to sample the eats at the hostels. The resort also has a kids club (ages three-12; $25 one-off fee) and a creche ($5 per hour).

Diving here is run by **Aqua-Trek Mana** (666 9309; www.aquatrekdiving.com).

❶ Getting There & Away

Mana is one of the few resort islands with a wharf. South Sea Cruises' catamarans service the island several times daily ($120), while the budget *Mana Flyer* transfer boat ($75 one way, 55 minutes) makes a daily trip to and from Nadi's New Town Beach.

Matamanoa

Matamanoa is a small island notable for its pointy volcanic cone and ludicrously white sand beach. It's just to the north of Mana Island. It's a private island, accessible only to resort guests. Most guests arrive on South Sea Cruises catamarans ($145); there's also a helipad on the island.

Matamanoa Island Resort   RESORT $$$
(672 3620; www.matamanoa.com; rm/bunga-low/villa incl breakfast $565/895/995; ❋ 🛜 ☀) As would be expected from an upmarket, adults-only resort, Matamanoa is stylish, sophisticated and peaceful. Its 33 beachfront *bures* and villas overlook a blindingly white, soft-sand beach, while cheaper studio-sized resort rooms have carved-wood interiors and private garden verandahs.

Its refined restaurant overlooks the ocean: meal plans are $170, or $110 for dinner only; there's also an à la carte option.

Activities include free use of non-motorised water sports gear, trips to the nearby pottery village on Tavua Island, champagne-fuelled island hopping trips, and resort diving with **Viti Watersports** (992 9474; www.vitiwatersports.com); intro dives $250, two-tank dive $350.

Modriki

Tiny, uninhabited Modriki (and ironically not Castaway Island) featured in the 2001 Tom Hanks movie *Cast Away,* and every resort worth its cabanas and cocktails sells day trips to what is increasingly referred to as 'Tom Hanks Island' (somewhat confusingly, it's also known as Monuriki). Trips cost around $100 to $140 depending on where you start out and what kind of lunch, if any, is included. The island is beautiful – it's a Hollywood star, after all – and the wide lagoon is perfect for snorkelling.

An ongoing program with local people to eradicate feral goats and rats has seen native crested iguanas and wedge-tailed shearwaters successfully reintroduced to the island, so keep your eyes open for them. BYO volleyball for 'Wilson' selfies.

The *Seaspray* schooner sails here as a day trip from Denarau and other island resorts.

Tokoriki

The small, hilly northern island of Tokoriki has a beautiful, fine-white-sand beach facing west to the sunset. It's home to two posh resorts: guests can walk a track around the point between the them.

South Sea Cruises catamarans service the island.

🛏 Sleeping

Tokoriki Island Resort   RESORT $$$
(672 5926; www.tokoriki.com; bungalow $1195-1495, villa $1695; ❋ 🛜 ☀) This orchid-strewn, adults-only playground makes for the ideal swoony getaway, with all manners of honeymoon packages, deserted-island picnics and photogenic proposal nooks on offer; there's even an on-site Romance Co-ordinator! All *bures* and villas have outdoor showers and divine interiors; many have private pools.

Naturally, dining options are romantic, including starlit dinners, free-flow champagne breakfasts and the intimate eight-seat teppanyaki restaurant.

If you can tear yourself away from moony gazes, all manners of activities are on offer, from diving (PADI Open Water Course $1230) to daytrips to the northernmost Mamanucas known as the Sacred Islands.

Sheraton Resort & Spa Tokoriki Island RESORT$$$

(☎666 7707; www.sheratontokorikiisland.com; rm $500-800, family ste from $950, retreats from $980; ❊🌐☈⚓) Formerly the Amanuca, this appears to be a work in progress: quality of the rooms, facilities and service varies wildly. When it's good, however, it's very good: more expensive rooms are beautifully appointed, and the Flying Fish restaurant is superb. The resort is divided into family-friendly and adults-only sides: the former has a movie theatre and kids club, the latter has posh 'retreats' with private plunge pools.

Castaway Island

Stunning, reef-fringed, 70-hectare Castaway Island, also known as Qalito, is 27km (1½ hours) from Denarau. The resort covers about one-eighth of the island – the best bit, on a wide tongue of sand stretching from a bush-clad hill.

Resort guests and daytrippers get here on South Sea Cruises' catamarans.

★Castaway Island Resort RESORT$$$

(☎666 1233; www.castawayfiji.com; bungalow $1140-1450; ❊🌐☈⚓) This is an oldie but a very-goodie. A huge hit with families (and couples, outside of school holidays), there's something for everyone here: great kids club, family-friendly pool with waterfall, adults-only pool with swim-up bar, free non-motorised water sports, bushwalks, village excursions, shadowboxing lessons and squillions more. All free-standing *bures* are spacious and stylish, with privacy screens between parents' and kids' bedrooms.

Dining options at its four restaurants range from wood-fired pizzas and sushi to gourmet Fijian-Asian fusion: all allergies and intolerances catered for. Meal plans are $129 for adults, $65 for kids.

The resort-operated dive centre here charges $198 for a single-tank dive and $1188 for a PADI Open Water Course. Kids aged eight and up can try out the Bubblemaker scuba experience ($132)

Wadigi

Pint-sized (1.2 hectares), picturesque and privately owned, Wadigi may beckon, but it's off limits to all but a few.

WORTH A TRIP

ON CLOUD NINE

A two-level floating platform just off Malolo Island, **Cloud 9** (☎869 7947; www.cloud9.com.fj) is a super-stylish daytrip destination. Home to a bar, wood-fire pizzeria and enticing sundeck scattered with daybeds, it's a top spot for languid lounging. The more energetic can swim and snorkel the gorgeous Ro Ro Reef. Kids are welcome, though non-swimmers and the very young might be bored (and parents might go insane making sure they don't jump/fall off the edge). Numerous daytrips leave from Denarau on the mainland and nearby islands: see Cloud 9's website for details.

Malolo

Malolo, an hour from the mainland, is the largest of the Mamanuca islands and has two villages from which the resorts lease their land. The island's highest point is Ul-uisolo (218m), which was used by locals as a hill fortification and by US forces in 1942 as an observation point; trekking to the top offers great panoramic views.

Subsurface Fiji (p115) offers diving trips and courses to all resorts; Malolo is also within striking distance of some great surfing spots.

South Sea Cruises' catamarans service Malolo.

🛏 Sleeping & Eating

In addition to the resorts listed here, construction of a new luxury hotel, The Island Grace, was underway in 2015, including a boutique marina and residential development (www.vunabaka.com); opening is scheduled for 2016.

Funky Fish Beach & Surf Resort RESORT$

(☎666 1500; www.funkyfishresort.com; dm $46, r $99-400, bungalow $279-500; ❊🌐☈) With some of Fiji's best breaks less than half an hour away, and top-notch kiteboarding spots a stroll from the door, Funky Fish is a thrillseekers' delight. Daily boats head out to spots including Cloudbreak, Restaurants and Swimming Pools, and stay until guests' wave-lusts are quenched. Ten-bed dorms and cheaper privates are clean but basic, while

CLOSE ENCOUNTERS

When American explorer Charles Wilkes sailed through the passage that now bears his name in 1840, Malolo wasn't quite the welcoming place it is today. According to Wilkes' log, when initial trade negotiations turned sour his landing party was forced to take a 'native' hostage and fire two warning shots. This upset the locals and two of Wilkes' crew were killed with throwing clubs. Seeking to set an example, Wilkes' retaliation was swift: both the island villages were razed, their plantations laid waste and their canoes scuttled before the vendetta ceased.

bures and Cloudbreak view rooms are a class above.

Optional meal plans (full/half $80/56) are available.

Funky Fish is owned by the same people who have the Beachcomber and Anchorage Beach (Vuda Point) resorts; transfers between the three are available.

Malolo Island Resort　　　　RESORT $$$
(☑666 9192; www.maloloisland.com; bungalow $821-1942; �﹢❄@❤🛥) This crisp, 100% Fijian-owned resort caters to both families (school holidays) and couples looking for a romantic escape (rest of the year). All 46 tropical-plantation-style *bures* have sea views; some are a footstep from the white sand. Young'uns like the kids club, their own pool and beach games; bigger folks love the adults-only pool (with swim-up bar and lounge), spa and intimate Tadra beach *bures*.

There are two fabulous restaurants (optional meal plans adults/children $155/77.50), one of which is open only to guests aged 13 and over, plus a sunset-view beach bar.

Tropica Island Resort　　　　RESORT $$$
(☑665 1777; www.tropicaisland.com; rm $699, bungalow $999, ste $1199; ❄🛜🛥) The Tropica has left its former incarnation as Walu Beach Resort (purpose-built for an Australian reality TV show) far, far behind to become a slick adults-only destination. There are 30 totally refurbished *bures,* suites and rooms (all but the latter have outdoor showers, patios and cosy deck swings), plus a 25m infinity pool, and spa. The restaurant serves gourmet Fijian cuisine; meal plans $160.

Malolo Lailai

Tranquil Malolo Lailai is, at 2.4 sq km, the second-largest island of the Mamanuca Group: its name means 'Little Malolo'. It has long been popular with yachties, who anchor in the protected lagoon and make use of the facilities at the marina. All three resorts are built on the shores of a beautiful, but extremely tidal, lagoon. The beach outside Musket Cove Island Resort is the most affected by these tides; Lomani Island Resort cops it the least. Get here on the Malolo Cat (p117).

◉ Sights & Activities

All the island's diving services are provided by Subsurface Fiji. Dive sites include the **Tavarua Wall**, **Gotham City** and the sharky **Supermarket**; all – and more – are close to the three island resorts.

Excellent surf breaks are accessible from here (and from neighbouring Malolo) and are about 20 minutes by boat: trips run between $70 and $90, and are for experienced surfers only.

Musket Cove Marina　　　　MARINA
(☑VHF Marine channel 68 666 2215; www.musketcovefiji.com/marina) This excellent marina attracts yachties from all over the world. There are 27 moorings ($15 per day), 25 marina berths (from $2 per metre, per day), dockside fuel and water (0.10 cents per litre, though this can be limited in the dry season), drop-mail services, a laundry, rubbish disposal, hot showers, a book swap, bike hire ($30/150 per day/week), a noticeboard and limited repair services.

The **Trader Market Store** (Musket Cove Marina; ◷8am-7pm) stocks fresh goods and groceries; the attached coffee shop makes a mean cuppa, and serves light lunches on the verandah overlooking the marina. Bulk alcohol is available at Dick's Place.

The Musket Cove Yacht Club hosts the famous Fiji Regatta Week every September.

Take A Break Cruises　　　　CRUISE, FISHING
(☑925 9469; www.takeabreakcruises.com; Musket Cove Marina) Offers a variety of outings, including day cruises (from $70, includes snorkelling and lunch), trips to Modriki ($120) and sunset cruises ($95, includes drinks and nibbles, minimum six people) on Tuesdays. Private cruises, plus fishing tours and charters are also available.

🛏️ Sleeping & Eating

Plantation Island Resort   RESORT **$$$**
(📞666 9333; www.plantationisland.com; r from $620, bungalow $470-985; ❄️🛜🏊👶) If children aren't your thing, be sure to check your calendar for school holidays: this huge place is a firm family favourite. While the littlies go berserk with the excellent Coconut Kids Club, waterslide, mini-golf course and dozens of squeal-inducing activities, parents relax with beachside massages, in the grown-ups pool or on the nine-hole golf course (from $32).

Rooms and *bures* come in a dizzying array of options: all are spotless and have enough space to accommodate families. Optional full meal plans (adult/child from $132/44) are available, though many guests prefer to spread their meals between the resort eateries and **Ananda's Restaurant** (mains $25-40) near the airstrip.

Musket Cove Island Resort   RESORT **$$$**
(📞664 0805; www.musketcovefiji.com; bungalow $720-950, villa $1190-1220; ❄️🛜🏊) With oodles of accommodation, eating, drinking and activity options, this sprawling resort is truly a world unto itself. Children are welcome in the garden *bures* and self-contained garden villas, but age limits apply at the beachfront *bures,* island villas and lagoon *bures* (a cluster of six airy cottages with private overwater verandahs).

There are free daily snorkelling trips to compensate for the low, low tides, along with free water sports, a village visit and farm tour; excursions to surf, dive and fishing spots can be arranged.

Dick's Place Bar & Bistro is a hit for its gourmet meals and theme nights; private picnics and beach dining can also be arranged. On-site bars and those at the attached marina are more sociable than most resort watering holes.

Lomani Island Resort   RESORT **$$$**
(📞666 8212; www.lomaniisland.com; bungalow $990, ste $740-810, breakfast incl; ❄️🛜🏊) This glamorous, adult-only resort has a long, lazy pool, a classy colonial-style bar and a twinkling outdoor restaurant (optional meal plan $140 per person): romantic on-sand meals can be arranged. There are only 24 rooms in the resort, and none are further than 30m from the sand (the impossibly stylish beachfront *bures* are but a stumble from it).

Owned by the same family as Plantation Island Resort, the two properties work closely together and guests here piggyback on the other's activities.

Namotu & Tavarua

Namotu and Tavarua are islands at the southern edge of the Malolo Barrier Reef, which encloses the southern Mamanucas. Namotu (www.namotuislandfiji.com) is a tiny (1.5 hectares) and pretty island; bigger Tavarua (www.tavarua.com) is 12 hectares, rimmed by beautiful white-sand. Both islands are primarily package surf resorts, geared to the American market. There is no public access.

YASAWA GROUP

POP 5000

Rugged, remote and more dramatic than the sugardrop islands of the Mamanucas, the mighty Yasawas were once off-limits to all but those determined to play out their Robinson Crusoe fantasies. Today, ferries, cruise ships and seaplanes make daily deposits of sun-and-fun-seekers keen to explore both its looming landscapes and eminently diveable depths.

The chain is composed of 20 or so sparsely populated and surprisingly barren islands. There are no roads, cars, banks or shops, and most of the locals live in small remote villages, surviving on agriculture and tourism for their livelihoods. Most resorts help make the tourist dollar go further by buying local crops or fish, supporting village schools or sponsoring older kids to get further education on the mainland.

While the majority of the Yasawas' beaches are uniformly divine, the quality of accommodation deviates dramatically: a *bure* could be anything from a hut that you could blow down with a hair dryer to an upmarket villa with an outdoor shower. The variety of digs on offer – nightly stays range from $40 all the way up to $4000 – now attracts families and well-heeled couples to what was once the sole stomping ground of backpackers. Whatever the budget, it doesn't take long for guests to fall into 'Fiji time', where two snorkels and a bash on the volleyball court constitutes a busy day at the beach.

Apart from ubiquitous island pastimes – book reading, hammock snoozing, cocktail sipping – the must-dos of the Yasawas

Yasawa Group

MAMANUCA & YASAWA GROUPS YASAWA GROUP

Yasawa Group

include swimming with manta rays (in season) and a jaunt out to the mysterious Sawa-i-Lau caves.

The Yasawas are mostly hilly; four of the larger islands have summits close to 600m above sea level. While the relatively dry climate is a plus for visitors, the land is prone to drought. During such times, the need to conserve water is a priority, and you may be asked to take fewer and shorter showers.

History

There is archaeological evidence to suggest that some of the Yasawa islands were occupied thousands of years ago, but with a paucity of fresh water and the threat of tribal war, people have come and gone frequently over that time. The present *mataqali* (extended family or land-owning group) of Waya island, for example, are believed to have arrived only about five generations ago.

At that time most people lived in the mountains, only occasionally venturing down to the foreshore in search of food and fish. Once Christianity was introduced and the wars subsided, the villagers moved down to the sea and have remained there ever since.

🏃 Activities

Diving

The northern Yasawas offer spectacular diving. Check out **Lekima's Ledge** (good for novice divers) and the popular **Bonsai, Maze** and **Zoo** sites. The adrenalin-rush shark-encounter dive is offered by most resorts in Nacula, Nanuya Lailai and Tavewa.

A two-tank dive in the Yasawas costs between $200 and $300, depending on the operator/resort; a PADI Open Water Course is between $850 and $1100.

Cruises

Blue Lagoon Cruises   CRUISE
(☑670 5006; www.bluelagooncruises.com)
Cruises on board the intimate 55m *Fiji Princess* allow for a maximum of 68 guests. The three-night (twin $1922-2513, single $2513-3252), four-night (twin $2562-3350, single $3350-4336) and seven-night (twin

THE YASAWA FLYER

Most people travelling to the Yasawas go by the *Yasawa Flyer* (also called the 'Yellow Boat') operated by **Awesome Adventures Fiji** (☑ 675 0499; www.awesomefiji.com; Port Denarau). Half the fun of staying in the Yasawas is getting on and off the *Flyer* as it works its way up the chain towards Nacula, and comparing notes with other travellers.

The comfortable high-speed catamaran departs at 8.30am daily from Denarau Marina, calling in at some of the Mamanuca islands (South Sea, Bounty, Beachcomber/ Treasure and Vomo) before reaching the Yasawa Group. It takes about two hours to Kuata or Wayalailai ($137), 2½ hours to Waya ($148), three hours to Naviti ($157), four hours to Yaqeta and Matacawalevu ($167), and 4½ hours to Tavewa, Nanuya Lailai and Nacula ($167). In the afternoon it follows the same route back to the mainland, again calling in at all of the resorts; it arrives in Denarau about 5.45pm. Children aged between six and 15 travel half price. For an extra fee (between $30 and $40, depending on the destination), you can upgrade to the air-conditioned Captain's Lounge, a boat-top cabin with comfortable loungers, TVs and free hot drinks and snacks. Upgrade or not, you'll want to BYO food if you're travelling the length of the islands in one hit.

Most islands don't have wharves, so the *Flyer* pulls up seemingly in the middle of the sea to meet a swarm of dinghies (called tenders) that bob and bounce alongside to take turns collecting and depositing guests, bags and mail. It's easy to be lulled by the passing seascape: listen out for island calls made over the loudspeaker. Keep an eye on your luggage: bags are occasionally offloaded onto the wrong boat.

If you haven't already booked your accommodation, the *Flyer* has a tour desk that can call ahead to do it for you. The service is excellent and accepts credit cards. Be warned that your choice may be limited to the budget end of the quality scale as some of the more desirable options get booked out well ahead.

If you want to linger in the islands without a prebooked itinerary then a **Bula Pass** (www.awesomefiji.com; 5/7/10/12/15/21 day pass $385/490/640/700/765/845) can be a good deal. The pass enables unlimited island-hopping within the purchased time period, but only one return trip to Denarau.

The pre-paid **Bula Combo Pass** (www.awesomefiji.com; 5-21 day pass $840-6000) covers boat transfers and island accommodation. Prices vary according to time period and type of accommodation; the latter is ranked by one- or two-coconut ratings. One coconut usually means a basic dorm or *bure*, while two coconuts signifies an upgrade in rooms and possibly resort facilities. Depending on where you stay, meals may or may not be included: see the website for full details.

The *Yasawa Flyer* welcomes rubberneckers for the nine-hour Denarau-Yasawas return trip (adult/child $183/84): be warned, though, as this is a long day and you won't be getting off.

Awesome Adventures also offers all-inclusive package holidays that span between five and 12 days.

The collection boxes on board the boat are for donations to the *Flyer's* Yasawa Trust Foundation. This foundation helps support villagers in the northern Yasawas with infrastructure such as water tanks and school repairs. More information is available at www. vinakafiji.com.fj.

$4138-5518, single $5518-7243) cruises meander through the Mamanucas and Yasawas; the company has exclusive use of the best part of Blue Lagoon beach. Transfers, on-board activities, village visits and food are included, but drinks and diving are extra. Cruises depart from Port Denarau.

Captain Cook Cruises CRUISE
(☑670 1823; captaincookcruisesfiji.com) Offers all-inclusive cruises ranging from three to seven nights (from $1950 per person) in various classes and sleeping arrangements on board *Reef Endeavour*. The 68m cruise boat has a swimming pool, bars, lounges and air-conditioned accommodation for 135 people spread over three decks. Cruises depart from Denarau Marina.

Sailing

Captain Cook Cruises (www.captaincook cruisesfiji.com/fiji-sailing-adventures) runs various sailing trips to the southern Yasawas aboard the tall ship *Spirit of the Pacific*; staff also organise sailing charters of the area.

To find about about chartering bareboat and crewed yachts, check with the marina offices in Denerau, Musket Cove and Vuda Point or have a look at www.yachtcharterguide.com.

Kayaking

Southern Sea Ventures KAYAKING
(www.southernseaventures.com) This Australian-operated group offers eight-day ($3600) and 11-day (from $4070) kayak safaris through the Yasawas between May and October. Prices include all meals, two-person fibreglass kayaks, and safety and camping gear. Expect to paddle for three to four hours daily, stopping along the way for snorkelling and village visits. Similar trips are also organised by **World Expedition** (www.world expeditions.com).

ℹ️ Information

The Yasawas are remote and isolated; there are no banks, postal or medical services, and no proper shops (resorts sometimes stock essentials, and there's a tiny store at Coralview on Tavewa Island). Although increased mobile phone range has made communications easier, it can still be a bit erratic when there's a mountain in the way.

Head to Lonely Planet (www.lonelyplanet.com/ fiji/yasawa-group) for planning advice, author recommendations, traveller reviews and insider tips.

ℹ️ Getting There & Around

AIR

Pacific Islands Air (☑672 5644; www.pacific islandair.com; from $360) and **Turtle Airways** (☑672 1888; www.turtleairways.com; from $330) run seaplane transfers between Nadi and the Yasawas.

If you do arrive by seaplane, be sure to inform your resort so they can send their boat out to collect you!

BOAT

Most people access the Yasawas by Awesome Adventures' *Yasawa Flyer* catamaran – it's the only public boat to make the daily trip up and down the island chain. As you cross over from the Mamanucas, keep an eye out for the guardian of the Yasawas: he's the tiny figure cavorting with a warrior's club on a small rocky outcrop above the waves.

Once in the islands, ask at your resort about getting a lift over to nearby islands, or enquire about a water taxi. Often these are local motorboats in varying stages of disrepair (and with scant regard for safety equipment); however, the boatmen know the water, reefs and weather like the back of their hand. **Joe's Water Taxi** (☑839 4841, 869 6485) is a dependable choice.

Prices are fixed depending on distance and current cost of fuel; in 2015 a one-way transfer from Nacula to Tavewa in the Northern Yasawas, for example, was about $25.

Kuata & Wayasewa

These two islands mark the first stop in the Yasawa chain. Kuata is separated from Wayasewa by a deep, narrow channel and kayaking between the two islands is a great way to spend a calm-water afternoon.

Both have unusual volcanic rock formations, with caves and coral cliffs in the waters off the southern end of little Kuata, which is also where you'll find that island's best snor-

---

ℹ️ GET A TASTE

If you're not ready to commit to an extended stay in the Yasawas, a resort daytrip (about $210/120 per adult/child) offers a good glimpse into what the islands have to offer. South Sea Cruises (p116) runs daytrips to Barefoot Kuata, Octopus and Botaira resorts. Lunch is included (though you'll have to tack on a bit extra if you decide on the spectacular lobster at Botaira), as is snorkelling gear and all transfers. Barefoot Kuata also offers a snorkelling with sharks option (adult/child $65/32.50).

kelling – the island is easily walkable. Kuata's **summit climb** (per person $15) takes a hot and sticky 30 minutes with a guide – great for sunrise and sunset views.

Wayasewa, also known as Waya Lailai (Little Waya), is dominated by a massive volcanic plug (Vatuvula; 349m) that towers dramatically over the beaches below. There's a sunrise and sunset **summit walk** (per person $12) here, too. The track passes a 'wobbling rock'; upwards is a good workout for the thighs and the downhill slopes are not for the fainthearted or weak-kneed. The views towards Kuata, Vomo and Viti Levu are phenomenal.

VIllage visits are available on Wayasewa: ask at your accommodation.

A 15-minute boat ride from the resorts is a spot renowned for shark snorkelling. The mostly white-tip reef sharks are harmless, though their sleek, stealth-like appearance might suggest otherwise: this is a heart-stopping trip. Snorkelling with the sharks with/without gear costs about $50/25: arrange it through your resort.

🛏 Sleeping & Eating

Naqalia Lodge   LODGE $

(📞932 2650; www.naqalialodge-fijiresort.com; Wayasewa Island; camping/dm/d bungalow incl meals $60/100/250; @) These wonderful, community-owned digs may not be fancy, but if you're looking to experience life as part of a Fijian family, drop your bags. Run by Wayasewa villagers, Naqalia (pronounced *nun-GA-lia*) has five traditionally built *bures* with handpainted interiors and wooden verandahs, and a simple 12-bed dorm; camping is also available.

The brightly coloured lodge that gives Naqalia its name is where guests gather for communal meals, low-key kava sessions and to grapple with local kids for use of the one computer with internet access. Guided walks, snorkelling trips and village visits – especially interesting on a Sunday morning – are all on offer. Electricity available during peak hours.

Waya Lailai Resort   HOSTEL $

(📞603 0215; www.wayalailairesort.com; Wayasewa Island; dm/r/bungalow from $120/200/270; @) Owned and operated by Wayasewa villagers, this rustic hostel enjoys a dramatic setting at the base of the Vatuvula volcanic plug. Accommodation is tiered over two levels above the beach, and includes dorms (five- or 26-beds), private singles and doubles in a for-

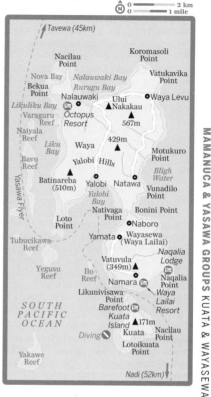

Kuata, Wayasewa & Waya

mer hilltop schoolhouse, and spacious traditional *bures* – two of which have cool lofts – with private balconies above the beach.

Village visits, snorkelling trips and diving are available, and you'll kick yourself if you miss out on a sunset hilltop trek; the views are spectacular. The resort is very popular with the sociable backpacking crowd. Meals are all included in the price.

Electricity available during peak hours.

★ Barefoot Kuata Island   RESORT $$

(📞896 2090; www.thebarefootcollection.com/kuata-island; Kuata Island; dm $90-130, bungalow $310; 🛜🏊) 🅿 This former beach-bum hostel has undergone a complete overhaul to become a spectacular, stylish hideaway (without the hefty price tag). New, spacious, beachside six- and eight-bed dorms offer million-dollar views; *bures* are modern with cute interiors; privates have fabulous outdoor showers. Beautiful design elements

MY ISLAND HOME: WAYA

Ruggedly ravishing Waya Island offers a miscellany of village homestays and experiences for those looking to get off the resort trail. Its friendly villages welcome visitors keen on immersing themselves in local life, while still enjoying the wonderful snorkelling and hikes of the more upmarket options.

In Yalobi, **Jone Sau** (☑735 5388) can arrange homestays and boats for pick-ups and island-hopping, as can **Trevor Withers Dawai** (☑755 0737); if you can't get through, try his daughter **Ateca** in Lautoka (☑805 6749). Trevor can arrange transport and hikes up to nearby Wayasewa's wobbling (balancing) rock.

In Natawa, contact **Simi Sivo** (☑766 8940).

For Waya Levu, call **Tomasi Sayavi** (☑780 3387) or email his son Ilaitia at isayavi@ hotmail.com; in his youth, Tomasi was Fiji's greatest shark catcher! You can also contact the village headman Naqaro via his daughter-in-law **Ivamere** (☑736 6198).

Be sure to bring along a *sevusevu* of kava root (if you arrange it in advance, your host can buy this for you) to present to the village chief or headman: you will be welcomed with a formal kava drinking ceremony before protocol relaxes. Just like on the mainland, modesty prevails at island villages: men can be shirtless on the beach but not in the village, and women should take along a *sulu* (sarong). Host-led excursions to nearby schools, villages and churches are a must; it's worth bringing donations of cash for the Village Funds or worthy supplies (cheap fishing handreels, toothbrushes, LED torches etc) along with you. Hosts can organise snorkelling gear, but many guests choose to bring their own and donate it to the village once they leave.

Obviously, visits must be booked in advance. Take the *Yasawa Flyer* to Octopus Resort, and your host should have a boat waiting for you: in some cases they can pick you up directly from Denarau or Lautoka Wharf. Prices vary for homestays (they're all cheap); discuss fees with your host when making arrangements.

are everywhere, from the seaside footprint-shaped pools to the carved handiwork lending major 'wow' to the sand-floored restaurant/bar.

The compulsory meal plan ($75) includes big breakfasts, lunch and three-course dinners; there are loads of vegetarian options. The island's dive shop has a strong focus on marine conservation; good value stay-and-dive packages are available.

At time of research, work was underway on a huge games room, rock-top spa and jungle tents.

Waya & Around

Waya is exquisite on the eyes, with picture-postcard scenery. It has rugged hills, beautiful beaches and lagoons, and a coastline that alternates between long, sandy beaches and rocky headlands. Waya is also unusually blessed with natural springs that percolate up through the volcanic rock, so it is unlikely you will face water restrictions here. There are four villages (Nalauwaki, Natawa, Yalobi and Waya Levu), a nursing station and a boarding school on the island.

Hiking unguided across the island is not recommended: land is privately owned, and many trails are overgrown. The best opportunity to work the pins is the summit trek to Ului Nakauka (three hours return). The track from Nalawauki village circles around the back of a huge rock outcrop before ascending to its summit. The views south across Waya and north towards Naviti are spectacular, and you may find yourself in the company of feral goats.

A thick rim of coral follows Waya's shoreline and provides good snorkelling just off the beach in front of Octopus Resort. Yachties often anchor on one side or the other (depending on the wind) of the natural sand bridge that has formed between Waya and Wayasewa.

🛏 Sleeping & Eating

★**Octopus Resort** RESORT $$
(☑777 0030; www.octopusresort.com; Waya Island; dm $38-68, bungalow $213-640, ste $915, family villa $1214-2080, 2-night minimum stay; ✲🛜🏊🐕) From good, no-bunk dorms to stand-alone *bures* in an array of configurations, all the way up to top-end suites and family villas,

Octopus offers something for everyone. Despite the disparity, it all works out: this is a favourite Yasawas getaway for both family and free-wheeling types. With a beach perfect for slacking or snorkelling, super-friendly staff and amenities galore, what's not to love?

The kids club frees up parents keen to unwind with daily yoga, spa treatments and Fijian cooking classes. Other activities include handline fishing, village visits and movies by the pool; a two-tank dive/PADI Open Water Course costs $235/895.

The compulsory meal package (adult/child $106/70) includes excellent à la carte lunches and ever-changing dinners: chefs cater to dietary requirements and allergies.

In addition to the *Yasawa Flyer,* guests can arrive via direct transfer from Vuda Point Marina (adult/child $177/88 one way, 1¼ hours).

Viwa Island Resort RESORT $$$

(☑603 0066; www.viwaislandresort.com; Viwa island; bungalow $832-976; ❄☎☀) Viwa is all about getting away from it all, 'it all' in this case being other islands and children. The upscale adults-only resort houses 11 absolute beachfront *bures* sleeping either two or four people. The island itself – home to three welcoming villages – is the stuff dreams are made of, and is ringed by a colourful reef teeming with life; snorkelling here is a must, and diving is available.

The *Yasawa Flyer* drops guests at Octopus Resort; they're then transferred via private boat to Viwa (30 minutes).

Naviti & Around

One of the largest (33 sq km) and highest (up to 380m high) islands of the group, Naviti has a rugged volcanic profile. Along with the three smaller islands of Drawaqa, Nanuya Balavu and Naukacuvu at the southern end, a collection of very different and equally inviting resorts welcomes travellers.

The islands' main draw is the chance to swim with manta rays, which cruise the channel between Nanuya Balavu and Drawaqa islands. The best time to see them is between June and August, although they may be around as early as May and as late as October. Resorts in the area offer manta ray snorkelling trips for around $45 per person plus snorkel hire, with spotters heading out in the mornings ahead of the tours to check where the animals are. If you're staying at

Mantaray or Barefoot Manta – the resorts closest to the channel – an island-wide call will go up once the rays are spotted, and you'll have to race to the boats.

It's up to you to keep up with the rays, which is not always easy, especially if they're swimming against the current. Those able to freedive the seven-or-so metres down to the rays may have a really close encounter, with 'look, don't touch' as the guiding principle.

🛏 Sleeping & Eating

White Sandy Beach HOSTEL $

(☑925 5370; www.whitesandybeachresort.com; Naviti Island; campsite/dm/bungalow incl meals $60/105/250; ☎) This is not a misnomer: the beach here is indeed white-sanded, as is the floor of the restaurant, bar and surely one of the world's most chilled-out common rooms. It's a wonderfully laid-back place overall, so much so that many guests, unable to drag themselves away from the mellow sea views, drag their mattresses onto the dorm's outdoor deck for the night.

Beachfront *bures* – some with outdoor showers and bathtubs – are also available.

Swimming is only possible at high tide here, though a steep, 10-minute walk leads to the secluded Honeymoon Beach. Visitors make a $2 donation to the village to visit this little cove, but the pay-off is tranquil waters and decent snorkelling.

Electricity available during peak hours.

SWIMMING WITH THE DEVIL

It's hard not to feel a little nervous at the sight of a large dark object approaching from the depths towards you, but the graceful flying carpet that emerges is something to admire, not fear. Also known as devil rays (because of their hornlike pectoral fin extensions), manta rays are the largest of the rays and typically measure 4m to 5.5m across at maturity. The largest recorded specimen was a massive 7.6m (2300kg) and, due to their size, only four aquariums in the world have ever kept them successfully. Despite their bulk, manta rays are capable of great speed and are known to leap out of the water, landing with a resounding slap – but mostly they glide effortlessly in seemingly synchronised swimming manoeuvres.

★ Mantaray Island Resort
RESORT $$

(☑776 6351; www.mantarayisland.com; Nanuya Balavu Island; dm $41, bungalow $150-285, villa $485; ❄️☎️) This happening hideaway can be whatever you want it to be: backpacker party central or high-end escape. Lodgings are spread across a small hill and two pretty beaches: the 32-bed dorm and treehouse *bures* are tucked away up a forested path, while self-contained jungle *bures* and posh new beachfront villas skirt the sand, far enough from the lively bar to be peaceful.

Many people come here for its proximity to the manta ray channel and excellent off-shore snorkelling; there are tons of other organised activities, including guided island treks, cooking classes, sunset tube cruises and diving.

The hilltop restaurant serves fresh, inventive and filling food ($87 compulsory meal plan); huge slices of wood-fired pizza ($5) are available during the twilight cocktail hour.

Barefoot Manta Island
RESORT $$

(☑707 7328; www.thebarefootcollection.com/manta-island; Drawaqa Island; dm $45-65, bungalow $310, compulsory meal package $75; ☎️) This refurbished and rebranded resort hasn't let its (continuing) upgrade go to its head: though magnificent, Barefoot Manta is decidedly low-key. Most guests are here to take part in underwater activities; as the name implies, this is a top spot for goggling at manta rays, with swim safaris running between May and October. Custom dive packages, kayaking, hikes and village visits are also available.

Comfortable, no-frills dorms and private tented *bures* are dotted between the island's Sunrise and Sunset beaches; the latter is also home to a simple but spectacular restaurant/bar. Many guests divide their holiday between here and sister resort, Barefoot Kuata.

Korovou Eco-Tour Resort
HOSTEL $$

(☑925 5370; www.korovouecotourresort.com; Naviti Island; dm/bungalow/villa incl meals $140/350/450; ☎️🍽️) This recently renovated spot attracts chatty backpackers and sociable families for its fish-filled reef, long activities list and super-friendly staff. Surprisingly spacious 17- and 31-bed dorms are notable for their solid beds and surplus of toilets, while *bures* and villas – some timber, some stone – have pleasant verandahs and ensuites. Guests gather by the pool, on the giant restaurant deck and at the good-timey Bula Bar.

Paradise Cove Resort
RESORT $$$

(☑776 8427; www.paradisecoveresortfiji.com; Naukacuvu Island; bungalow from $405, villa $600-1260, ste $1120, beach house $1010-1400, 2-night minimum stay; ❄️☎️🍽️🏊) This dazzling resort opened in 2013, and has been attracting hordes of families and cashed-up couples ever since. Beautifully built *bures,* villas and suites (with plunge pools and hanging daybeds) come in a variety of configurations; all have outdoor showers, private verandahs and gorgeous interiors. There's a great kids club and family activities; the adults-only side of the resort is private and peaceful.

Luxury one- and two-bedroom beach houses offer exclusive seclusion; they're just a quick zip across the channel from the resort.

There's a compulsory meal plan (adult/child $147/81 per day; kids under four eat

---

TAKING TIME TO GIVE BACK

Spend any time in the Yasawas and you'll quickly realise that its not just its scenic attributes that make the islands so beautiful: it's their people. But behind the *bulas* and beaming countenances, the reality of life in the Yasawas isn't always an easy one. Many island villages subsist at third-world levels, with limited access to clean water, power and education.

The **Yasawa Trust Foundation** (www.vinakafiji.org.fj) aims to change that. Its Vinaka Fiji volunteer programs accept people (aged 16 and up) from all over the world, who come on placements lasting between one and 26 weeks. Programs cover areas including education, sustainability and marine conservation; volunteers do everything from working as teachers' aides to constructing water tanks in drought-prone villages. Weekends are free to explore the islands, and most people take the opportunity to travel in-country for a while before or after their placement.

If volunteering isn't your thing, donations can be made online, or on-board the *Yasawa Flyer.*

free); the Black Rock Restaurant is exceedingly good.

★ Botaira Beach Resort
RESORT $$$

(☏ 670 7002; www.botaira.com; Naviti Island; bungalow $636-390; ☞) Botaira makes a great day-trip destination – the open-air deck restaurant serves spectacular seafood lunches and there's fab snorkelling right off the beautiful beach. For overnighters, the *bures,* scattered along the beach and lush garden, are certainly stylish and spacious, but they are expensive, considering the resort doesn't have 24-hour power and you can never be sure when your shower will spurt cold seawater. Staying at the resort also includes a compulsory $105 meal plan.

There is a dorm here ($150), but it's usually reserved for students or group bookings.

Matacawalevu & Yaqeta

Matacawalevu is a 4km-long hilly volcanic island protected by the large Nasomo Bay on its eastern side. Nanuya Levu (Turtle Island) is to the east, and to the south, across a protected lagoon used for seaweed farming, is Yaqeta. The island has two villages: Matacawalevu on its northeast end and Vuake in Nasomo Bay.

🛏 Sleeping

Long Beach Backpackers
HOSTEL $

(☏ 925 5370; www.longbeachresortfiji.com; Matacawelevu Island; dm $105/bungalow $180-260 incl meals) If you're looking to party, avert your eyes: this low-key, family-run hostel is all about seclusion and serenity. There are garden and beachfront *bures* and a clean eight-bed dorm: both are liveable, but the big draw here is the long, horseshoe-shaped beach and a breezy deck overlooking tiny Deviulau island – you can wade over at low tide and scramble to the top for great views.

Electricity available during peak hours.

Bay of Plenty Lodge
HOSTEL $

(☏ 925 5370; www.bayofplenty-yasawa.com; Matacawalevu Island; dm/bungalow incl meals $105/250) This humble hostel attracts adventurous guests keen on experiencing island life like a local. It's far from fancy, and not the place to stay if you want to walk out and snorkel – the mangrove-fringed beach is extremely tidal and resembles an estuary for much of the day. But the staff is friendly, a welcoming village is next door, and there's

wildlife galore to contemplate. Electricity available during peak hours.

★ Navutu Stars
BOUTIQUE HOTEL $$$

(☏ 664 0553; www.navutustarsfiji.com; Yaqeta Island; bungalow incl breakfast $747-1264; ☀☞☼) This intimate resort specialises in Pacific-style decadence: think petal-sprinkled baths, romantic sunset dining and complimentary massages on arrival. The nine whitewashed *bures* have exquisitely detailed 8m-high roofs, space galore and fantastic views. If you can haul yourself out of your king-sized bed, there's free yoga every morning. Food is fabulous, a fusion of Italian specialties with local ingredients. Optional full/half meal plans are $185/120.

Energetic guests can take part in coral restoration dives, kayak, join various island-hopping tours and go on night-time lobster hunts.

Tavewa, Nanuya Lailai & Nacula

These islands are right in the middle of the Yasawa Group, but house some of the group's northernmost resorts. Nacula marks the end of the *Yasawa Flyer* route. Travelling between the resorts by water taxi costs around $25 per trip.

All the resorts can arrange boat trips to the Blue Lagoon (around $20 per person) and trips to Sawa-i-Lau caves ($60 to $100 per person); give Joe's Water Taxi (p128) a call if you want to go it alone.

Recommended dive spots include the big wall dives at the Zoo and Bonsai and the swim-throughs and tunnels at the Maze. The dive companies also run weekly shark dives, where you are likely to see two resident 4m lemon sharks and, occasionally, 2m grey reef sharks. A two-tank dive/PADI Open Water Course costs around $185/800, including equipment.

Tavewa

A pleasant beach unfurls itself on the southeastern coast of this small island (3 sq km) but it's often plagued by buffeting trade winds (which are great, however, for kiteboarders). You need to head west to the beach around the bend of Savutu Point to find relief from the gales and you're best off doing so at low tide. The snorkelling just offshore here is excellent. An ambling

Tavewa & Around

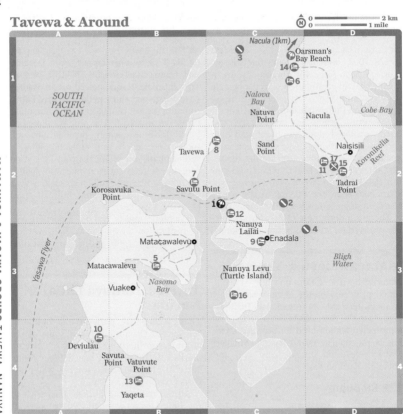

Tavewa & Around

⊙ Sights
1 Blue Lagoon	C2

✪ Activities, Courses & Tours
2 Bonsai	C2
3 Maze	C1
Vertical Blue Diving	(see 6)
4 Zoo	D3

⌂ Sleeping
5 Bay of Plenty Lodge	B3
6 Blue Lagoon Beach Resort	C1
7 Coconut Beach Resort	B2
8 Coralview Resort	C2
9 Gold Coast Inn	C3
10 Long Beach Backpackers	A4
11 Nabua Lodge	D2
12 Nanuya Island Resort	C2
13 Navutu Stars	B4
14 Oarsman's Bay Lodge	C1
15 Safe Landing Resort	D2
16 Turtle Island Resort	C3

⊗ Eating
17 Travellers Tea House	D2

ascent of the central crest affords photogenic views of the Yasawa chain, which is particularly spectacular at sunset; the track crosses several stretches of private land, so ask your accommodation to get the OK from the owners before you head up.

🏨 Sleeping & Eating

Coralview Resort HOSTEL $
(☑666 2648; www.coralview.com.fj; Tavewa Island; dm $55/bungalow $156-194; ❄🞕) This well-run budget resort is popular with the party people (though adventurous families are joining their ranks): with a ripper bar, twice-weekly

lovo/disco/knife-and-fire dance show, and loads of adrenalin-spiking activities – including jet-skiing, shark diving and steep sunset hikes – it's easy to understand why. Air-conditioned dorms with partitions offer a semblance of privacy; garden and beachfront *bures* have patios and nice interiors.

Other bonuses include 24-hour power, meals (compulsory $89 plan) made with organic produce from Coralview's mainland farm, a small on-site store and roaming goats.

★Coconut Beach Resort   RESORT $$
(☑945 7505; www.coconutbeachfiji.com; Tavewa Island; bungalow $250-350; ☎) Occupying one of the best beaches in the Yasawas, this brand-new resort is an up-and-coming star. Set on a huge former copra plantation, its five stylish *bures* (more, to be dotted along the preposterously enticing shoreline, are planned) are super-spacious, comfortable and feature king-sized beds and stunning outdoor bathrooms; none are closer than 40m to each other, guaranteeing an immensely laid-back, private-paradise feel.

It's not a 'resorty' resort – there's no pool or kids club – but rather an ideal spot to unwind, snorkel (there's a vibrant marine sanctuary right off the sand) and eat yourself into a happy stupor: the chef is renowned for his hearty meals and legendary afternoon teas (compulsory meal plan adult/child $89/49).

Nanuya Lailai

This is it, folks – home to the most famous of all the Yasawas' beaches, the **Blue Lagoon** (Nanuya Lailai). Crystalline and glossy, it doesn't disappoint the bevy of swimmers, snorkellers, divers, and people on cruise boats or yachts who dabble in its gorgeous, lucent depths. Actually, it's not dissimilar to many of the lagoons scattered around the Yasawas. The snorkelling here is rich in fish but the coral has taken a hammering over recent years. Travellers are advised by signs, and enforced at times by security staff, to stay off the section of Blue Lagoon beach used by Blue Lagoon Cruises.

The settlement of Enadala is on the eastern side of Nanuya Lailai, and the beach here is buffeted by strong winds. Connecting the Blue Lagoon and Enadala beaches, and snaking over the mass of gently sloping hills of the island's interior, is a well-trodden track. It takes about 30 minutes to walk from one beach to the other by using this track or following the coastline at low tide. But what could possibly draw anyone away from the Blue Lagoon's bright water? How about cake? Lo's Tea Shop – a blue shack on the edge of the water – sells homemade cakes with sugary sauce for $3 a slice. Both Lo's and Grandma's Shell Market, a few sandy footprints down, sell seashells (along with sarongs and jewellery). Opening hours are Fiji time.

🛏 Sleeping & Eating

Gold Coast Inn   HOMESTAY $
(☑925 5370; www.goldcoastinn-yasawas.com; dm/bungalow incl meals $105/250) This is a smallish affair – there are only five *bures* and a small 10-bed dorm – but it's run by a lovely family with a big heart. It's not the place for those expecting luxury: showers are cold and electricity can be sporadic. The beach, however, is gorgeous, and the Fiji-style meals are wholesome. A plus for parents: free babysitting!

Nanuya Island Resort   BOUTIQUE HOTEL $$$
(☑666 7633; www.nanuyafiji.com; villas incl breakfast $389-1250; 2-night minimum stay; ❋☎) A short walk from the azure waters of the Blue Lagoon, this swish spot is the epitome of holiday indulgence and serenity (no kids under seven). The new Australian owners have given the romantic resort a makeover, with the addition of a luxurious honeymoon villa, four thatched-roof 'superior' villas (with spas and sundecks) and 24-hour solar power.

The cosy treetop villas that overlook the lagoon are rightfully popular (book far ahead), but beware: the path up to them is very steep.

The Boathouse at Nanuya complex is attached to the resort and is aimed at visiting yachties and island-hoppers looking for cheaper accommodation. Moorings, a general store, and a bar are all planned.

Nacula

Nacula, a hilly volcanic island, is the third largest in the Yasawas. Blanketed with rugged hills and soft peaks, its interior is laced with well-trodden paths leading to villages and small coves. It is possible to follow a trail inland through mangroves from the resorts on the southern point to those at Long Beach. Keep an eye out for mudskippers, a not-particularly-pretty amphibious fish living in the tidal streams among the mangroves; despite their primordial-swamp appearance, they apparently go very well in a coconut curry. For a broader view of your surrounds, a two- to three-hour return hike above Nabua Lodge provides 360-degree views across the islands.

There are four villages on Nacula island, including Nacula, home of Ratu Epeli Vuetibau Bogileka, the high chief of Nacula Tikina. The tikina (group of villages) includes the islands of Nacula, Tavewa, Nanuya Levu, Nanuya Lailai and Matacawalevu, and is home to about 3500 people. Catching a Sunday church service in one of the villages is a real treat; most resorts will arrange free transport for their guests.

Nacula has some of the finest beaches, swimming and snorkelling in Fiji, particularly at Long Beach.

🛏 Sleeping & Eating

South Coast

The two budget resorts are separated by a few hundred metres of waterfront. Sandwiched between them is the wonderfully wonky **Travellers Tea House** (Nacula Island; ⊙3pm-5.30pm, Mon-Sat). It's nothing more than a few wobbly benches and plastic tablecloths held down by rocks, but the view is sublime, as are the homemade cakes and tea ($6).

Nabua Lodge   HOSTEL $
(☑925 5370; www.nabualodge-yasawa.com; dm $110, bungalow from $260; ⊛) Nabua's utterly relaxed vibe and welcome-to-the-family sociability make this budget spot stand out from the crowd almost as much as their pink *bures* do. Staring down at the sea from a well-maintained, hammock-strewn grassy plot, this is a good place for catching up on holiday reading, taking part in nightly Fiji-flavoured events or hopping out on a cave tour. All meals are included.

The 12-bed dorm is basic but bunkless; work was underway in 2015 on a second dorm. *Bures* are clean, roomy and simple.

Electricity available during peak hours.

Safe Landing Resort   HOSTEL $
(☑625 3746; dm/bungalow incl meals $90/240; @) Several small *bures* dot the waterfront here, overlooking the resort's trademark sandy cove, a pretty little beach framed by two rocky outcrops. The resort was quiet when we visited, due to expansion, refurbishments and construction (including that

of another dorm). Owned and operated by villagers, the hostel is friendly and offers lots of cultural activities, as well as snorkelling and cave trips.

Long Beach

With a long swath of powdery sand easing into a glassy, cerulean sea, this is easily one of the Yasawas' finest beaches. Unlike at many others nearby, it's possible to swim here at low tide without trudging over an exposed coral shelf to do so.

★**Blue Lagoon Beach Resort**   RESORT $$
(☑603 0223; www.bluelagoonbeachresort.com. fj; dm $30, r from $172, bungalow $316-870; ❄❢⊛⋒) Blue Lagoon ticks all the right boxes: its beach is gorgeous, the staff is friendly but unobtrusive, and while it's small enough to be low-key, it's big enough (about 100 guests when full) to have a bit of buzz. It caters for all budgets in a compatible way; *bure* are stylish (the beachfront digs are divine) and the two eight-bed, air-conditioned dorms are sparkling.

Excellent, ever-changing meals (daily plans adult/child $99/67) are served in the sand-floored restaurant/bar with bean bags, lounges and hammocks over the water: parents praise the 5.30pm dinnertime for kids. There's also a very good kids club.

Their **Vertical Blue** (dive@bluelagoon beachresort.com.fj; Blue Lagoon Resort) dive shop caters to guests and those staying at nearby resorts.

Oarsman's Bay Lodge   RESORT $$
(☑628 0485; www.oarsmanbayfiji.com; campsite/ dm $45/60, bungalow $250-350; ⊛) Plonked between a village and a fabulous slice of shoreline, Oarsman's Bay occupies two worlds. The same can be said about its accommodation: *bures* and the dorm – perched above the restaurant overlooking the sea – are incredibly basic, but have trillion-dollar views. Renovations were underway at the time of research, though they hadn't interrupted the filling meals (compulsory meal plan adult/child $85/45) at the communal restaurant, village visits and cave/snorkelling trips.

Nanuya Levu (Turtle Island)

Nanuya Levu is a privately owned island (2 sq km) with protected sandy beaches and rugged volcanic cliffs. The 1980 film *The Blue Lagoon,* starring Brooke Shields,

BEACH BUSINESS

All the resorts in the Yasawas are on the waterfront, but not all can claim idyllic beaches. If white sand, turquoise depths and simmering in a sun-coma are what you came for, here is our Top 5:

Coconut Beach Resort (p135; Tavewa) The former copra plantation sits on an absurdly gorgeous curving beach, with soft, white sand looking over a horizon of stripey blue/green/purple waters.

Blue Lagoon Beach Resort (p136; Nacula) Definitely one of best of the Yasawas' resort-based beaches. Protected from the trade winds, the water is still, clear and deep. A large bank of coral provides excellent snorkelling.

Nanuya Island Resort (p135; Nanuya Lailai) The resort occupies an enviable and isolated position on a quiet beach in front of the renowned Blue Lagoon.

Octopus Resort (p130; Waya) The beach in this protected cove is beautiful for swimming at high tide and great for sunbaking and wandering at low tide.

Botaira Beach Resort (p133; Naviti) Botaira's beach is a length of soft white sand with ample room to park a towel. The calm water has a good stretch of shallows before it drops into the deep.

was partly filmed here, as was the original 1949 version starring Jean Simmons. It is off-limits to all but Turtle Island Resort guests.

Sawa-i-Lau

Must-see Sawa-i-Lau is a stand-out limestone island – housing two caves – amid a string of those formed by volcanos. The gorgeous grottoes attract visitors by the dingy-ful. Known as the 'heart of the Yasawas', they're rich in legend as they are in looks: among other tales, they are reputed to be the final resting place of Ulutini, the 10-headed ancient Fijian god.

The underwater limestone is thought to have formed a few hundred metres below the surface and then uplifted over time.

Shafts of daylight enter a great dome-shaped cave – its walls soar 15m above the water surface – where you can swim in a mind-bogglingly beautiful natural pool. With a guide, a torch and a bit of courage, you can also swim through an underwater passage into an adjoining chamber. The walls have carvings, paintings and inscriptions of unknown meaning.

Most Yasawa resorts offer trips to the caves from about $60 per person.

Yasawa

Yasawa, the 22-km-long, northernmost island in the group, has six small villages and the fabulous, five-star **Yasawa Island Resort** (☑ 672 2266; www.yasawa.com; from $1665-3500).

Ovalau & the Lomaiviti Group

POP 12,065

Best Sights

➡ Levuka (p143)

➡ Snake Island (p148)

➡ Lovoni village (p140)

➡ Niubasaga (p148)

➡ Nadelaiovalau Peak (p140)

Best Places to Stay

➡ Levuka Homestay (p145)

➡ Bobo's Farm (p147)

➡ Caqalai Island Resort (p148)

➡ Leleuvia Island Resort (p148)

Why Go?

Despite its proximity to Viti Levu, the Lomaiviti Group is often overlooked as a tourist destination, which is a shame. It was in Levuka, the capital of the main island Ovalau, that the first Europeans settled and eventually made this the country's first capital. Its wild and immoral colonial days are long over but you'll be seduced by its charms and welcoming atmosphere – not forgetting its historic centre that won Fiji's first World Heritage site listing in 2013.

The tiny coral islands of Leleuvia and Caqalai have sandy beaches, good snorkelling and simple budget resorts. To the north is Koro with its fantastic diving, family-oriented Naigani and the luxury resort of Wakaya island. Hawksbill turtles visit to lay their eggs, and a pod of humpback whales passes the east coast of Ovalau on their annual migration between May and September. Unfortunately Ovalau and the Lomaiviti Islands were badly damaged by 2016's Cyclone Winston.

When to Go

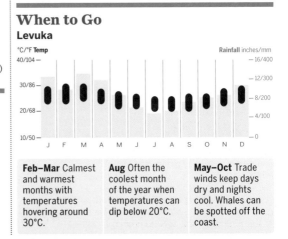

Levuka

Feb–Mar Calmest and warmest months with temperatures hovering around 30°C.

Aug Often the coolest month of the year when temperatures can dip below 20°C.

May–Oct Trade winds keep days dry and nights cool. Whales can be spotted off the coast.

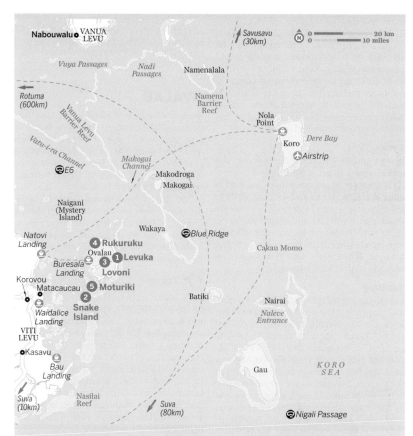

Ovalau & the Lomaiviti Group Highlights

❶ Enjoying the rickety colonial architecture of colourful **Levuka** (p143) and easily imagining its rowdy outpost atmosphere of times past.

❷ Spotting Napoleon wrasses, banded sea snakes, phenomenally big schools of fish and psychedelic gardens of soft corals while snorkelling **Snake Island** (p148).

❸ Hiking through river jungles to the proud and remote village of Lovoni with **Epi's Tours** (p140).

❹ Eating homegrown organic food in the rainforest at **Bobo's Farm** (p147).

❺ Getting spiritual with a melodious church service at **Niubasaga village** (p148) on remote Moturiki.

🏃 Activities

Diving & Snorkelling

The Lomaiviti waters offer some wonderful, little-visited dive sites where you can encounter manta rays, hammerheads, turtles, white-tip reef sharks and lion fish, but at the time of writing few resorts offered diving trips. **Blue Ridge**, off Wakaya Island, is famous for its bright-blue ribbon eels. There is stunning soft coral at **Snake Island**, just off Caqalai, in the Moturiki Channel, and excellent hard coral at **Waitovu Passage**. The **Pipeline**, two minutes by boat from town at Levuka Passage, is for experienced divers only. Here the fishy waste from the Pafco tuna plant attracts giant groupers, eagle rays and bull sharks. The famous **E6** in the Vatu-i-Ra Channel is a huge pinnacle with soft corals and plenty of big pelagics. **Nigali Passage** off Gau island is a narrow channel in the reef that has a concentration of pelagics such as gray reef sharks and barracuda. E6 and Nigali Passage can usually only be accessed on a live-aboard. Naigani Island Resort and Wakaya Resort both offer diving. Sadly there are no dive shops on Lomaiviti itself. Snorkelling off the outer islands is fantastic, especially around Snake Island. Napoleon wrasses, banded sea snakes and flourishing corals are highlights.

Cycling

Levuka and its surrounding area is compact and it is easy to get around by bike – especially if you're heading south, as the road is quite flat. Head north and the road starts to get very hilly around Cawaci. If you're reasonably fit, it will take you about a day to cycle around the island. No one was officially renting out bikes at the time of research, but ask around and you're sure to find someone who will rent or lend you one.

Yachting

Levuka is a port of entry into Fiji for yachties and there are a few good spots to put down anchor in the Lomaiviti Group. You can anchor in Levuka harbour to explore Ovalau, and good desert-island spots to park include Leleuvia island and Dere Bay on Koro island. You will find resort facilities at both of these spots. Formalities are usually simpler here than in Suva. There is a customs house by the main wharf, and ship supplies and repairs are available here. Call ahead if arriving outside normal working hours.

❶ Getting There & Around

AIR

From Suva **Northern Air** (☑ 347 5005; www. northernair.com.fj) flies to Bureta Airstrip on Ovalau ($86 one way, 12 minutes, Monday to Saturday) at 8am and returns to Suva at 8.40am. The airstrip is about 40 minutes' drive from Levuka. A taxi costs about $30. On Wednesday and Friday afternoons, Northern Air's Suva–Savusavu flight also stops at Bureta, but only if there is demand – call ahead to book, as this service cannot be booked online.

BOAT

Patterson Brothers Shipping (☑ 344 0125; Suite 2, Level 2, Epworth Arcade, Nina St, Suva; ⊙ 8.30am-4.30pm Mon-Fri, to noon Sat) has a daily combined bus-ferry service from Suva to Levuka via Natovi Landing ($35, four to six hours), leaving from Suva Bus Station at 1.30pm, and from Levuka at 5am. Arrive 30 minutes before departure.

The resorts on the islands near Ovalau (all except Koro) offer private transfers in their own boats to either Natovi, Bau or Waidalice Landings on Viti Levu and to Levuka.

OVALAU

Ovalau is the largest island in the Lomaiviti Group. At the centre of the island is an extinct volcano and several mountains which offer nice hiking. There's also the captivating old colonial centre of Levuka, which is the only place in the Lomaiviti Group with decent banks, shops and services.

The Bureta Airstrip and Buresala Landing (for ferries) are on the western side of Ovalau, while Levuka is on the eastern coast. A gravel road winds around the perimeter of the island and another follows the Bureta River inland to Lovoni village.

☞ Tours

Epi's Tours   TOUR
(☑ 746 0700, 977 9977; epistours@gmail.com; Levuka historical tour $10, Lovoni day trip $50-80, Nadelaiovalau Peak $20-30) Offers historical tours of Levuka town, day trips to the volcanic crater or Lovoni (with river swimming and a traditional Fijian lunch), and a half-day hike to The Peak (487m), a summit overlooking Levuka, where you can learn about Ovalau's wild foods and medicinal plants as well as a trek up Nadelaiovalau Peak (626m), the highest point on the island.

Prices depend on the number of clients: tours require a minimum of two people, or four for the town tour.

Tours with Nox   WALKING TOUR
(☑ 344 0777) Offers historical walking tours of Levuka ($10) and hikes to waterfalls in the hills. Contact Nox through Levuka Homestay (p145).

Levuka

POP 3750

There's no denying Levuka's visual appeal. It's one of the few places in the South Pacific that has retained its colonial buildings (though many were damaged by Cyclone Winston in 2016): along the main street, timber shop-fronts straight out of a Hollywood western are sandwiched between blue sea and fertile green mountains. The effect is quite beguiling – you can almost taste the

Ovalau & Moturiki

| | 0 | 5 km |
| | 0 | 2.5 miles |

Ovalau & Moturiki

wild frontier days of this former whaling outpost.

It is an extremely friendly place and you will be warmly welcomed by the mixture of indigenous Fijians, Indo-Fijians, Chinese Fijians, part-European Fijians and the clutch of expats who inhabit this sleepy town. Nearly everyone is welcoming to visitors, and if you stay for a few days, you'll meet half the town.

In 2013, Unesco listed Levuka as Fiji's first World Heritage Site, and there are hopes that a focus on the town's unique history will provide a boost for a unique destination that's often overlooked in favour of Fiji's tourist headline acts.

Sights

Levuka is small enough that you can see the sights in a single day of walking. Start your walking tour at Nasova, about 10 minutes' stroll south of the Pafco cannery. The Deed of Cession, handing over Fiji to Britain, was signed here in 1874. Cession Site, a memorial commemorating the event, is a pair of anchors and a scattering of plaque-bearing stones.

Across the road are faded Nasova House, once the governor's residence, and the thatched Provincial Bure. Prince Charles made his headquarters in the Provincial Bure when he represented Her Majesty's government during the transition to independence in 1970. It later served as a venue for Lomaiviti council meetings. A large, new meeting venue has been built next door, constructed in time for a 2006 Great Council of Chiefs meeting that never got off the ground because of the 2006 coup. According to our guide, it has yet to be used.

The Pafco tuna cannery at the southern end of Levuka employs almost 1000 townspeople and gives the whole town its distinctive odour. It was occupied by Lovoni villagers during the 2000 coup as part of a dispute about unloading cargo.

Head north along Beach St where the streetscape dates from the late 19th and early 20th centuries. Just in front of the post office is the site of the original Pigeon Post, marked by a nondescript drinking fountain in the centre of the road. From the timber loft that stood here, pigeons provided the first postal link between Levuka and Suva. The birds flew the distance in less than 30 minutes, and were considerably faster and more reliable than Post Fiji.

A few doors away stands the 1868 former Morris Hedstrom (MH; Beach St) trading store, the original MH store in Fiji. Behind its restored facade are the Levuka Community Centre, a library and the small but fascinating **Levuka Museum** (admission $2; ⏲8am-1pm & 2-4.30pm Mon-Fri, 9am-1pm Sat), which holds a small exhibition detailing the history of the town, including some wonderful old photos from colonial days.

Sacred Heart Church (Beach St) dates from 1858. The clock strikes twice each hour, with a minute in between. Locals say the first strike is an alarm to warn people who are operating on 'Fiji time'. The light on the spire guides ships through Levuka Passage. From the church, head west along Totoga Lane to explore the backstreets.

The Marist Convent School (1882) was a girls' school opened by Catholic missionaries and run by Australian and French nuns. It is now a lively co-ed primary school. It was built largely out of coral stone in an attempt to protect it from the hurricanes that have claimed so many buildings in town, and it remains an impressive monument against the mountain backdrop.

LEVUKA'S WILD WEST HISTORY

In the 19th century the town of Levuka was a bolt-hole where embittered sailors jumped ship, escaped convicts hid out, polygamous drunks took strings of island brides and disputes were settled with the musket.

As early as 1806 European sandalwood traders stopped at Levuka in search of supplies. However, foreigners did not begin to settle here until the 1830s, when it became a popular whaling centre. The newcomers built schooners and traded for *bêche-de-mer* (sea cucumber), turtle shells and coconut oil. Some settled down with several Fijian women at a time, explaining to the local people that this was the custom where they came from.

The Lovoni people, warriors of the caldera in the centre of Ovalau, saw the settlers as interlopers and repeatedly burned down their timber town. The Europeans lived under the protection of the chief of Levuka, who was murdered by raiding Lovoni in 1846.

Levuka grew, and by the 1850s it had a reputation for drunkenness, violence and immorality. It attracted beachcombers and freebooters, con men and middlemen, dreamers and crooks. In the 1870s a flood of planters and other settlers came to Fiji, and the booming town reached a population of about 3000 Europeans, with 52 hotels for them to drink in. Although the port was protected by a reef, such was Levuka's reputation that it was claimed that ships could navigate their way by following the gin bottles floating out from the town.

In 1825 the coastal villagers ended their alliance with the chief of Verata (a village on Viti Levu's Rewa Delta) and gave allegiance to Ratu Seru Cakobau, the powerful chief of Bau (an island off the southeast coast of Viti Levu). Cakobau attempted, unsuccessfully, to form a national government in 1871. In 1874 Great Britain acted on an earlier offer by Cakobau and Fiji was ceded to the Crown. Fiji thus became a British colony and Levuka was proclaimed its capital. The government was officially moved to Suva in 1882, and by the end of the 19th century trade was also shifting to Suva. With copra markets plummeting in the 1930s, Levuka declined further.

While the northern end of town was swept away in the hurricanes of 1888 and 1905, many of the boom-time buildings remain.

The little weatherboard building on the corner of Garner Jones Rd and Totoga Lane was Levuka's original police station (1874), and across Totoga Creek in Nasau Park you'll find Fiji's first private club – the 1904 colonial-style timber Ovalau Club – which is now sadly closed. Next door to the Ovalau Club is the former town hall (1901), built in typical British colonial style (although not to celebrate Queen Victoria's silver jubilee as is commonly thought), and under renovation to restore it to community use.

Alongside the former town hall you'll find the stone shell of the South Pacific's first Masonic lodge (1875). It was once Levuka's only Romanesque building, but it was burnt to a husk in the 2000 coup by God-fearing villagers. Local Methodists had long alleged that Masons were in league with the devil and that tunnels led from beneath the lodge to Nasova House, the Royal Hotel and through the centre of the world to Masonic headquarters in Scotland. This turned out not to be the case.

Return across the creek and follow Garner Jones Rd west to the Levuka Public School (1879). This was Fiji's first formal school and many of Fiji's prominent citizens were educated here, including Percy Morris and Maynard Hedstrom. Walk back down to Garner Jones Rd, turn left into Church St and pass Nasau Park. There are many old colonial homes on the hillsides, and the romantically named 199 Steps of Mission Hill are worth climbing for the fantastic view – although if you count them, you might find there are closer to 185 steps. The very simple, coral-and-stone, Gothic-style Navoka Methodist Church (1864), near the foot of the steps, is one of the oldest churches in Fiji.

Head down Chapel St then left along Langham St. The Royal Hotel (1860s) is Fiji's oldest hotel, rebuilt in 1903. It is the lone survivor of the once-numerous pubs of that era. Originally it had an open verandah with lace balustrading, but this was built in to increase the size of the rooms. Check out the fantastic old snooker room, and play a game of hunt-the-Royal-Hotel-staff.

Back on Beach St, continue north to Niukaube Hill, on a point near the water. This was once the site of Ratu Cakobau's Supreme Court and Parliament House. This is also where the first indentured Indian labourers landed in Fiji, after being forced to anchor offshore for several weeks in an attempt to control an outbreak of cholera.

The site now has a memorial to locals who fought and died in WWI and WWII.

North of here is the Anglican Church of the Holy Redeemer (1904), with its colourful stained glass and altar of yaka and dakua wood. Tidy little Levuka village, once the home of Tui (Chief) Cakobau, is about 200m further north. In the cemetery next to the village's Methodist Church is the grave of former American consul John Brown Williams. It was his claim for financial compensation that started Cakobau's financial troubles which ultimately led to the chief handing Fiji over to Britain.

With the chief's permission you can climb one of two local sites known as Gun Rock for a great view over Levuka. In 1849 Commodore Charles Wilkes, of the US exploring expedition, pounded this peak with canon fire from his ship in an attempt to impress the chief of Levuka. Commodore James Graham Goodenough repeated the 'entertainment' in 1874. You can still find cannonball scars on the rock. (The other Gun Rock is much smaller, and named for the canon mounted upon it in the 1850s.) Gun Rock is a good place to spot whales, which swim past between May and September.

Walk, cycle or take a taxi 8km north to Cawaci, where you'll find the Bishops' Tomb (1922), a beautiful, fading, Gothic-style construction on a grassy point overlooking the ocean. Fiji's first two Roman Catholic bishops are entombed here – it's a lovely spot to rest one's bones. From here you can see the limestone-and-coral St John's College (1894), originally where the sons of Fijian chiefs were educated in English. These days girls are educated here too. The boys' and girls' dormitories are separated by a bridge that no student is allowed to cross after 6pm.

🛏 Sleeping

Royal Hotel   HOTEL $
(☎344 0024; www.royallevuka.com; s/d/tr $32/53/73, cottages $90-150; 🌀🏊) The Royal is the oldest hotel in the South Pacific, dating back to the 1860s (though it was rebuilt in the early 1900s after a fire) and it's got the character to back it up. This proud timber building is thick with colonial atmosphere, although the creaking wooden floorboards are sometimes matched by a similarly creaky approach to customer service.

Upstairs each room is different and full of quirky old furniture, with iron bedsteads and sloping floors. The semi-enclosed

Levuka

Levuka Creek

VAKAVITI

LEVUKA VILLAGE

Ovalau Holiday Resort (3km);
Cawaci (5km);
Rukuruku (16km)

Beach St

Levuka Hospital

Mission Hill (60m)

Koro Sea

Hill Rd

Church St

Chapel St

King St

Langham St

Nasau Park

Patterson Brothers Shipping

Hennings St

Totoga Creek

Garner Jones Rd

Levuka Public School (100m)

Totoga La

Bentley's La

Beach St

Pafco Tuna Cannery (50m);
Provincial Bure (500m);
Cession Site (500m);
Nasova House (500m);
Natokalau (6km);
Airport (17km)

0   100 m
0   0.05 miles

Levuka

◉ Sights
1	199 Steps of Mission Hill	A3
2	Church of the Holy Redeemer	A2
	Former Morris Hedstrom	(see 5)
3	Former Town Hall	A5
4	Gun Rock	A1
5	Levuka Museum	B6
6	Levuka Village	A2
7	Marist Convent School	A6
8	Masonic Lodge Ruins	A5
9	Navoka Methodist Church	A3
10	Niukaube Hill War Memorial	B3
11	Old Police Station	A5
12	Pigeon Post Site	B7
13	Sacred Heart Church	A5

⊜ Sleeping
14	Clara's Holiday Lodge	B5
15	Gun Rock Cottage	A1
16	Levuka Homestay	A4
17	New Mavida Lodge	A3
18	Royal Hotel	A4
19	The Sailor's Home	A3

✴ Eating
20	Horizon Restaurant	B7
21	Kim's Paak Kum Loong	B6
22	Whale's Tale	B6

⊜ Drinking & Nightlife
23	Ovalau Club	A5
	Vintage Bar	(see 20)

⊕ Shopping
24	Handicrafts Market	B4

ⓘ Information
	Ovalau Tourist Information Centre	(see 5)

private verandahs come complete with old-fashioned white cane chairs and wooden shutters. There are also some modern cottages with kitchenettes in the grounds – less characterful but certainly more comfortable.

New Mavida Lodge HOTEL $
(☏344 0477; Beach St; incl breakfast dm $25, d $80-125; ☏) The New Mavida is an imposing (by Levuka standards) cream building sitting behind a white picket fence. Pass through the plain lobby to find comfortable rooms with hot-water bathrooms, TV and balconies, and a six-bed dorm.

Gun Rock Cottage COTTAGE $
(☏344 0745; noby@owlfiji.com; monthly rental $650) This tiny cottage is about a 15-minute walk north of town. There's a well-equipped kitchen and hot water, and it's right in the

middle of a pretty, tropical garden under the imposing Gun Rock cliff – in season you can pick your own fruit. Just the place to escape from it all and finally write that novel.

Clara's Holiday Lodge   HOSTEL $
(☑344 0013; clarasholidaylodge@rocketmail.com; Beach St; dm/s/d with shared bathroom incl breakfast $25/40/50) The whitewashed wooden rooms at Clara's Holiday Lodge are pretty basic, as are the shared bathrooms. It's friendly enough though and central, and meals can be prepared on request ($15).

Ovalau Holiday Resort   RESORT $
(Map p141; ☑344 0329; ohrfiji@connect.com.fj; cottage $120, with air-con $140, 3-bedroom house $250; P 🛜 ☝) Three kilometres north of town, this resort consists of a cluster of cosy cottages on a gentle slope across from the beach. There's a licensed restaurant, and nonguests may use the small pool for $3. Cottages sleep up to four, while the house on the panoramic hill above takes eight ($30 per person supplement for more than five guests).

The resort is built on the site where Fiji's first governor general lived in the 1880s.

⭐**Levuka Homestay**   B&B $$
(☑344 0777; www.levukahomestay.com; Church St; s/d incl breakfast $60/180, extra person $50; 🛜) Far and away the most chic choice in Levuka – a multilevel house with four large, comfortable, light-filled rooms with terraces, each one on its own level. The laid-back owners live on the highest level, where guests come to eat a truly spectacular breakfast or swap stories with them on their enormous deck overlooking the sea. The homestay can also arrange historical walking tours and hiking with staff member and local guide Nox.

The Sailor's Home   COTTAGE $$
(☑360 9569; thebaystayfiji@gmail.com; s/d $100/130, whole house rental $180; 🛜) Its sea views and sometimes-sloping wooden floors make you think you're aboard a ship in the Sailor's Home. This cheery, bright blue wooden house dates from the 1870s, making it one of Levuka's older properties. There's a kitchen for self-caterers, and while the decor is simple, everything is kept reassuringly ship-shape for guests.

✕ Eating

⭐**Whale's Tale**   WESTERN $
(☑344 0235; Beach St; mains around $13.50; ☺9.30am-2pm & 5-9pm Mon-Sat) This perennial Levuka favourite is a charming little place with big windows for watching the world go by and a bamboo thatched kitchen at the back. The fish and chips is a classic, but look out for local river prawns, deliciously light cassava cakes, and other specials. It doesn't sell alcohol but allows BYO (the mini market next door sells booze).

Kim's Paak Kum Loong   CHINESE $
(☑344 0059; Beach St; mains $9-15, breakfast $4-10.50; ☺7am-3pm & 5-9pm Mon-Sat, 11am-2pm & 6-9pm Sun) This is the best place to get Chinese food in Levuka, situated above the Westpac Bank. The menu has a bit of Thai and Fijian influence thrown in, while if you come in the morning it does a good line in cooked breakfasts. There's a good street-side balcony for voyeurs. Serves alcohol.

Horizon Restaurant   PIZZA $
(☑344 0429; Beach St; mains $9-17, pizza from $13.50; ☺8am-2pm & 5-9pm Mon-Sat, 5-9pm Sun) You can get curries, fish and chips, and other European meals here, but locals recommend it because of the pizza, which is, apparently, very hit and miss – 'either one of the best pizzas you've ever tasted or a total disaster' was one comment. If you're willing to take the risk, go for one of the many fishy toppings – the tuna is the most fitting since the cannery's right on the doorstep.

🍸 Drinking & Nightlife

Ovalau Club   BAR
(Nasau Park) This white timber colonial-style building is a sight in its own right. Once Levuka's favourite drinking spot, it's currently closed due to a dispute over ownership, but we list it here in the hope that its door may re-open soon.

Vintage Bar   BAR
(Beach St; ☺10am-2-pm & 4pm-1am Mon-Sat, 4pm-1am Sun) In the same building as the Horizon Restaurant, but tucked around the back, this is currently Levuka's main place to drink.

🛍 Shopping

Handicrafts Market   HANDICRAFTS
(Beach St; ☺Mon-Sat) This small covered market has a variety of traditional Fijian handicrafts for sale.

ℹ Information

There are Westpac and BSP Bank ATMs right next to each other on Beach St.

Levuka Hospital (⌨ 344 0221; Beach St; ☺ outpatient treatment 8am-1pm & 2-4pm Mon-Fri, to noon Sat, emergencies only after hours) A good, new hospital at the northern end of town.

Ovalau Tourist Information Centre (⌨ 330 0356; Levuka Community Centre, Morris Hedstrom Bldg; ☺ 8am-1pm & 2-4.30pm Mon-Fri, to 1pm Sat) Has an information board detailing Ovalau's accommodation and food options and also organises Levuka town tours.

Patterson Brothers Shipping (⌨ 344 0125; Church St) Ticket office for the bus-ferry service from Levuka to Suva.

Police Station (⌨ 344 0222; Totoga Lane)

Post Office (Beach St) Near Queen's Wharf at the southern end of town; there's a cardphone outside.

VM Nargey (Beach St; per hr $2; ☺ 8am-6pm Mon-Sat) This general store has an internet cafe at the back of the shop.

Lovoni

Lovoni village is surrounded by thick, green rainforest in the centre of a flat-bottomed valley that is actually an extinct volcano crater. It is the island's beating heart and the centre of indigenous culture. There's no accommodation for travellers here, but guided tours are available from Levuka – you need to go with a guide to visit the village. Wear sturdy shoes and be prepared to face down some serious mud if it rains (which it does

often, and suddenly). Your guide should provide a *sevusevu* (gift) for the chief (if the chief's around) and point out the chiefs' burial site opposite the church and the Korolevu hill fortification high on the crater rim, where villagers took refuge in times of war.

The Lovoni villagers are extremely proud of their heritage and often describe themselves as the strongest and bravest people in all of Fiji. The fact that Chief Cakobau was only able to defeat them with trickery is held up as proof of this. On 7 July each year the enslavement of the Lovoni people is remembered. People of all religions gather in one church and the history is read out.

Rukuruku

Rukuruku village is a 17km drive north of Levuka, up a rough road with fantastic ocean vistas along the way. It's best to arrange a day out there with Bobo (of Bobo's Farm) to avoid trespassing on village property. Schoolchildren might sing you a song and old people will share a bowl of kava. Tours are free for houseguests at Bobo's Farm.

You can walk to a black-sand beach (about 15 minutes), the local waterfall or natural waterslides and there's a freshwater stream for bathing or prawn catching. Bobo will gladly escort you to all of these and the village. He can also arrange island-hopping, fishing trips and a hike that can meet up

WARRIORS IN CHAINS: FIJI'S ONLY SLAVES

The saddest exhibit in the Fiji Museum at Levuka is the photograph of a 'dwarf' priest and two Lovoni warriors who were sold by Tui (Chief) Cakobau to the Barnum & Bailey circus in the USA. In 1870 and 1871 Cakobau fought battle after battle with the ferocious Lovoni highlanders, who regularly sacked the settlement of Levuka and did not accept Cakobau's claim to be king of all Fiji. After repeated failed attempts to penetrate their hill, Cakobau sent a Methodist missionary to subdue the people. The Lovoni put their trust in a 'dwarf' (actually just a short bloke) priest who had the ability to foresee the future. The priest was the first to notice the approaching missionary and, seeing a brightness emanating from him, believed he came in peace. The missionary read from the Bible in Bauan, referring to the Lovoni villagers as the lost sheep of Fiji. He then invited them to a reconciliation feast with Cakobau.

On 29 June 1871 the Lovoni people came down from the safety of their village to Levuka and, in good faith, put aside their weapons. However, as they started their meal, Cakobau's warriors caught them off guard, quickly surrounding and capturing them.

Cakobau humiliated his captives horribly, then sold them as slaves for £3 a head. His takings helped him form his government. Families were separated as the villagers were dispersed as far as Kavala (in the Kadavu Group), Yavusania (near Nadi on Viti Levu), Lovoni-Ono (in the Lau Group) and Wailevu (on Vanua Levu). The Lovoni were the only Fijians ever to suffer this fate. When the British administration took over Fiji it freed the Lovoni slaves, and the blackbirding of other Pacific Islanders began instead.

with Epi's Tours. The snorkelling here is wonderful, but you'll need to bring your own kit.

★ **Bobo's Farm** GUESTHOUSE $
(Map p141; ☑ 362 3873; www.bobosfarm.com; s/d $60/80, whole cottage $120-150) ✆ Bobo's Farm is a clean, tranquil, solar-powered, two-room timber cottage 15 minutes from Rukuruku, all on an organic farm carved out of the thick rainforest by personable hosts Bobo and Karin. There's a shared living room and tiny kitchen, so you can self-cater if you wish, but the organic, homemade meals here are excellent (breakfast $13, lunch $15, dinner $20).

Rukuruku is closer to the ferry station at Buresala than Levuka, so when booking ask in advance to arrange a transfer if needed.

Rukuruku Resort RESORT $
(Map p141; ☑ 360 9569; thebaystayfiji@gmail.com; Rukuruku; bungalow $120) Sat on Rukuruku Bay, this tiny resort wasn't quite finished when we visited, and had just two very basic thatched *bures* (wood-and-straw hut). Meals will be available on request.

Arovudi & Silana

These small, delightful twin villages have their own little patch of pebbly beach. Poles were just going up to supply the area with electricity when we passed. The Methodist village church (1918) is made of coral cooked in a lovo (a pit oven). A tabua (whale's tooth) hangs by the side of the altar; it was presented to the village by the first missionaries to come here. There is one place to stay, run by the enterprising Seru, who also organises regular tours from Levuka.

Silana Ecolodge RESORT $$
(☑ 835 9260; sala_nagalu@yahoo.com; dm $70, bungalow full board $155-185) Off in a pretty beachside corner about a minute's walk from Silana Village, there are a few choices at this tranquil homestay, all set in a big, lush family compound. There's one light-filled, two-room *bure* that sleeps four, with a rudimentary shared bathroom; another *bure* is bigger, with its own hot-water bathroom; and there's a six-bed dorm.

Hosts Seru and Sala can arrange fishing and bush-walking trips. There's a carrier from Levuka, which takes around 40 minutes and costs $3.

EPI'S LOVONI TOUR

Visit Lovoni village in the crater of an extinct volcano deep in the heart of Ovalau (although it resembles a flat valley floor surrounded by hills rather than anything else). Epi, who runs the tour (p140), is a Lovoni married to an Englishwoman and will take you through forest and past streams, pointing out all kinds of plants, bush food and local medicine along the way. The scenery is beautiful and Epi will regale you with the history and legends of the island and the Lovoni people. Once you've reached the village and presented your *sevusevu* (gift) to the village chief – assuming the chief is around – you can take a dip in the river. A delicious lunch in one of the village homes is laid on. The price includes transfers and lunch but requires a minimum of two people; the cost per person goes down with each additional person.

OTHER LOMAIVITI ISLANDS

Lomaiviti's smaller islands are simply breathtaking. If you've been craving empty white-sand beaches and world-class snorkelling, look no further.

Naigani

Naigani (Mystery Island) is a mountainous island about 10km offshore from Ovalau. The island has white-sand beaches, lagoons, a fringing coral reef, the remains of a pre-colonial hillside fortification and 'cannibal caves'.

There's good snorkelling at Picnic Beach, the next bay over from Naigani Island Resort. You can walk over at low tide (take a sturdy pair of shoes), take a kayak or get the resort boat to drop you off and pick you up a couple of hours later.

Naigani Island Resort RESORT $$
(☑ 995 7301, 603 0613; www.naiganiresort.com; dm $160, studio $190, 1-/2-bedroom villa $210/335, boat transfer return $100; ☏☀♨) A former copra plantation and a friendly, unpretentious family resort, Naigani Island Resort is popular with antipodean time-sharers. The villas have clean, white, airy interiors

and are strung out along palm-lined paths in an arrangement that's reminiscent of a retirement village. There's a pretty beach and good snorkelling about 50m out from the shore.

The food here is OK (European-style food) and there's a *lovo* at the weekend. There's a small pool with a kids' slide, a baby pool and several inflatables. There's also a kids' club in the holidays. The dorm accommodation includes all meals and boat transfers.

Yanuca Lailai

Yanuca Lailai (Lost Island) is the nearest to Ovalau of the small islands. Much of the shoreline is rocky but there is a patch of golden sand, good snorkelling from the shore, and a small mountain at the island's centre, which you can clamber up for fantastic views out to sea and of Ovalau. You'll need to arrange a private boat as there is currently no accommodation on the island.

Moturiki

The lush, hilly island of Moturiki is just southwest of Ovalau and home to 10 villages. Although it has no accommodation for travellers, both Leleuvia and Caqalai resorts will take guests to the village of Niubasaga for a typical Sunday church service, with beautiful singing and plenty of welcoming smiles. Be prepared: one of your party will have to get up and introduce the group to the congregation.

Caqalai

Teeny little Caqalai island (pronounced 'Thangalai') lies just south of Moturiki. It only takes 15 minutes to walk around the island perimeter's beautiful golden-sand beaches, which are fringed with palms, electric-blue water and spectacular reefs.

For some of the best snorkelling in Fiji walk out to Snake Island (named after the many black-and-white-banded sea snakes here) at low tide and swim around the reef. Take some reef shoes though (and something to secure them while you're swimming), as the walkway can be hard on the feet. Underwater is a veritable wonderland of soft and hard corals and a mind-boggling array of fish including massive Napoleon wrasses. Watch for currents, though, and

make sure you get in and out at the designated spot (marked with a buoy) so you don't damage the environment.

★ **Caqalai Island Resort**   RESORT **$**
(Map p141; ☎ 362 0388; www.fijiislandresort caqalai.com; camping (own tent)/dm/bungalow per person full board $55/65/75, boat transfers $40) Caqalai Island Resort is a gem of a backpackers and is run by Moturiki's Methodist Church, but don't let that scare you – you'll find more kava here than kumbaya (but bring your own alcohol if you prefer dirt to the muddy stuff). Accommodation is in big, basic *bures* scattered between the palm trees and hibiscus. Cold-water showers are in a shared block.

Locals come over from Moturiki or Leleuvia in the evenings and there's often some singing and dancing and a kava session. The resort offers village trips to Moturiki ($10), boat trips to tiny Honeymoon Island ($15) and day trips to Leleuvia ($10). Boat transfers from the mainland are from Waidalice Landing, a 90-minute bus ride from Suva.

Leleuvia

Just south of Caqalai sits beautiful Leleuvia, another stunning palm-fringed coral island (slightly larger than Caqalai) wrapped in white powdery beaches with outstanding views out to sea, and some great snorkelling.

Boat transfers to/from Waidalice or Bau Landing are $25 each way (call in advance for a pick-up; Waidalice is about a 1½-hour bus ride from Suva). Transfers to/from Levuka (one hour) also cost $30 each way. Call in advance for a pick-up.

★ **Leleuvia Island Resort**   RESORT **$$**
(Map p141; ☎ 999 2340; www.leleuvia.com; dm $40, bungalow $160, meal package $50, boat transfers adult/child return $84/42; ⚙) Leleuvia Island Resort is a decent choice for couples looking for comfort and a fantastic choice for families thanks to the sandy bottom and shallow swimming at the island's point. Thatched *bure* here are basic but classy with views of the sea and trade winds pouring through for natural ventilation.

A large, open, sand-floored bar and restaurant area serves cold beer and tasty meals, and at the resort's 'entrance' is a gorgeous wide stretch of beach with sun loungers and kayaks. There's even an art gallery. The staff put on all kinds of entertainment (such as kava drinking and beach bonfires).

While the snorkelling is not on a par with Caqalai, it is still excellent and you can hire equipment. Village trips, diving and fishing excursions are also possible. Leleuvia is popular with the weekend crowd from Suva, so advance booking is recommended. Boat transfers from the mainland are from Waidalice Landing, a 90-minute bus ride from Suva.

Wakaya

About 20km east of Ovalau, Wakaya is a privately owned island visible from Levuka. It has forests, cliffs, beautiful white-sand beaches and archaeological sites, including a stone fish trap. In some areas you'll find feral horses, pigs and deer roaming freely; in others there are millionaires' houses.

Wakaya Club RESORT **$$$**
(☑ 344 8128; www.wakaya.com; all-inclusive bungalow US$2900-7600; ❄ 🕸) Wakaya Club is possibly Fiji's most exclusive resort, and is owned by the founder of Fiji Water. If you've got several thousand dollars to spare, you can enjoy this utterly sublime private island with the world's one percent. You'll be flown there from Nadi via Cesna aircraft, served chilled champagne on arrival and pampered to the absolute maximum.

WHAT LIES BENEATH

Don't tempt the spirits of Gavo Passage. If you head out to the islands south of Ovalau, your boat will likely travel through a break in the reef. Many indigenous Fijians believe that beneath the waters of Gavo Passage lies a sunken village inhabited by ancestral spirits. Stories of fishermen hooking newly woven mats are whispered around Levuka. When passing over the *tabu* (sacred) site, Fijians remove their hats and sunglasses and talk in hushed tones. They believe the spirits will avenge any act of disrespect. Stay on the safe side, take off your baseball cap and give your sunnies a rest. Even if there are no spirits to annoy, irreverent behaviour might put the wind up your boatman.

Koro

Many villages are nestled in the lush tropical forests of Koro, northwest of Ovalau. Roads over the mountainous interior provide plenty of thrills and wonderful views. A portion of the island is freehold, so plenty of foreigners have bought up land to build their second homes – the community has its own website (www.koroisland.org).

At Dere Bay a wharf allows you to walk out to good swimming and snorkelling; inland there's a waterfall and natural pool. The co-run resorts are surrounded by residential developments and have been aimed at people visiting or building real estate on the island, although they are gearing up to be more tourist friendly.

Koro was badly affected by Cyclone Winston in 2016.

🛏 Sleeping

Dere Bay Resort RESORT **$$**
(☑ 331 1075; http://derebayresort.com; d bungalow per person full board $200; ❄) Dere Bay Resort has three well-designed, intimate *bure* with soaring ceilings, 360-degree outlooks and spacious verandahs right on the beach. There's also a fantastic deck, a pier and a bar next door. Children stay for half-price.

Koro Beach Resort RESORT **$$**
(☑ 331 1075; http://korobeachresort.com; d bungalow per person full board $150; ❄) Koro Beach Resort has simple thatched, solar-powered *bure* with terraces and attached bathrooms lining a white sandy beach. Transfers are not included and cost $35/50 from the ferry wharf/airport.

ℹ Getting There & Away

Fiji Link (p231) flies from Koro to Suva on Wednesdays ($135, 35 minutes).

Patterson Shipping (p140) has a bus-ferry service to Koro from Suva via Natovi Landing ($60, seven hours) every Wednesday. It leaves Suva every Wednesday at 9am. The return ferry leaves Koro every Wednesday at 6am.

Goundar Shipping (p232) has a slow weekly sailing from Suva every Monday and Friday, leaving Suva at 6pm ($60/70/170, 12 hours, economy seating/1st class seating/cabin), and continuing on to Savusavu ($55/60/100) and Taveuni ($60/70/180).

Vanua Levu & Taveuni

Best Dive Sites

➡ Namena Marine Reserve (p154)

➡ Great White Wall (p167)

➡ Nasonisoni Passage (p154)

➡ Rainbow Reef (p167)

➡ Dreamhouse (p154)

Best Places to Stay

➡ Namena Island Resort (p162)

➡ Maqai Resort (p178)

➡ Dolphin Bay Divers Retreat (p173)

➡ Salt Lake Lodge (p158)

➡ Gecko Lodge (p157)

➡ Bibi's Hideaway (p174)

Why Go?

With welcoming settlements, year-round warmth and genuine local hospitality, it's not for nothing that Vanua Levu and Taveuni are billed as Fiji's 'friendly north'. The country's second- and third-biggest islands, respectively, are clean, green havens languidly trapped in a time before 'hectic' was invented: even their epithets – Vanua Levu was once called Sandalwood Island and Taveuni's nickname is the Garden Island – evoke the scents and sights of a land left wild.

Though dusty Labasa is Vanua Levu's largest town, it's in beautiful, stay-a-little-longer Savusavu where most visitors drop their bags. Across the Somosomo Strait, Taveuni's 9000 residents spread themselves between jungle villages and microscopic hamlets along the coast. Everyone on both islands, from the locals to the numerous expats, smile and act as if they've just awoken from a long nap – and they probably have.

When to Go

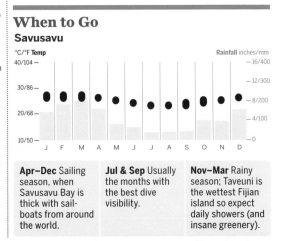

Savusavu

Apr–Dec Sailing season, when Savusavu Bay is thick with sailboats from around the world.

Jul & Sep Usually the months with the best dive visibility.

Nov–Mar Rainy season; Taveuni is the wettest Fijian island so expect daily showers (and insane greenery).

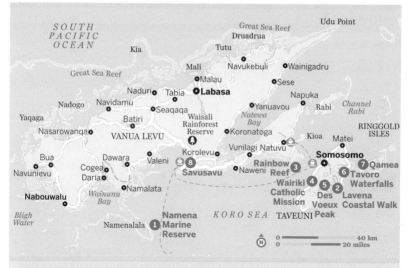

Vanua Levu & Taveuni Highlights

❶ Making bubbles around the pristine **Namena Marine Reserve** (p154).

❷ Exploring the lush beauty of the **Lavena Coastal Walk** (p176).

❸ Diving the soft-coral wonderland of the **Rainbow Reef** (p167).

❹ Getting goosebumps at the powerful Sunday services at **Wairiki Catholic Mission** (p171).

❺ Finding the rare, delicate, red-and-white *tagimaucia* flower high on the slopes of **Des Voeux Peak** (p171).

❻ Swimming in all three glorious pools of the **Tavoro Waterfalls** (p177).

❼ Lounging on white sands, snorkelling and surfing at **Qamea** (p178).

❽ Having a waterside sunset cocktail with yachties in **Savusavu** (p160).

VANUA LEVU

POP 130,000

Though it's Fiji's second-largest island, Vanua Levu (Big Island) is one of the tropics' best-kept secrets. It's another world from the bustle of Viti Levu and the more-touristed islands: many roads are little more than rutted dirt tracks, and Labasa, the island's largest 'city', is a one-street strip of shops. To the south, Savusavu entices yachties, divers and dreamers looking for a tropical idyll. The rest of 'Big Island' is given over to sugarcane and copra plantations, hideaway villages, mountain passes streaming with waterfalls, endless swaths of forest and an ever-changing coastline forgotten by the world. Take it slow, keep a smile on your face and savour rural Fiji on its grandest scale.

❶ Getting There & Away

AIR

Flying is the easiest way to get to Vanua Levu. **Fiji Airways** (☑330 4388, 672 0888; www.fijiairways. com) – billed as Fiji Link for domestic services – runs regular flights to/from Labasa, Nadi, Suva and Taveuni; for the brave (landings are notoriously bumpy), there are also flights in and out of Savusavu. The smaller **Northern Air** (p231) flies to Labasa and Savusavu from Suva.

The Labasa airport is about 11km southwest of Labasa. There's a bus that passes the airport about every hour, but it doesn't link up with flights and you'll have to go out to the main road to flag it down. A taxi from Labasa costs about $15.

Savusavu's airstrip is 3km south of town.

BOAT

To/from Suva

The *Lomaiviti Princess*, run by **Goundar Shipping** (☑330 1035; www.goundarshipping.com; Kong's Shop, Main St, Savusavu), departs Suva every Monday and Friday at 6pm, arriving in Savusavu at 6am. Tickets for this route start at $55/25 for adults/kids, and go up to $400 for a 1st-class cabin. Goundar expects to put a second boat on the route in 2016: check the website for updates.

Bligh Water Shipping (☑999 2536; www. blighwatershipping.com.fj) goes to Savusavu

Vanua Levu

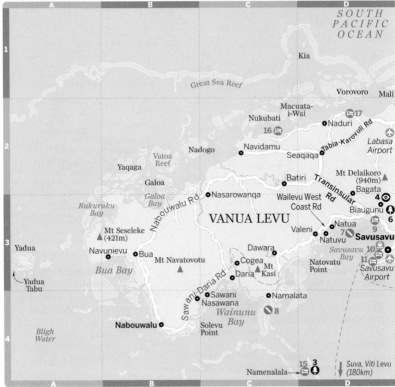

Vanua Levu

from Natovi Landing, half an hour from Suva (buses run there from Suva's main bus station; fares are included in boat ticket prices) a few days a week: keep an eye on the website's schedule, as departure days and times change frequently. Tickets start at $55; sleepers are $150 and cabins $500.

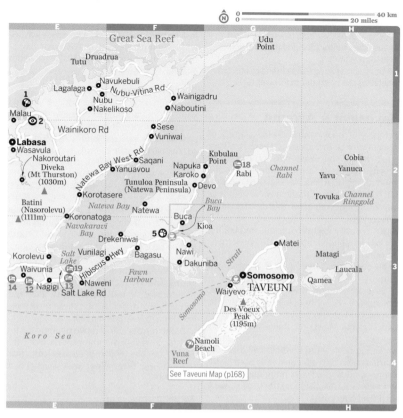

See Taveuni Map (p168)

To/from Taveuni

Two ferries ply the waters between Natuvu (Buca Bay) on Vanua Levu's east and the 'Korean Wharf' at Lovonivonu in Taveuni.

Grace Ferry (✆995 0775; ☺Sun-Fri) runs every day but Saturday ($15 each way). It leaves Taveuni at 8am (boarding at 7.30am) and arrives at Natuvu on Vanua Levu at 9am; it returns to Taveuni at 9.30am. Express buses leave Labasa (bus and ferry tickets $35) at 4.30am and Savusavu (bus and ferry tickets $25) at 7am and arrive at Natuvu with plenty of time before the ferry departs. In Savusavu, buy tickets at Ravin's (hole-in-the-wall restaurant on the main drag); in Labasa, get them at the Gifts & Fashion shop on Nasekula Rd.

The **Egi One** (✆708 0390; ☺Mon-Sat) ferry ($10 each way) runs between Monday and Saturday. It leaves Taveuni at 7.30am, and departs Vanua Levu for the return trip between 9.30am and 10am (get there early just in case). The company runs a bus from Savusavu to Natuvu ($7) at 7am. Buy your ferry ticket on the bus or on the ship.

In addition to the ferries, the *Lomaiviti Princess* run by **Goundar Shipping** (p151) leaves Savusavu for Taveuni (adult/child $30/10) on Tuesday and Saturday mornings around 9am as part of its Suva route.

ⓘ Getting Around

Vanua Levu's remote, tropical roads are crying out to be explored by 4WD. Hire cars are available in Labasa and Savusavu. Given the bumpy terrain, though, the available vehicles won't always be in top condition. There are unsealed roads around most of the island's perimeter. The road from Labasa to Savusavu is sealed but showing plenty of wear and you'll have to do a fair amount of pothole dodging. The first 20km of the Hibiscus Hwy from Savusavu along the scenic coast is similarly paved. The rest of the highway is much rougher.

Avoid driving at night: there are lots of wandering animals and often fog in the mountains. Petrol stations are scarce and usually closed on Sundays, so fill up in Labasa, Savusavu or

Seaqaqa. It's also a good idea to take some food with you on the road.

Just remember, you cannot wander on foot through the countryside without permission from the landowners.

It's possible to navigate the island by bus, but timetables can be erratic and it takes far longer.

Savusavu & Around

Before you book your tickets, a word of warning: once in Savusavu, there is a very good chance you won't ever want to leave. Preposterously picturesque and affable beyond all expectations, Savusavu is a swashbuckling throwback to the days of high-seas adventure and tall tales told in rollicking, rickety taverns. The storybook Savusavu Bay was once a gigantic volcano, and boiling springs still bubble up across town, perhaps accounting – at least in part – for the palpable energy that surrounds this enchanted outpost.

Savusavu's main drag is a shabby-chic hotchpotch of cosmopolitan restaurants, secondhand shops, well-stocked supermarkets, eclectic watering holes and a busy market. As the sole point of entry for yachts on Vanua Levu – and home to two excellent marinas – Savusavu is constantly abuzz with dropped-anchor old salts mingling with lively locals and travellers looking to escape the well-trodden trail.

East of Savusavu, the Hibiscus Hwy stretches for 112 km up the coast. It's a lazy drive to a clutch of relaxed resorts through avenues of palm trees, past blue bays and old plantations.

◎ Sights & Activities

Hot Springs HOT SPRINGS
Those vents of steam you see along the water's edge are evidence of the volcanic activity that simmers below Savusavu's surface. The main springs are just down from the aptly named Hot Springs Hotel. They are literally boiling: locals come to cook food in them. You'll scald yourself if you touch them. The Savusavu Medical Centre (p160) next door has three therapeutic spa baths (40°C), and welcomes visitors. No appointment necessary.

Flora Tropica Gardens GARDENS
(www.floratropica.com; Lesiaceva Point Rd; $20; ☉10am-5pm) Take a guided tour through these gorgeous gardens, home to 300 types

of palms and countless tropical flowers and fruit trees. Birds and butterflies love it here just as much as visitors, who are rewarded with stunning views over Savusavu Bay at the end of the timber boardwalk. It's about 5km out of town.

Diving & Snorkelling
Far and away the best diving around Vanua Levu – and arguably in all of Fiji – is at **Namena Marine Reserve** (www.namena.org; park fees $30, valid one year), a protected 70 sq km park housing corals so vibrant and marine life so plentiful that it's become the poster child for Fiji's underwater world. It's about a two-hour boat ride from Savusavu.

The best sites closer in are just outside Savusavu Bay (about a 20-minute boat ride) and include the suitable-for-all-levels **Dreadlocks** with its multicoloured hard- and soft-coral garden; **Dreamhouse**, home to hammerheads, great schools of barracuda, jacks and tuna at a coral outcrop; **Dungeons and Dragons**, a towering maze of dive-throughs; and **Nasonisoni Passage**, an incredible drift dive that sucks thrill seekers along by a strong current.

Some resorts can arrange diving trips for guests. Live-aboard options that visit the region include **Nai'a** (www.naia.com.fj; from US$3626) and **Siren Fleet** (www.sirenfleet.com; from €2995).

KoroSun Dive DIVING
(☑934 1033, 970 6605; www.korosundive.com; Savasi Island resort) Colin and Janine run an attentive and professional centre that caters just as well to beginners as it does to advanced divers. Two-tank dives/PADI Open Water Courses, including all gear, cost $230/850; snorkelling trips are $35. Multiday dives are recommended, as discounts apply. In addition to spectacular dives just 15 minutes from shore, they also offer trips to the Somosomo Strait and Namena Marine Reserve.

Transfers are free between Savusavu and their base at Savasi Island resort.

Jean-Michel Cousteau Diving DIVING
(☑885 0694; www.jeanmichelcousteaudiving. com) As befitting the name, this is a topnotch centre that gets rave reviews from seasoned divers from around the world; it's also the only outfit that regularly visits the drift-dive Nasonisoni Passage. It's based at Jean-Michel Cousteau Fiji Islands Resort. Two-tank dives/PADI Open Water Courses cost $335/1145.

Namena Divers DIVING
(✏️885 3389; www.namenadiversfiji.com; Main St) This popular outfit whisks divers and snorkellers to Namena Island each morning for three guided drift dives of vibrant sites, including the teeming-with-big-fish Grand Central Station; the all-inclusive trip is $573. It also offers five- and seven-day packages ($2815 to $3866); the PADI Open Water Course is $1050.

Tui Tai Expeditions DIVING
(✏️999 6365; www.tuitai.com; five nights from s $4045-12,090, d $8956, seven nights s $3191-9208, d $6821) A voyage with Tui Tai Expeditions is a fantastic way to see and do a lot in a short time. Sailing between Vanua Levu, Taveuni and remote islands including Kioa, Rabi and the Ringgold Attols, you'll get to snorkel, kayak, bike, trek, swim, fish, dive or just lounge on deck to your heart's content. Prices include all meals and activities except diving.

Diving on the five-/seven-night trips costs $1160/1480; individual dives are $150.

Aboard A Dream DIVING
(✏️828 3030, 929 7041; www.aboardadream.com) This highly regarded outfit offers two- to five-day charters (two/four people from $2000/2800; includes diving for those certified) and half- and full-day snorkelling charters ($1100/1800) of Namena Marine Reserve and other fantastic nearby spots. These are intimate trips: there's a maximum of four guests on live-aboard trips, and 14 on day tours. Hosts Tommy and Nadine have a wealth of local diving experience.

Other Activities

Rafa's Adventure Tours ADVENTURE TOUR
(✏️838 0406; www.rafasadventuretours.weebly.com) These fun tours get top marks for their friendly and knowledgeable guides. Set trips include an island adventure (including snorkelling, hiking and *lovo* (feast cooked in a pit oven) lunch for $150), village and snorkelling tours ($125), waterfall visits ($95) and four-hour hikes up the Nakula Trail ($95); you can also customise your own tours.

J Hunter Pearls BOAT TOUR
(✏️885 0821; www.fijipearls.com; $25; ⏰tours 9.30am & 1.30pm Mon-Fri) Learn all about how black pearls are farmed before heading out on a glass-bottom boat to the floating farm. If you want to snorkel the oyster lines, bring your own gear and jump in; otherwise you can see everything from the boat. During seeding seasons (April to May and October to November), watch 'pearl technicians' implanting and harvesting pearls from the oysters.

Bagata Eco Tours CULTURAL TOUR
(✏️961 5942; www.bagatavillage.com; $200) If you've had your fill of water-based activities, try a deep-end dive into village life. These tours explore Bagata, a small settlement 20km from Savusavu. Guests are welcomed into village homes and the church, and are treated to a *meke* (traditional dance) and afternoon tea. Dress modestly and bring a *sevusevu* (customary gift for the chief) of dried kava: pick this up at the Savusavu markets.

Tours are $200 per group of six. Money from the tours funds village projects and provides scholarships for local kids.

You'll have to make your own way to Bagata: taxis ($40) or buses ($3) run regularly. The tours run from 2pm to 4pm daily.

Trip n Tour ISLAND TOURS
(✏️992 8154, 885 3154; tripntour@connect.com.fj; Copra Shed Marina) These friendly folks offer a range of tours around Vanua Levu, including trips to a copra plantation and Waisali Rainforest ($69; minimum two people). They can also organise fishing trips and rent scooters.

Marinas

Use VHF Marine channel 16 for assistance in locating moorings on arrival. The marinas can arrange for the relevant officials to visit your boat to process your arrival into Fiji.

Copra Shed Marina MARINA
(✏️885 0457; www.coprashed.com) Starting life as a copra mill back in the late 1800s, this charming marina now attracts yachties and passersby for its range of services and laid-back waterfront vibe. Moorings in the pretty harbour between Savusavu and Nawi Island cost $13.25/342.45 per day/month; berths per foot per day/week $0.50/3. Salty dogs will appreciate the hot showers and laundry facilities.

Waitui Marina MARINA
(✏️835 3913, 885 3057; www.waituimarinafiji.com) This endearingly ramshackle marina is atmospheric as all-get-out. It has 25 well-maintained helix moorings, plus showers, laundry and a wonderful club in a beautiful, restored boat shed. Moorings cost $12/80/300 per day/week/month.

Savusavu

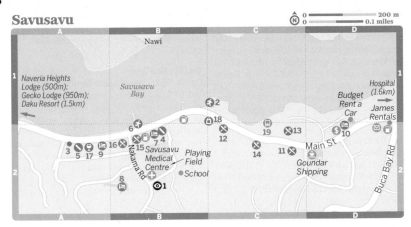

🛏 Sleeping

Stay in town to soak up South Sea sailor charm, or venture out to some incredible resorts, either on Lesiaceva Point to the southwest, Savusavu Rd to the northwest or along the Hibiscus Hwy to the east. Buses service all locations regularly.

If you're going to stick around for a while, a self-contained apartment may be worthwhile. Check out **Copra Shed Marina Apartments** (☑885 0457; www.coprashed. com; Copra Shed Marina; apt from $180; ❋🖛) or the **Waterfront Apartment** (☑885 2327; Waterfront Complex; r $180; ⊜❋) on top of the Surf and Turf Restaurant. There are also lots of holiday home rentals – from basic *bures* (wood-and-straw hut) to posh palaces – available: www.fiji-savusavu.com is a good place to start looking at listings.

🛏 In Town

Savusavu Budget Lodge   GUESTHOUSE $

(☑999 3127; www.savusavubudgetlodge.com; Main St; s/d with fan $45/60, with air-con $65/75, f $95; ❋🖛) The best low-budget option in Savusavu, this place is clean, welcoming and just a skip from the centre of town. Rooms are small but bright, with private hot water bathrooms, and there's an upstairs lounge and a balcony overlooking the street and the water. Breakfast is included.

Hidden Paradise
Guest House   GUESTHOUSE $

(☑885 0106; Main St; s/d $45/75, with air-con $60/90; ❋) Though far from schmick, this is nevertheless a good place to meet other budget travellers. It's a no-frills deal, with a shared bathroom and cold-water showers, but it's got a great, central location and you can watch life pass by from the Sea View Café at the front of the guesthouse. Breakfast is included.

Naveria Heights Lodge   B&B $$

(☑885 0348; www.naveriaheightsfiji.com; r incl breakfast $200-500; 🖛🏊) This boutique B&B can be as active or as chilled as you want it to be: choose between yoga classes, river tubing, mountain biking, snorkelling, hiking or doing sweet nothing at all. It can also organise diving trips. Perched on a jungly hill, the lodge's three elegant, polished-wood rooms have stunning bay views and open up to a fabulous sun deck.

Meals are prepared to order; owner Sharon is a nutritionist and can tailor a menu for you. The B&B is a steep, 15-minute hike up the hill; otherwise, it does free pick-ups from Savusavu airport and the ferry terminal.

Hot Springs Hotel   HOTEL $$

(☑885 0195; www.hotspringsfiji.com; Nakama Rd; r with fan/air-con $105-165, studio $215, f from $310, apt $370; 🅿❋🖛🏊) Every room in this huge hotel has a balcony with picture-postcard views over Savusavu Bay and an expanse of technicolour-green lawn. The rooms don't have a world of personality, but they are very clean and spacious; good-sized studios and apartments have well-equipped kitchenettes. It's a great option for families and self-caterers. The hotel also has a bar, restaurant and a pool overlooking the bay.

Savusavu

Lesiaceva Point Road & Savusavu Road

★ **Gecko Lodge**　　　　　　　　LODGE $
(✆921 3181; www.geckolodgefiji.com; r from $100; P❋☎) Gecko's is a fantastic new budget option that couples Savusavu convenience (it's a three-minute drive to town) with away-from-it-all serenity and scenic vistas. The three colourful rooms-with-a-view are all very big, air-conditioned, and have their own en suite and fridge: there's a great communal kitchen too, though the hugely hospitable owners prepare fantastic meals upon request ($15). It also offers Indian cooking lessons.

Bikes and kayaks are complimentary; unusually for Fiji, so is the wi-fi.

It's a pleasant 15 minute walk to town.

Bayside Bure　　　　　　　　BUNGALOW $
(✆992 8154, 885 0556; Lesiaceva Point Rd; bungalow $120; ☎) This sweet, bright-white little cottage sleeps two and has a decent kitchen with a gas stove and TV and DVD player. There's a beach across the road that is excellent for snorkelling and kayaking. It's 6km out from Savusavu.

Daku Resort　　　　　　　　RESORT $$
(✆885 0046; www.dakuresort.com; Lesiaceva Point Rd; bungalows & villas $235-555; ❋☎⊗) A resort-cum-self-improvement centre, Daku offers a diverse array of courses from gospel singing and watercolour painting to meditation and yoga. If doing nothing makes your chakras sing, flop down by the inviting pool or book a massage. Accommodation is in neat *bures*, villas with plunge pools, or private three- or four-bedroom houses (from $365) that are ideal for groups. All have wonderful views.

The beach across the road is pebble rather than sand, but there's good snorkelling and kayaking to be had.

Jean-Michel Cousteau Fiji Islands Resort　　　　RESORT $$$
(✆885 0188; www.fijiresort.com; bungalow $1850-5515; ☎⊗⋔) ⊘ This outstanding luxury eco-resort was started by the son of Jacques Cousteau. Unsurprisingly, it attracts divers, but families love it too: the kids club is exceptional, and practically a mini-resort unto itself, with a pool, flying fox, cooking classroom, play areas galore and a nanny-per-child for everyone under

five. The beautiful *bures* are massive and feature handmade furnishings, large decks and private garden areas.

Fabulous gourmet meals are included in the price, as are all activities except diving: they'll even ferry you over to the exclusive Naviavia Island for private picnics. Though very family-centric, the resort has dedicated 'serenity zones' for adults only.

Its dive shop is one of the best in Fiji; there's also a full-time marine biologist on site.

Emaho Sekawa
Luxury Resort RESORT **$$$**
(☑995 3576; www.emahofiji.com; villas $2870-390, residence $9730; ❋❂❅) If you're looking for your own private slice of rainforest, tawny beach and decadence with your own staff, gourmet chef and dive master, then this retreat hits the dream mark. Accommodation is Balinese Crusoe-chic with heart-stopping sunset views; you get a golf cart to tool around the 2-hectare grounds. It's a five-minute walk to a 2km-long private beach where kayaks await.

No kids under 12. All meals are included, and there is a three-night minimum stay.

🏠 Hibiscus Highway

Dolphin Bay Divers Retreat, Remote Resort and Sau Bay Fiji Retreat are southeast of Buca Bay; accessible only by boat, they are most easily reached from Taveuni.

Vosa Ni Ua Lodge LODGE **$$**
(☑820 8648; www.flyseastay.com; bungalow from $200; ❂) The *bures* here are classy, comfortable and have insane sea views, but you'll likely be so busy you won't have time to appreciate them. The lodge is adrenaline HQ on this stretch of coast: from its wonderfully windy spot, staff offer professionally run kitesurfing courses, and arrange paragliding, diving, surf safaris and heaps more. Mountain bikes are available to rent. The snorkelling out the front is superb.

Siga Siga Sands Resort RESORT **$$**
(☑885 0000; www.theultimateparadise.com; Hibiscus Hwy; bungalow per night/week $200/1200 villa per night/week $480/2845) Situated on 119 acres just back from the best beach in the area (1.6km of white sand), these better-than-basic oceanfront cottages are 11km from Savusavu. The two *bures* and one villa are totally self-contained, but you can order the trademark Indian Fijian specialities if you don't feel like cooking. It's a $13 taxi ride from town and the bus passes by as well.

⭐**Salt Lake Lodge** LODGE **$$$**
(☑828 3005; www.saltlakelodgefiji.com; per night from $395; ❂) 🏊 For peace and personalised service, this remote lodge is tough to beat. Sitting on a 5-acre organic farm beside the Qaloqato River, the timber complex is yours alone, as are a personal chef, maid and all the fresh fruits and vegies you can pick. It's an absolutely idyllic location, and opportunities abound to explore it on fishing, snorkelling and kayaking trips.

There's a strong eco ethos here: all toilets are compost, rainwater is used for bathing and cooking, and there's 24-hour solar power.

Savasi Island RESORT **$$$**
(www.savasiisland.com; villas from $1255; ❋❂❅) This is the place to come for seclusion, scenery and getting spoiled senseless. The seven gorgeous villas all have incredible sea views, cloistered gardens and decks and impeccably designed interiors; most have their own pool. Gourmet meals are served in the tasteful restaurant or, in keeping with the privacy theme, on a deserted stretch of sand (or in a beach cave!). The excellent KoroSun Dive (p154) is based here.

Savasi Island is connected to Vanua Levu by a causeway: it's about 10-minutes' drive from Savusavu.

Koro Sun Resort RESORT **$$$**
(☑885 0262; www.korosunresort.com; Hibiscus Hwy; bungalow/villa from $765/1275; ❋❂❅⚓) This refurbished resort welcomes families and romantics by the drove; with 64 beautifully landscaped hectares, there's room for them all. There are 51 *bures* and villas in varying sizes, shapes and locations sprinkled across the grounds, the most exciting of which are the new adults-only Edgewater *bures* floating above a gorgeous lagoon. From here, kayak out to the magnificent grotto at nearby Bat Island.

Food, kids club and nannies are included in the price, as is use of tennis courts, a nine-hole golf course, kayaks, bikes and snorkelling gear. Diving is with Namena Divers (p155).

La Dolce Vita Holiday Villas RESORT **$$$**
(☑828 0824, 991 3669; www.ladolcevitaholiday villas.com; Hibiscus Hwy; villas incl meals from $760; ❂❅) This sweet place blends Italian touches – from the superb food right down

VANUA LEVU & TAVEUNI SAVUSAVU & AROUND

to the Botticelli replica on one of the *bure*'s ceilings – with Fiji-style hospitality and architecture: as incongruous as it sounds, it's a winning combination. The five round *bures* are stylish – *certamente*! – and have exceptional sea views; there's even a thatched-roof pizza oven.

If the six-hole golf course isn't your thing, there's a *bocce* court, paddleboating, bush-walking, snorkelling and dolphins to watch in Natewa Bay. The resort runs on 24-hour solar power.

Namale Resort   RESORT $$$
(☑ 885 0435; www.namalefiji.com; Hibiscus Hwy; bungalow from $3380; ❀ 🕿 ❀) Namale is a hugely exclusive and pricey resort right by the water, with accommodation ranging from delicious *bures* hidden among the rainforest to a jaw-droppingly luxurious grand villa complete with a mini-movie theatre and private stretch of beach. There's even an on-site bowling alley. Don't think about dropping by for a gander, however: no daytrippers allowed.

🍴 Eating

Savusavu is blessed with exceptional eateries that belie their low-key appearances. Unless otherwise mentioned, they're all on Main St. For lunch on the go, hit up the sprawling **market** (Main St), with its prepackaged lunches (usually fish, egg and vegies), bakery and more-ish roti wraps.

There are three or four large supermarkets along Main Street: look out for the IGA and Morris Hedstroms (closed Sundays).

Savusavu Wok   CHINESE $
(☑ 885 3688, 836 6898; mains $7-15; ☺ 11am-9pm; ❀) Like so many eateries in Savusavu, this place looks a bit woebegone from the outside. But don't be fooled by the flaky paint and misspelled signs: the Wok dishes up incredible, authentic Chinese food. It's a locals' favourite for its low prices and huge portions. The menu is extensive: we tried to eat our way through it and found every dish divine.

Taste of Hidden Paradise Restaurant   INDIAN $
(☑ 920 9781; curries from $8; ☺ 10am-7pm) This modest-looking joint is a strong contender for having the best curries in town. There's a good selection, and all dishes are very flavourful, but do be prepared to wait, as they cook everything – slowly – from scratch.

BYO. Despite the name, this is not attached to the central Hidden Paradise Guesthouse: it's at the far end of Main St, towards the wharf.

Decked Out Café   INTERNATIONAL $
(☑ 885 2929; meals from $6-15, pizzas from $20; ☺ lunch & dinner; 🕿) This no-frills, friendly pad is one of the more popular yachty hangouts: there's always a few old (or young) salts yakking over a beer and nosh in its street-facing covered beergarden. It dishes up all the standards: curries, fish and chips, pizzas and burgers. Daily happy hours run between 5pm to 7pm, and there's live music from Thursday to Sunday evenings.

Mum's Country Kitchen   INDIAN $
(☑ 927 1372; meals $3.50-10; ☺ 8am-6pm) One step up from a hole-in-the-wall, this place is popular with local Indo-Fijians for its curries. It's not a creative menu, but it's a solid one. Takeaway meals come in plastic bags (and *dahl* is poured into old juice bottles), but don't be put off: this is the real, delicious deal. If you like it super-spicy, staff are happy to oblige.

Sea View Café   INDIAN $
(☑ 885 0106; Hidden Paradise Guest House; meals $7-12; ☺ 8am-9pm Mon-Sat) In front of the Hidden Paradise Guesthouse, this cute place serves surprisingly excellent curries and Fijian specialities just above the roadside where you can watch life go by. The jovial owners also offer cooking classes ($15) so you can re-create your meal at home.

Arpaan's Blue Sea Restaurant   INTERNATIONAL $
(☑ 885 3057; Waitui Marina; meals $3-7.50; ☺ 7.30am-9pm) This quaint restaurant at Waitui Marina dishes up fish and chips, chicken and Indian and Chinese staples; good, basic breakfasts are available until 11am. It's a popular place on Thursday nights during cruising season for its Fijian buffet ($15, from 6pm).

Chong Pong   CHINESE $
(☑ 885 0588; meals $5-10; ☺ 11am-7pm) What this place lacks in ambience, it makes up for with good, filling food and astonishingly quick service.

Captain's Table   INTERNATIONAL $$
(☑ 885 0457; Copra Shed Marina; meals $8-20; ☺ 8am-9pm) Dine overlooking the bay on a creative assortment of international and Indian fare, like chicken stuffed with spinach,

steaks and seafood. It's not silver service, but it's more upmarket than most Savusavu offerings. If you're feeling more casual, try the street-side Captain's Café for pizzas, pancakes, quesadillas and sandwiches from $9.

★**Surf and Turf** INTERNATIONAL $$$
(☑885 3033; Waterfront Bldg; mains $25-65; ⊗10am-9.30pm Mon-Sat) This is the poshest restaurant in town, though you wouldn't know it from its dilapidated entrance. It has a beautiful deck overlooking the water, great wine list and lobster on the menu, yet it's as laid back as Savusavu itself. Tasty pastas, curries and exceptional fish and chips are to be had; it also has pricier steaks and upmarket seafood dishes. The homemade ice cream is a must.

If you're travelling with little ones who get squirmy while waiting for food, there's a good local playground out the back and to the left of the restaurant.

🍷 Drinking & Nightlife

Savusavu Yacht Club BAR
(Copra Shed Marina; ⊗10am-10pm Sun-Thu, to midnight Fri & Sat) Tourists are considered temporary members of this friendly little drinking hole. There are tables out by the waterside, plenty of cold beer and lots of mingling between yachties and expats.

Waitui Marina BAR
(☑835 3913; ⊗10am-10pm Mon-Sat) Sit on the balcony upstairs to enjoy classic South Pacific views of the yacht-speckled, palm-lined bay. The bar is well-stocked and all foreigners on holiday are welcomed. Expect locals playing guitars and heavy drinking as the night wears on.

Planters' Club BAR
(⊗10am-10pm Mon-Sat, to 8pm Sun) This was traditionally a place for planters to drink when they brought in the copra, and some of their descendants can still be found clustered around the bar. It's got a whiff of colonialism and teems with expats. Happy hour is from 5.30pm to 6.30pm. It holds a monthly Sunday *lovo*. Ignore the 'members only' placard; staff will happily sign in visitors.

Savusavu Wines & Spirits LIQUOR STORE
(☑885 3888; Main St; ⊗9am-5pm Mon-Thu, to 9pm Fri & Sat) It's amazing what you can find in this little bottle shop: a great wine and international spirits selection as well as im-

ported gourmet coffees, cheeses, cereals and more. There are a couple of tables outside if you wish to sit down and imbibe; many do.

Mahi Bar BAR
(Hot Springs Hotel) Attached to the Hot Springs Hotel, this open-deck bar has fabulous panoramic bay views. Hotel guests as well as drop-in yachties mingle here. Be careful on your way back down the steep hill.

White Stork BAR
(⊗10am-11pm) This wonky green building houses the rowdiest place in town: everyone is blind drunk by around 11pm and fights are common.

Uros CLUB
(admission $5; ⊗8pm-midnight) Meaning 'sexy' in Fijian, this is where everyone comes to bump and grind to local and international music. It's a smallish room up a dark flight of stairs and great fun.

🛍 Shopping

Across the road from the Copra Shed is a handicrafts stall where a local man sells his wooden carvings. At the back of the market is Town Council Handicrafts, devoted to local woven and wooden handicrafts.

Savusavu has loads of great, extremely cheap secondhand clothing shops: look out for them all along the main street.

ℹ Information

Being an official point of entry for yachts, there are customs, immigration, health and quarantine services available. ANZ, BSP and Westpac banks all have branches in the main street.

Customs (☑885 0727; ⊗8am-1pm & 2-5pm Mon-Fri) Located west of the marinas on the main street.

Hospital (☑885 0444; Cross Island Rd) The hospital is 1.5km east of town on the road to Labasa. Call the hospital if an ambulance is required.

Police (☑885 0222) The police station is 600m past the Buca Bay Rd turn-off.

Post Office At the eastern end of town near Buca Bay Rd.

Savusavu Medical Centre (☑923 9043; savu savumedicalcentre@yahoo.com; $15; ⊗8am-4pm Mon-Fri) The Savusavu Medical Centre, beside the Hot Springs, has three therapeutic spa baths (40°C), and welcomes visitors. No appointment necessary.

ℹ️ Getting There & Around

BUS

Savusavu's bus station is in the centre of town, beside the market. Buses travelling the scenic, sealed (yet bumpy) highway from Savusavu over the mountains to Labasa ($10, three hours, four times daily) depart from 7.30am to 3.30pm. Some buses take the longer route from Savusavu to Labasa along Natewa Bay, and these should depart at 9am ($18, six hours).

Buses from Savusavu to Napuca ($9, 4½ hours), at the tip of the Tunuloa Peninsula, depart three times daily. The last bus stays there overnight and returns at 7am. A 4pm bus only goes as far as Naweni ($3). There is no bus from Savusavu to Nabouwalu; catch a morning bus to Labasa and change buses there.

From Monday to Saturday there are five bus services from Savusavu to Lesiaceva Point ($1.20, 15 minutes) between 6am and 5pm. For confirmation of bus timetables, ring **Vishnu Holdings** (📞885 0276; admin@vhlbuses.com)

CAR

Car-rental agencies include **Budget** (📞881 1999; www.budget.com.fj), **Carpenters** (📞885 0274; www.carprentals.com.fj) and **James Rentals** (📞867 3375; www.jamesrentalsfiji.com). **Trip n Tour** (p155) rents scooters for $75.

TAXI

Taxis are easy to find in Savusavu; the main stand is right next to the bus station.

North & East of Savusavu

Nestled in the mountains north of Savusavu, the 120-hectare **Waisali Rainforest Reserve** (📞828 0267; Savusavu Rd; adult/child $8/2; ⏱8am-5pm Mon-Sat) is home to thousands of birds, flowers, trees and plants, some of which are used in local traditional medicines. There's a pleasant 30-minute walk through dense greenery down to a waterfall (watch out for its slippery death-trap rocks).

You can enter the park 20km north of Savusavu, directly off the road to Labasa. Bus drivers should know where to drop you off (ask before you board), as should most carrier and taxi drivers. It's a very scenic drive.

Drekeniwai to Dakuniba

About 20km east of Savusavu, the Hibiscus Hwy veers right (south). The turn-off to the left (north) follows the western side of Natewa Bay, an alternative 4WD route to Labasa. About 35km further along the highway

NUKUBOLU

Deep in the mountains north of Savusavu, reachable by 4WD, lies the ruins of Nukubolu, an ancient Fijian village whose old stone foundations, terraces and thermal pools are in surprisingly good condition. The setting is lovely: a volcanic crater with steaming hot springs in the background. Nukubolu has myriad uses for the local villagers, who dry kava roots on corrugated-iron sheets laid over the pools and use the hot springs as a healing aid. The ruins are on the property of the village of Biaugunu, so take a *sevusevu* (gift; kava is a good option) for the chief and ask permission before wandering around. The turn-off is about 20km northwest of Savusavu; continue about 8km inland and over a couple of river crossings. You can also rent a carrier from town to take you there; combine it with a trip to Waisali Rainforest Reserve.

from this intersection is the turn-off into the village of Drekeniwai, where former prime minister Sitiveni Rabuka was born.

If you follow the Hibiscus Hwy to Buca Bay, the highway turns left (north), becoming more potholed as it heads through the **Tunuloa Silktail Reserve**, the habitat of the rare silktail bird. Found only on this peninsula and on Taveuni, the silktail is an endangered species: it remains under threat by continued logging. The average bird is about 8cm high and is black with a white patch on its tail.

If you turn right (south) at Buca Bay, you'll head through Natuvu village and then up over the mountain to the next village, Dakuniba. The road is one big pothole and the going is slow, but you'll be rewarded with dazzling views over the forest and out to sea. In a beautiful forest setting, just outside Dakuniba, **petroglyphs** are inscribed on large boulders. They are thought to be of ceremonial or mystical significance. Be sure to bring a *sevusevu* (gift) for the village chief and read up about village etiquette before you arrive. The people of Dakuniba are very friendly and may offer to take you to a nearby beach to swim, fish or snorkel. The famous Rainbow Reef is offshore from Dakuniba, but is more easily accessible from Taveuni.

THE SACRED PRAWNS OF NAWENI

While in Fiji, you'll no doubt encounter prawns on the menu. But while you can enjoy crustaceans in coconut or a curry, touch the red ones at your peril. Known locally as *ura-buta* (cooked prawns) for their distinctive boiled-red colour, these rare prawns exist in Fiji only in Naweni village (40 minutes from Savusavu) and the small island of Vatulele, off the southern coast of Viti Levu. According to legend, the daughter of a chief angrily rejected a suitor's offering of a prawn supper, and threw them – and him – off a cliff. Upon hitting the water, the prawns miraculously returned to life, and retained their cooked colour. The boring version? They probably get their colour from the iron oxide in their limestone pools. Even more remarkable than their curious colouring is the fact that villagers can 'call' the prawns with chants and claps... and the prawns respond.

Nobody – not even a chief – may touch *ura-buta;* to do so is *tabu,* and will surely bring a shipwreck upon you.

Some resorts offer tours of the sacred prawn pools, or otherwise can arrange them: ask at your accommodation for details.

Offshore Islands

Namenalala

The volcanic island of Namenalala rests on the Namena Barrier Reef, now one of the most spectacular protected marine reserves in the country, 25km off the southeastern coast of Vanua Levu and about 40km from Savusavu. Namenalala has the best diving and snorkelling in the region: sights include the shallow isolated offshore **Chimneys**, covered with soft and hard corals as well as plenty of nudibranchs, and **Grand Canyon**, a drop off at least a mile deep along **Save-A-Tack Passage** where there are great drift diving opportunities and plenty of marine life. The island also has lovely beaches and is a natural sailors' refuge. There's just one small, upmarket resort, which also runs daytrips to the island.

★**Namena Island Resort**   RESORT **$$**
(☑828 0577, 885 3389; www.namenaislandresort. com; bungalow $360, round-trip transfers $200; ☏) This small dive and snorkel retreat is outrageously located on Namenalala Island in the paradisaical Namena Marine Reserve. Namena was badly damaged in 2016's Cyclone Winston, and was closed at the time of research. Contact the resort for updates.

Kioa

POP 600

The island of Kioa (25 sq km) is inhabited by Polynesians originally from the tiny, coral-reef island of Vaitupu in Tuvalu. Because of weak soil and overcrowding on their home island, they decided that the best idea would be to buy another, more fertile island and start a relocation program. The people of Vaitupu had earned some money during WWII working for American soldiers who had occupied their islands, and in 1947 they purchased Kioa for the grand sum of $15,000. It was with some trepidation, however: those living on Kioa today speak wryly of their initial fears about how they would deal with the climate and whether they would be eaten by Fijian cannibals.

The residents of Kioa were finally granted Fijian citizenship in 2005. They are a very warm and traditional people. Women make woven handicrafts that are sold to tourists on Taveuni and Vanua Levu, and fishing is done from small, traditional *drua* (double-hulled canoes). The people of Kioa have a speciality called *toddy,* which is a tradition that they imported from Tuvalu. It's a sweet syrup taken from coconut sap and can be made into a thick, spreadable syrup or fermented into a pungent alcoholic drink.

Read more about the island and its community here: www.kioaisland.org.

There is no official accommodation or facilities for tourists, though if you email the council on kioacouncil@gmail.com, they may find a homestay for you. Tui Tai Adventure Cruises (p155) and various international cruise ships make stops here. Alternatively, the Taveuni ferry might be able to drop you off on its way past, though remember, this is a private island and it's best to seek permission before just lobbing up. For snorkellers and divers, the Farm, off the most easterly point of the island, has fantastic corals.

Rabi

POP 5000

Rabi (66 sq km), east of the northern tip of the Tunuloa Peninsula, has four villages populated by Micronesians originally from Banaba, in Kiribati. At the turn of the 20th century the islanders of Banaba were first tricked and then pressed into selling the phosphate mining rights of Banaba for a small annual payment, and their tiny island was slowly ruined by the subsequent mining and influx of settlers. WWII brought further tragedy when the Japanese invaded Banaba and massacred many villagers. Following the war, Rabi was purchased for the Banabans by the British Government – with money from the islanders' own Provident Fund, set up by the British Government in 1931 for phosphate royalties – and 2000 survivors were resettled here. However, as they were dropped in the middle of the cyclone season with only army tents and two months' rations, and had never been so cold (Banaba is on the equator), many of the original settlers died.

To visit Rabi, you must first ask permission from the **island council** (☏820 1961). If you're extended an invitation, catch a bus from Savusavu to Karoko where small boats wait for passengers to Rabi (about $80 one way).

Rabi Island Council Guesthouse (☏820 1961; dm $50; ☺Mon, Wed & Fri) has beds in basic, four-bed rooms. You'll eat with the villagers.

Labasa

POP 27,950

Labasa (pronounced '*Lam-basa*'), Vanua Levu's administrative centre, is a dusty sugar and timber town that doesn't hold much allure for the average traveller. Sitting about 5km inland on the sweltering banks of the Labasa River and reclaimed mangrove swamps, the top sights in town are a large sugar mill and the seasonal trains that *ka-chunk* bushels of cane through Labasa's centre. The local population is predominantly Indo-Fijian, many of whom are descendants of *girmitiyas* (indentured labourers brought from India to work on the plantations); you'll find good curries here, and can shop for trinkets, bangles and saris in

colourful shops blasting out Bollywood hits. Vanua Levu's main airport is also here.

Out of town are nearly undeveloped coastal areas that are rumoured to get great surf and have awesome diving

⊙ Sights & Activities

Wasavula Ceremonial Site　　HISTORIC SITE

This site has a cryptic – and cannibalistic – history. At the entrance, there's a sacred monolith that villagers believe grew from the ground; behind is a cemetery and the area that was used during cannibalistic ceremonies, with a *vatu ni bokola* (head-chopping stone), another rock for the severed head and a bowl-like stone where the brain was placed for the chief. The site is found in Wasavula village (Vunimoli Rd) south of town; a taxi should be about $7.

Once there, ask the first villager you see for permission to visit. Everyone should dress modestly, especially women, who are required to wear a *sula* (no pants or shorts allowed) and cover their shoulders. Don't forget a *sevusevu* of kava for the chief.

🛏 Sleeping

Hotel Northpole　　HOTEL **$**

(☏881 8008; www.northpole.com.fj; Nasekula Rd; r $85-110; P☀🌐) Smack in the middle of town, the refurbished Northpole is an

---

DRUA

For assisting him in a war against the people of Rewa, Ratu Cakobau presented King George of Tonga with a *drua* (traditional catamaran). Named Ra Marama, the *drua* was built in Taveuni in the 1850s. It took seven years to complete, was over 30m long and could carry 150 people. Hewn from giant trees, it could outsail the European ships of the era.

Building *drua* could involve entire communities; some boats could carry up to 300 people. Their construction often involved ceremonial human sacrifices, and the completed vessel was launched over the bodies of slaves, which were used as rollers under the hulls. The last large *drua* was built in 1913 and is on display at the Fiji Museum in Suva. If you visit the island of Kioa, north of Taveuni, you can still see fishermen out in small, one-person *drua*.

Labasa

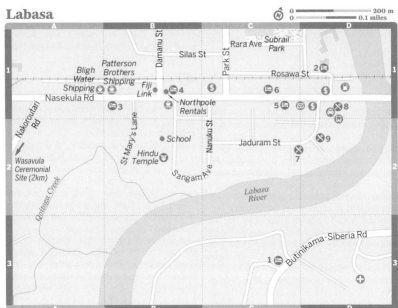

excellent option: it's friendly, clean and as modern as it gets in Labasa. You can rent 4WDs from here; they do worthwhile room and rental deals. The hotel is atop The Lunch Box fast food joint; don't be surprised if the wafting dinner smells induce a fried chicken craving.

Friendly North Inn   HOTEL $
(☎990 8611; www.cjsgroup.com.fj/friendly.html; Butinikama-Siberia Rd; r $75-95; ❄) A 15-minute walk to town, this well-maintained hotel offers a rare peace in Labasa. There are several surprisingly classy duplex villas set in a mellow, flower-studded garden; guests have free access to a large pool a couple of minutes' walk away. Breakfasts are included, and if you order in advance, staff can arrange other meals as well. A taxi to town is $5.

Northwinds Hotel   HOTEL $
(☎881 1057; cenhotel@connect.com.fj; Nasekula Rd; r $80-110; ❄🖥) Bang in the centre of town, this place has large, if uninspiring, rooms with bathrooms. It's basic but friendly. Rates include breakfast.

★Grand Eastern Hotel   HOTEL $$
(☎881 1022; www.cjsgroup.com.fj/grand_eastern. html; Rosawa St; r $90-200; P❄🖥🏊) This is the plushest hotel in Labasa. There's an airy, somewhat colonial atmosphere and the staff is helpful. Standard rooms have porches facing the river, but it's worth paying the extra for the deluxe rooms that open out onto the courtyard swimming pool. All rooms are clean but slightly careworn. There's also a decent restaurant and bar.

Hotel 88   HOTEL $$
(☎881 1839; hotel88labasa@gmail.com; 43 Nasekula Rd; r $90-180; P❄🖥) Labasa's newest hotel (opened 2015) is clean, comfy and, thanks to double-glazed windows and triple-layer walls, very quiet for central digs like these. Hot showers are solar-powered. There's a communal kitchen, though you may not be able to tear yourself away from the attached Colour Dragon restaurant.

Hotel Takia   HOTEL $$
(☎881 1655; www.hoteltakia.com; Nasekula Rd; r $75-155, ste $235; ❄) Rooms here are large and clean, there's a restaurant that dishes out hefty servings of Chinese and Indian food for around $15, and a bar – though the drinkers can get rowdy. Be sure to book a room farthest from the street, as sound carries. It can also arrange tours and daytrips.

Labasa

🛌 **Sleeping**		🍴 **Eating**	
1 Friendly North Inn	C3	Colour Dragon	(see 3)
2 Grand Eastern Hotel	D1	7 Horse Shoe	C2
3 Hotel 88	B1	8 Market	D1
4 Hotel Northpole	B1	9 Oriental Seafood Restaurant	D2
5 Hotel Takia	C1		
6 Northwinds Hotel	C1		

✖️ Eating

Labasa is full of basic cafes serving cheap plates of Indian and Chinese food. Note: most restaurants, although open for dinner, close by 7pm. There's also a cavernous market next to the bus station and a few well-stocked supermarkets.

Horse Shoe   FAST FOOD **$**
(Reddy Place; mains $3-15; ⊘8am-7pm) This place is locally famous for its creative burgers, homemade chicken nuggets and vegetarian options. It gets especially packed at lunchtime: you can amuse yourself by chortling at the cheeky menu.

Colour Dragon   CHINESE **$$**
(☑881 1839; 43 Nasekula Rd; mains $6-20; ⊘9am-8pm Mon-Sat) Cheap, tasty and so clean it shines (it *is* owned by an ex-surgeon), the Colour Dragon is a long-time Labasa favourite. The long menu includes all the usual favourites; staff willl also whip up whatever else takes your fancy. Service is incredibly brisk for Fiji.

Oriental Seafood Restaurant   CHINESE **$$**
(☑881 7321; Jaduram St; meals $5-23; ⊘10am-3pm & 6-10pm Mon-Sat, 6-10pm Sun) Look for the bright-orange door and pink balcony overlooking the bus station. Although you wouldn't guess it from the outside, this is one of Labasa's most upmarket and atmospheric restaurants, with a well-stocked bar and a wide choice of tasty, well-portioned Chinese dishes, including plenty of veggies and a few Fijian options.

🍷 Drinking & Nightlife

There's not much going on in town. You might try the bar at the Grand Eastern Hotel for a poolside drink; the brave can venture to the bar and club at Hotel Takia. The Labasa Club can get pretty rough. The Pontoon and Fusion nightclubs, both on Nasekula Rd and open from 6pm-1am, are worth checking out if you like to boogie to Bollywood beats.

ℹ️ Information

ANZ, BSP and Westpac banks all have branches in the main street and have 24-hour ATMs.

Hospital (☑881 1444; Butinikama-Siberia Rd) The hospital is southeast of the river.

Police (☑881 1222; Nadawa St)

Post Office (Nasekula Rd) There are several cardphones outside.

ℹ️ Getting There & Around

There are regular buses that chug along the scenic mountain route between Labasa and Savusavu ($10, three hours, five times Monday to Saturday, four on Sunday) departing between 7am and 4.15pm. There is also a daily bus that takes the long route ($18, six hours) to Savusavu around the northeast, following the scenic Natewa Bay. Buses to Nabouwalu depart three times per day Monday to Saturday ($14, six hours). Call Vishnu Holdings (p161) to confirm timetables.

The majority of shops, businesses and hotels in Labasa are within walking distance of the centre. If you are going further afield, there is no shortage of taxis; the main rank is by the bus station.

Northpole Rentals (☑777 7224; www.northpole.com.fj/rentals.html; Hotel Northpole) has an office at the hotel of the same name on the main drag. You can rent 4WD Suzuki Jimnys from $120 per day. Free airport pick-up and drop-off.

Around Labasa

The area around Labasa is a great place for 4WD exploration. There are some interesting things to see, though it's definitely the adventure of finding them rather than the sights themselves that make it worthwhile. For all of these, you'll need to turn left onto Wainikoro Rd, just past the sugar mill and across from a secondary school. This is the main road out of town to the east.

👁️ Sights & Activities

Naag Mandir Temple   TEMPLE
The sacred 3m-high Cobra Rock is housed inside the vibrant Naag Mandir Temple. It's draped with flower-and-tinsel garlands, and

MONOLITHIC GODS

Although the Wasavula Ceremonial Site is shrouded in mystery, it is thought to be related to similar sites of the *naga* (snake) cult found in Viti Levu's Sigatoka Valley. In the old religion those who betrayed ceremonial secrets would face insanity and death from the ancestral spirits and gods, so what is known about such places is mostly based on hearsay and vague memories.

Before the arrival of Christianity, ceremonial sites were venues for communicating with ancestral gods. Rituals performed at the sites provided a spiritual link between the people and the earth, time, crops and fertility. It's believed that this was where chiefs and priests were installed, where male initiation rites took place and where a *bokola* (the dead body of an enemy) was offered to the gods.

Stone monoliths at the sites were seen as actual gods or as the shrines of gods. These stones were often used for refuge; if someone who had committed a crime made it to the monolith before being caught, their life would be spared.

While the rituals of long ago are no longer practised at Wasavula Ceremonial Site, the ancestral gods haven't been evicted so easily. It is still revered as a sacred place by the village people and is where they bury their dead. Some people continue to see the monolith as supernatural; it is said that in photos of villagers with the monolith, the villagers have often vanished from the developed pictures.

offerings are placed at its base; locals believe the rock can cure the sick and the infertile. The rock also – apparently – grows; locals say the roof has had to be raised four times since the 1950s. Remove your shoes outside the beautifully tiled temple and try to make it there on a Sunday, when the temple is heaving.

A few buses pass the temple, including those to Natewa Bay ($1.60). A taxi costs about $20. If you're driving, the temple is 10km from the turn off for Wainikoro Rd.

Korovatu Beach   BEACH
(per car $5) From Naag Mandir Temple, head down through dense coconut trees and past the lounging cows to Korovatu Beach. It's the closest stretch of sand to Labasa and makes a decent side trip if you're in the area for a few days.

Floating Island   ISLAND
This house-sized island floats on a pond during high winds or, if you believe local lore, when a priest chants at it. The real reason to come here is to say you have; if you're the type who loves a challenge, you'll like it too as it's very remote and you'll have to find a local willing to slog through the mud with you. The island is found near Nakelikoso Village, about 50km northeast of Labasa.

You'll need a 4WD, strong walking legs and a local guide, plus permission from local villagers. Ask around in Labasa to find someone to take you out.

🛏 Sleeping

Palmlea Farms Resort   RESORT $$
(☏828 2220; www.palmleafarms.com; Tabia-Naduri Rd; bungalows incl breakfast from $295; ❄☎☺) ✐ This remote-feeling resort makes for a gorgeous getaway. Overlooking the Great Sea Reef, simple *bures* with verandahs sit on a gentle green slope a short walk from the resort's jetty – from here you can kayak to a private white-sand beach or enjoy fantastic snorkelling. Organic fruit and veg is grown on-site and every effort is made to manage the resort in an ecofriendly fashion.

Other activities include hiking, diving ($250 two-tank dive), fishing and crabbing with a local guide.

It's a 20-minute drive from Labasa; there are also frequent buses passing daily, making it easy to get to Savusavu.

Nukubati Island Resort   RESORT $$$
(☏603 0919; www.nukubati.com; bungalow incl meals & activities $1677-2420; min 5-night stay; ☎) ✐ If you're looking for seclusion, this private island should do the trick. The seven *bures* each have private verandahs facing a white-sand beach and clean, whitewashed interiors. Prices include gourmet meals, all drinks (including alcohol) and most activities; game fishing, diving and massages cost extra. No kids are allowed, unless you book the whole island.

Guided surf trips to the Great Sea Reef are possible from November to March.

Nabouwalu & Around

Nabouwalu is a small settlement on the island's southwestern point. Early in the 19th century, European traders flocked to nearby Bua Bay to exploit yasi dina (sandalwood), which grew in the hills. Today, the ferry landing – not active at time of research – is its only draw. Nabouwalu has administrative offices, a post office, a small market and a store. Offshore to the northwest, the island of Yadua Tabu is home to the last sizeable population of the rare and spectacular crested iguana. It became Fiji's first wildlife reserve in 1980. Landing here is not allowed.

Nabouwalu has a basic, clean **government guesthouse** (883 6027; r per person $15). It's often booked out with government workers; call ahead to reserve a room. There is a kitchen; bring your own supplies. There are no eateries nearby.

Nabouwalu can be reached by bus from Labasa, but not from Savusavu.

The road from Nabouwalu around the southern coast to Savusavu (127km) is barely passable by 4WD or carrier.

Wainunu Bay

Hardly any travellers make it over to Wainunu Bay. The road here is poor and the land has escaped commercial logging, so the surrounding landscape – a patchwork of forest and waterfalls – remains untouched for the most part. Wainunu River, the third-largest river in Fiji, flows into Wainunu Bay. Today it's mostly populated with Fijian subsistence farmers who make money selling timber and kava.

Wainunu is three hours by very, very bad road from Savusavu, and about an hour from Nabouwalu. (It's actually closer to Viti Levu than Savusavu.)

TAVEUNI

POP 12,000

Taveuni is renowned as Fiji's Garden Island, though its tangled, steamy interior is more reminiscent of a prehistoric jungle than anything that might yield to a hedgetrimmer and set of pruning shears. Hot and often wet, this impossibly green volcanic bump is covered by a riotous quilt of palms, monster ferns and tropical wildflowers, one of which

– the *tagimaucia* – is found nowhere else on earth. Its dense rainforest is a magnet for colourful bird life.

Much of Taveuni's coastline is rugged: Des Voeux Peak reaches up to 1195m and the cloud-shrouded Mt Uluigalau, at 1241m, is Fiji's highest summit. A massive swath of the island's east is protected national park: here, you can get sweaty on hillside hikes, cool off under waterfalls, tramp along a coastal walk beside impossibly beautiful beach or glide through clear waters on a traditional *bilibili* (bamboo raft).

Taveuni's beauty doesn't fade at the water's edge: the dazzling corals and diverse marine life of the Somosomo Strait, Waitabu Marine Park and Vuna Reef draw divers and snorkellers from around the world.

🏃 Activities

Diving & Snorkelling

Taveuni has achieved mythical status among divers, who come to the Somosomo Strait to see vibrant coral, a profusion of fish and the occasional shark, turtle or pilot whale. The most famous soft-coral site is **Rainbow Reef**, which fringes the southwest corner of Vanua Levu but is most easily accessed from Taveuni. Highlights include the luminescent **Great White Wall** (vertical drop-off covered in white corals resembling wavering, glimmery snow), the **Purple Wall** (covered in purple corals, gorgonia fans and sea whips) and **Annie's Brommies**, a fantastic outcrop teeming with fish. The island is especially hot and humid in January and February and the water clarity is reduced due to plankton blooms and northerly winds from the equator.

There is plenty for snorkellers, too. Vuna Reef, off southern Taveuni, boasts psychadelic coral and improbable creatures. The three small islands immediately offshore from Naselesele Point in Matei also have good snorkelling (the third is known locally as 'Honeymoon Island'). You can also snorkel at Prince Charles or Beverly Beaches.

ⓘ PACK A TORCH

All of Taveuni's electricity is supplied by generator. Upmarket resorts have 24-hour power; however, some budget and midrange places only run their generators in the evening, usually between 6pm and 10pm.

Taveuni

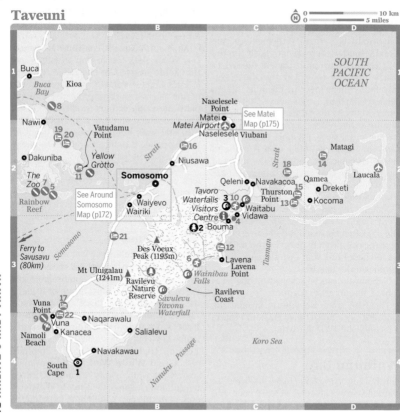

There are a number of good dive operators on Taveuni. The average price for a two-tank dive/PADI Open Water Course runs from $250/950.

Taveuni Ocean Sports DIVING
(☑888 1111; www.taveunioceansports.com) 🖉 The centre is dedicated to protecting the environment; each dive starts with a short lesson on local marine biology. With group maximums at four people per dive you'll want to reserve in advance. It's based at Nakia Resort and Dive (p172).

It also offers snorkelling (from $125) and surf tours (from $265; experienced boarders only).

Taveuni Dive DIVING
(☑828 1063; www.taveunidive.com) This long-running centre offers diving and snorkelling tours, plus cultural, fishing and other watersports tours. It's based at Taveuni

Dive Resort (p172) but does pickups from across the island.

Dolphin Bay Divers DIVING
(☑992 4001, 828 3001; www.dolphinbaydivers. com) Located at Dolphin Bay Divers Retreat (on Vanua Levu but best accessed from Taveuni), this is a well-regarded outfit with excellent gear.

Garden Island Dive Centre DIVING
(☑888 0286; www.gardenislandresort.com) Professional place with a good reputation; it's based at the Garden Island Resort.

Hiking

Taveuni's wild interior is perfect for exploring on foot. Bouma National Heritage Park is the place to head for hiking; you can amble beachside on the Lavena Coastal Walk, tramp up hills to the Tavoro Waterfalls or trek the guided Vidawa Rainforest Trail. If

Taveuni

that's not hardcore enough, slog it up to Des Voeux Peak or around Lake Tagimaucia.

Wildlife Watching

Taveuni is one of Fiji's best areas for birdwatching. More than 100 species of bird can be found here. Try Des Voeux Peak at dawn for a chance to see the rare orange dove (the male is bright orange with a green head, while the female is mostly green) and the silktail. Avid birdwatchers also recommend the Vidawa Rainforest Trail. On the Matei side of the village, follow a 4WD track for 3.5km up the mountain. Here you might see parrots and fantails, particularly in August and September when they're nesting. The deep-red feathers of the kula parrot were once an important trade item with the Tongans. The forested Lavena coast is also a good spot to see orange or flame doves, Fiji goshawks, wattled honeyeaters, and grey and white herons.

Other Activities

Civa Pearl Farm   TOUR
(☑935 6168; www.civafijipearls.com; $40)
Founded by two Canadian expats, Civa pro-

duces black – as well as unusual blue, green and pink – pearls from their 55-hectare farm. Ninety-minute boat tours explore the farm hut and nursery; afterwards, guests are welcome to have a snorkel and, of course, buy pearls. Book tours through your Taveuni accommodation.

The **Peckham Pearl Farm** (☑888 2789; Matei; $25) in Matei may or may not be working; if you're in the area, drop in and see if it's offering tours.

Makaira Sports Fishing   FISHING
(☑888 0680; www.fijibeachfrontatmakaira.com; half/full day $950/1700) Captain John Llanes Jr, who has over 30 years' experience on the water, will take you fishing for big game. Book through Makaira Resort in Matei.

Exotic Holidays Fiji   TOUR
(☑625 3792; www.exoticholidaysfiji.net) Though it's based in Viti Levu, this outfit knows Taveuni – particularly its natural attractions – inside out. If you're keen on making a short visit to the Garden Isle, staff can arrange accommodation and tours of all the must-sees on the island. A four-night stay (with tours included) starts at $499.

Sailing Fiji   SAILING
(☑906 8600; www.sailfarnorthfiji.com; Matei) Offers exclusive chartered day cruises and overnight packages on board the 43-ft yacht *Looping*. Full-day excursions ($2915, six people max) include snorkelling, morning and afternoon tea and gourmet lunch; liveaboard charters ($5036 per night, two-night minimum) take in the islands, atolls and fringing reef of the far northern and Lau island groups.

Trips depart from Vacala Bay Resort (www.vacalabay.com; still under construction at research time); this company also offers kiteboarding and SUP trips and lessons; contact them for information.

⊙ Getting There & Away

AIR

At Matei airport, **Fiji Airways** (p151) has at least one flight a day to/from Nadi (1½ hours) and Suva (45 minutes). **Northern Air** (p231) has daily flights between Taveuni and Suva.

Be aware that routes are often heavily booked and are cancelled at the hint of bad weather. Leave yourself a grace period between Taveuni and your international flight in case you get stuck a day or two.

VANUA LEVU & TAVEUNI TAVEUNI

BOAT

The Wairiki Wharf, for large vessels such as the MV *Suliven* and *Lomaviti Princess,* is about 1km south of Waiyevo. Smaller boats depart from the Korean Wharf, about 2km north

The *Lomaiviti Princess,* operated by **Goundar Shipping** (✆ in Savusavu 330 1035; www.goundarshipping.com), arrives and departs Taveuni on Tuesdays and Saturdays on its Suva–Savusavu–Taveuni run: a ticket between Taveuni and Savusavu is $30. Goundar is expected to put on a second boat in 2016.

Boat-bus trips run from Taveuni to Savusavu and Labasa ($17 to $25). Boats depart from the Korean Wharf at 7.30am. You may be able to buy tickets on-board, but it's best to book ahead at the wharf. Operators are **Grace Ferry** (p153) and **Egi One** (p153).

❶ Getting Around

The one main road in Taveuni follows the coast, stretching from Lavena in the east, up north and around to Navakawau in the south. It is sealed from Matei to Wairiki, and there's also a sealed (though slightly potholed) section through Tave-euni Estates. There are also a couple of inland 4WD tracks. Getting around Taveuni involves a bit of planning – the main disadvantage being the sporadic bus service. To get around cheaply and quickly you need to combine buses with walking, or take taxis – the driver will probably act as a tour guide too!

TO/FROM THE AIRPORT

From Matei airport expect to pay about $30 to Waiyevo, and $90 to Vuna (about one hour) in a taxi. Most upmarket resorts provide transfers for guests.

BUS

Pacific Transport (✆ 888 0278) has a depot in Naqara, opposite the Taveuni Central Indian School. Buses start at the depot and travel north to Matei and beyond to Lavena in the southeast,

as well as south to Navakawau, just past Vuna. They run three times per day Mondays to Satur-days, and once on Sundays.

You can find a schedule here: www.taveuni. au/services/bus.htm. Be aware that times can and do change; buses may show up early or an hour late. Double-check the time of the return bus when you board, just to make sure there is one.

CAR

Give **Budget Rent a Car** (p161) a call, though keep in mind the roads here can be really rough. Locals are often willing to hire out their cars for around $130 per day. This of course means that there is no rental agreement and you will not be insured.

TAXI

It's easy to find taxis in the Matei, Waiyevo and Naqara areas, though on Sunday you might have to call one in advance. Hiring a taxi for a negotiat-ed fee and touring most of the island's highlights in a day will work out cheaper than hiring a car. You should be able to get one from around $140 for the day, depending on how far you want to go. For destinations such as Lavena you can go one way by bus and have a taxi pick you up at the end at a designated time: arrange this before you go.

Alternatively, your accommodation will be able to procure a private driver for you.

Waiyevo, Somosomo & Around

This isn't the most beautiful part of Taveuni, but it holds most of the island's facilities. It's also politically important – Somosomo is the largest village on Tave-uni and headquarters for the Tui Cakau (high chief of Taveuni). The Great Coun-cil of Chiefs' meeting hall (bure b*ose)* was built here in 1986 for the gathering of chiefs from all over Fiji.

ORIENTING YOURSELF ON TAVEUNI

The majority of visitors fly into Matei airport at the island's northernmost point, where most of the island's hotels, restaurants and dive shops are based. Head southeast from Matei and you'll eventually hit Bouma National Heritage Park, where the road stops at Lavena. Head southwest from Matei and you reach the towns of Somosomo, Naqara and Waiyevo, where there's some budget accommodation, shops and services but not much of interest. If you arrive by boat it will be at one of the two wharves in the Waiyevo area. Further south there are a few resorts near the village of Vuna. The road then goes only as far as the blowhole on South Cape, making much of the southeast coast almost inac-cessible. Some locals believe that the Federal Government's 'Look North' policy might finally deliver on road upgrades (and electricity) in the next couple of years; others aren't holding their breath.

Just south of Somosomo is Naqara, Taveuni's metropolis – if you take metropolis to mean a few supermarkets, a budget hotel and the island's only bank. Head another 2km down the coast and you'll hit Waiyevo, which is Taveuni's administrative centre and home to the hospital, police station, more ferry links and a resort. About 2km further south of Waiyevo is Wairiki village, which has a general store and a beautiful old hilltop Catholic mission.

◉ Sights

International Dateline   LANDMARK
Though Fiji adheres to the single time convention, the International Dateline cuts straight through Taveuni, offering visitors a great photo-op and the chance to jump from one day to the next. Take the road uphill from Waiyevo (towards the hospital) and cross the field on the right: you'll find a big Taveuni map split in two to mark both sides of the dateline.

Waitavala Water Slide   WATERFALL
Wahooo! This awesome natural slide is a ton of fun. Slide down on your bum or attempt it standing up, like the local kids. Either way, you'll end up in a small pool at the bottom. Don't start your slide from the very top of the falls – it's too dangerous – or slide if there's too much water. Watch and learn from the locals. The slide is a 20-minute walk from Waiyevo.

With the Garden Island Resort on your left, head north and take the first right at the bus stop. Take another right at the branch in the road, pass a shed and then go left down a hill. You'll see a 'waterfall' sign. The river is on the Waitavala estate, which is private land: if you pass anyone, ask if you can visit.

Lake Tagimaucia   LAKE
Lake Tagimaucia is in an old volcanic crater in the mountains above Somosomo. Masses of vegetation float on the lake (823m above sea level), and the national flower, the rare *tagimaucia* (an epiphytic plant), grows on the lake's shores. This red-and-white flower blooms only at high altitude from October to December. It's a difficult trek around the lake as it is overgrown and often very muddy. You'll need a guide; ask in Naqara or arrange one through your accommodation.

The track starts from Naqara. Take lunch and allow eight hours for the round trip.

WORTH A TRIP

WAIRIKI CATHOLIC MISSION

This faded beauty has bags of colonial charm, and the setting is equally beguiling – standing on a slope peering over the Somosomo Strait. Its interior has an impressive beam ceiling and beautiful stained glass, reputedly from France. In the presbytery there's a painting of a legendary battle in which a Catholic missionary helped Taveuni's warriors defeat their Tongan attackers. It's worth attending Mass on Sundays when the congregation lets rip with some impressive vocals. There are no pews here, though: the congregation sits on woven mats on the floor; take off your shoes. Some resorts offer Sunday trips.

The mission is about 20 minutes' walk south along the coast from Waiyevo. You can't miss it on the hill to the left. A dirt track behind leads up to a huge white cross. The views from here are superb.

Des Voeux Peak   MOUNTAIN
At 1195m, this is the island's second-highest mountain. On a clear day the views from the peak are fantastic: it's possible to see Lake Tagimaucia and the Lau Group. Birdwatching is great every day. Allow three to four hours to walk the 6km up, and at least two to return. It's a steep, arduous climb in the heat; start early. Take the inland track just before you reach Wairiki Catholic Mission (coming from Waiyevo), or arrange for a lift up and walk back.

⌂ Sleeping

The resorts listed here have fantastic restaurants that are open to nonguests. Otherwise, there are a few basic eateries in Waiyevo serving standard island fare.

First Light Inn   GUESTHOUSE $
(☑888 0339; firstlight@connect.com.fj; Waiyevo; r with fan/air-con $75/85; ❄☏) Convenient for the ferries, this place has kitchen facilities available and satellite TV. Try to ring before you turn up as it might not always be staffed.

Chottu's Motel   GUESTHOUSE $
(☑888 0233; Naqara; budget s/d/tr $50/60/70, deluxe s/d $65/80) Chottu's has two types of room: budget, which are basic and share

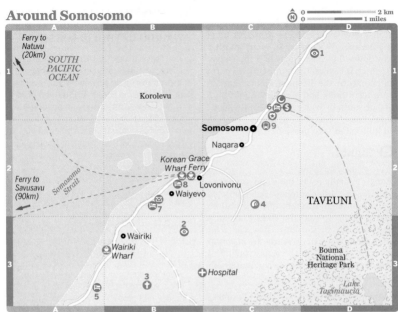

Around Somosomo

◎ Sights

1 Great Council of Chiefs' Meeting Hall	D1
2 International Dateline	B3
Shiri Laxmi Narayan Mandir	(see 9)
3 Wairiki Catholic Mission	B3
4 Waitavala Water Slide	C2

◎ Activities, Courses & Tours

Garden Island Dive Centre	(see 8)

◎ Sleeping

5 Aroha Resort	A3
6 Chottu's Motel	C1
7 First Light Inn	B2
8 Garden Island Resort	B2

◎ Transport

9 Pacific Transport	C2

cold-water bathrooms; and deluxe, which are still pretty bare bones but have small TVs, private facilities and kitchenettes.

Garden Island Resort HOTEL $$
(☑888 0286; www.gardenislandresort.com; r $245-490; ❄️📶🏊) The oldest resort on Taveuni (built 1971), this place has a plain block-like exterior, which opens to a surprisingly chic, streamlined interior. All rooms have balconies or patios; more expensive rooms have private spas. There's a stylish pool, good snorkelling off the rocky beach and a wonderful tree dripping with sleeping bats at the water's edge. It has an on-site dive shop.

Nakia Resort and Dive BUNGALOW $$$
(☑888 1111; www.nakiafiji.com; bungalow $470-850; 📶) 🍃 Four simple, dark, yet comfortable *bure* sit on a grassy hillside looking out to sea at this raved-about ecoresort. It uses alternative energy wherever possible, is into composting and recycling, and has a large organic garden growing fruit and veg for its restaurant (optional meal plans from $106). The dive shop is excellent and takes the same eco-bent.

Taveuni Dive Resort RESORT $$$
(☑891 1063; www.taveunidiveresort.com; bungalow from $400; 📶📶🏊) 🍃 If you're a diver, this spanking new resort may well prove impossible to beat. Built by the well-respected Taveuni Dive outfit, it's the closest digs on Taveuni to Rainbow Reef: from *bure* to bubbling takes just 15 minutes. There are eight luxury *bures* available, but don't be fooled by the opulence: this is an ecoresort, running on solar power and constructed out of sustainable materials.

Its super-sociable **Salty Fox Bar & Grill** (mains $14-40; ☺7am-10pm) is proving popular with guests and visitors, who congregate over burgers and beers to swap diving notes and tall tales.

Aroha Resort BUNGALOW $$$
(☑888 1882; www.arohataveuni.com; bungalow $300-420; ☢☣) This quiet spot (max 12 guests) offers simple but elegant varnished-wood rooms with louvred windows looking out over a black-sand beach. Each *bure* has its own airy kitchen and outdoor showers. The new **Kai Time restaurant** (mains $15 to $35) does fantastic meals. There's a small infinity pool, a barbecue, bikes and kayaks. Diving is through Taveuni Dive. It's a short walk to Wairiki.

ⓘ Information

Bank South Pacific (BSP; Naqara; ☺9.30am-4pm Mon, from 9am Tue-Fri) The only bank on the island will exchange currency and travellers cheques and has an ATM, which has been known to run out of money.

Hospital (☑888 0444; Waiyevo) For emergencies.

Police (☑888 0222; Waiyevo) The main police station is at the government compound behind the Garden Island Resort in Waiyevo. There is also a police station in Naqara.

Post Office (☑888 0019; Waiyevo; ☺8am-1pm & 2-4pm Mon-Fri) Among the shops beneath the First Light Inn.

Southern Taveuni

The southern part of the island isn't well-serviced by public transport but it's a beautiful place to visit. Check out the blowhole on the dramatic, windswept South Cape. As the water jumps up through the volcanic rock it creates rainbows in the air. Southern Taveuni is also home to Vuna Reef, which is perfect for snorkellers and novice divers. The main villages on southern Taveuni are Naqarawalu in the hills and, on the southern coast near Vuna Reef, Kanacea, Vuna and Navakawau.

🛏 Sleeping

★**Dolphin Bay Divers Retreat** RESORT $
(☑992 4001, 828 3001; www.dolphinbaydivers.com; Vanaira Bay, Vanua Levu; safari tent $35-85, bungalow $150-210; @) ✎ Tucked away in a jungly cove on Vanua Levu (but best accessed from Taveuni), this is a fantastically remote place with simple *bure* and permanent safari tents. Divers, aware of the excellent location and great reputation of the diving outfit here, make up most of the guests; there's also good snorkelling from the stunning beach. The food is delicious (optional meal plan $105).

The resort is only accessible by boat, and transfers must be arranged in advance. Transfers from Taveuni Wharf are $40, and $65 from Buca Bay; in a pinch, staff will also pick you up from Savusavu (extra costs apply).

The resort is in the process of moving to Viani Bay (about 10 minutes south); dive operations are set to commence there in April 2016, with accommodation to open in December; the present location will remain fully operational until then. It also plans on building 20 yacht moorings.

Vuna Lighthouse Lodge GUESTHOUSE $
(☑822 1963; dm/s/d $25/50/75) This simple blue wooden house is a few steps from a black volcanic rock beach. Run by a local

---

THE LEGEND OF THE TAGIMAUCIA

Fiji's emblem flower, the *tagimaucia (Medinilla waterhousei),* only grows above 600m in the mountains of Taveuni and in tiny, isolated areas of Vanua Levu. The unusual and very rare flower hangs off a vine and has white petals with a layer of leaf-like crimson red petals underneath. It blooms from October to December and its legend is a Fijian favourite.

There once lived a young girl with a wild spirit. One day her mother lost patience with the girl and beat her with a bundle of coconut leaves, saying she never wanted to see her face again. The distraught girl ran deep into the forest. She came upon a large vine-covered *ivi* (Polynesian chestnut) tree and climbed it. The higher she climbed, the more entangled she became in the vine and, unable to break free, she began to weep. As giant tears rolled down her face they turned to blood and, where they fell onto the vine, they became beautiful white-and-red *tagimaucia* flowers. Calmed by the sight of the flowers, the girl escaped the forest and, upon returning home, was relieved to find an equally calm mother.

family, there's a self-catering kitchen and laundry facilities. It's just a couple of minutes from Vuna Village and it's a great place to hang out and make friends with the locals. Good, home-cooked meals are available for between $7 and $12. Definitely call and book ahead.

Remote Resort
RESORT $$$

(📞979 3116; .www.fijiresort.com.fj; Vanua Levu; villas $1465-1740; ❄️🛜🏊) Private villas on the doorstep of the Rainbow Reef (it's only a 10-minute boat ride to the Great White Wall) make this luxury diving heaven. There's a spa, private plunge pools and as much or as little activity you could hope for on a beach like this. All meals are included and the views are beyond the imagination.

Paradise Taveuni
RESORT $$$

(📞888 0125; www.paradiseinfiji.com; bungalow/r incl all meals & transfers from $550/600; ❄️🛜🏊) Set on a former plantation, this aptly named oceanfront place has stunning sunset views and plenty of hammocks and loungers from which to enjoy them. The *bures* and *vales* (rooms) are luxury all the way; all have outdoor Jacuzzis and rock showers, while *bures* and larger *vales* boast large private sundecks, some with locally handmade day beds. There's incredible snorkelling right off the shore on the house reef, although there's not much of a beach. Activities include fishing, diving, guided walks and cave trips; there's also a spa overlooking the water.

Sau Bay Fiji Retreat
BUNGALOW $$$

(📞992 0046; www.saubay.com; Vanua Levu; cottage $480-850, luxury tent $995; ♿) This gorgeous, private place is in a sheltered bay on Vanua Levu (best accessed from Taveuni; contact them in advance for transfers) and offers easy access to exceptional diving spots, including the famous Great White Wall. There are four light wooden cottages (one with two bedrooms) with private decks and outdoor showers, and a highly covetable luxury safari 'glamping' tent.

There's no actual beach, but there is excellent hiking (it's surrounded by rainforest), good snorkelling at the house reef and you can take the kayaks to paddle in the mangroves up a small river. Food is fresh and local; compulsory meal plans $127.

Matei

A residential area on Taveuni's northern point, Matei is the main 'tourist hub', with a scarcely visible string of guesthouses, hotels and rental properties strewn along a long stretch of beachside road: sardonic sorts will snort at the 'densely populated area' street sign.

The airport is tiny and, if you're travelling light, you can step off the plane and wander down the street five minutes later. Only a couple of beaches are suitable for swimming and sunbathing, but this is a good and friendly place to base yourself for diving and other activities.

🛏️ Sleeping

⭐ Bibi's Hideaway
BUNGALOW $

(📞888 0443; paulinabibi@yahoo.com; bungalow $40-150; 🅿️🚼) A rambling, quiet 2-hectare hillside plot hides a selection of adorable, colourful *bure* in varying sizes among the fruit trees. Charming host Paulina will welcome you with a heaving fruit platter; once you've polished that off, you're welcome to pick as much as you can gorge. There are fantastic self-catering facilities here and plenty of room for exploring. A brilliant choice, especially for families.

Tovu Tovu Resort
BUNGALOW $

(📞888 0560; www.tovutovu.com; bungalow from $95; 🛜) This friendly place has a selection of ageing *bure* with wooden verandahs, hot-water bathrooms and fans: some have kitchenettes. It's built on a subdivided copra estate, and owned by the Petersen family, which once ran the plantation. The resort is a 20-minute walk southeast of Matei airport, past the Sun City Supermarket. The attached **Vunibokoi Restaurant** (mains $15 to $20) does superb Fijian food.

Maravu Lodge
HOSTEL $

(📞888 0555; www.maravulodge.com/; dm $25-35, d $90, bungalow $120-150, villa $180; 🛜🏊) This is a little slice of backpacker heaven, with fun, frivolity and lots (and lots) of kava. Accommodation is clean and comfy, but what draws the crowds are the convivial ambiance, huge home-cooked meals and the majestic view over offshore islands. There's a good bar here; if you can tear yourself away from it, the awesome staff can organise heaps of activities and tours.

Beverly's Campground
CAMPGROUND $

(📞888 0684, 907 4933; www.beverlys campground.geewhiz.me; sites per person/permanent tent/dm/r $15/17/20/50) This is one of those magical spots where everybody makes friends easily and camping isn't a

Matei

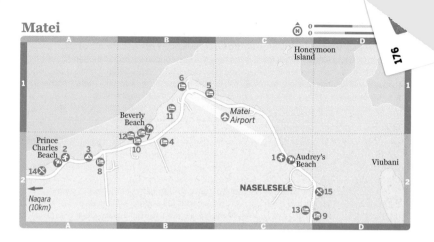

Honeymoon Island

Beverly Beach

Matei Airport

Prince Charles Beach

Audrey's Beach

Viubani

NASELESELE

Naqara (10km)

chore. The small site sits on a white-sand beach beneath huge rustling trees: basic facilities include flush toilets, showers and a sheltered area for cooking and dining.

Karin's Garden GUESTHOUSE $$
(☑888 0511; www.karinsgardenfiji.com; cottage $310) This wooden, two-bedroom cottage is in the grounds of the owner's house. It has views out towards the reef and beach (which you can access from the property); rooms are big and cosy and, though there's a kitchen, the affable owners will cook delicious meals for guests with enough notice.

Makaira by the Sea BUNGALOW $$
(☑888 0680; fijibeachfrontatmakaira.com; bungalow $415-530; ☎) Makaira has three *bures*, two of which have private plunge pools. All have kitchenettes but there's also a small cafe where you can get breakfast and dinner. The family that runs the resort operates Makaira Sports Fishing; alternatively, try your luck on a fishing kayak trip ($110 per day). Guests are also invited to take part in their coral gardening program to help regenerate damaged reef.

Taveuni Palms VILLA $$$
(☑888 0032; www.taveunipalms.com; d villas all inclusive except alcohol $3190-5320; ❄☎❄🐾) Breathtakingly beautiful and *very* private, Taveuni Palms boasts three villas, each with its own beach, pool and seven-strong staff, including a personal chef and nanny. The cook will prepare a five-course meal for you every night, but the villas also have kitchens. All have huge decks, ridiculous views and incredible entertainment cen-

tres with big TVs, DVD players and loaded iPods. Activities include kayaking, diving, snorkelling and cooking lessons. All fruit and veggies are organically grown on the sprawling, manicured property.

Coconut Grove Beachfront Cottages BUNGALOW $$$
(☑888 0328; www.coconutgrovefiji.com; bungalow $390-565; ☎) These three tasteful, bright cottages enjoy beautiful beach views and tranquility by the truckload. All are breezy, tasteful and hard to leave, even

LAVENA COASTAL WALK

The 5km Lavena Coastal Walk follows the forest edge along stunning white-sand Lavena beach, a volcanic black-sand beach and past peaceful villages before climbing up through a landscape straight out of *Jurassic Park* to a gushing waterfall. There's some good snorkelling and kayaking here and Lavena Point is fine for swimming.

The path is well maintained and clearly marked. About halfway along the trek, watch for the *vatuni'epa*, bizarre rock pedestals formed by the erosion of the coral base along the coast, which locals aptly refer to as 'mushrooms'. Past these the path seems to disappear at Naba settlement: follow the path onto the beach, then follow the shore past the *bure* (wood-and-straw hut) and cross the stream to where the path reappears. Further ahead is a suspension bridge and eventually the trail takes you up the ancient valley of Wainibau Creek.

To reach the falls at the end of the trail, you have to clamber over rocks and swim a short distance through two deep pools. Two cascades fall at different angles into a deep pool with sheer walls. The hardy can climb up the rocks to the left-hand side and jump into the deep pool. If you're visiting in the rainy season, the rocks near the falls can be slippery, if not flooded; it can be difficult and dangerous to reach the falls at this time. Ask at Lavena Lodge for current conditions. At any time of year (even if it hasn't been raining), violent flash floods can occur; stay to the left of the pool, where you can make an easier getaway.

The walk is managed through Lavena Lodge (p178). Entrance is $20. You can also take a guided kayak journey and coastal walk for $40 (including lunch) or arrange to take a boat one way and walk back ($220 for the whole boat). Usually you can order a meal for when you return to the lodge, but it's a good idea to bring along some food – definitely bring water.

Lavena village is about 15 minutes' drive past Bouma and 35 minutes from Matei. However, by local bus it takes about one hour from Matei or just under two from Waiyevo. Expect to pay about $75 for a taxi to/from Matei.

for the tempting golden-sand beach just footsteps away. The attached restaurant (mains $12.50 to $39) is possibly the best on the island. The owners can arrange diving, snorkelling, sightseeing and bird-watching trips. No children under 12.

Dolphin Bay Divers Matei   BUNGALOW $$$
(www.dolphinbaydivers.com/taveuni.html; bungalow $390, return diving transfers per day $50; 🛜) Owned by the same fabulous folk that run Dolphin Bay Divers Resort on Vanua Levu, the cute, self-contained Yanuyanu *bure* lets guests take advantage of the group's renowned diving trips and facilities, while enjoying accommodation in a less-roughing-it locale. It's a nice, private spot, even if you're not a diver. A chef and maid can also be arranged.

Taveuni Island Resort & Spa   RESORT $$$
(☑888 0441; www.taveuniislandresort.com; bungalow $1760-1960, villa $4230; 🛜🌊) This extravagant jaw-dropper has 12 luxury *bure* with polished wood walls, floor-to-ceiling windows, outdoor rock showers and complete privacy, all balanced on a hilltop. The private villa has a plunge pool and private staff. Meals are gourmet and included in the price. Children under 15 aren't allowed.

Tides Reach Resort   RESORT $$$
(☑888 2080; www.tidesreachresort.com; villa incl meals $2325-3390; 🅿✳🛜🌊) This new upscale resort is intimate (there are just four villas) and very modern; minimalism is the go here. But who needs busy furnishings with ocean views like those on offer from the private teak decks here? The open-air restaurant dishes up local, seasonal cuisine; it has a weekly *lovo* and *meke*. Each guest has their own private staff.

Taveuni Rental Properties   HOLIDAY RENTAL $$$
(☑888 0522; www.fiji-rental-accommodations.com; houses from US$280) This local group has six holiday homes available for rent; all have a full kitchen, polished wood floors, great outside deck areas, plenty of lush garden as well as beach access. Rates, which vary wildly depending on location and length of stay, include a housekeeper.

✗ Eating

If you're here on a Wednesday, try the *lovo* (feast cooked in a pit oven) or buffet (complete with entertainment) at Naselesele village; your accommodation can arrange this for you. Profits go to the local school.

Really good rotis ($1.50) can be had at Matei airport.

Sun City Supermarket　　　GROCERY $
(Matei; ⊙7.30am-6pm Mon-Sat, 8am-11am Sun) Sells a range of groceries (including disposable nappies), and accepts credit cards. It has a public phone and a petrol pump (no petrol on Sundays). There's a bottle shop next door.

★ Restaurant Tramonto　　　WESTERN $$
(✆888 2224; pizza from $25, meals $12-25; ⊙lunch & dinner) If you're in the market for a pizza the size of a small child, Tramonto won't disappoint – they're huge, delicious and mightily topped. The gasp-inducing sunset views are equally scrumptious; get there early to secure a table. It also does superb seafood. Book in advance for the roasts on Sunday and buffets on Wednesday.

Vunibokoi Restaurant　　　FIJIAN $$
(✆888 0560; www.tovutovu.com; dinner mains $15-20; ⊙breakfast, lunch & dinner) This down-home restaurant serves incredibly good, wholesome meals with a strong emphasis on Fijian flavours: think crabs, coconut cream and chillis. It's attached to the Tovu Tovu Resort, but everyone is welcome. Come hungry for the Friday buffet (and live tunes) or special Sunday roast.

Coconut Grove Restaurant　INTERNATIONAL $$$
(✆888 0328; www.coconutgrovefiji.com; lunch $10-30, dinner $22-50; ⊙breakfast, lunch & dinner) Enjoy the sea views from the deck of this popular restaurant. The menu includes fresh vegetarian dishes, homemade pasta, soups, salads and fish. You can just turn up for breakfast or lunch, but you'll have to let them know you're coming for dinner. If you're lucky, you'll be serenaded by local lads and their ukeleles.

Eastern Taveuni

The local landowners of beautiful eastern Taveuni have rejected logging in favour of ecotourism, under the banner of the Bouma Environmental Tourism Project.

Bouma National Heritage Park

This national park (✆867 7311; www.bouma fiji.com) protects over 80% of Taveuni's total area, covering about 150 sq km of rainforest and coastal forest.

⊙ Sights & Activities

Tavoro Waterfalls　　　WATERFALL
(✆820 4709; adult/child $20/10; ⊙visitors centre 9am-4pm) Framed by thick, ridiculously green jungle, these three waterfalls (also known as the Bouma Falls) epitomise the 'Garden Island' epithet Taveuni is famous for. The first waterfall (24m) has a change area, picnic tables and barbecues; it's an easy stroll from the visitors centre. It's a 30-minute climb (and river-rock hop) to the second one; the third involves a hike along an oft-muddy forest path for another 20 minutes. Rocks and paths leading to the last two falls can get very slippery; they can be cut off during wet season.

All waterfalls have natural swimming pools; at the third – if you bring a snorkel – you'll see hundreds of prawns.

You must sign in (and pay) at the visitors' centre before heading off. Do *not* go alone: this is a very isolated spot.

Vidawa Rainforest Trail　　　WALKING
(✆820 4709; $60) If you're a keen, fit walker, try this full-day, guided trek led by shamans. Beginning at Vidawa village, it passes through ancient, fortified village sites and follows trails into the rainforest where you'll see lots of birdlife and learn about medicinal plants; it ends at the Tavoro Waterfalls. Tours (eight people max) include guides, lunch, afternoon tea and park admission fee. Reservations are essential; book through the Tavoro Waterfalls visitors centre (p177) or your accommodation.

Waitabu Marine Park　　　MARINE PARK
(✆820 1999, 888 0451; www.waitabu.org; campground per person with own tent $12, incl hire tent $17) This area has decent snorkelling and a gorgeous white-sand beach. It is only possible to visit with a guide. Waitabu village has set up a half-day tour ($60 per person) that includes a guide, snorkelling, a *bilibili* (lashed bamboo raft) ride, and afternoon tea. There's also a Backpackers' Tour ($40 per person) with guided snorkelling. You must book in advance; trips depend on daily tides. You can arrange to sleep at ᵗʰᵉ

THE CURSE OF THE AMERICAN IGUANA

It's thought that the first *iguana iguana* (usually called the common/green iguana but known as the American iguana in Fiji) arrived in Fiji with a foreign national on Qamea in 2000, who set it free. Twelve years later the species has spread to Laucala, Matagi, Taveuni, Viti Levu and Vanua Levu. The incredibly destructive animal can grow up to 2m in length, weighs up to 15kg and has no natural predators in Fiji. Besides regularly scaring the bejesus out of islanders, the iguanas eat *dalo* (taro), kava and other staples, and risk spreading disease to the country's three native and endangered iguana species.

Iguanas generally avoid people, but when threatened they can become vicious. People have been bitten by the lizards and in these cases the risk of salmonella infection is very high. There are also concerns that iguanas could infect the crops they frequent.

Some islanders have started eating the iguanas, though the local government has warned against this: the salmonella they carry may cause food poisoning. Fines have been set for the possession of the animals or their eggs (up to $50,000) and resorts that keep them as pets can be fined up to $250,000; moving American iguanas from one island to another can get you 15 years in prison.

The iguana remains a huge threat to Fiji. The Biosecurity Authority of Fiji runs eradication programs – sometimes involving the country's military and police forces – though nary a dent has been made in the lizards' apparent plan for world (or at least Fijian) domination. If you see one, contact the BAF immediately on ☑ 331 215.

campground (own/hired tent $15/20); contact them for homestay options.

🛏 Sleeping & Eating

Lavena Lodge GUESTHOUSE $
(☑ 877 9825; camping per person $25) Run by friendly, informative staff, the lodge was destroyed by Cyclone Winston in 2016. By the time you're reading this, it may have been rebuilt; contact them for updates. Otherwise, those with tents are welcome to camp on the beach.

Offshore Islands

Qamea, Matagi and Laucala are clustered just east of Thurston Point, across the Tasman Strait from northeastern Taveuni. All three islands have lovely, white-sand beaches.

Qamea

The closest of the three islands to Taveuni is Qamea (34 sq km), only 2.5km east of Thurston Point. Its coastline is riddled with deep bays and lined with white-sand beaches; the interior is fertile and rich in bird life. The island is also notable for the *lairo* (annual migration of land crabs). For a few days from late November to early December, at the start of their breeding season, masses of crabs move from the mudflats toward the sea.

🛏 Sleeping

★ **Maqai Resort** HOSTEL $
(☑ 990 7073; www.maqai.com; dm/bungalow from $80/185; @) A private white-sand beach, excellent snorkelling, epic waves and nightly entertainment: believe it or not, this is a backpackers. Accommodation is in sturdy, clean safari tents and shared *bures:* meals (compulsory meal plan $89) are taken in a common area with sand floors, couches and a pool table. There's a boat to take you out to the breaks as well as snorkelling, village visits and hiking.

Nadilo Bay Resort RESORT $$
(☑ 820 8242; www.nadilobaysustainableresort.com; d bungalow $175-195; ☎) ⌀ This surf resort bills itself as sustainable, and it really does walk the walk. Power is via water turbine, all fruits and veggies are from its garden, and local fishermen provide their daily catches for the menu. *Bures* are super-traditional, and cut from the island's rainforest: they have not only thatched roofs, but the walls are thatched as well.

The bay has top-notch right- and left-hand surf breaks; the resort rents long and short boards.

Kids are welcome and are encouraged to play with local village children.

Qamea Resort & Spa RESORT $$$
(☑ 888 0220; www.qamea.com; bungalow $1240-2070; ❄☎❄) These magnificently thatched

bures lie on a long stretch of beautiful white-sand beach. Some have plunge pools, spa baths or rock showers. Rates include meals and transfers to and from Taveuni; children under 16 are not accepted unless you book the entire resort. There's excellent snorkelling just offshore, plus all manners of watersports, walks and village visits.

Matagi

Tiny, horseshoe-shaped Matagi (1 sq km), formed by a submerged volcanic crater, is 10km off Taveuni's coast and just north of Qamea. Its steep rainforest sides rise to 130m. The bay faces north to open sea and there is a fringing reef on the southwest side of the island.

Matangi Island Resort   RESORT **$$$**
(☏888 0260; www.matangiisland.com; bungalow $995-1610; 🛜⛴) The light-soaked *bures* here are huge, vaulted-ceilinged affairs with massive beds and private verandahs; each one is surrounded by a neat tropical garden. It's romance run amok in the 'treehouse', perched 5m up in the tree canopy with wraparound decks, top views, outdoor Jacuzzis, lanterns aplenty and day beds. The pretty restaurant looks over Qamea and out to the ocean.

There are dozens of dive spots within 10 to 30 minutes of here. The resort is not suitable for children under 12.

Laucala

Just 500m east across the strait from Qamea, 30-sq-km Laucala was once owned by the estate of the late US millionaire Malcolm Forbes. It's now owned by Red Bull billionaire Dietrich Mateschitz, who has turned it into his own resort, **Laucala Island** (www.laucala.com; villas from US$5520), complete with an 18-hole championship-standard golf course and private international airport.

Kadavu, Lau & Moala Groups

POP 20,850

Best Places to Stay

➡ Oneta Resort (p185)

➡ Matava Resort (p184)

➡ Papageno Eco-Resort (p185)

➡ Koro Makawa (p186)

➡ Mai Dive Astrolabe Reef Resort (p186)

Best Dive Sites

➡ Naiqoro Passage (p183)

➡ Manta Reef (p182)

➡ Eagle Rock (p183)

➡ Yellow Wall (p182)

➡ Broken Stone (p183)

➡ Pacific Voyager (p182)

Why Go

This is where you wish you were right now. Remote and authentic yet easily accessed from Viti Levu and home to comfortable, ecofriendly resorts, Kadavu blends Fiji's best assets. As your plane lands on a tiny airstrip surrounded by luminescent sea, volcanic peaks and intense forest, you'll feel like an adventurer. Your flight will be followed by a boat ride to your resort past prehistoric-looking coves, and when you reach your destination you can grab your snorkel or dive gear to get below the waves and explore the incredible Great Astrolabe Reef – the world's fourth-largest barrier reef.

Meanwhile, the Lau and Moala Groups are for those who have the time and endurance to seek out even more pristine environments: think turquoise waters, hardly touched jungle and traditional villages. Only the truly dedicated need apply – there are few facilities for travellers, and getting there is a logistical exercise in itself.

When to Go

Kadavu

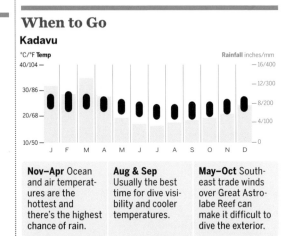

Nov–Apr Ocean and air temperatures are the hottest and there's the highest chance of rain.

Aug & Sep Usually the best time for dive visibility and cooler temperatures.

May–Oct Southeast trade winds over Great Astrolabe Reef can make it difficult to dive the exterior.

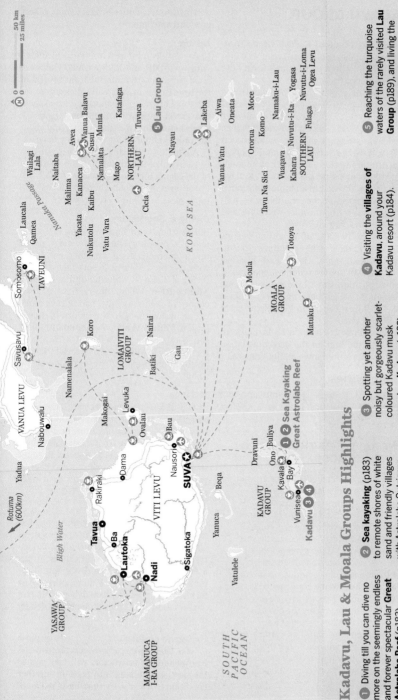

Kadavu, Lau & Moala Groups Highlights

① Diving till you can dive no more on the seemingly endless and forever spectacular **Great Astrolabe Reef** (p183).

② **Sea kayaking** (p183) to remote shores of white sand and friendly villages with Astrolabe Outrigger Adventures.

③ Spotting yet another noisy but gorgeously scarlet-coloured Kadavu musk parrot on **Kadavu** (p183).

④ Visiting the **villages of Kadavu**, around your Kadavu resort (p184).

⑤ Reaching the turquoise waters of the rarely visited **Lau Group** (p189), and living the slow village life.

KADAVU GROUP

Sitting sleepily 100km south of Viti Levu, the ruggedly beautiful Kadavu Group (pronounced 'Kandavu') offers a slice of wild and untamed Fiji. There is one small town here and next to no roads.

Snaking its way around the islands, the Great Astrolabe Reef is justifiably renowned in diving circles. People come from all over the world to sample its underwater delights. Handsome stretches of long, sandy beach and sheltered coves ring the islands' perimeters. In the interior you'll find all manner of bird life, including the colourful Kadavu musk parrot, thriving in an impossibly green rainforest that's ripe for scrambling up hillsides, splashing about under waterfalls and kayaking through mangroves.

The group is made up of several islands including Kadavu (the country's fourth-largest island), Ono, Galoa and Yaukuve Levu. Kadavu is irregular in shape and is almost split into three by deep bays along its length. At its southern tip sits its highest peak, the impressive 838m-high Nabukelevu (Mt Washington).

Most visitors will stay on Kadavu, where you'll find the bulk of the accommodation and the group's only town, petite Vunisea.

🏃 Activities

The Kadavu Group's rich landscape and underwater seascapes make it a perfect destination for nature lovers, divers, hikers and birdwatchers.

Hiking

Kadavu's hilly rainforest interior is sprinkled with waterfalls and hiking trails. There are good treks into the interior from several of the resorts. Resort staff will act as guides for the tougher treks. For shorter journeys you can set off on your own, but be sure to ask locals beforehand if a track is safe and about the proper etiquette for visiting a village.

A popular walk offered by most resorts is to Naikorokoro Waterfall. On the southeast of the island, the two gorgeous waterfalls are linked by a deep pool. There are few swimming spots in Fiji that are so perfect.

Diving & Snorkelling

Buliya island, just north of Ono, is a great manta snorkelling site, where you're pretty much guaranteed an amazing encounter with the rays. Matava Resort takes people diving at a site off Kadavu accurately called **Manta Reef**, where divers have a good chance of seeing massive manta rays cruising alongside the reef. Novice divers should head to **Yellow Wall**, with abundant yellow soft corals among a series of arches, and the **Pacific Voyager**, 61m wrecked tanker on the more-protected western side of the island.

Mai Dive DIVING
(☑603 0842; http://maidive.com) Located at Mai Dive Astrolabe Reef Resort, this extremely professional place is the best-located dive centre for the Great Astrolabe Reef. Groups are small, the boat is clean, fast and sheltered, and the equipment is excellent. A two-tank dive/PADI Open Water Course including equipment costs $218/710.

Mad Fish Dive Centre DIVING
(☑333 6222; http://matava.com) 🐟 At the Matava Resort, this gem of a centre offers dives all over the reef system, including fantastic manta ray, cave and shark dives. It has a fleet of big comfortable dive boats. Two-tank dives/PADI Open Water Courses cost $245/850. The centre strongly supports reef conservation and environmentally friendly diving practices.

Papageno Eco-Resort DIVING
(☑603 0466; www.papagenoresortfiji.com) 🐟 Knowledgeable instructors will take you to the best sites, taking into account weather conditions. It's also within easy reach of

---

THE BATTLE OF THE SHARK & OCTOPUS GODS

Dakuwaqa, the Shark God, once cruised the Fiji islands challenging other reef guardians. On hearing rumours of a rival monster in Kadavu waters, he sped down to the island to prove his superior strength. Adopting his usual battle strategy, he charged at the giant octopus with his mouth wide open and sharp teeth prepared. The octopus, however, anchored itself to the coral reef and swiftly clasped the shark in a death lock. In return for mercy the octopus demanded that the people of Kadavu be forever protected from shark attack. In Kadavu the people now fish without fear and regard the shark as their protector. Most won't eat shark or octopus out of respect for their gods.

the tanker wreck *Pacific Voyager*. A two-tank dive/PADI Open Water Course costs $220/800 including equipment. It uses fixed moorings for its dives and encourages tourists to help protect the reefs.

Dive Kadavu   DIVING
(☑ 368 3502; www.divekadavu.com) A favourite haunt is Namalata Reefs, which is about 5km off the west coast of the island and more sheltered from the prevailing winds than the Great Astrolabe Reef. Expect to pay $190/700 for a two-tank dive/PADI Open Water Course including equipment.

Tiliva   DIVING
(☑ 747 6976; www.tilivaresortfiji.com) New dive shop at the recently reopened Tiliva Resort. Very close to the Naiqoro Passage on the Great Astrolabe Reef, and the diving on the eastern side of Ono island. Prices start at $210/175 for a two-tank dive/PADI discover scuba course.

Fishing

The Great Astrolabe Reef is a great location for blue-water sport and big game fishing. Dogtail tuna, giant trevally and red bass are regulars on the line and many of Kadavu's resorts (Ono's Oneta Resort and Kadavu's Matava Resort in particular) will take you out beyond the reef for some serious fishing action. You may be able to take some of your catch home for dinner, too.

Surfing

The best surfing in Kadavu is found around Cape Washington, at the southernmost end of Kadavu. It gets plenty of swell activity year-round, including the excellent **King Kong Lefts**, off Nagigia island. **Vesi Passage**, near Matava Resort, also has powerful surf, but the waves often get blown out. Sadly, there is currently no organised surfing on Kadavu, but that shouldn't deter the most dedicated wave chasers.

Sea Kayaking

Organised kayaking trips take place from May to September and all of the resorts have two-person ocean kayaks free or for hire.

Astrolabe Reef Outrigger Adventures   KAYAKING
(☑ 744 1144, 713 6726; http://paddlefiji.com/) Fiji's original canoes were outriggers, so you're following in a fine tradition by exploring Kadavu in their modern descendants. This

THE GREAT ASTROLABE REEF

The famous Great Astrolabe Reef, which is a major pull for most visitors to Kadavu and is the fourth-largest barrier reef in the world, hugs the eastern side of the group. It is bisected by the **Naiqoro Passage**, home to brilliantly coloured soft and hard corals, a fantastic assortment of tunnels, caverns and canyons, and a variety of marine life, including plenty of reef sharks and graceful manta rays. Particularly recommended dive sites are **Eagle Rock**, a group of rock pinnacles with abundant hard corals and masses of fishlife including pelagics; and **Broken Stone**, which is a beautiful underwater landscape with a maze of swim-throughs, caverns and tunnels. The weather often dictates which sites are suitable to dive, and visibility can range from 15m to 70m. Most of the resorts will also take snorkellers out to the reef.

great operation has trips for novice and experienced paddlers alike. You can arrange multiday adventures or simple day trips from your resort – itineraries are planned to allow lunch on deserted beaches and paddling home with the wind behind you.

Trips are organised from the owner's base a short boat trip away from the Mai Dive resort.

Tamarillo Sea Kayaking   KAYAKING
(☑ 761 6140; www.tamarillo.co.nz/fiji) These interesting and well-organised jaunts run five to seven days. All tours include meals and accommodation (at one of the Kadavu resorts) as well as a village stay. It also offers day and overnight trips. There's a two-person minimum.

Birdwatching

The lush rainforests, especially on Kadavu's eastern side, are home to a wide variety of bird life, including the islands' four endemic species: the Kadavu honeyeater, Kadavu fantail, velvet fruit dove and the colourful Kadavu musk parrot (also known as the Kadavu shining parrot). Most of the resorts will be able to arrange a guide, but you'll see many species fluttering around the resorts as well.

Kadavu Group

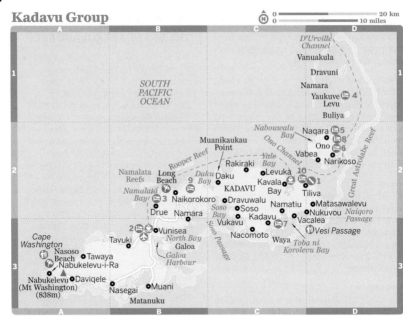

Kadavu Group

🛏 Sleeping

Take into account the time and cost of transfers when choosing your accommodation. In Kadavu, most of the places to stay are a fair way from the airport, and the only way to get there is by boat. Most places have a three-night minimum and offer package rates from their websites that are more economical than per night rates. Prices listed include boat transfers.

The Kadavu resorts are all pretty much off-grid: if you're wondering where your fresh food and clean water comes from, staff are usually keen to show off their organic gardens and mini-farms, solar arrays and pumping stations that are part of the self-sufficient lifestyle the islands demand.

🛏 Kadavu

Cooksley's Homestay GUESTHOUSE $
(📞 782 2505, 360 7970; osbornemck@yahoo.com; Vunisea; self-catering/full board $50/80, tent pitch $10) A minute's walk away from both Kadavu airstrip and the beach, this homely guesthouse is a basic but highly welcoming place from which to explore Kadavu if you're looking more for regular island life than a dive resort. Rooms are partitioned by simple bamboo and woven palm walls. If you're self-catering, bring extra supplies from Suva.

The hosts are extremely congenial – Mere will cook up dinner while David talks through his extensive vinyl LP collection, and you can play with the friendly dogs.

⭐ **Matava Resort** RESORT $$
(📞 333 6222; www.matava.com; d per person incl meals & transfers from $320; 📶) 🍃 Matava is a social, active and impeccably run place. An-

ything you want to do, from diving to sport-fishing, birding or hiking, the team here can set you up. Meanwhile, stay in spacious and clean hard-wood *bure* (wood-and-straw hut) with heaps of windows to maximise the views (there are both garden and hillside options) and good solid beds.

The resort runs on solar power, has a large organic garden and employs strict recycling policies. Fantastic meals, using vegetables and herbs from the organic garden, are eaten communally in the big restaurant-bar *bure,* which is beautifully lit by lanterns in the evening. There's no beach to speak of, but there are suitable spots a short kayak away and there is plenty of space to lounge on ample decks or in the grassy grounds. A reef links Matava to Waya, a picturesque offshore island, which makes for a great snorkelling or kayaking trip – or it's a short walk to the village and its magnificent waterfall where local kids try to impress with their high-diving skills.

Papageno Eco-Resort RESORT $$

(✆ 603 0466; www.papagenoresortfiji.com; garden room s/d $232/292, bungalow incl meals s/d $339/515; ☎ ⚓) *Low-key Papageno is the stuff of island fantasies. Large, dark-wood *bure,* with decks looking out to sea, are spread sparingly around manicured tropical gardens. Towards the back of the resort are four connected 'garden rooms', which share a single verandah, are surrounded by greenery and overlook a small stream. All rooms are decked out with local artwork and have bigger-than-average bathrooms.

The welcoming central lodge has a small bar, some comfy chairs and an excellent selection of books. The resort prides itself on its eco-credentials, using solar and micro-hydro energy to complement its generator, composting organic waste on site, and investing heavily in environmental and local community development projects. The food is excellent and plentiful. Sea kayaking and hiking are all free. Snorkelling, fishing and surfing are extra, along with excursions from the dive shop. There are family rooms here and a babysitting service is available.

Dive Kadavu RESORT $$

(✆ 368 3502; www.divekadavu.com; bungalow per person incl meals & transfers s/d/tr/q $340/520/700/850; ☎ ⚓) This resort has *bure* with nearly all the walls covered in louvres so you can open them up for plenty of ventilation. They all have comfortable beds,

verandahs, hot water and tidy bathrooms, but the brighter choices are the smaller units at the southern end. It boasts an excellent sheltered beach where the snorkelling and swimming is wonderful.

There's a dive shop, focusing on the sheltered northwestern side of the island, which is often overshadowed by the Great Astrolabe Reef. There are also myriad other activities available from massage to village tours, and bird nerds will happily spot most endemic species at the resort itself. There's also a social, oceanfront bar that hosts regular *lovo* (a feast cooked in a pit oven), barbecue and curry nights.

Tiliva Resort RESORT $$

(✆ 333 7127; www.tilivaresortfiji.com; incl meals s $405, d $535-605; ☎) *There are six *bure* at the recently re-opened Tiliva. The gregarious new owners have taken an idiosyncratic approach to decoration, filling the place with a lifetime's worth of collecting: expect Italian suits of armour in the honeymoon suite and every wall covered with art (and yes, you will be advised that the Picasso and Chagalle paintings are real).

Plenty of activities that revolve around the village as well as the dive shop are on offer. The place prides itself on its fine cuisine – the kitchen considers it a point of honour to serve up the national dish of any guest, no matter their country.

Ono

★ Oneta Resort RESORT $$

(✆ 603 0778; www.onetafiji.com; d per person incl meals from $300; ☎) *The architecturally lovely thatched *bure* with hard-wood floors, woven walls and louvred, netted windows are among this region's classiest accommodation. Mattresses have been imported from Italy and beds are draped with gauzy white mosquito nets and topped with Southeast Asian embroidered linens. All units from the private honeymoon suite to the stylish six-bed dorm complex have giant open-to-sky bamboo showers.

All this wonderfulness sits in an artfully landscaped garden complete with fruit trees and organic vegies, and there's a lush white-sand beach out front. This place is mostly meant to be a fishing lodge but with diving (at nearby Mai Dive) and so many other activities are on offer, anyone would be happy here.

KADAVU, LAU & MOALA GROUPS KADAVU GROUP

★**Mai Dive Astrolabe
Reef Resort** RESORT $$
(☑ 603 0842; www.maidive.com; r incl meals from $390; ☎) ✈ Pretty tongue-and-groove-built bungalows line the beach at this very tidy, streamlined resort (just a few minutes' boat ride from the fantabulous Great Astrolabe Reef) run by an Australian-Fijian family. All *bure* have polished timber floors and wooden verandahs and are right by the water; they are simple but stylish and have an incredibly happy feel to them.

Some units have showers that are open to the elements so you can wash under the stars. Underfoot you'll find either white sand or Japanese grass, and frangipani trees perfume the air with tropical bliss. The dive centre here has become one of the island's most respected. There's plenty to do for nondivers, but honestly you'd be better off elsewhere; serious divers, however, should make this their first choice. There's a one-week minimum stay.

Koro Makawa HOLIDAY RENTAL $$$
(☑ 603 0782; www.koromakawa.com.fj; d per night all inclusive US$500; ☎ 🏠) This lavish two-bedroom pad with a wraparound deck, plunge pool and private sea views really offers a slice of luxury island living. If you're not content with enjoying the good life on your private white-sand beach, your private staff can arrange secluded beach picnics and nature walks among other things. All nonmotorised activities are included.

You can snorkel with manta rays five minutes away or head underwater through their dive shop (which offers PADI open-water certification). The name means old village – the owners found the remains of a long-abandoned defensive settlement near the site when they were building the property.

🏘 Yaukuve Levu

This beautiful, reef-fringed volcanic island may one day be the site of a luxury resort – if it doesn't hit any more snags.

Kokomo Yaukuve Island RESORT $$$
(☑ 327 0011; www.yakuve.com; ☎) The much-delayed opening of this glamorous resort has been something of a saga, but we're assured that its doors will finally open in 2016. Guests will arrive by seaplane, and can expect 21 luxurious *bures* and five private villas (all with personal infinity pools),

a spa, gym, restaurants and a dive shop. The resort occupies the whole of the uninhabited island.

Dollops of well-finished contemporary Fijian design and attention to detail means that Kokom Yakuve Island is bidding to be one of Fiji's most exclusive resorts.

🍴 Eating

The airport has a kiosk selling snacks, drinks and rotis. There are small grocery stores in Vunisea and Kavala Bay, and a regular weekday market in Vunisea. Most of the resorts are very remote, so even if all your meals are provided it may be an idea to take along snacks.

ℹ Information

Many resorts offer wi-fi but service is very slow. Some resorts, especially the more upmarket ones, accept credit cards, but check before you fly out. You can't change foreign currency in Vunisea and there's no ATM, so bring however much money you'll need.

The **Vunisea post and telephone office** (☺ 8am-3pm Mon-Fri) is on top of the hill, a short walk from the airstrip. It also sells some groceries, clothes and stationery. Kavala Bay, at the northeastern end of the island, also has a post office.

Emergency & Medical Services

Hospital (☑ 333 6008) Opened in 1996 with the help of Australian aid, Vunisea's hospital only has limited services. For more serious ailments you're better off heading back to Viti Levu. Divers suffering from the bends can be transferred to the Fiji Recompression Chamber Facility in Suva by Medivac helicopter service.
Police (☑ 333 6007)

ℹ Getting There & Away

AIR

Fiji Airways (☑ 672 0888; www.fijiairways.com) has flights to Kadavu from Nadi (from $195 one way, 45 minutes) every day except Sunday and Suva ($240 one way, 40 minutes). Prices can vary wildly, so book as far ahead as possible, but check timetables and confirm flights the day before departure as they are often late or cancelled.

Book your accommodation and transfers in advance, otherwise you could be stranded in Vunisea.

BOAT

Goundar Shipping (☑ 330 1035; http://goundarshipping.com) runs the clean and

KADAVU CONNECTIONS

The ferry trip to Kadavu from Suva can be rough, but the MV *Lomaiviti Princess,* run by Goundar Shipping, is relatively comfortable and it can be more reliable than flying. Flights are sometimes cancelled for the slightest reasons and travellers can find themselves stuck in paradise a few days longer than they anticipated. If you end up stranded at the airport try booking into Cookley's Homestay (p184) – just a minute's walk from the airstrip, or Dive Kadavu (p185), the closest resort, which sometimes offers special 'cancelled flight' rates (prices are negotiable).

The boats used by budget resorts for transfers to/from the airstrip often don't have covers, life jackets or radios. The islands often fall prey to rough weather and the southeast coast in particular is often buffeted by wind and rain. Be prepared for a sometimes bumpy ride. It's a good idea to dress with the expectation that you'll get wet – not just from spray, but you'll almost certainly have to wade ashore at least a short way when you arrive at the resort. Packing your clothes in plastic bags inside your luggage isn't a bad idea. If all this sounds concerning, rest assured that the transfer is also very scenic, and may be one of the most beautiful boat trips you take in Fiji.

reliable MV *Lomaiviti Princess,* which departs Suva every Wednesday at 10pm and arrives at Vunisea eight or nine hours later (economy seat/1st-class seat/cabin $50/$70/$170); it departs Kadavu Thursday afternoon and arrives in Suva that night connecting onwards to Vanua Levu and Taveuni. Venu Shipping (p232) operates the more basic MV *Sinu-i-Wasa* to Suva from $55 per person one way on Tuesday nights.

❶ Getting Around

Kadavu's few roads are restricted to the Vunisea area, except for one rough, unsealed road to Nabukelevu-i-Ra around the southern end of Kadavu. Small boats are the island group's principal mode of transport. Each resort has its own boat and will pick up guests from Vunisea airstrip, but make sure you make arrangements in advance. Boat trips are expensive due to fuel costs. In rough weather it can be a wet and bone-crunching trip to the more remote resorts.

To get to Ono island you'll have to fly to Vunisea on Kadavu, where you'll be picked up by your resort. Transfers take anything from one to two hours.

LAU & MOALA GROUPS

Fiji's final frontier, the Lau islands are strewn across the southwest corner of Fiji's vast archipelago like green champagne bubbles on the blue Pacific. Few visit here, but those who do report countless bays; deserted, reef-rimmed atolls; and sparsely populated islands with hilly interiors. For the hardened and patiently adventurous, Lau

and Moala offer the opportunity to create your own trail and go where few outsiders have been.

Vanua Balavu and Lakeba in the Lau Group are the only two of the 30 or so inhabited islands that see a thin dribble of visitors. Both have basic amenities, weekly flights and a simple guesthouse.

Although much closer to the mainland, the Moala Group is even further removed from the reaches of tourists and has no facilities whatsoever.

🏃 Activities & Tours

The biggest draw is the isolation of the islands: a chance to interact with local communities and experience a way of life seldom seen by outsiders. Hiking is the most accessible activity and easily arranged, as long as you follow polite etiquette.

Lau Group is still relatively unexplored in terms of diving. The Fijian Government protects the waters, and commercial fishing is prohibited in the area. In the absence of diving companies, snorkelling is the next best way to experience the sizeable reefs and their marine life. Guesthouses should be able to arrange for local boats to run you out to the reefs.

Sailing around the Lau Group requires a cruising permit, which is now relatively easy to obtain and is issued at any official port of entry (you cannot legally enter Fiji via the Lau Group). Yachts are charged an anchorage fee of $10 per day. These poor islands need the funds so if the anchorage fee isn't asked for offer it anyway.

KADAVU, LAU & MOALA GROUPS LAU & MOALA GROUPS

ROTUMA

Far flung and isolated, the 43-sq-km volcanic island of Rotuma drifts in the Pacific 460km northwest of Viti Levu. The vast distance between its tiny frame and the mainland is what has allowed the Rotumans to develop such an inimitable culture.

Ethnically and linguistically distinct from Fiji, the Rotuman culture resembles that of Tonga and the Polynesian islands to the east. Strong emphasis on communal sharing and *kainaga* (kinship), combined with a slow pace of life, mean that visitors encounter a close-knit people with an elastic sense of time. And that is how the Rotumans prefer it to remain.

In 1985, wary of Western influence, 85% of Rotumans voted against opening the island up to organised tourism and, while it's perfectly feasible to visit, genuine travellers here are few. Most who do so have been invited or are returning residents visiting 'home'.

There are more than twice as many Rotumans living abroad than there are left on Rotuma. Most have left to find work and opportunities in Fiji, New Zealand and Australia, and this exodus means that young people can seem relatively scarce on this island outpost.

Hiking, Archaeology & Beaches

Rotuma's volcanic curves offer excellent hiking and there are spectacular views from Solroroa Bluff and Mt Suelhof (256m), Rotuma's highest peak. Between Losa and Solroroa Bluff is Mamfiri, a volcanic vent that drops around 25m. The islets of 'Agaha and Solkope are lovely picnic spots.

Twenty stone tombs were recorded at Sisilo Hill in 1824 at the archaeological site known as the **Graveyard of Kings**. If you're lucky you may spot some endemic wildlife including the Rotuman gecko and the red-and-black Rotuman honeyeater.

Rotuma also has some of the loveliest beaches in Fiji. The best are at Oinafa, Losa and Vai'oa, west of Solroroa Bluff. Other popular beaches and picnic spots on the main island include Joro, Lulu and 'Ana-te-Fapufa (Fapufa cave). There are also some fine surfing areas around the island and pristine snorkelling.

Fara Festival

An annual festival Fara begins on 1 December, leading into six weeks of dancing, parties and revelry. The emphasis is on hospitality and celebrating friends, family, visitors, life and love. At this time the population increases by around one-third; it's the best time to be on the island.

Where to Stay

The easiest way to stay on Rotuma is to organise a homestay. If you're lucky enough to be invited to the island, discuss with your Rotuman contact how best to compensate the family during your stay. You can also contact the Fiji Visitor Bureau in either Nadi or Suva to get the contact details for the Rotuman Island Council, which is the group you should contact if you want to visit. You can also simply ask the visitor's bureau for their advice.

Another option would be to post a message on the Rotumans' Facebook group (www.facebook.com/groups/rotumans/) or at www.rotuma.net. These online forums are used by Rotumans to keep in contact across the globe and somebody there may be willing to offer a homestay.

Getting There

Fiji Airways (Fiji Link; ☑ 330 4388, 672 0888; www.fijiairways.com) flies from Nadi to Rotuma ($640) on Wednesdays; the trip takes 1½ hours.

Goundar Shipping (☑ 330 1035; http://goundarshipping.com/) sails to Rotuma (tickets $200) once a month the first Saturday of every month. The journey takes 36 hours and the conditions on board are pretty basic.

There's a ferry between Suva and Rotuma on the first Saturday of every month (tickets $200). There's no set company that provides the service (the government decides on a monthly basis) but check with Goundar Shipping in the first instance.

Yachts occasionally visit the island and to anchor they must obtain permission from the Ahau government station in Maka Bay, on the northern side of the island. Rotuma is not a designated port of entry.

ℹ️ Information

There is little infrastructure for locals, let alone for travellers, but you'll find a couple of general stores in Lomaloma and on Lakeba. Currently there is only spotty Vodafone mobile coverage on Vanua Balavu. There is the **Lomaloma post office** (☑ 889 5000) on Vanua Balavu, and the **Tubou post office** (☑ 882 3001) on Lakeba. Tubou also has a **police station** (☑ 882 3043) and **hospital** (☑ 882 3153).

ℹ️ Getting There & Away

Fiji Airways (p186) flies between Suva and Vanua Balavu on Wednesdays ($283 one way, one hour) and to Lakeba on Thursdays ($283 one way, 1½ hours). There's also a flight every Thursday from Suva to Cica ($272). There are no flights between islands.

Goundar Shipping (p188) operates a monthly trip to Vanua Balavu ($160) and Cicia ($150). Call well in advance to find out when the next sailing is. A new ship, the MV *Sea Rakino,*was coming into service as we went to press, offering a more regular service linking the Lau group to Suva, with the possibility of a stop at Savusavu and Taveuni.

Seaview Shipping (p232) has two ferries (the *Sandy* and the *Lady Sandy*), which sail from Suva to the southern Lau group. Schedules are a moveable feast.

Lau Group

The 57 isles of Lau are subdivided into northern and southern Lau. It is said that on the southernmost island of Ono-i-Lau you can see Tonga on a clear day. This proximity to its Pacific neighbour has had a profound influence on the group's cultural development. The southeast trade winds made it easy for Tongan warlords to reach Fiji and with them came Tongan language, food, decoration and architecture. The winds that blew them so favourably over were less inclined to blow them back and Lau islanders still bear the names and physical traits of their Tongan ancestors.

Vanua Balavu

Vanua Balavu, 355km east of Nadi, about halfway to Tonga, is northern Lau's largest island, and has a grass airstrip.

Arguably the most scenic of Lau's islands, Vanua Balavu averages about 2km wide and resides with eight other smaller islands inside a barrier reef. The islands curl their way around the surrounding water, creating sheltered bays and corridors of calm sea. The interior of Vanua Balavu is scattered with rugged hills and pristine, sandy beaches ring the group's perimeter. The celebrated Bay of Islands, also known as Qilaqila, sits in the northwest pocket and is a spectacular site for snorkelling, kayaking and swimming. It's also a lovely place for yachties to draw anchor and is a known hurricane shelter. Within the rugged limestone hills is Vale Ni Bose (literally, the 'Meeting House of the Gods'), a gaping cave with limestone walls and a pool of crystalline water.

Vanua Balavu's largest village is Lomaloma on the southeast coast. In the mid-19th century Tonga conquered the island, and the village of Sawana was built next to Lomaloma. Fifth-generation Tongan descendants still live in Sawana, and the houses with rounded ends show the influence of Tongan architecture.

At one time, ships trading in the Pacific regularly visited Lomaloma and it had the first port in Fiji. In its heyday Lomaloma had many hotels and shops, as well as Fiji's first botanical gardens, though little remains of its past grandeur.

One week after the full moon in November, the people of Vanua Balavu witness the annual rising of the balolo (tiny green and brown sea worms). At sunrise the Susui villagers collect worms by the thousands. The fishy-tasting baked worms are considered a delicacy.

FATAL ATTRACTION

There's a freshwater lake near the village of Mavana, on the northeast corner of Vanua Balavu, where the people of Mavana gather annually for a fun ceremony authorised by their traditional priest. Naked except for a leaf skirt, they jump around in the lake to stir up the muddy waters. This provokes the large fish known as *yawa* (a type of mullet usually only found in the sea) to spring into the air. It's believed that the male fish are attracted to the female villagers and thus easily trapped in the nets. Legend has it that the fish were dropped into the lake by a Tongan princess while flying over the island on her way to visit her lover on Taveuni.

ℹ️ KNOW BEFORE YOU GO

➡ The Lau and Moala islands are Fiji's wild frontier. There are no hotels, bars, restaurants, dive shops, banks or tourist shops. Only two islands, Vanua Balavu and Lakeba, have guesthouses. Neither accepts credit cards.

➡ Meals will be mostly whatever the locals can catch or grow. Expect fresh seafood of various kinds, local fruits and (often starchy) vegetables.

➡ Book flights well in advance and confirm your reservation. Flights are infrequent, sometimes rescheduled and generally full. If it rains and the grass on the landing strip is dangerously slippery, the plane will return to Suva.

➡ Boats can run weeks behind their published timetables and, if they do, the local shops will run out of goods. BYO snacks.

🛌 Sleeping

Moana's Guesthouse　　　　GUESTHOUSE $
(☑916 2684, 719 0929; r per person incl meals $95, children under 12yr $50; @) This hospitable place (the only accommodation on Vanua Balavu) covers all the basics with beach *bure* and guesthouse options. The simple *bure* are a 1km walk from Sawana village and mere metres from the lovely beach on Lomaloma Bay. The *bure* are simple, thatched affairs with mosquito nets, solar power, private bathrooms and mats laid over concrete floors.

Husband and wife owners Tevita Fotofili and Alumita can arrange boat, snorkelling and fishing trips, and collect travellers from the airstrip.

Other Northern Lau Islands

Mago island made headlines in 2005 when Hollywood actor Mel Gibson bought the former copra estate for nearly US$15 million from a Japanese hotel chain, making it one of the largest privately owned islands in the world. The Yavusa Vuaniivi clan, who claimed their ancestors were cheated by 19th-century British settlers who allegedly gave the islanders 2000 coconut plants in return for Mago, challenged the sale's validity.

Kaibu is another privately owned island in the northern Lau Group, 55km west of Vanua Balavu. It has a grass airstrip, shares a fringing reef with the larger island of Yacata and is home to the now defunct, but previously exclusive, Kaimbu Island Resort. It has been in a state of renovation and sale for several years and conflicting rumours of its imminent operation or demise abound.

Cicia is a 34-sq-km dot in the Pacific southwest of Vanua Balavu that's covered in coconut palms.

Lakeba

Lakeba, being the hereditary seat of the Tui Nayau (Chief of Lau), is the most important island in southern Lau. It is a roughly circular volcanic island, approximately 9km in diameter, with a small peninsula at its southern end. Its 54-sq-km area is home to about 2000 people. In days of yore the islanders lived in an interior hilltop fort, far from marauding neighbours. Today, they live in the eight coastal villages that are connected by a road that circles the island. To the east is a wide lagoon enclosed by a barrier reef.

Lakeba was historically a meeting place for Fijians and Tongans; it was also the place where Christian missionaries first entered Fiji via Tonga and Tahiti. Two missionaries, Cross and Cargill, developed a system for written Fijian here and produced the first book in that language. Lakeba was frequently visited by Europeans before the trading settlement was established at Levuka in the Lomaiviti Group.

The **provincial office** (☑882 3164) for the Lau Group is in Tubou at the southern end of Lakeba. There is also a guesthouse, a post office, a police station and a hospital here, and some of the nearby beaches are good for snorkelling and swimming. For transport you can utilise the carriers and buses that circle the island.

The island has caves worth visiting, especially Oso Nabukete, which translates as 'too narrow for pregnant women'. Adorned with huge pillars of limestone stalactites and inhabited by bats, it's an awesome example of nature's might.

🛌 Sleeping

Jeke Qica's Guesthouse　　　GUESTHOUSE $
(☑882 3188; r per person incl meals $65) In Tubou, this small guesthouse offers two rooms with private bathroom inside 'Jack's house'.

Jack can provide interesting commentary on the area's culture and history.

Other Southern Lau Islands

There are 16 other southern Lau islands, mostly within a radius of 100km southeast of Lakeba. Vatoa and Ono-i-Lau are more isolated and much further south.

The islanders of southern Lau are well known for their crafts: Moce, Vatoa, Ono-i-Lau and Namuka-i-Lau produce *masi* (bark cloth) and the artisans of Fulaga are excellent woodcarvers. You may be able to purchase crafts from villages on the islands or from handicrafts shops in Suva.

Moala Group

The three islands of this group – Moala, Totoya and Matuku – are geographically removed from Lau, but administered as part of the Eastern Division. The islands are the eroded tops of previously submerged volcanic cones that have lifted more than 3km to the sea surface. Totoya's horseshoe shape is the result of a sunken volcano crater forming a land-locked lagoon. Matuku has rich volcanic soil, steep wooded peaks and a submerged crater on its western side. However, this beautiful island is generally inaccessible to visitors. Each of the islands has villages.

Moala

Moala (65 sq km) is the largest and most northerly of the group and is about 160km from Suva. The highest peak reaches 460m and has two small crater lakes. It has extremely fertile soil and supports nine villages that produce copra and bananas.

Moala has no tourist infrastructure and although you don't need to be formally invited as such, your only option for accommodation is with a local family and you'll need to organise this before you arrive.

Understand Fiji

Fiji Today

Fiji's image as a tourist paradise was tempered for a decade while the army stuck its nose (and guns) into politics. But in 2014 the country finally returned to democracy. Fiji was looking more stable than it had for years, even as it was facing the challenges of globalisation, climate change and – of course – a struggle for international rugby glory. Just as Fiji's fortunes turned, the Category 5 Cyclone Winston arrived causing widespread destruction. Visitors may notice residual damage to smaller villages, especially on remote islands.

Best on Film

Cast Away (2000) Tom Hanks is all washed up on a desert island. Shot in Fiji.
The Blue Lagoon (1979) Tropical teen romance that made Brooke Shields – and Fiji – a movie star.
His Majesty O'Keefe (1954) Adventure film in which Yankee seadog Burt Lancaster swashbuckles his way through Fiji.

Best in Print

Kava in the Blood: A Personal & Political Memoir from the Heart of Fiji (Peter Thomson; 2008) Engaging memoir of Fiji's cultures and coups.
Getting Stoned with Savages (J Maarten Troost; 2006) Humorous travelogue centred on Fiji.
Worlds Apart: A History of the Pacific Islands (Ian C Campbell; 2003) Excellent guide to Fiji's place in the Pacific.

Back to the Ballot Box

In September 2014, Fiji finally held the elections that brought it back into the fold of democratic nations. A few months earlier, coup leader Commodore Voreqe (Frank) Bainimarama stepped down from the military to contest the election. His Fiji First party swept the board, winning 32 of the 50 seats in the national parliament. Although the opposition parties called foul on certain aspects of the election, international observers certified the process – for which 84% of the electorate turned out – to be free and fair.

The election came on the back of a new constitution published in 2013. It enacted new rules to protect indigenous Fijian land, and the compulsory teaching of Fijian and Fiji-Hindi languages at primary school level, alongside English. While critics also noted that it gave the prime minister broad powers to impose a state of emergency, it also mandated the setting up of the Fiji Human Rights Commission – one of the few such bodies in the Pacific Region.

After the elections, Fiji was returned to the Commonwealth, from which is had been expelled after the 2006 coup. But Bainimarama was equally quick to show his willingness to reorient Fiji's international relations to suit the changing 21st century. Within two months of his election, he hosted the Indian prime minister and Chinese president in Fiji and looked to strengthen Fiji's ties with their countries, as well as Asian powerhouses such as Indonesia. This went hand in hand with a cooling in relations with Australia and New Zealand. Bainimarama threatened to boycott future meetings of the regional Pacific Islands Forum unless the antipodean nations, which fund the body, were expelled. During the coup years, he had set up the rival Pacific Islands Development Forum, funded by China, to combat what he saw as colonial meddling in the region.

Noble Banner Blue
Bainimarama's plans for a new Fiji free of its old colonial ties came to a head in 2015, when his government unexpectedly announced the national flag – which has the British Union Jack in the corner – would be replaced. A public competition was held to design the new flag, and the national conversation drew sharp opinions both for and against the move. However, there was almost universal disappointment when the shortlist of finalists was published. When church leaders criticised the entries as being unworthy of representing the nation, the government suggested that there was still time to go back to the drawing board to get the process right. The new flag was due to be unveiled in 2016.

Sporting Glory
If the flag debate provoked divisions, there is at least one constant in Fijian life that proves a great unifier: rugby. There was an immense outpouring of national pride when Fiji were crowned winners of the 2014–15 Sevens World Series, their first international title for 10 years. With Fiji currently the top-ranked Sevens side in the world, there was even more excitement when they were one of the first teams to qualify for the 2016 Rio Olympics. Locals joke that if the Fijian rugby team win the gold medal there, a month-long national holiday would probably be declared.

Future Challenges
Fiji faces challenges to diversify its economy. Around 200,000 Fijians depend directly or indirectly on the sugar industry, but in 2017 EU quotas that have helped sustain sugar production are due to be abolished, and the economy is due to take a hit. Visitor numbers are slowly growing (more than 750,000 arrivals in 2015) and the closer ties to India and China include increased marketing to encourage tourists from destinations.

At the same time, Fiji tries to prepare itself for the inevitabilities of global warming and rising sea temperatures and sea levels. Extreme weather events are becoming both more frequent and less predictable in the South Pacific. Fiji was battered by Cyclone Winston in early 2016, and rare is the speech by a Fijian politician in an international arena that doesn't draw attention to climate change in the region.

POPULATION: **881,065**

LIFE EXPECTANCY: **69.6 YEARS**

POPULATION BELOW POVERTY LINE: **25.5%**

GDP: **7.29 BILLION (2014)**

COUPS SINCE 1987: **4**

if Fiji were 100 people

57 would be Fijian

38 would be Indo-Fijian

4 would be other (European, Pacific Islander or Chinese)

belief systems
(% of population)

64.5 Christian

0.5 Sikh

6 Muslim

28 Hindu

1 Other

population per sq km

FIJI   AUSTRALIA   USA

≈ 3 people

History

The Fijian islands are strewn across the Pacific's southwest corner and it is the vastness of that mighty ocean that has defined and helped the country become the nation it is today. Since humans first arrived 3500 years ago, the trade winds have blown in people from Melanesia, Polynesia, and finally Europe and the Indian subcontinent, all of whom have played their part in shaping Fiji's history and culture.

The first traders to reach Fiji were Tongan who came to trade colourful *kula* (a type of parrot) feathers, *masi* (printed bark cloth) and weapons with the eastern Fiji islands.

The First Fijians

According to oral folklore, the indigenous Fijians of today are descendants of the chief Lutunasobasoba who, along with his companions, reached Vuda (near Lautoka on Viti Levu) in their canoe *Kaunitoni*. Though this story hasn't been independently substantiated, the Fijian government officially promotes it, and many tribes today claim to be descended from Fiji's first chief. What is clear however, is that Fiji's early culture was shaped by several waves of seafarers from across the region.

Crossroads of the Pacific

Fiji was settled by a wave or waves of Polynesians and Melanesians from Papua New Guinea who had descended from earlier Austronesian migrations from Southeast Asia.

The so-called Lapita people, possibly arriving from New Caledonia, left the earliest mark in the archaeological record through their distinctive pottery. It is theorised that a thousand years later new arrivals from Melanesia assimilated, displaced or killed the descendants of the first Polynesian colonists and that it was the blending of these two cultures that gave rise to the indigenous Fijian culture of today.

Around 500 BC a shift from a coastal, fishing lifestyle towards an agricultural one occurred; this, along with an expansion of population – probably due to further immigration from other parts of Melanesia – led to an increase in intertribal feuding. War was a highly ritual and organised business, and cannibalism eventually developed as a ceremonial way of humiliating defeated foes. New architecture developed around this martial culture, with villages moving to ring moat-fortified sites

TIMELINE	1220 BC	500 BC	AD 1000
	The Austronesian people arrive, choosing to settle only along the coast and to live off fishing, just as they did in Tonga before gradually moving to Samoa.	Melanesians from elsewhere in the Pacific arrive and establish permanent settlements, which includes moving inland and establishing farms and other more sustainable ways of life.	Tongan and Samoan warriors begin a series of incursions into Vitian territory, forcing Fijians to create fortified sites and adopt a warlike lifestyle.

during times of war. Spirit houses were a central part of every village; here priests would commune with ancestor spirits and keep consecrated objects such as war clubs and flesh forks (used in ritual cannibalism). Polygamy was widespread, as was the practice of strangling widows on the death of their chiefly husbands.

Fiji was part of a well-developed network of western Polynesian islands. Its Samoan and Tongan neighbours were sources of trading goods, cultural exchange and intermarriage. Political alliances were sealed by the presentation of *tabua* (polished whale tooth; see boxed text for more information) and exchange of *masi* – intricate hand-printed cloth made from the paper bark tree, brought over by the original Fijian settlers. Travel between island groups was by enormous double-hulled canoes (*drua*). The largest reached over 30m and could carry over hundred people, and were sources of great chiefly prestige – as well as vehicles of war.

While there were extended periods of peace, by the end of the 18th century, Fiji was undergoing intense social upheaval due to the consolidation of chiefly power blocks in Viti Levu, and external pressure from the powerful Tongan kingdom next door.

In ancient times a war club was a warrior's most treasured possession and came in many forms. Some were bulbous, ideal for braining your opponent, while others were designed to be thrown or jabbed. Clubs that had killed many acquired their own *mana* (prestige) and were both feared and revered.

When Cultures Collide

In the early 19th century, Fiji was dominated by two great chiefly confederacies, Rewa and Bau, who were fighting for dominance of the islands. Into this mix came the first European explorers, who came looking for natural resources and brought gunpowder – and the word of their Christian god in return. Fiji's trajectory took a brand new path.

TABUA

Tabua (carefully polished and shaped whales' teeth) were originally believed to be shrines for the ancestor spirits, but subsequently became powerful diplomatic symbols. The acceptance of a *tabua*, which is a powerful *sevusevu* (a gift presented as a token of esteem or atonement), binds a chief to the gift-giver. Originally *tabua* were rare, obtained only from washed-up sperm whales or through trade with Tonga. However, European traders introduced thousands of whale teeth and replicas made of whalebone, elephant tusk and walrus tusk. These negotiation tools became concentrated in the hands of a few dominant chiefdoms, increasing their power – traditionally, a chief's body was accompanied to the grave by a *tabua*.

They were, and still are, highly valued items and essential to diplomacy. In 1995 Colonel Sitiveni Rabuka presented Queen Elizabeth with a *tabua* as a gesture of atonement and apology for leading the two 1987 military coups; in the following month Fiji was readmitted to the Commonwealth.

1643	1774	1789	1804
The ship of Dutch explorer Abel Tasman is almost wrecked off the northern islands; he charts the eastern portion of Vanua Levu so that others can avoid it.	After landing at Australia, Captain Cook visits – although he limits his contact, due to the islands' reputation as the 'Cannibal Isles'.	Captain William Bligh and 18 others make rough navigation charts while drifting between the Vitian islands after being cast adrift near Tonga following the *Bounty* mutiny.	After trading with Tongans, Europeans discover sandalwood on Vanua Levu and begin a direct trade, which utterly depletes the supply by 1813; some chiefs become briefly wealthy.

The indigenous name for Fiji is 'Viti'. The name Fiji comes from European explorers mishearing the Tongan name for the islands, which is 'Fisi'.

Early European Encounters

Europeans sailed the Pacific during the 17th and 18th centuries, ostensibly to find *terra australis incognita*, the great 'unknown southern land' later called Australia. Some of them bumped into Fiji on the way.

The first European to sail the area was a Dutch explorer Abel Tasman, who sailed past in 1643 on his way back to Europe from Van Diemen's Land. His descriptions of treacherous reefs kept mariners away for the next 130 years. English navigator James Cook stopped over on Vatoa in the southern Lau Group in 1774 and his countryman, Captain Bligh, passed between Vanua Levu and Viti Levu after he was thrown off the *Bounty* in 1789. The channel is known as Bligh Water in memory of the mutinied captain.

By the early 19th century European whalers and traders of sandalwood and *bêche-de-mer* (sea cucumbers) began to visit as better maps of the surrounding reefs were developed. Fragrant sandalwood was highly valued in Europe and Southeast Asia. Tongans initially controlled the trade, obtaining sandalwood from the chiefs on Vanua Levu and then selling it to the Europeans, but when a shipwrecked survivor of the *Argo,* Oliver Slater, discovered the location of the supply, news quickly spread of its whereabouts. In 1805 Europeans began to trade directly with Fijians, bartering metal tools, tobacco, cloth, muskets and gunpowder. By 1813 the sandalwood supply was exhausted, but firearms and the resulting increase in violent tribal warfare were lasting consequences.

The other commodity that brought trade to the area, *bêche-de-mer*, was an Asian delicacy. The intensive harvesting and drying required to process the seafood required hundreds of workers at each *bêche-de-mer* station. Chiefs who sent their villagers to work boosted their own wealth and power, with an estimated 5000 muskets traded during this period. *Bêche-de-mer* was a short-lived trade, lasting only from 1830 to 1850.

A New God

In the 1830s London Missionary Society (LMS) pastors and Wesleyan Methodist missionaries arrived in southern Lau to find converts and preach against cannibalism, helped by the recently converted Tongans.

Conversion of chiefs became the most successful strategy, with the powerful Cakobau adopting Christianity in 1854, on the recommendation of the king of Tonga. Acceptance of Christianity was further made palatable by its similarity with existing beliefs of *tabu* (sacred prohibitions) and *mana* (spiritual power). Early adoption, however, usually meant that Christianity was infused with traditional spirituality rather than supplanting it outright. Villagers attended church but also continued to worship ancestral gods through such practices as the kava ceremony, and codes of conduct.

1822	1830	1840	1867
Fiji's first modern town, Levuka, is established by European settlers. Its population consists mostly of traders, missionaries, shipwrights, opportunists and drifters.	The first London Missionary Society pastors arrive from Tahiti and begin to devise a written language, which they will teach in schools and use to record early-contact culture.	The first US navy visit, commanded by Captain Charles Wilkes, occurs; an incident at Malolo island results in the deaths of two sailors and more than 70 Fijians.	After several conversions in coastal areas, Methodist minister Reverend Thomas Baker heads into the Western Highlands, but after disagreements with villagers, the pastor is killed and eaten.

Commercial Settlers

A whaling settlement was established at Levuka, on Ovalau, in the 1830s, and became a major port in the South Pacific for traders and warships. In 1840 Charles Wilkes led a US expedition that produced the first reasonably complete chart of the Fijian islands. He also negotiated a port-regulation treaty under which Cakobau and his subchiefs were paid for the protection of foreign ships and the supply of provisions.

However, this seemingly mutually beneficial relationship was fraught with tension. Relations began to deteriorate in 1841 when Levuka was razed by fires, which the settlers suspected Cakobau of instigating. Later, during the 1849 US Independence Day celebrations, the Nukulau island home of US consul John Brown Williams was also destroyed by fire, and locals helped themselves to his possessions. Williams held Cakobau (as nominal king of Fiji) responsible for the actions of his people and sent him a substantial damages bill, which was a significant source of Cakobau's debts.

Samples of Lapita pottery found at the Sigatoka Sand Dunes, which is now open to the public, suggest that this was one of the earliest settlements in Viti.

HISTORY WHEN CULTURES COLLIDE

THE REVEREND BAKER'S LAST SUPPER

Thomas Baker, a Wesleyan Methodist missionary, was killed on 21 July 1867 by the Vatusila people of Nabutautau village deep in Viti Levu's isolated Nausori Highlands. A few years earlier Baker had been given the task of converting the people of the interior to Christianity. Baker's predecessors had been able to convert many groups peacefully, and he was advised to keep to these areas. But whether due to impatience, martyrdom, foolhardiness or the urge for success, he ignored the advice and, with it, crucial cultural know-how.

The highlanders associated conversion to Christianity with subservience to the chiefdom of Bau. As they were opposed to any kind of extended authority, knocking off the reverend may well have been a political manoeuvre. However, a second and more widely believed theory maintains that it was Baker's own behaviour that brought about his nasty end. Apparently, the local chief had borrowed Baker's comb to festoon his voluptuous hairdo. Insensitive or forgetful of the fact that the chief's head was considered sacred, Baker grabbed the comb from the chief's hair. Villagers were furious at the missionary for committing this sacrilege and killed and ate him and seven of his followers in disgust.

In 2003, believing they had suffered a curse of bad luck as a result of their ancestors' culinary habits, the people of Nabutautau held a tribal ceremony to apologise to the descendants of the missionary. Around 600 people attended, including Thomas Baker's great-great-grandson, and Prime Minister Lasenia Qarase.

1871	1874	1875	1879
On arriving on Levuka, European settlers establish the Kingdom of Fiji as a constitutional monarchy and name Ratu Cakobau as the king of Fiji.	After much debate and negotiation, Cakobau and 12 other chiefs cede Fiji to Queen Victoria and Britain on 10 October in a ceremony at Levuka.	Without the benefit of the immunity that Europeans had to the disease, a third of the population is killed by a savage measles outbreak, creating further tensions in the colony.	Following the outlawing of blackbirding, Britain introduces the first group of *girmitiyas* (Indian indentured labourers) to work in the labour-intensive sugar-cane fields of the main island.

Blackbirding

When the American Civil War created a worldwide cotton shortage, Fiji enjoyed a cotton boom that indirectly stimulated blackbirding, a trade in labourers. Europeans brought Melanesian Pacific Islanders, particularly from the Solomon Islands and New Hebrides (now Vanuatu), to labour on the Fijian cotton (and copra and sugar) plantations.

Initially, people were coaxed, bribed and tricked into agreeing to work for three years in return for minimal wages, food and clothing. Later, however, chiefs were bribed and men and women traded for ammunition.

On completion of the three-year contract, regulations required that labourers be given passage back to their villages, but more often than not they were dropped at the first island the captain saw fit outside of Fijian territorial waters.

By the 1860s and '70s the practice had developed into an organised system of kidnapping. Stories of the atrocities and abuses inflicted by recruiters resulted in pressure on Britain to stop the trade, and in 1872

CHIEF CAKOBAU: KING OF FIJI

By the middle of the 19th century the chiefdom of Bau, in eastern Viti Levu where European trade was most intense, had accumulated great power, with the help of European muskets and the war canoes of Tongan allies. Chief Seru Epenisa Cakobau (pronounced *Tha-kom-bau*) was at the height of his influence by the 1850s and asserted himself as the king of Fiji *(Tui Viti)*, although this claim wasn't accepted by all chiefs and many regarded him as, at best, first among equals.

By 1862 Cakobau has acquired some large debts, and with the Tongans now eyeing up his territory, he proposed to Britain's consul that he would cede the islands to Queen Victoria in return for financial aid. The consul declined, doubting Cakobau's claims on the kingdom, but the rumours caused a large influx of settlers to Levuka, who bickered among themselves. Disputes also erupted with Fijians over land ownership, and the town became a lawless and greedy outpost that was on the verge of anarchy and racial war.

And what of Cakobau's huge debt? This was not cleared until 1868 when the Australian Polynesia Company agreed to pay it in exchange for land. Clearing his bills encouraged Cakobai to form a government in Levuka in 1871, but it quickly ran into trouble when it tried to pass laws and raise taxes in the previously lawless town. Money and political troubles again drove Cakobau to look to the British for support. 'If matters remain as they are, Fiji will become like a piece of driftwood on the sea, and be picked up by the first passer-by,' he wrote to the colonial secretary. 'Of one thing I am assured, that if we do not cede Fiji, the white stalkers on the beach, the cormorants, will open their maws and swallow us.' And with that, Fiji finally passed into British hands.

1882	1916	1951	1958
As Levuka's difficult geography impedes further expansion, the government is forced to relocate; Suva officially becomes the capital, although the town has barely a dozen buildings.	The importation of indentured Indian labourers ends after agitation within India and the visit to Fiji by Anglican clergyman Rev Charles Freer Andrews.	Fiji Airways, called Air Pacific after 1971, is founded by Australian aviator Harold Gatty, offering one of the first services to another new capital: Canberra, Australia.	Fiji's favourite statesman, Ratu Sir Lala Sukuna, dies. Born a chief of the Bau Royal House, he is best remembered for his tireless work creating the Native Land Trust Board.

the Imperial Kidnapping Act was passed, but it took the interception of Royal Navy ships to finally bring blackbirding to an end.

The Colonial Period

The end of the American Civil War in 1865 brought a slump in the world cotton market, which severely affected the Fijian economy. In the following years new arrivals brought diseases to Fiji, such as measles, which had dramatic effects on the Fijian population.

By 1873 Britain was finally interested in annexing Fiji, citing the need to abolish blackbirding as justification. In reality, they were also interested in protecting Commonwealth commercial interests and bailing out an economy that was drastically overspent. Taking advantage of this interest, Cakobau, who had acquired new debt, again approached the British consul to cede the islands to Queen Victoria. Besides financial stability, Cakobau believed cession to British rule would also bring Christianity and civilisation to the islands. Fiji was pronounced a British crown colony on 10 October 1874, at Levuka.

From Girmitiyas to Indo-Fijians

To maintain good relations with its subjects, the colonial government combated exploitation of indigenous Fijians by prohibiting their employment as plantation labourers. However, plantation crops such as cotton, copra and sugar cane, while extremely profitable, demanded large pools of cheap labour. If the colony were to avoid blackbirding, then a new labour source had to be found.

In 1878 negotiations were entered into with the Indian colonial government for indentured labourers to come to Fiji on five-year contracts. After this term the labourers (known as *girmitiyas*) would be free to return home. Indian indentured labourers soon began arriving in Fiji, at a rate of about 2000 per year.

The *girmitiyas* were a diverse group from all over India, with 80% Hindu, 14% Muslim and the remainder mostly Sikhs and Christians. Overcrowded accommodation gave little privacy, different castes and religions were forced to mix, and social and religious structures crumbled. Despite the hardship, most *girmitiyas* decided to stay in Fiji once they had served their contract, and many brought their families from India to join them.

By the early 1900s India's colonial government was being pressured by antislavery groups in Britain to abolish the indenture system. In 1916 recruitment stopped and indenture ended officially in January 1919. By this time 60,537 indentured labourers were in Fiji.

Fiji's first coup took place 108 years to the day after the arrival of the *Leonidas* carrying the first group of Indian indentured labourers.

Contact with the firearms and diseases of Europeans had a marked impact on Fiji's ethnic population, which has only recently returned to its 18th-century level.

1963	1970	1973	1977
Indigenous Fijian men and women are given the vote, and the 38-member Legislative Council is divided almost equally into indigenous Fijian, Indo-Fijian and European groups.	After 96 years of colonial rule, Fiji becomes independent on 10 October, adopting a British model of parliament with two houses, including a 'House of Lords' made up of Fijian chiefs.	Ratu George Cakobau, great-grandson of Cakobau, the chief who ceded Fiji to the UK in 1871, is sworn in as the country's first Fijian governor-general.	The National Federation Party wins an election but fails to form a government, so election results are overturned by the governor-general. The following election is a landslide for the Alliance Party.

Independent Fiji

Most Indians stayed in Fiji after their period of indenture and leased land from indigenous Fijians or organised through newly formed trades unions. These moves brought them increasing political clout, particularly after World War II and India's independence from Britain in 1947. Although Fiji's Legislative Council expanded to allow locally elected members in 1953 (splitting power between Europeans, indigenous Fijians and Indo-Fijians), the calls for the British to leave Fiji completely grew ever louder. Indian voices often led the way – much to the consternation of many indigenous Fijians.

A New Political Landscape

On 10 October 1970, Fiji became independent after 96 years of colonial administration. Ratu Sir Kamisese Mara was the country's first prime minister, and he led Fiji for 17 years. In the rush towards independence, important problems, such as land ownership and leases and how to protect the interests of a racially divided country, were not resolved. Despite an economic boom in the immediate post-independence years, by the early 1980s the price of sugar had fallen, and given the country's dependence on it, the drop resulted in massive foreign debt.

Economic woes exacerbated ethnic tensions. In Fiji most shops and transport services were (and still are) run by Indo-Fijian families. Stereotypes developed portraying Indo-Fijians as money-obsessed, despite the fact that most belonged to poorer working classes and, Indo-Fijians – unlike indigenous Fijians – could never secure land tenure on their farming leases.

Fiji's first government (the Fijian Alliance Party) became associated with economic failure, and greater unity among workers led to the for-

WHERE ARE THE CHIEFS?

One of Fiji's most powerful institutions was the Great Council of Chiefs, which was founded by British colonisers in 1876 to advise the government on indigenous matters. It was comprised of hereditary chiefs, although its paramount chief was, of course, Queen Victoria. Its hereditary nature was abolished after independence, including the right to nominate members, but it remained an exclusively indigenous organisation. Its powers grew after the military coups of the 1980s and introduction of the 1990 constitution, which gave it the right to nominate members of the senate. The council refusal to recognise Frank Bainimarama's seizure of power in 2006 led to its suspension, and ultimately, its abolishment in 2012 – bringing to a close nearly 130 years of formal political power for the chiefs. These days, the political influence of Fiji's chiefs is restricted primarily to the social and cultural spheres.

1979	1987	1990	1997
A remake of *The Blue Lagoon*, in the Yasawas, catapults Brooke Shields to teenage stardom and puts Fiji on the top of the romantic-holiday list.	Two military coups take place in quick succession under the leadership of Lieutenant Colonel Sitiveni Rabuka; Fiji is expelled from the Commonwealth and becomes a republic.	A new constitution is created that asserts ethnic Fijians' role in the political system, marginalises Indo-Fijians and reserves two seats for the army in the cabinet.	Under increasing pressure, Rabuka unveils a new constitution calling for a return to multiethnic democracy; this leads to democratic elections and a Bill of Rights that outlaws racial discrimination.

FIJI IN ARMS

Fiji had only a minor involvement in WWI, as colonial authorities prevented many Fijians from enlisting. Most famous among these was Ratu Sir Lala Sukuna, Fiji's great states-man of the 20th century, who fought for the French Foreign Legion after his enlistment papers in England were refused.

The conflict in the Pacific during WWII was much closer to home. Fiji itself was used as an Allied training base from an airstrip at Nadi that today has become the international airport. Around 8000 Fijians were recruited into the Fiji Military Force (FMF) and from 1942 to 1943 fought against the Japanese in the Solomon Islands.

Today Fiji, considering its size, has fairly large armed forces and has been a surprisingly major contributor to UN peacekeeping missions in various parts of the world. In 2004 Fiji was the first country to volunteer troops to protect UN officials in Iraq, while in 2014, 45 Fijian peacekeepers in Syria's Golan Heights dominated the news when they were kidnapped by Islamist fighters in that country's civil war. All were later released unharmed.

UN Peacekeeping is an important income stream for the country, but while the over-seas role of Fijian soldiers also generates national pride, some critics have noted Fiji's post-independence history of coups and suggested that peacekeeping may have given the army an outsized picture of the role it has to play at home.

mation of the Fiji Labour Party (FLP). In April 1987 an FLP government was elected in coalition with the National Federation Party (NFP). De-spite having an indigenous Fijian prime minister, Timoci Bavadra, and a cabinet comprising an indigenous Fijian majority, the new government was labelled 'Indian dominated' because the majority of its MPs were Indo-Fijian.

The Early Coups

With the FLP labelled 'Indian dominated', racial tensions got out of hand. The extremist Taukei movement played on Fijian fears of losing their land rights and of Indo-Fijian political and economic domination. On 14 May 1987, one month after the elections, Lieutenant Colonel Sitiveni Rabuka took over from the elected government in a bloodless coup and formed a civil interim government supported by the Great Council of Chiefs.

In September 1987 Rabuka again intervened with military force. The 1970 constitution was invalidated, Fiji was declared a republic and Rabuka proclaimed himself head of state. The following month Fiji was dismissed from the Commonwealth of Nations.

The excellent Fiji Museum (p88) in Suva is the best place to get up to speed on Fiji's national story.

1998	2000	2001	2004
Mahendra Chaudhry becomes the first Indo-Fijian prime minister, promising change, which unnerves many indigenous Fijians and leads to protests in the capital and around the country.	Failed businessman George Speight heads a 19 May coup; 30 hostages are held in parliament for eight weeks as Speight demands the resignation of Mahendra Chaudhry and the president. Speight is later jailed.	In a tough election campaign, interim Prime Minister Lasenia Qarase defeats Mahendra Chaudhry; George Speight (using the name Ilikimi Naitini) is also briefly elected before being prevented from taking his seat.	Fiji becomes the first country to volunteer troops to protect UN officials in Iraq, sending 155 soldiers to protect UN buildings and 24 bodyguards for officials.

The coups returned power to an elite minority, with Indo-Fijians effectively removed from the political process. Conflicts resurfaced: between chiefs from eastern and western Fiji, between high chiefs and village chiefs, between urban and rural dwellers, and within the church and trade-union movement. Economically the coups were disastrous, with the two main industries – tourism and sugar – severely affected. Development aid was suspended, and from 1987 to 1992 about 50,000 people, mostly Indo-Fijians, emigrated.

Rewriting the Constitution

In 1995 a Constitutional Review Commission (CRC) presented its findings. It called for a return to a multiethnic democracy and, while concluding that the position of president should be reserved for an indigenous Fijian, proposed no restriction on ethnicity for the prime minister. The government acted on most of the CRC's recommendations and a new constitution was declared in 1997. After Rabuka made a formal apology for the 1987 coups, Fiji was readmitted to the Commonwealth.

The 2000 Coup

In the May 1999 elections voters rejected Rabuka's slate. The FLP won the majority of seats, and its leader, Mahendra Chaudhry, fleetingly became Fiji's first Indo-Fijian prime minister.

Many indigenous Fijians feared for their traditional land rights and began protesting. Many refused to renew expiring 99-year land leases to Indo-Fijian farmers. On 19 May 2000 armed rebels entered the parliamentary compound in Suva and took 30 hostages, including Prime Minister Chaudhry. Failed businessman George Speight quickly became the face of the coup, demanding the resignation of Chaudhry and President Ratu Sir Kamisese Mara. He also wanted the 1997 multiethnic constitution rescinded.

Support for Speight was widespread, and Indo-Fijians suffered such harassment that many fled the country. Although the coup lasted only around eight weeks, increasing lawlessness resulted in the army – led by Commodore Josaia Voreqe 'Frank' Bainimarama – instituting martial law. After long negotiations between Speight's rebels and Bainimarama's military, the 1997 constitution was revoked.

In March 2001 the appeal court decided to uphold the 1997 constitution and ordered that Fiji be taken to the polls to restore democracy. Lasenia Qarase, heading the Fijian People's Party (SLD), won 32 of the 71 parliamentary seats in the 2001 elections. Claiming that a multiparty cabinet would be unworkable, Qarase defied the constitution by including no FLP members in his 18-strong cabinet.

In 2006 the discovery of an ancient Fijian village, possibly dating back as far as the 13th century, brought excitement to the village of Kuku in Nausori. Locals have been rebuilding the site in the hopes of creating a tourist attraction.

2006	2007	2009	2009
Commodore Voreqe 'Frank' Bainimarama begins military manoeuvres in Suva that eventually depose the government of Lasenia Qarase; he then declares himself acting president of Fiji.	Bainimarama restores Ratu Josefa Iloilo to the presidency, who in turn appoints Bainimarama prime minister.	The Fijian constitutional crisis sees President Iloilo abrogate the constitution and remove all constitutional office-holders. He then reappoints Bainimarama as prime minister under his 'new order'.	Fiji is suspended from both the Pacific Islands Forum and the Commonwealth for failing to hold democratic elections.

The Bainimarama Years

While Speight's coup was quick, there was much that was unresolved. The Qarase government's draft Promotion of Reconciliation, Tolerance and Unity (PRTU) Bill divided the country during 2004 and 2005. Though the aim was to heal the wounds of the past, opponents saw the amnesty provisions for those involved in the coup as untenable. One of the opponents of the bill, Commodore Voreqe 'Frank' Bainimarama, presented a list of demands including dropping the PRTU and other controversial bills. In late 2006 he gave a deadline to Qarase and began military exercises around Suva to support his intention.

Qarase met several of the demands, agreeing to put three contentious bills on ice, but it wasn't enough. Fiji's fourth coup since independence took place on 5 December 2006, when President Ratu Josefa Iloilo dissolved Bainimarama's order and Qarase was put under house arrest. Several key groups did not approve of Bainimarama's coup, including the Methodist Church and the Great Council of Chiefs, who refused to meet without Qarase, but it was to little avail when Bainimarama declared a state of emergency.

In 2009, the constitution was annulled, and the Court of Appeal was disbanded after it ruled the 2006 coup illegal. The same year, Fiji was suspended from participation in the Pacific Islands Forum and dismissed (again) from the Commonwealth of Nations for failing to return to democracy. In 2012, Bainimarama consolidated power even further by abolishing the Great Council of Chiefs.

A new constitution was promulgated in 2013, promising a popular vote in 2014. When elections were finally held, Bainimarama was returned as prime minister with a large mandate, with hopes that this time Fijian democracy could be made to stick.

In 2013, the old colonial capital of Levuka was named Fiji's first World Heritage Site.

HISTORY INDEPENDENT FIJI

Fiji's most notorious cannibal was Ratu Udre Udre. The 19th-century chief is the holder of the *Guinness World Records* title for the most people eaten: 872. His tomb is in Rakiraki on Viti Levu.

2013	2014	2015	2016
A new constitution is signed into law, removing race-based electorates and increasing protection for indigenous Fijian land.	Elections see Bainimarama return as democratically elected prime minister, and Fiji's re-admittance to the Commonwealth.	A proposal to redesign Fiji's flag, minus the British Union Jack, prompts a national debate over symbols of Fijian identity.	Fiji's men's rugby seven team wins the country's first ever medal at the Rio Olympic Games. In the inaugural tournament Fiji resoundingly beat Great Britain 43-7 in the final to take gold.

Environment

Fiji has long been defined by the ocean that surrounds it, and the vast stretches of the South Pacific have both protected and isolated the locals for much of their history. In Fiji's vast territorial waters, laced around the hub of Viti Levu, are 332 other islands, of which 110 are permanently inhabited. These are fertile islands, with the richness of tropical rainforests – a richness mirrored below the waves by Fiji's astonishing coral reefs.

Fiji is an archipelago of 332 islands and a further 500 smaller islets; they cover an enormous 1.3 million sq km, but only about 18,300 sq km of this – less than 1.5% – is dry land.

Fiji's Landscape

Islands

Fiji owes its existence to plate tectonics. Volcanoes formed when the Pacific plate was pushed under the Australian plate, and it was these that gave Fiji its backbone and laid down the building blocks for the creation of further islands. Fiji's oral tradition sees things differently. According to legend, the snake-god, Degei, created Viti Levu as a home for the two humans (and their progeny) who hatched from eggs he had found in an abandoned hawk's nest. Degei now sleeps in Viti Levi's Nakauvadra Range and it is the opening and closing of his eyes that prompt day and night.

Fiji no longer has any active volcanoes, but in Savusavu on Vanua Levu locals still tap into some of that geothermal energy by using the hot springs for cooking.

Reefs

The geological uplift that raised Fiji left its islands surrounded by more reefs than it's possible to count. The Coral Coast, which runs along the southern edge of Viti Levu, is a classic fringing reef, linked to the island shore, with sections exposed at high tide. At the opposite end of the spectrum are the long barrier reefs, separated from land by channels of deep water. Cakaulevu Reef (also known as the Great Sea Reef) is the world's third-longest barrier reef, stretching 200km from the north coast of Vanualevu to the Yasawas; in the south the Great Astrolabe Reef circles Kadavu. Both hold a staggering amount of biodiversity.

On occasion, the combined actions of waves and wind on exposed reefs can produce coral islands. Beachcomber and Treasure Islands in the Mamanucas, and Leleuvia and Caqalai in the Lomaiviti Group are all examples of coral islands.

Wildlife

Like many isolated oceanic islands, Fiji's native wildlife includes a few gems but is otherwise relatively sparse. Many of the plants and animals are related to those of Indonesia and Malaysia and are thought to have drifted in on the winds and tides.

Native Animals

The only native terrestrial mammals in Fiji are six species of bat. You'll almost certainly see *beka* (large fruit bats or flying foxes) flying out at sunset to feed, or roosting during the day in colonies in tall trees. Two species of insectivorous bats are cave-dwellers and are seldom seen.

More than 130 species of birds live or pass through Fiji, making birdlife the main wildlife attraction; birdwatching is best during the dry season. There are 27 endemic, with members of the pigeon and parrot families well represented. The beautiful orange dove is particularly striking, as is the red-and-green Kadavu parrot – once highly threatened but making a comeback thanks to local conservation efforts. The collared lory is the most common parrot species, easily seen in the trees of most towns.

Fiji's 27 species of reptiles are mostly lizards. The endemic crested iguana, a startling green lizard with white bands, is found on the Yasawas and on Yadua Taba off the west coast of Vanua Levu. Its ancestors are thought to have floated to Fiji on vegetation from South America. There are also two terrestrial snakes – a small, nonvenomous Pacific boa (*gata*) and the Fiji burrowing snake.

Introduced Animals

Besides the bats, all other land-dwelling mammals have been introduced from elsewhere. More than 3500 years ago the first settlers introduced poultry, Polynesian rats, dogs and pigs to Fiji. In the 19th century Europeans brought additional domestic animals and, inadvertently but inevitably, brown and black rats and house mice.

The common Indian mongoose was introduced in 1883 to control rats in sugar-cane plantations. Unfortunately, the mongoose mostly chose to eat Fiji's native snakes, frogs, birds and eggs, while the rats continued to prosper. Mongooses are a common sight – keep an eye out for them scampering across the highway into the undergrowth. Taveuni and Kadavu are mongoose-free, making them the best islands for birdwatching.

Undaunted by the consequences of these early introductions, authorities imported the cane toad in 1936 to control insects in the cane plantations. Sadly, it too, has now become a pest, preying upon native ground frogs in coastal and lowland regions, as well as competing with them for food.

In 2000 a small number of common iguana (known locally as the American iguana) were smuggled into Fiji and released on Qamea Island. They have since spread to several other islands, including

Top Bird-watching Spots

Bouma National Heritage Park (p177)

Colo-i-Suva Forest Park (p91)

Kadavu (p183)

Des Voeux Peak (p171)

ENVIRONMENT WILDLIFE

FIJI'S FLYING FOXES

Fruit bats (flying foxes) are a pretty common sight, particularly when they take to the wing at sunset. Most of them are Pacific flying foxes, a species found across the region. Fiji has one purely endemic species, the Fijian monkey-faced bat, although you'll be very lucky to see one, as they are restricted to just one area of montane cloud forest around Des Voeux Peak in the highlands of Taveuni. As its name suggests the bat has an appealingly cute face, with large orange eyes. There are thought to be fewer than 1000 individuals extant, although their low numbers and remote habitat make surveys a tricky prospect. The bat is listed as critically endangered by the International Union for Conservation of Nature.

Faring a little better, but still under threat, is the Fijian blossom bat species unique among fruit bats for roosting in caves. There are just four known roost sites in Viti Levu, putting it in a potentially precarious situation. Working with local communities is vital for their protection; at the Snake God Cave (p102) at Wailtoua, local guides lay down strict guidelines for visitors to avoid disturbing the roost – a good omen in a country with a long tradition of hunting bats for food.

Taveuni, although environmental groups working in conjunction with teams from the Fijian army are currently working on an eradication program.

Marine Life

Fiji's richest animal life is underwater. There are hundreds of species of hard and soft coral, sea fans and sponges, often intensely colourful and fantastically shaped.

As coral needs sunlight and oxygen to survive, it's restricted to depths of less than 50m. Corals on a reef break are generally of the densely packed varieties, such as brain coral (which looks like a human brain), which are able to resist the force of the surf. Fragile corals such as staghorn grow in lagoons where the water is quieter.

Fiji's tropical fish are exquisite. Among the many you're likely to see are yellow-and-black butterflyfish; coral-chomping, blue-green parrotfish; wraithlike needlefish; and tiny, territorial, black-and-white clownfish guarding their anemone homes. Fat-fingered blue starfish and delicate feathered starfish are common. Some marine creatures, such as fire corals, scorpionfish and lionfish, are highly venomous; if in doubt, don't touch! And watch where you put your bare feet.

Fiji is also good for spotting sharks and rays. On the reefs, small black-tip and white-tip sharks are the most common, with the larger (and more aggressive) bull shark also frequently seen. The enormous and graceful manta ray, whose wingspan can reach 4m, can be encountered in several spots in the Yasawas and Kadavu.

Of the four sea snakes found in Fiji, most are rarely seen, except for the *dadakulaci* (banded sea krait), which occasionally enters freshwater inlets to mate and lay its eggs on land. Although the *dadakulaci* is both placid and shy, and can't open its jaws wide enough to bite humans, its venom is highly potent, so it is worth being careful if you spot one when diving.

Five turtle species are found in Fijian waters: the hawksbill, loggerhead, green (named after the colour of its fat), Pacific Ridley and leatherback. Traditional Fijian culture venerated the turtle as one of the few species that could bring together the land and the sea, and the world of the living to that of the spirits.

Plants

Most of Fiji is lush with fragrant flowers and giant, leafy plants and trees; 1596 plant species have been identified, of which about 60% are endemic. Many are used for food, medicine, implements and building materials.

Rainforest Plants

Around 40% of Fiji is forested. Forest giants include valuable timbers such as *dakua* (Fijian kauri), a hard, durable timber with a beautiful grain used for furniture. Of the many different fern species in Fiji, a number are edible and known as *ota*.

You'll see *noni* (evergreen) products – cordials and soaps – for sale throughout Fiji. *Noni* produce a warty, foul-smelling, bitter-tasting fruit, which, despite its unattractive properties, is gaining credibility worldwide for its ability to help relieve complaints including arthritis, chronic fatigue, high blood pressure, rheumatism and digestive disorders.

The *tagimaucia,* with its white petals and bright red branches, is Fiji's national flower. It only grows at high altitudes on the island of Taveuni and on one mountain on Vanua Levu.

Can't tell a batfish from a butterflyfish? *Tropical Reef Life – A Getting to Know You & Identification Guide* by Michael AW, gives an informally detailed overview of underwater life, plus photographic tips.

Suva's beautiful (but underfunded) public gardens, opened in 1913, are named after botanist John Bates Thurston, who introduced many ornamental plants to Fiji.

Not all Fiji's trees are native. The African tulip tree, easily spotted by its pretty red flowers, is spreading widely and outcompeting many native species. Wherever there are people, you'll see land that's been cleared for cultivation of the crops that thrive in the lush environment: cassava, *dalo* (taro), and the all-important kava.

Coastal & River Plants

Mangroves are the most distinctive plant communities along the coasts of Fiji. They provide important protection against erosion for seashores, and are breeding grounds for prawns and crabs.

Casuarina, also known as ironwood or *nokonoko,* grows on sandy beaches and atolls. As its name suggests, the timber is heavy and strong and was used to make war clubs and parts of canoes.

An icon of the tropics, the coconut palm continues to support human settlement. Coconuts provide food and drink, shells are used for making cups and charcoal, leaves are used for baskets and mats, and oil is used for cooking, lighting and as body and hair lotion.

Other common coastal plants include the beach morning glory, with its dawn-blooming purple flowers, the beach hibiscus, with its large, yellow flowers, and the night-flowering *vutu* tree.

National Parks & Reserves

Fiji has several protected conservation areas. Lack of resources means that conservation is often difficult, but the Bouma National Heritage Park now protects more than 40% of Taveuni.

➡ **Sigatoka National Park** (p75) Self-guided trails along impressive sand dunes, blustery coast, rolling grassland and young mahogany forest. On the Coral Coast.

➡ **Koroyanitu National Heritage Park** (p69) Easily accessible from Nadi, this park is rich with native forest and open grassland, as well as the peak of Mt Batilamu.

RESPECT & PROTECT

Many of Fiji's endangered animals and plants are protected by the Convention on International Trade in Endangered Species (CITES). Others are protected by national legislation. If you buy a souvenir made from a protected or endangered species and don't get a permit, you're breaking the law and chances are that customs will confiscate it at your overseas destination. In particular, remember the following:

➡ *Tabua* are *tabu* (sacred) – whales' teeth are protected.

➡ Turtle shell looks best on live turtles.

➡ Leave seashells on the seashore; protected species include giant clams, helmet shells, trochus and tritons.

➡ Tread lightly. Stepping on live coral is like stepping on a live budgie (parakeet): you'll kill it.

➡ Many plants, including most orchids, are protected.

Trash & Carry

Your litter will become someone else's problem, especially on small islands; where possible, recycle or remove your own.

Don't Rush to Flush

Fresh water is precious everywhere, especially on small islands; take short showers and drink treated water or rainwater rather than buy another plastic bottle.

For more information on local conservation efforts, check out Nature Fiji (www.naturefiji.org), the island's only dedicated environment NGO.

⇒ **Bouma National Heritage Park** (p177) A rainforest-rich park on Taveuni threaded with walking trails and dotted with waterfalls.

⇒ **Colo-i-Suva Forest Park** (p91) A small park just outside Suva, with lush rainforest and plenty of birdlife.

Other significant (but smaller) sites include Tunuloa Silktail Reserve near Navua on Vanua Levu, and Yadua Taba (off Taveuni), which is home to the crested iguana. Visiting requires permission from the National Trust for Fiji in Suva.

Fiji has several marine parks, with plans for many more. Its most notable are Waitabu Marine Park in Taveuni and Namena Marine Reserve in Vanua Levu. In 2014, the Shark Reef Marine Reserve at Beqa was declared a national park – the first dedicated shark-protection area in the country.

Environmental Concerns

Along with other Pacific island nations, Fiji finds itself on the frontline of global warming. Extreme weather events are becoming more frequent and unpredictable. In 2016 Fiji was hit by Category 5 tropical cyclone Winston, the strongest cyclone to ever hit the Southern Hemisphere. Rising sea levels also threaten coastal life, and increased sea temperatures have led to the phenomenon of coral bleaching. As the seas warm, corals lose the symbiotic algae that provide their colour and nutrition, which can lead to complete die-off. Two-thirds of Fiji's reefs have experienced large amounts of bleaching.

It's not all doom and gloom. On the islands, a reforestation program for the sandalwood tree, logged out by 19th-century merchants, is meeting with success. In many areas threatened by overfishing, Fijian environmental groups working in partnership with local communities are finding increasing success protecting fishing grounds by declaring them *tabu* (sacred) at particular times such as spawning season. On a larger scale, the Fijian government has declared its intent to protect 30% of its waters as marine parks by 2020 – potentially the largest marine park network in the world.

Culture

Fiji has been an important Pacific crossroads over the centuries, and its culture reflects the manifold influences that have touched the nation. Indigenous island culture, based on the communal values of the village, still holds sway, rubbing up against (sometimes with friction) the Indian culture brought by indentured labourers and the influences of Western colonialists in everything from Christianity to rugby.

Who are the Fijians?

Since Fijian independence, there have frequently been tensions between Fiji's two main communities – those of island descent and those from the Indian communities who settled in the islands in the late 19th and early 20th centuries. These tensions have spilled over into disputes over who holds political power and whether all communities are equal in the eyes of the law. Until 2010, Fiji was divided into 'indigenous Fijians' and 'Indo-Fijians', with only the former officially allowed to call themselves Fijian. Under current law, all citizens are finally now referred to as being Fijian, with the appellation iTaukei used to refer to members of the original native community. According to the most recent survey, 57% of the population are iTaukei, 38% Indo-Fijians and the remainder a mix of Chinese, Pacific Islander and European.

The iTaukei

In most places you go in Fiji you'll be met with a cheery '*bula*' (cheers! hello! welcome!; literally 'life') and a toothy grin. It's your first introduction to the iTaukei language, the most important word you'll learn in Fiji. Foreigners (*kaivalagi;* literally 'people from far away') are welcomed warmly and openly, helping to give Fiji a reputation as one of the friendliest nations on earth.

iTaukei culture is based in Fiji's villages (for more information see p219). Traditional customs, from drinking *yaqona* (kava) to village law remain crucial to maintaining iTaukei identity, even (or especially) in the face of globalisation and 24-hour media culture.

Village life is subject to complex rules of etiquette and land (*vanua*) is owned collectively by the community and cherished. Land can be leased but never sold – nearly 90% of land in Fiji is owned by the iTaukei and overseen by a government commission. These land leases help provide Fijians in rural areas with income to maintain their traditional farming and fishing lifestyles.

Clan chiefs still wield great influence in society. Unlike other Melanesian societies where chiefs are appointed on merit, in Fiji a chief's position is hereditary (though the title may pass to a relative and not necessarily the chief's own son or daughter). This is common in nearby Polynesian societies and illustrates how Fiji, as the crossroads of the Pacific, has been influenced by those around it, most notably the Tongans and Rotumans. Chiefs represent clans rather than villages, who elect or choose their own administrator (*turaga ni koro*) to represent them to the government and to visitors.

To visualise the lives of Fiji's early Indian settlers, visit the Fiji Museum's Indo-Fijian gallery in Suva. It reconstructs the history of indentured labourers, and their customs and traditions, with the help of family heirlooms, artefacts and personal belongings.

The Indo-Fijians

The early indentured-labourer experience and post-coup reflections have inspired countless pages of Indo-Fijian poetry and fiction by authors such as Satendra Nandan, Raymond Pillai, Subramani, Sudesh Mishra, Mohit Prasad and Kavita Nandan.

The first Indians came to Fiji in the late 19th century, brought by the British, who wanted indentured labourers to work on their plantations. Those who stayed on after their period of indenture settled as farmers or gravitated to the towns to open small businesses, and they helped transform Fiji's social and political traditions, as well as influencing the nation's cuisines.

The Indian nature of Fijian life was forged in the sugar-cane belts of Viti Levu and Vanua Levu, and many of the large cane farms remain leased and managed by Indo-Fijians. However, as Indians have never been allowed to legally own land, many have faced eviction as their leases on native land have expired. The towns, particularly on Viti Levu, are strongholds of Indo-Fijian life, even more so as younger generations follow the call of urbanisation. However, even in the countryside you can look out for roadside Hindu shrines and mosques that illustrate the deep ties that Indo-Fijians have to the soil.

Towns like Ba, Lautoka, Labasa and Levuka are still caught in a time warp with old-style shopfronts and aisles cluttered with Indian homewares, fashions and pantry essentials. Billboards entice you to shopping meccas such as New Delhi Fashions and promise great deals from the Tappoos, Khans and Motibhais.

The explosion of Indo-Fijian commerce really happened when Indians from the state of Gujarat set up shop, tapping into the needs of the rural folk. Today they still own many of the shops lining the streets of Fiji as well as the upmarket malls in cities like Suva. Their business acumen has sometimes worked against them. During coups, nationalist leaders have harnessed anti-Indian sentiment by conjuring caricatures of stingy, acquisitive Indians about to take over the country.

KAVA

Few visitors will spend time in Fiji without being offered to join a kava ceremony at least once. This drink (more correctly called *yaqona,* and colloquially called 'grog') is made from an infusion of powdered roots from *Piper methysticum,* a type of pepper plant. Before the arrival of Christianity, *yaqona* was a ritual drink reserved for chiefs and priests; nowadays gathering around a kava bowl for conversation with friends is an essential part of Fijian social life.

The ritual aspect of kava remains important. When visiting a village, you'll usually be welcomed with a *sevusevu* ceremony, centred on *yaqona* drinking. Visitors sit cross-legged facing their hosts and a large central wooden bowl (*tanoa*). Never walk around across the circle or turn your back to it, or step over the coir cord that ties the white cowrie shell to the *tanoa* (it represents a link to the ancestors).

The powdered *yaqona* is wrapped in cloth and mixed with water in the *tanoa*. The resulting infusion looks a little like muddy water. You'll be offered a *bilo* (coconut shell cup) with the drink. Clap, then accept the *bilo* and drink it down in one swig: bear this in mind if your hosts offer to fill your cup 'low tide' or 'high tide'. On drinking, everyone claps three times, and the *bilo* is passed back to the server. You needn't drink every *bilo* you're offered, but it's polite to at least drink the first. Bear in mind that once a kava session starts, it doesn't end until the *tanoa* is empty.

Kava is only very mildly narcotic. After a few drinks you might feel a slight numbness on the lips, but stronger mixes can induce drowsiness (kava from Kadavu is said to be the most potent). In 2014 a local drinks company started selling Tāki Mai, an 'anti-stress' shot drink with kava extract. Some Fijians were skeptical, though: if you really want to de-stress they say, is to sit around all night chatting with your mates while drinking grog. Pass the *bilo*!

Cuisine

Starchy carbohydrates play a big part in Pacific diets. Traditional Fijian foods include *tavioka* (cassava) and *dalo* (taro) roots, boiled or baked fish, and seafood in *lolo* (coconut cream). Meat is usually fried and accompanied with *dalo* and *rourou* (boiled *dalo* leaves in *lolo*), though you'll often find the colossally popular corned beef substituting for the real thing. *Kokoda* is a popular dish made of raw fish marinated in *lolo* and lime juice, with a spicy kick.

A *lovo* is a traditional indigenous Fijian banquet where food is prepared in an underground oven. A hole is dug in the ground and stones are put inside and heated by an open fire. The food – whole chickens, legs of pork, fragrant stuffed *palusami* (meat or corned beef, onions and *lolo*) or *dalo* – is wrapped in banana leaves and slowly half baked and half steamed on top of the hot stones. Delicious! Traditionally, *lovo* is served for family get-togethers as well as for more formal occasions, such as church festivals and funerals. Lots of resorts offer a weekly *lovo* for guests.

Indo-Fijian dishes are usually spicy, and a typical meal comprises meat (but never beef or pork, which are avoided by Hindus and Muslims respectively), curry with rice, dhal (lentil soup) and roti (a type of Indian flat bread). Chinese food is generally a Western-style takeaway affair with stir-fries, fried rice, chop suey, chow mein and noodle soups.

Fiji's most famous drink is *yaqona* (kava; see boxed text opposite), followed by the internationally branded Fiji Water, a mineral water sourced from a deep aquifer in northeast Viti Levu. Fiji's rainy, mountainous terrain also makes it ideal country for growing coffee – look out for the rich, dark blends from Bula Coffee.

Fiji Gold and Fiji Bitter are the country's two leading beers. Despite the latter's name, both are lagers, as is the premium Vonu brand. Local rum is also freely available, originally produced as a by-product from the sugar industry. Refreshing coconut water is widely available, especially in markets, where vendors just slice off the top of a nut. If you've got a sweet tooth, look out for freshly squeezed sugar-cane juice or pineapple juice.

Markets

Every large town in Fiji has a fresh fruit-and-vegetable market and at least one supermarket where you can buy basic groceries. Those like the central market in Suva are visitor attractions in themselves, with stalls piled high with fresh produce and areas reserved for bundles of *yaqona* roots and sacks of aromatic spices. Most villages have a small shop, but since villagers grow their own fresh produce, stock is often limited to items such as tinned fish, corned beef and packets of instant noodles.

If your accommodation has cooking facilities, it will generally sell (very) basic supplies, but you'll be better off stocking up in town.

Restaurants

There are plenty of cheap restaurants in Fijian towns, serving a mix of Indian and Chinese cuisine, although Western fast food and takeaway baked goods like pies are also popular. Only in Suva, Nadi and Denarau (and resort restaurants) will you generally find great variety in types of cuisine being offered, from Italian and Japanese to contemporary fusion takes on Fijian dishes. It's also common for resorts offer a weekly *lovo* night, with a traditional Fijian buffet. Many Indo-Fijians are strict vegetarians, so there are usually plenty of vegie options available.

Dinner is usually taken early. In smaller towns many restaurants close by 9pm.

The late Epeli Hau'ofa, who died in 2009, was one of Fiji's most celebrated writers. Grab a copy of *We Are the Ocean*, an essential collection of his essays, short fiction and poetry.

Arts

Traditional arts and crafts such as woodcarving and weaving, along with dancing and music, remain an integral part of life in many villages, as well as a draw for tourists. These traditions have inspired much of the small but thriving Fijian contemporary arts scene, of which Suva is the epicentre.

The University of the South Pacific's Oceania Centre for Arts & Culture (p92) in Suva provides working space for artists, musicians and dancers, as well as regular performances. Suva is also the literary hub for Fiji, hosting occasional readings by members of the Pacific Writing Forum (http://www.usp.ac.fj/index.php?id=2585) and poetry slams.

Pottery

Pottery is thought to have initially been brought to Fiji by the Lapita people over 3000 years ago, and some modern potters still use traditional techniques. The pots are beaten into shape with wooden paddles of various shapes and sizes, while the form is held from within using a pebble anvil. Coil and slab building techniques are also used. Once dry, pots are fired outdoors in an open blaze on coconut husks and are often sealed with resin varnish taken from the *dakua* tree.

Woodcarving

Traditional woodcarving skills are largely kept alive by the tourist trade, providing a ready market for war clubs, spears and cannibal forks. *Tanoa* (drinking bowls) and *bilo* (kava cups of coconut shell) remain part of everyday life. *Tanoa* shaped like turtles are thought to have derived from turtle-shaped *ibuburau,* vessels used in indigenous Vitian *yaqona* rites.

The best *tanoa* come from the southern Lau islands. They are carved from a solid piece of *vesi* wood, and are traditionally the domain of certain Lau clans who are descended from Tongan woodcarvers who settled in the islands in the 18th century.

See traditional potters at work at Nasilai (p101) and, on Tuesdays and Thursdays at the Fiji Museum (p88).

Bark Cloth

Masi is bark cloth with rust-coloured and black printed designs. In Vitian culture *masi* was invested with status and associated with celebrations and rituals. It was worn as a loincloth by men during initiation rituals and renaming ceremonies, and as an adornment in dance, festivity and war. *Masi* was also an important exchange item, used in bonding ceremonies between related tribes. Chiefs were swathed in a huge puffball of *masi,* later given to members of the other tribe.

While men wore the *masi,* production has traditionally been by women. Made from the inner white bark of the paper mulberry bush that has been soaked in water and scraped clean, it's then beaten and felted for hours into sheets of a fine, even texture. The unprinted cloth is called *tapa.* Intricate designs are added to the *tapa* by hand or stencil and often carry symbolic meaning. Rust-coloured paints are traditionally made from an infusion of candlenut and mangrove bark; pinker browns are made from red clays; and black from the soot of burnt *dakua* resin and charred candlenuts.

It is difficult to see *masi* being made, though you'll see the end product used for postcards, wall hangings and other decorative items. Textile designers have begun incorporating traditional *masi* motifs in their fabrics – or even using *masi* to make wedding dresses for fashion-forward brides who want to keep close to their traditions.

Mat & Basket Weaving

Most indigenous Fijian homes use woven *voivoi* (pandanus leaf) to make baskets, floor coverings and fine sleeping mats. Traditionally, girls living in villages learned to weave and many still do. Pandanus leaves are cut and laid outdoors to cure, stripped of the spiny edges, and boiled and dried. The traditional method of blackening leaves for contrasting patterns is to bury them in mud for days before reboiling. The dried leaves are made flexible by scraping with shells and then split into strips of about 1cm to 2cm and woven. Mat borders are now often decorated with brightly coloured wools instead of the more traditional parrot feathers.

Fiji's Treasured Culture (www.museum.vic.gov.au/fiji) is an online exhibition of Fijian artefacts held in Museum Victoria (in Melbourne, Australia) and Suva's Fiji Museum.

Music & Dance

Traditional Fijian music blends Melanesian and Polynesian rhythms. Along with native slit drums, guitar and ukelele are widespread accompaniments. Many visitors will experience this by hearing a rendition of *Isa Lei,* the lullaby-like national farewell song, with which many resorts serenade their guests on departure.

Modern Fijian music has been influenced by the currents of reggae, rock and even hip hop. Hindi pop and Bollywood soundtracks are also heard everywhere due to India's deep influence on Fijian culture. Church music, particularly gospel, is also popular.

One of the most notable names in Fijian music include Laisa Vulakoro, the queen of *vude,* a genre blending old Fijian songs with modern R&B. Other names to listen out for include Lagani Rabukawaqa, Lia Osborne, Daniel Rae Costello (who makes a Fijian reggae blend), and bands such as Delai Sea and Voqa ni Delai Dokidoki. Rosiloa (formerly Black Rose) is one of Fiji's most successful rock bands. For some Fijian musicians, success means moving overseas, such as for hip hop artists D Kamali.

However, in recent years there has been a move to rediscover the popular Fijian music of the 1960s and '70s and reignite the live music scene. Makare, a Lautoka-based band have been spearheading the revival: if you catch them playing oldies auch as the impossibly catchy *Mai Gaga Voli* (written by 1980s star Lela Seruvakula), you'll be humming the melody for the remainder of your trip.

Meke

Most visitors first encounter Fijian dance when they're welcomed at resorts and hotels with *meke,* a performance that enacts ancient lore. Traditionally, *meke* were accompanied by a chanting chorus or by

MELODIOUS MEASURES

Replaced by guitars and keyboards, traditional indigenous instruments are a rare find in Fiji these days. Yet once upon a time, nose flutes were all the rage. Made from a single piece of bamboo some 70cm long, the flute would be intricately carved and played by a laid-back Fijian, reclining on a pandanus mat and resting his or her head on a bamboo pillow. Whether it was the music or the pose, flutes were believed to have the power to attract the opposite sex and were a favourite for serenading.

Other traditional instruments had more practical purposes, such as shell trumpets and whistles, which were used for communication. Portable war drums were used as warnings and for communicating tactics on the battlefield. One instrument you are still likely to see (and hear) is the *lali,* a large slit drum made of resonant timbers. Audible over large distances, its deep call continues to beckon people to the chief's *bure* (traditional thatch dwelling) or to church.

THE MILAAP PROJECT & MORE

There is now a growing volume of works in print, film and online reflecting the Indo-Fijian experience. Dr Satish Rai is among the more prolific producers. In his films he has documented the growing interest in ancestral history among Indo-Fijians as well as recorded testimonials and commentaries about Fiji's recent political and social history. His films include *Milaap: Discover Your Indian Roots* (2001), *Once Were Farmers* (2004) and *In Exile at Home: A Fiji Indian Story* (2008). Other writers and raconteurs have posted stories on sites such as www.girmitunited.org, which is also a comprehensive guide to publications and films about Indo-Fijians.

'spiritually possessed seers'. Rhythm was supplied by clapping, the thumping and stamping of bamboo clacking sticks and the beating of slit drums. The whole community participated in *meke*. In times of war, men performed the *cibi* (death dance), and women the *dele* or *wate,* a dance in which they sexually humiliated enemy corpses and captives. Dancing often took place by moonlight or torchlight, with the performers in costume, their bodies oiled, faces painted and combs and flowers decorating their hair.

Vilavilairevo (Fire-Walking)

Although famous throughout Fiji and performed in many of the Coral Coast resorts, *vilavilairevo* (fire-walking) was originally performed only by the Sawau tribe of Beqa, an island off Viti Levu's southern coast. Traditionally, strict taboos dictated the men's behaviour leading up to the ceremony, and it was believed adherence to these protected them from burns.

Architecture

Since colonial times some communities have grown to sizeable towns and small cities. Today these urban centres are more heavily influenced by modern building practices than rural villages, which still retain some aspects of traditional architecture.

Traditional

Fijian villagers once resided in traditional thatched dwellings known as *bure*. In the past these homes were dark and smoky inside, with no windows, usually only one low door and hearth pits for cooking. The packed-earth floor was covered with grass or fern leaves and then finely woven pandanus-leaf or coarse coconut-leaf mats. Sleeping compartments were at one end, behind a bark-cloth curtain, with wooden headrests.

Traditional *bure* are usually rectangular in plan, with timber poles and a hipped or gabled roof structure lashed together with coconut-fibre string. Thatch, woven coconut leaves or split bamboo is used as wall cladding, and roofs are thatched with grass or coconut leaves. Most villages still have some traditional-style *bure* but, as village life adapts and changes and natural materials become scarcer, most Fijians find it easier and cheaper to use concrete blocks, corrugated iron and even flattened oil drums.

The village of Navala, nestled in the Viti Levu highlands, is an exemplar of traditional Fijian architecture. It's the only village remaining where every home is a *bure*.

Indian

Among the more colourful reminders that Indian communities thrive in Fiji are the myriad temples, mosques and family shrines. The architecture and rituals of the Hindu temples, Muslim mosques and Sikh *gurdwaras* are an integral part of the Fijian landscape.

A must-see is the extravagantly decorated South Indian–style Sri Siva Subramaniya Swami Temple (p56) in Nadi. It's packed with brightly painted statues of Hindu deities and ceiling frescoes and is by some way the most colourful building in the country. A North Indian–style temple (p165) near Labasa on Vanua Levu boasts a large rock that devotees believe has been growing in the form of a snake, which is sacred to Hindus. Mosques are visually more restrained affairs, often with the simplest of domes and modest minarets, decorated with trims of green, the colour of Islam. Meanwhile, the major Sikh temples across Fiji follow Indian tradition and regularly offer free meals to all visitors and devotees.

While the large shrines are hard to miss, the red flags atop bamboo poles next to Hindu family homes are subtler. They mark tiny personal shrines, which are often decorated with statues, marigold garlands and offerings.

Colonial & Modern

Historical Levuka was once the capital of Fiji, and a number of its buildings date from its heyday of the late 19th century, particularly the main street, which is surprisingly intact. In 2013 it was was given Unesco World Heritage status.

The British influence is particularly visible in Suva, which has many grand colonial buildings. The most celebrated is the gorgeous white edifice of the Grand Pacific Hotel, built in 1914. Other notable buildings include Government House and Suva City Library.

The best of modern Fijian architecture has sought to blend elements of traditional design with the best in current practice. Many resorts play with iTaukei themes, but the Fijian Parliament building in Suva, built in 1992, takes the *bure* concept and really runs with it – free tours are available if arranged in advance.

Sport

Almost a religion among indigenous Fijians, rugby union is the one sport that has continually put Fiji on the world stage since the first match between Fijian and British soldiers in 1884. Fijians players are prized internationally, often having contracts in Europe, NZ or Australia that prevent them from playing for Fiji. Despite this, Fiji has won the most Pacific Tri-Nations titles and is a tough draw for any international side. Its rugby sevens squad is even more formidable. They were world champions in 2005 and won the series again in 2015, and they are currently the top-ranked sevens side in the world.

The rugby season is from April to September, and every village in Viti Levu seems to have its own rugby field – the abundance of giant bamboo means that even those with the most limited means can quickly put up a set of goalposts. Even if you're not a footy fan, it's worth going to a local Friday-afternoon or Saturday-morning match just to watch the excited crowd. During international tournaments, the whole country seems to grind to a halt.

Athletics is increasingly popular. The Coca Cola Games, a youth athletic championship, are held every April and attract national attention and widespread television coverage. School teams converge on Suva from across the country to seek glory.

Netball has the same popularity among Fiji's women as rugby does with men. The national squad, known as the Pearls, consistently rank highly on the world stage: their 11th-place finish in the 2015 World Championships was their first time finishing out of the top 10 in 15 years, although they remain the reigning Pacific champions.

Fiji is more urbanised than many might imagine, and two-thirds of the population now live in urban centres – principally Suva, the capital, and Viti Levu towns.

CULTURE SPORT

BURE KALOU

In the days of the old religion, every village had a *bure kalou* (spirit house), which was also used as a meeting house. These buildings had high-pitched roofs and usually stood on terraced foundations. The *bete* (priest), who was an intermediary between the villagers and spirits, lived in the temple and performed various rituals, including feasting on slain enemies and burying important people. A strip of white *masi* (decorated bark cloth) was usually hung from the ceiling to serve as a connection to the spirits. The construction of such a temple reputedly required that a strong man be buried alive in each of the corner-post holes.

Religion

Since the 1830s Christianity has been developing in Fiji and is an important part of cultural and political life. Indigenous Fijians maintain their traditional culture, but practices such as cannibalism and ancestor worship were erased by Christian teachings long ago. Tongan missionaries were particularly important in bringing Christianity to the islands.

Today 60% of Fijians are Christian, the majority of whom are Methodist, and the church remains a powerful force in internal affairs. There's a Catholic minority within this group of around 7%, and evangelical Christian churches are becoming increasingly popular.

Religion and politics have often gone hand in hand in Fiji, and church approval has been sought as a way of legitimising power structures, particularly after coups. Although there has been increased separation between church and state, religious leaders still carry a lot of soft power in society. Sunday is a day to worship and rest and a time spent with family. Most businesses close for the day and streets are deserted. If you find yourself at loose ends, consider attending a Sunday service. It is a real treat; Fijians love to sing and choir groups don't hold back. Many resorts now incorporate church services into their cultural tours.

Around 30% of Fijians are Hindu, 6% are Muslim and nearly 1% are Sikh. Adherence to these religions helped unify the new Fiji Indian communities after indenture, and Hindu, Muslim and Sikh schools have often been some of the best-performing academies in the country. The remainding 3% are a mix of Chinese religions and non-religious Fijians.

Even though they are far away from the heartland of Vedic astrology in India, many Indo-Fijians regularly consult with pundits (priests) for readings and predictions about the future.

Village Life

Although parts of Fiji – and particularly Viti Levu – are becoming increasingly urban-ised, Fiji's heart still beats strongest in its villages. If you get invited to someone's village (it's rude to just turn up unannounced), you're in for a treat. Life here is often governed by complex codes of behaviour, although Fiji's famous hospitality is likely to shrug off with a joke any social faux pas you may accidentally make.

Village Structures

Fijian villagers live in land-owning *mataqali* (extended family groups) under a hereditary chief, who allocates land to each family for farming. Land rights are central to traditional identity, and 'native' land can only ever be leased, and never sold. Village life is more conservative than its urban counterpart. Fiercely independent thinking is not encouraged, and generally being too different or too ambitious is seen as a threat. Concepts such as *kerekere* and *sevusevu* are still strong, especially in remote areas. *Kerekere* is unconditional giving based on the concept that time and property is communal. *Sevusevu* is the presentation of a gift such as kava for, say, permission to visit a village, or more powerfully, a *tabua* (whale's tooth) as a token of reconciliation or wedding gift.

Another important concept is *solevu*. This is a social gathering between two groups or villages: the hosts provide food, while the guests offer gifts than can range from yams and woven mats to gasoline. Once an important part of local political life, these days *solevu* tend to be restricted to the weddings or funerals of prestigious people.

In a Fijian village you will see few, if any, fences between homes, and children run from one home to the next at will and without thought. This communal sense of living forms the cornerstone of village life, and most Fijians would find it downright unneighbourly to erect a fence or wall between their homes.

> Legend has it that the plant that kava is made from sprung from the grave of a Tongan princess who died of a broken heart.

Village Etiquette

Finding your way around village etiquette may initially seem complicated, but the best way to gauge what is appropriate is to simply ask your hosts. The following tips will stand you in good stead.

➡ **Bring a gift** Always offer *sevusevu* (gift) to the village headman (*turaga-ni-koro*).

➡ **Dress to impress** Sleeves and *sulu* (skirt or wrapped cloth, worn to below the knees) or sarongs are appropriate for both men and women. Both sexes should cover their shoulders. Wear slip-on shoes: they're easier to take off when entering houses.

➡ **Mind your head** Fijians regard the head as sacred – never ever touch a person's head. Take off your hat and don't wear sunglasses pushed up on your head. Carry bags in your hands, not over your shoulder; it's considered rude to do otherwise.

> Fiji's most common garden plant is the hibiscus. Its large, beautiful flowers only last a day but are in plentiful supply. You'll find them everywhere – tucked behind ears, decorating tables and adorning pillows. Don't be afraid to tuck one behind your own ear – you know you want to.

➡ **Keep it low** Stoop when entering a *bure* (traditional thatch dwelling) and quietly sit cross-legged on the mat. It is polite to keep your head at a lower level than your host's.

➡ **Photography** Check with your host if you can take photos. It's impolite to take photos during the *sevusevu*.

➡ **Ask to be shown around** Never wander around unaccompanied: gardens and beaches are all someone's private realm.

➡ **Cover up** If you'll be bathing in the river or at a shared tap, wear a *sulu* while you wash. You will rarely see adult Fijians swimming and when they do they cover up with a T-shirt and *sulu*.

➡ **No kissing** It is rare to see public displays of affection between men and women, so curtail your passions in public to avoid embarrassing or offending locals.

➡ **Camping** If you're staying overnight, and had planned to camp but are offered a bed, accept it; it may embarrass your hosts if they think their *bure* is not good enough for you.

➡ **Sunday** This is a day for church and family, so avoid visiting then unless invited.

Daily Life

Fijians are early risers, and if you spend a night in a village expect to hear the first clatter of pots and pans and hushed tones of conversation at around 5.30am. As a recipient of Fijian hospitality, you may well be given the best, and in some cases only, bed in the house (many people still sleep on woven pandanus mats on the floor).

Most homes are no longer built in the traditional thatched *bure* style but are simple, rectangular, pitched-roof houses made from industrialised materials requiring less maintenance. Rural homes may not have electricity or plumbing, and people wash and get water from a communal tap fixed above a concrete square. Cooking is done over small kerosene stoves. Toilets may be of the long-drop variety, usually in a row of tin sheds tucked away behind the houses.

The women tend to most of the domestic duties – washing, cooking, cleaning and looking after the children. Men spend their days farming, fishing and performing communal obligations. Evenings are often spent sitting in the chief's (or another elder's) house talking and drinking *yaqona*.

The *balabala* (tree ferns) of Fiji are similar to those in Australia and New Zealand; once used on the gable ends of *bure* (traditional thatched dwellings), the trunks are now commonly seen carved into garden warriors – the Fijian counterpart of the Western garden gnome.

Survival Guide

Directory A–Z

Accommodation

Five-star hotels, B&Bs, hostels, motels, resorts, treehouses, bungalows on the beach and village homestays – there's no shortage of accommodation options in Fiji.

The peak visitor periods coincide with holidays in Australia and New Zealand (July/August, Christmas/New Year and Easter), and prices at this time are usually at their highest. Outside these times you'll frequently find useful discounts and lower walk-in rates.

Resorts

Resorts can cover almost any sort of accommodation in Fiji. As a rule of thumb a resort is any accommodation option that offers a complete package to guests, from room to food to activities. This can be anything from a top-end hotel on the Coral Coast to a boutique offering on an island in the Yasawas to a self-contained guesthouse specialising in scuba diving in Kadavu.

Most resorts price by the room rather than person. Packages for multiple-night

occupancies are common. If you're booking a long-term stay in Fiji, many places also offer a local resident price. The best prices are almost always found online and in advance; walk-in rates are usually higher. Check what's on offer at the time of booking. Many resorts are run on a cash-free basis, so you settle up the meals, drinks and activities you've had during your stay when you pay your bill on checkout.

Hotels & Guesthouses

Hotels and private guesthouses are more common on Viti Levu, Taveuni and Ovalau and are good bases for exploring Fiji's towns and rural areas away from the resorts.

Prices start at $50 per night and usually include breakfast.

Backpacker Resorts

Hostels in Fiji are usually called backpacker resorts. They primarily have dorm accommodation but usually have a handful of private rooms as well. A host of activities and excursions are part of the offering, and there's usually a bar and pool

as well (or failing that, access to the beach). They're a lively scene in which to meet other backpackers.

Prices are usually around $15 to $20 a night.

Homestays

Organised village homestays are possible in some areas and offer a great opportunity for visitors to learn about traditional Fijian life. Village etiquette is important during a homestay – for more information see p219. Prices start from around $50 per night for homestays but vary widely. Bringing a gift such as kava is often recommended.

Camping

Camping isn't popular in Fiji. If you're on village land, locals may commonly interpret a decision to sleep under canvas as a slight against their community as not being good enough to stay in.

Customs Regulations

Visitors arriving in Fiji may bring the following:

➡ 2.25L of liqueur or spirits, or 4.5L of wine or beer

➡ No more than 250g of tobacco products.

➡ You can bring as much currency as you like into the country, but you will need to declare any amount over $10,000 and you can't take out more than you brought in.

BOOK YOUR STAY ONLINE

For more accommodation reviews by Lonely Planet writers, check out lonelyplanet.com/fiji/hotels. You'll find independent reviews, as well as recommendations on the best places to stay. Best of all, you can book online.

Be aware that Fiji operates strict biosecurity measures. Importation of vegetable matter, seeds, animals, meat or dairy produce is prohibited without a licence from the Ministry of Agriculture & Fisheries. Bins are provided at customs for disposal of food items you may have inadvertently brought with you.

Restricted items

Pottery shards, turtle shells, coral, trochus shells and giant clamshells cannot be taken out of the country without a permit.

Tourist VAT Refund Scheme

Tourists can reclaim VAT on many items bought in Fiji, through the Tourist VAT Refund Scheme (TVRS). Refunds may be claimed at Nadi International Airport or Suva Wharf only. You need to have spent $500 at a registered VAT refund outlet (these include Jack's and Tappoo shops). Present your receipt at a Tourist VAT Refund Inspection Counter on departure. For more information vist the Fiji Revenue & Customs Authority (www.frca.org.fj).

Electricity

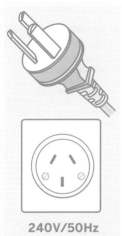

240V/50Hz

Embassies & Consulates

Generally speaking, your country's embassy won't be much help if the trouble you're in is remotely your own fault. Remember, you are bound by the laws of the country you are in.

A number of countries have diplomatic representation in Fiji (a complete list can be found at www.fiji.gov. fj). All embassies are in Suva.

Australian High Commission (Map p89; ☎338 2211; www.fiji.highcommission.gov. au; 37 Princes Rd, Tamavua)

Chinese Embassy (Map p89; ☎330 0251; http:// fj.china-embassy.org/eng; 183 Queen Elizabeth Dr)

European Union Embassy (Map p90; ☎331 3633; 4th fl, Fiji Development Bank Centre, Victoria Pde)

Federated States of Micronesia Embassy (Map p90; ☎330 4566; 37 Loftus St)

French Embassy (Map p90; ☎331 0526; www.ambafrance-fj. org; 7th fl, Dominion House, Thomson St)

Japanese Embassy (Map p90; ☎330 4633; www.fjemb-japan.go.jp; 2nd fl, Dominion House, Thomson St)

Korean Embassy (Map p90; ☎330 0977; 8th fl, Vanua House, Victoria Pde)

Nauruan High Commission (Map p90; ☎331 3566; 7th fl, Ratu Sukuna House, Macarthur St)

Netherlands Consulate (Map p90; ☎330 1499; 1st fl, Crompton Solicitors Suite, 10 Victoria Arcade)

New Zealand Embassy (Map p90; ☎331 1422; 10th fl, Reserve Bank Bldg, Pratt St)

Tuvaluan High Commission (Map p90; ☎330 1355; 16 Gorrie St)

UK High Commission (Map p90; ☎322 9100; www.british highcommission.gov.uk/fiji; Victoria House, 47 Gladstone Rd)

US Embassy (Map p89; ☎331 4466; http://suva.us embassy.gov; 158 Princes Rd, Tamavua)

Food

For more on Fijian cuisine, see the Culture chapter, p211.

GLBT Travellers

Fiji is one of the the more progressive countries in the Pacific region when it comes to the legal status of homosexuality and laws banning discrimination based on sexual orientation and gender identity were introduced following the implementation of the 2013 constitution.

Same-sex marriages and civil unions are not recognised in Fijian family law, which means visiting gay couples are unable to marry while on vacation.

There is a strong LGBT movement in Fiji, but the local scene remains fairly closeted. Nonetheless, a large number of openly gay men and women work in the hospitality industry, and some nightclubs in Lautoka, Nadi and Suva are gay-tolerant.

Fiji is socially conservative: any public displays of affection are frowned upon. For gay or lesbian couples the risks of receiving unwanted attention for outwardly homosexual behaviour is high.

Gay singles should exercise some caution; don't give anyone an excuse to even think you are paying for sex, and be very careful not to give the impression you are after young Fijian men.

Resources

Useful local NGOs include:

Drodrolagi Movement (www.facebook.com/Drodrolagi.Movement)

Haus of Khameleon (www.facebook.com/HausOfKhameleonFiji)

DIVA for Equality (www.divafiji.com)

Health

There is no malaria or rabies in Fiji. Health facilities are good; however, this is a small country with a limited budget, so 'good' does not necessarily compare with the facilities of a well-developed country.

The overall risk of illness for a normally healthy person is low; the most common problems are diarrhoeal upsets, viral sore throats and ear and skin infections – all of which can mainly be treated with self-medication. For serious symptoms, eg sustained fever, chest or abdominal pains, it is best to go to the nearest clinic or doctor.

Dengue Fever

Dengue fever is a virus spread by the bite of a day-biting mosquito. It causes a feverish illness with headache and severe muscle pains similar to those experienced with a bad, prolonged attack of influenza. Another name for the disease is 'break-bone fever' and that's what it feels like. Danger signs include prolonged vomiting, blood in the vomit and a blotchy rash. There is no preventive vaccine, and mosquito bites should be avoided whenever possible. Dengue fever requires medical care.

Recommended Vaccinations

There are no compulsory vaccinations needed for Fiji. The World Health Organization (WHO) recommends that all travellers be covered for diphtheria, tetanus, measles, mumps, rubella and polio, regardless of their destination. Most vaccines don't produce immunity until at least two weeks after they're given, so visit your physician at least six weeks before departure. A recent influenza vaccination is always a good idea when travelling, as are vaccinations for hepatitis A, hepatitis B and typhoid fever.

If you have been in a country affected by yellow fever within six days of arriving in Fiji, you will need an International Certificate of Vaccination for yellow fever to be allowed entry into the country.

Availability of Health Care

Fiji has readily available doctors in private practice and standard hospital and laboratory facilities with consultants. Private dentists, opticians and pharmacists are also available. The further you get from the main cities, the more basic the services.

Private consultations start from around $30. Fees for government-provided services vary from modest to negligible, but waiting times can be very long. Direct payment is required everywhere except where a specific arrangement is made, eg in the case of evacuation or where a prolonged hospital stay is necessary; you will need to contact your insurer.

Medications

Most commonly used medications are available. Private pharmacies are not allowed by law to dispense listed drugs without a prescription from a locally registered practitioner, but many will do so for travellers if shown the container or a prescription from home.

Water

The municipal water supply in Suva, Nadi and other large towns is chlorinated and can usually be trusted, but elsewhere avoid untreated tap water. After heavy rain it's worth boiling the water before you drink it.

Insurance

Worldwide travel insurance is available at www.lonelyplanet.com/travel-insurance. You can buy, extend and claim online anytime – even if you're already on the road.

A good travel insurance policy covering theft, loss and medical problems is essential. Some policies specifically exclude designated 'dangerous activities', such as scuba diving, so make sure the policy you choose fully covers you for your activity of choice.

You may prefer a policy that pays doctors or hospitals directly rather than

---

EATING PRICE RANGES

The following price ranges refer to a standard main course meal:

$	Less than $15
$$	$15–$25
$$$	More than $25

requiring you to pay on the spot and claim later. If you have to claim later, make sure you keep all documentation. Check that the policy covers ambulances and emergency medical evacuations by air.

Internet Access

If you can get a phone signal in Fiji, you can normally find somewhere to get online. In remote areas, prepare for internet access to be limited, expensive (due to the need for connection by satellite) or completely non-existent.

➡ Budget resorts in Nadi also have internet access, some using prepay cards that deduct credits in 15-minute allotments (which works out at around $10 an hour).

➡ If you're carrying your own laptop or iPad, you can sign up for a prepay account with a service provider such as **Connect** (www.connect.com.fj), **Unwired Fiji** (www.unwired.com.fj) or **Vodafone** (www.vodafone.com.fj). The latter sells modem sticks for $79, and 1GB of data costs $15.

➡ Many midrange and top-end resorts have internet connections, so you simply need to plug in your computer.

Internet cafes

Internet cafes are fairly common in Suva, Lautoka and Nadi; competition means that you can jump online for as little as $3 per hour. Outside of urban centres, access is more limited, slower and pricier, reaching up to $8 per hour.

Modems

If you want to carry the internet with you, consider buying a local modem from either **Unwired Fiji** (www.unwired.com.fj; sold in Digicel shops) or **Vodafone** (www.vodafone.com.fj). Free-standing modems or USB stick modems

are available, connecting at up to 4G. Prices start from around $50 per month for 14GB on a pay-as-you-go plan.

Wi-fi

Wi-fi is increasingly widespread in Nadi and Suva. Hotels may or may not offer it as standard, and there's often a fee to get online. On island resorts, wi-fi is more likely to be restricted or expensive.

Legal Matters

Drugs are not uncommon in Fiji, including marijuana and amphetamines. All are illegal. The consequences if you are caught in possession can be serious – it is not uncommon for drug users in Fiji to be imprisoned in the psychiatric hospital.

Most travellers manage to avoid any run-ins with the local authorities. If you are arrested, though, you have the right to contact your

embassy or consulate, which will be allowed to provide you with legal representation but can do little else.

Maps

Specialist marine charts are usually available at Fijian ports but are expensive.

Map Shop (Map p90; ☑321 1395; www.lands.gov.fj; Lands & Surveys Department, Southern Cross Rd, Suva; ☺8am-3.30pm Mon-Thu, to 3pm Fri) Beyond the maps found at the front of each telephone book, this shop in the Government Buildings stocks a good map of Suva and the surrounding areas, as well as big (1:50,000) and detailed topographic maps of each island or island group.

Money

The local currency is the Fiji dollar ($); it's fairly stable relative to Australian and New Zealand dollars. All prices quoted here are in Fiji dollars unless otherwise specified.

The dollar is broken down into 100 cents. Bank notes come in denominations of $100, $50, $20, $10 and $5. There are coins to the value of $2, $1, $0.50, $0.20, $0.10 and $0.05.

It's good to have a few options for accessing money – take a credit card, a debit card, and a small amount of foreign currency. The best currencies to carry are Australian, New Zealand or US dollars, which all freely exchangeable.

Before you head out to remote parts of Fiji, always check to make sure you can access money, use your plastic or change currency.

ATMs

ATMs are common in major urban areas, and most accept the main international debit cards including Cirrus and Plus. Although they are increasingly commonplace, you won't find ATMs in remote areas, including the Yasawas, so plan ahead.

Credit Cards

Restaurants, shops, mid-range to top-end hotels, car-rental agencies and tour and travel agents will usually accept major credit cards. Visa, Amex and MasterCard are widely used. Some resorts charge an additional 5% for payment by credit card. Cash advances are available through credit cards at most banks in larger towns.

Tipping

Tipping is not expected or overtly encouraged in Fiji; however, if you feel that the service is worth it, tips are always appreciated.

Opening Hours

Fijians are not known for their punctuality – 'Fiji time' is a highly elastic concept, derived from the languid pace of island life. A few shops are open for limited hours on Sunday, but the general rule is to assume everything will be closed. Many places in Fiji close for lunch from 1pm to 2pm.

Banks 9.30am to 4pm Monday to Thursday and 9.30am to 3pm Friday

Government offices 8am to 4.30pm Monday to Thursday and 8am to 4pm Friday

Post offices 8am to 4pm Monday to Friday and 8am to 11.30am Saturday

Restaurants lunch 11am to 2pm, dinner 6pm to 9pm or 10pm

Shops 9am to 5pm Monday to Friday and 9am to 1pm Saturday

Post

Post Fiji (www.postfiji.com. fj) is generally quick with its actual delivery, if a little slow at the counter, and has offices throughout the country.

If you're posting souvenirs home that include woven grass or wood, you'll need to have your parcel cleared by the **Fiji Biosecurity Authority** (☑331 2512; www.baf. com.fj; Renown St, Suva). This is a free and usually quick procedure – give their biosecurity seal sticker to the post office clerk with your parcel.

DHL (Map p89; ☑337 2766; www.dhl.com; Grantham Rd, Suva) has representatives throughout the country, with its head office in Suva. **FedEx** (☑672-2933; www.fedex.com/fj;

Nadi International Airport) has an office in Nadi only.

Public Holidays

Fijians celebrate a variety of holidays and festivals.

Exact dates vary from year to year but are given a year in advance on the government's website (www.fiji.gov.fj) in the 'About Fiji' section.

Annual public holidays include the following:

New Year's Day 1 January

Prophet Mohammed's Birthday December or January

Easter (Good Friday & Easter Monday) March/April

National Sports Day March

Fiji Day (Independence Day) 10 October

Diwali Festival October/November

Christmas Day 25 December

Boxing Day 26 December

Safe Travel

Fiji is a very safe place for travellers, and common sense is all you really need to ensure a safe and happy holiday. That said, Fiji isn't immune to crime, and occasionally tourists are targeted. It is worth keeping the following in mind.

➡ When you're in Nadi or Suva do not walk around at night, even in a group. Locals catch cabs after dark and you should do the same.

GOVERNMENT TRAVEL ADVICE

For the latest travel warnings and cautious advice, log onto the following websites:

Australian Department of Foreign Affairs & Trade (www.smartraveller.gov.au)

New Zealand Ministry of Foreign Affairs & Trade (www.safetravel.govt.nz)

UK Foreign & Commonwealth Office (www.fco.gov.uk/en/travel-and-living-abroad)

USA Department of State – Bureau of Consular Affairs (www.travel.state.gov)

➡ Male travellers in particular are often approached and asked if they want marijuana and/or prostitutes – it's illegal to buy either (both sex work and buying sex are criminalised in Fiji).

➡ If your stay is long-term, be aware that burglaries are not uncommon. Always make sure you have good locks on all doors and windows of rental properties.

Shopping

The main tourist centres of Nadi, the Coral Coast and Suva have lots of handicraft shops. Savusavu (on Vanua Levu) and Lautoka also have lots of handicraft shops, which are quieter and where the salespeople are less pushy. Also, you can often buy interesting handicrafts direct from villages, particularly woven goods and carvings.

Look out for the 'Made in Fiji' label, a government-run initiative to support Fijian crafts and industries. For more information see www.fijianmade.gov.fj.

Be cautious about buying wooden artefacts. A label reading 'treated wood' doesn't guarantee an absence of borers. Inspect items closely for holes or other marks, or you may end up paying more for quarantine in your own country than you did for the actual piece.

Popular souvenir items include:

➡ Traditional artefacts such as war clubs, spears and chieftain cannibal forks, as well as kava bowls of various sizes, woven pandanus mats, baskets from Kioa, sandalwood or coconut soap, and *masi* (bark cloth) sold in the form of wall hangings, covered books and postcards.

➡ Pottery can be a good buy – if you can get it home in one piece.

➡ Clothing shops in Suva and Nadi have bula shirts (a *masi*- or floral-design shirt) and fashion items by local designers. There are also vibrant saris and Indian jewellery on sale.

➡ Stuffed, *masi*-patterned teddies called Bula Bears are Taveuni specialities and are quite cute.

Bargaining

Indigenous Fijians generally do not like to bargain; however, it's customary in Indo-Fijian stores, especially in Nadi and Suva. Indo-Fijian shop owners and taxi drivers consider it bad luck to lose their first customer of the day, so you can expect an especially hard sales pitch in the morning.

Telephone

There are no area codes within Fiji. Smaller and more remote islands often lie outside the phone network.

Country code	679
International access code	00
Operator assistance	010
International operator assistance	022

Mobile Phones

Mobile phones in Fiji use the GSM system. There are two mobile phone companies, **Digicel** (www.digicelfiji.com) and **Vodafone** (www.vodafone.com.fj), both of which offer international roaming agreements. Alternatively, you can pick up a plan or pre-paid SIM card (ID required) at any phone shop. Prices start from $10, but look out for offers.

Phonecards

Fiji has distinctive public phone booths, their shapes inspired by traditional *drua* (masted canoes). They take telecards, which can be purchased from post offices, phone shops and many general stores in denominations ranging from $3 to $50.

Time

Fiji is 12 hours ahead of GMT/UTC. When it's noon in Suva, corresponding times elsewhere are as follows:

CITY	TIME
SAME DAY	
Sydney	10am
Auckland	noon
Honolulu	2pm
PREVIOUS DAY	
London	midnight
Los Angeles	4pm
New York	7pm

Add one hour to these times if the other country has daylight saving time in place.

Tourist Information

The **Fiji Visitors Bureau** (Map p60; 672 2433; www.fiji.travel; Suite 107, Colonial Plaza, Namaka; ⊙8am-4.30pm Mon-Thu, to 4pm Fri) in Nadi is the only tourist information body in Fiji. The website is excellent, but the office deals mainly with promoting Fiji abroad and has little to offer walk-in travellers.

The **South Pacific Tourism Organisation** (Map p90; 330 4177; www.spto.org; 3rd fl, Dolphin Plaza, cnr Loftus St & Victoria Pde, Suva) promotes cooperation between the South Pacific island nations for the development of tourism in the region, including Fiji.

Travellers with Disabilities

In Pacific countries people with disabilities are simply part of the community, looked after by family where necessary. In some cities there are schools for children with disabilities, but access facilities such as ramps, lifts, accessible toilets and Braille, are rare. Buses do not have wheelchair access and pavements have high curbs.

Nevertheless, people will go out of their way to give you assistance when you need it. This includes scooping you up in their arms so that they can carry you on and off boats.

Most top-end hotels have at least one disabled-friendly room with wheelchair access, paths, walk-in showers and handrails, but this may be tucked away at the back of the resort. It's a good idea to check exactly what facilities a hotel has to ensure it suits your needs.

Even if the resort is disabled-friendly, consider how you plan to reach your destination. Mamanuca and Yasawa resorts are commonly accessed by catamarans, which are met by small dinghies that run guests to the beach. Those with mobility impairments may find arriving this way challenging. Instead opt for islands that can be reached by plane or, at the very least, have a wharf.

Organisations

The **Fiji Disabled People's Association** (Map p89; ☑330 1161; www.fdpa.org.fj; 3 Brown St, Toorak, Suva) may be able to offer pretrip planning advice.

Visas

Entering Fiji is very straightforward. To get a visa you'll need an onward ticket and a passport valid for at least three months longer than your intended stay. A free tourist visa for four months is granted on arrival to citizens of more than 100 countries, including most countries belonging to the European Union, British Commonwealth, North America, much of South America, India,

Indonesia, Israel, Japan, Mexico, the Philippines, Russia, Samoa, Solomon Islands, South Korea, Tonga, Tuvalu, Vanuatu and many others.

Nationals from countries excluded from the list will have to apply for visas through a Fijian embassy abroad prior to arrival. More information can be found on the website of the **Department of Immigration** (Map p90; ☑331 2622; www.immigration.gov.fj; Government Bldgs, Suva).

Visitors cannot partake in political activity or study, and work permits are needed if you intend to live and work in Fiji. Foreign journalists will require a work visa if they spend more than 14 days in Fiji.

Arriving by Boat

Those entering Fiji by boat are subject to the same visa requirements as those arriving by plane. There are other requirements for those entering Fiji by yacht.

Visa Extensions

In theory, tourist visas can be extended for up to six months by applying through the **Department of Immigration** (Map p90; ☑331 2622; www.immigration.gov.fj; Government Bldgs, Suva). You'll need to show an onward ticket and proof of sufficient funds, and your passport must be valid for three months after your proposed departure. Processing can be slow, and success is not automatic.

Volunteering

Several organisations offer volunteering opportunies in Fiji, mostly for extended periods of time. Different organisations are on the lookout for different skill sets, so do your research well and

if at all possible, make contact with the volunteers who went before.

Volunteering often takes place in fairly remote locations under fairly basic conditions. If you are liable to faint at the sight of a gecko clinging to the roof of your thatched hut, it may not be for you.

For more information, see Lonely Planet's *Volunteer: A Traveller's Guide*.

Trusted organisations with volunteer opportunities in Fiji include:

Fiji Aid International (www.fijiaidinternational.com)

Peace Corps (www.peacecorps.gov)

Australian Volunteers for International Development (www.dfat.gov.au/australianvolunteers)

Women Travellers

Fiji is a fairly male-dominated society, but it is unlikely that solo women travellers will experience any difficulties as a result.

If you're travelling alone, you may experience whistles and stares but you're unlikely to feel threatened. Nevertheless, some men will assume lone females are fair game and several female readers have complained of being harassed or ripped off, particularly in touristy areas.

On rare occasions lone women have been harassed and even attacked on mainland beaches and forest trails. We haven't heard of any incidents on the small outlying islands, but while on Viti Levu, exercise caution before visiting a secluded spot by yourself.

Generally speaking, though, female travellers will find Fijian men friendly and helpful.

Transport

GETTING THERE & AWAY

Fiji's central location in the South Pacific makes it one of the main airline hubs in the region, and as a result it often features as an extended stopover on travellers' itineraries as they travel between Australia or New Zealand and the northern hemisphere.

Flights and tours can be booked online at www.lonelyplanet.com/bookings.

Entering the Country

All visitors require a passport valid for more than three months after their proposed date of departure. Most nationalities can obtain visas on arrival. For more information, see p228.

Air

Airports & Airlines

The national carrier is **Fiji Airways** (☑672 0888; www.fijiairways.com), formerly Air Pacific. As well as offering international connections, it codeshares flights with Qantas, Air New Zealand, Cathay Pacific, American Airlines and Etihad.

Most visitors to Fiji arrive at the small but well-organised **Nadi International Airport** (NAN; Map p54; www.airportsfiji.com/nadi_aiport.php; Queens Rd), situated 9km north of central Nadi. **Nausori Airport** (Map p54), about 23km northeast of Suva, is used primarily for domestic flights but receives a small number of regional international connections.

REGIONAL CONNECTIONS

Fiji Airways serves the following Pacific capitals: Port Vila (Vanuatu), Honiara (Solomon Islands), Port Moresby (Papua New Guinea), Nuku'alofa (Tonga), Apia (Samoa), South Tarawa (Kiribati), Funafuti (Tuvalu), as well as Honolulu in Hawaii.

Airlines serving the Pacific region from Nadi International Airport:

Air Vanuatu (www.airvanuatu.com) Flights to Port Vila, Vanuatu.

Air Niugini (www.airniugini.com.pg) Flights to Port Moresby, Papua New Guinea, via Honiara (Solomon Islands).

Solomon Airlines (www.flysolomons.com) Direct flights to Honiara, Solomon Islands, or via Port Vila (Vanuatu).

Tickets

➡ High-season travel to Fiji is between April and October, as well as the peak Christmas and New Year period.

➡ Airfares peak between April and June, and in December and January.

➡ Fiji is a popular destination for Australian and New Zealand families; school

---

CLIMATE CHANGE & TRAVEL

Every form of transport that relies on carbon-based fuel generates CO_2, the main cause of human-induced climate change. Modern travel is dependent on aeroplanes, which might use less fuel per kilometre per person than most cars but travel much greater distances. The altitude at which aircraft emit gases (including CO_2) and particles also contributes to their climate change impact. Many websites offer 'carbon calculators' that allow people to estimate the carbon emissions generated by their journey and, for those who wish to do so, to offset the impact of the greenhouse gases emitted with contributions to portfolios of climate-friendly initiatives throughout the world. Lonely Planet offsets the carbon footprint of all staff and author travel.

holidays in these countries are considered high periods in Fiji.

Sea

Travelling to Fiji by sea is difficult unless you're on a cruise ship or a yacht.

Cruise Ships

Fiji doesn't feature in many cruising itineraries, and few cruise ships call here. A notable exception is **P&O Cruises** (www.pocruises.com.au), which calls into Fiji as part of a larger South Pacific circuit from Brisbane or Sydney.

Yacht

Strict laws govern the entry of yachts into Fiji, and skippers should immediately make for one of designated ports before exploring Fijian waters. Fiji's five designated Ports of Entry are: Suva, Lautoka, Levuka, Savusavu and Oinafa (Rotuma). Advance applications must be made to request Port Denarau as a port of entry.

The **Pacific Puddle Jump** (www.pacificpuddle jump.com), also sometimes known as the Coconut Milk Run, is a popular route cruising from California to French Polynesia (and sometimes on to New Zealand) via Hawaii, Tahiti, Rarotonga, Vava'u and Fiji. To make the most of the weather, most yachts depart California in February and reach Fiji in July or August.

Boats from New Zealand often time their departure to coincide with the Auckland-to-Fiji yacht race in June. By the end of October most yachts head south to Australia and New Zealand via New Caledonia to spend the summer there.

Yacht Help Fiji (☑675 0911; http://fijimarineguide. com; Shop 2, Port Denarau Terminal Building, Port Denarau, Nadi) provides a useful online guide to sailing to and around Fiji.

PORT PROCEDURES

➡ Vessels must be cleared by immigration and customs and are prohibited from visiting any outer islands before doing so.

➡ 48 hours' notice must be given in advance of arrival. Failure to do so attracts heavy fines. Download and complete an Advanced Notice of Arrival Form (C2C) from the **FRCA** (Fiji Revenue & Customs Authority; www.frca. org.fj).

➡ Fees payable on arrival are $150 (quarantine) and $172.50 (health). There is no charge for immigration or customs.

➡ Border facilities operate Monday to Friday 8am to 4.30pm. Arrival outside these hours incurs extra fees and must be arranged in advance.

➡ To complete customs formalities when you arrive, you will require a certificate of clearance from the previous port of call, a crew list and passports for everyone on board except children travelling on their parent's passport.

➡ If you wish to visit any place beside a port of entry, a cruising permit from the Ministry of Fijian Affairs is required. These are easily obtained and free of charge.

➡ On arrival contact Port Control on VHF channel 16 to be directed to the quarantine area and await the arrival of customs officials.

➡ Before departing you'll need to complete clearance formalities (within 24 hours), providing inbound clearance papers, your vessel's details and your next port of call.

GETTING AROUND

By using local buses, carriers (small trucks) and ferries you can get around Fiji's main islands relatively cheaply and easily. If you'd like more com-

fort or are short on time, you can utilise air-conditioned express buses, rental vehicles, charter boats and small planes.

Air

Viti Levu's airports at Nadi and Nausori (near Suva) are the main domestic hubs. Other domestic airports include:

➡ Savusavu and Labasa (Vanua Levu)

➡ Vunisea (Kadavu)

➡ Matei (Taveuni)

➡ Bureta (Ovalau)

➡ Koro (Lomaiviti)

➡ Vanuabalavu and Cicia (Northern Lau)

➡ Lakeba (Southern Lau)

➡ Rotuma

Some other small islands also have airstrips, including Yasawa island and Malolo Lailai and Mana in the Mamanucas; otherwise, chartered seaplanes or helicopters can get you almost everywhere in the Mamanuca and Yasawa Groups.

Airlines in Fiji

Domestic flights are in small, light planes. Some may find them scary, especially if it's windy or turbulent, but the views of the islands, coral reefs and lagoons are fantastic.

Most flights are turnaround flights that return to Nadi or Suva after unloading and reloading passengers. Some flights only go once a week, so it is advisable to book well in advance to secure a seat.

Arriving before or after your possessions is not an uncommon occurrence. It's a smart policy to take a change of clothes and all your valuables in your carry-on luggage.

Fares vary widely according to destination demand. Sample one-way fares include:

➡ Nadi–Suva $89

→ Nadi–Kadavu $230

→ Nadi–Savusavu $320

Fiji Link ([☎]672 0888; www. fijiairways.com) The domestic subsidiary of Fiji Airways, with the widest network of connections.

Northern Air ([☎]347 5005; www.northernair.com.fj) Flights from Suva to Levuka, Vanua Levu, Taveuni and various destinations in the Lau Group, as well as charters.

Charter Services

Charter services are most commonly used by those wishing to maximise their time at island resorts.

Island Hoppers (Map p66; [☎]672 0410; www.helicopters. com.fj) Offers helicopter transfers to most of the Mamanuca islands resorts from Nadi Airport and Denarau; charter planes also fly to Taveuni, Savusavu and Kadavu.

Turtle Airways (Map p60;[☎]672 1888; www.turtleairways.com) Has a fleet of seaplanes departing from New Town Beach near Nadi. As well as joy flights, it provides transfer services to the Mamanucas and Yasawas.

Pacific Island Air ([☎]672 5644; www.pacificislandair.com) Offers helicopter, plane and seaplane transfers and scenic flights in the Mamanuca and Yasawa Groups.

Heli-Tours Fiji ([☎]675 0255; www.helitoursfiji.com) For resort transfers from Nadi and Denarau to the Mamanuca and Yasawa island groups and the Coral Coast, as well as scenic flights.

HeliPro Fiji ([☎]770 7770; helipro.com.fj) For superfast helicopter transfers to pretty much anywhere in Fiji you'd like to go.

Bicycle

Cycling allows you to see the countryside at your own pace and reduces your carbon footprint at the same time. It's a particularly good way to explore Viti Levu, Vanua Levu

(the Hibiscus Hwy) and parts of Ovalau and Taveuni.

→ With the exception of the Kings and Queens Roads, most roads, especially inland, are rough, hilly and unsealed, so mountain bikes are the best option.

→ The best time to go is the drier season (May to October); note that the eastern sides of the larger islands receive higher rainfall.

→ Bring your own bike, helmet, waterproof gear, repair kit and all other equipment. It is difficult to get bike parts in Fiji. If you wish to take a bike on a domestic flight, make sure it is demountable.

→ Drivers are not used to cyclists and can be manic in towns or a menace on highways. Avoid riding in the evening when visibility is low. Travel light but carry plenty of water – it can be hot and dusty or humid.

→ The cheapest place to store bikes is at backpacker hostels.

→ On Viti Levu, bike hire can be arranged through **Stinger Bicycle Tours** ([☎]992 2301; www.stingerbikes.com; ☺8am-6pm) in Nadi.

Boat

With the exception of the ferries listed here, often the only means of transport between neighbouring islands is by small local boats or pricey water taxis. These rarely have radio-phones or life jackets. If the weather looks ominous or the boat is overcrowded, consider postponing the trip or opting for a flight.

Ferry

Regular ferry services link Viti Levu to Vanua Levu, Taveuni, Ovalau and Kadavu. Ferry timetables are notorious for changing frequently, plus boats sometimes leave at odd hours with a lengthy

waiting period at stopovers. The worst thing about the longer trips is that the toilets can sometimes become disgusting (take your own toilet paper). There are irregular boats that take passengers from Suva to the Lau Group and Rotuma.

NADI–MAMANUCA GROUP

Every day a small flotilla of high-speed catamarans departs Denarau Marina to the resorts on the Mamanuca islands. All boats have a free pick-up and drop-off service between the port and Nadi Hotels. Mana, Malolo and Malolo Lailai all have wharves; at the other islands the arriving catamarans are met by a swarm of resort dinghies that take turns to pull alongside the bigger catamaran and deposit or collect travellers.

Luggage is colour-coded with tags, but it's a good idea to check that your bags have followed you into the dinghy. In calm weather the transfer of passengers from big boat to little boat goes smoothly, but when there is motion in the ocean, things become interesting.

Awesome Adventures Fiji (Map p66; [☎]675 0499; www. awesomefiji.com) Calls into five Mamanuca islands on its daily run to the Yasawas.

Malolo Cat (Map p66; [☎]675 0205) Runs four daily transfers between Port Denarau and Plantation, Musket Bay and Lomani resorts on Malolo Lailai Island.

South Sea Cruises (Map p66; [☎]675 0500; www.ssc.com.fj) Operates two fast catamarans from Denarau Marina to most of the Mamanuca islands.

NADI–YASAWA GROUP

Awesome Adventures Fiji (Map p62; [☎]675 0499; www. awesomefiji.com) Owned by the same company as South Sea Cruises, it operates the lurid-yellow *Yasawa Flyer*, a large catamaran that services all of the resorts on the Yasawa islands. It's a large boat with a comfortable interior that has a snack shop and toilets, but you'll still feel the swell on choppy days.

SUVA–VANUA LEVU & TAVEUNI

Two shipping companies, Bligh Water Shipping and Goundar Shipping, connect Suva and Savusavu, often via Koro, Taveuni and/or Ovalau.

It takes around 12 hours to reach Savusavu. For those bound for Labasa, a bus often meets the boats at Savusavu, and tickets can be bought in Suva that include the Labasa bus transfer. Sometimes the boats depart from Natovi Landing, a half-hour bus ride north of Suva. Two daily ferries run between Natuvu in Vanua Levu and Taveuni (see p153).

Bligh Water Shipping (☑in Suva 331 8247; www.blighwatershipping.com.fj; 1-2 Matua St, Walu Bay) Has regular Natovi–Savusavu departures aboard the MV *Westerland* in three classes, including supercomfy cabins, double bunks and economy seats. The ferry usually arrives in Savusavu in the wee hours of the morning.

Goundar Shipping (Map p89; ☑in Suva 330 1035; http://goundarshipping.com; 22-24 Tofua St, Walu Bay) The comfortable *Lomaiviti Princess* departs Suva every Monday and Friday for a 12-hour voyage to Savusavu, and onwards for 2-3 hours to Taveuni. Accommodation ranges from economy seating to first-class cabins; facilities include a theatre room, kids' playground and cafe. A second ferry was due to be added to the route at the time of writing. It also has a branch in **Savusavu** (Map p156; ☑in Savusavu 885 0108, Kong's Shop, Main St).

NATOVI (SUVA)–OVALAU (LEVUKA)

Suva ferries actually leave from Natovi Landing, which is 90 minutes north of the city, and land at Buresala Landing on Ovalau.

Patterson Brothers Shipping (☑331 5644; 1st fl, Epworth Arcade, Nina St, Suva) Operates a daily service between Suva and Levuka. Tickets are for a combined bus-ferry through service, with a journey time of around four to five hours.

SUVA–KORO

Goundar Shipping (☑in Suva 330 1035; http://goundarshipping.com; 22-24 Tofua St, Walu Bay) Weekly ferry every Monday from Suva to Koro, on the *Lomaiviti Princess*.

SUVA–KADAVU

Viti Levu is connected to Kadavu by only two companies. Both sail out of Suva.

Goundar Shipping (☑in Suva 330 1035; http://goundarshipping.com; 22-24 Tofua St, Walu Bay) Overnight voyage from Suva to Vunisea every Wednesday on the *Lomaiviti Princess*, departing 10pm and arriving around 6am. Accommodation ranges from economy seating to first-class cabins; facilities include a theatre room, playground and cafe.

Venu Shipping (☑339 5000; Narain Jetty, Walu Bay, Suva) Weekly overnight service every Tuesday evening from Suva to Vunisea and Kavala Bay on the *Sinu-i-Wasa* cargo ship. The ferry is basic, but there is a small number of cabins with bunk beds.

OUTER ISLANDS

There are very few services to the Lau, Moala and Rotuma Groups. Those that run are slow, uncomfortable and erratic. Many islands only receive one ferry a month, making this an unreliable option for anyone with a fixed timetable.

Goundar Shipping currently visits Vanuabalavu and Cicia in the Lau Group, and Rotuma once a month – call ahead for the schedule. A new ship, the MV *Sea Rakino*, was coming into service as we went to press, offering a more regular service linking the Lau Group to Suva, with

the possibility of a stop at Savusavu and Taveuni.

Seaview Shipping (☑in Suva 330 9515; www.seaviewshippingfiji.com; 37 Matua St, Walu Bay) MV *Sandy* regularly travels from Suva to Upper Southern Lau and Lower Southern Lau.

Cruise Ship

Only one local company so far has taken advantage of Fiji's potential as a cruise destination.

Captain Cook Cruises (☑670 1823; www.captaincookcruisesfiji.com) Offers three- to seven-night cruises around the Yasawas, a seven-night cruise around Vanua Levu (also taking in Levuka), and an 11-night cruise around Kadavu and the Lau Group. All departures sail from Port Denarau.

Yacht

Yachting is a great way to explore the Fiji archipelago, but remember: if you wish to visit any place except a port of entry, a cruising permit from the Ministry of Fijian Affairs is required. These are free of charge and usually issued on the spot.

For more information, **Yacht Help Fiji** (☑675 0911; http://fijimarineguide.com; Shop 2, Port Denarau Terminal Building, Port Denarau, Nadi) has an excellent online guide as well as a base at Port Denarau.

Bus

Fiji's larger islands have extensive and inexpensive bus networks. Local buses are cheap and regular and a great way to mix with the locals. While they can be fairly noisy and smoky, they are perfect for the tropics, with unglazed windows and pull-down tarpaulins when it rains.

➡ There are bus stops, but you can hail buses along the road, especially in rural areas. Most drivers prefer to go downhill at the maximum speed their vehicle allows to make up for the excruciatingly slow speed they travel going uphill. It's a lot like being on a roller coaster, only cheaper.

➡ Reservations are not necessary for local buses.

➡ On Viti Levu, there are several companies with comfortable air-conditioned express buses: **Pacific Transport** (☑330 4366; www.pacifictransport.com.fj), **Sunbeam Transport** (☑338 2122; www.sunbeamfiji.com) and **Coral Sun** (☑672 3311; www.touristtransportfiji.com/coral-sun-express-booking). Timetables can be checked online.

➡ Pacific Transport also operates services on Taveuni. Local companies operate buses on Vanua Levu, but they can be slow and their timetables are often erratic.

➡ If you are on a tight schedule or have an appointment, though, it's a good idea to buy your ticket in advance, especially for bus trips and tours over longer distances (eg Suva to Nadi).

Car & Motorcycle

About 90% of Fiji's 5100km of roads, of which about one-fifth are sealed. are on Viti Levu and Vanua Levu. Both of these islands are fun to explore by car, 4WD or motorcycle.

Driving Licence

If you hold a current driving licence from an English-speaking country, you are entitled to drive in Fiji. Otherwise you will need an international driving permit, which should be obtained in your home country before travelling.

Fuel

Petrol stations are common and easy to find on Viti Levu and Vanua Levu. They are most prolific and competitive in the cities. Once you get off

the beaten track, however, they become fewer and farther between. If you plan to do some driving by 4WD into Viti Levu's interior, you should take a full tank with you. Fuel may be available in village shops, but don't assume so.

Hire

Rental cars are relatively expensive in Fiji. Despite this, it is a good way to explore the larger islands, especially if you can split the cost with others.

Check the rental conditions: some agencies do not allow their cars to be driven on unpaved roads, limiting your ability to explore the highlands. Also check if the agency allows you to take the vehicles on roll-on, roll-off ferries to Vanua Levu, Taveuni or Ovalau, if these are on your itinerary. If you do take a car on to Vanua Levu, it's best to hire a 4WD.

The shorter the hire period, the higher the rate. Delivery and collection are often included in the price. Rates for a week or more with an international company start at around $125 per day, excluding tax, but the same car can cost an extra 50% per day for just one or two days' hire. Some companies will hire at an hourly rate or per half day, while some have a minimum hire of three days. It's usual to pay a deposit by credit card. If you don't have a credit card, you'll need to leave a hefty cash bond.

The minimum-age requirement is 21, or in some cases 25.

Generally, the larger well-known companies have better cars and support but are more expensive. Consider what's appropriate for you, including how inconvenienced you might be if the car breaks down, what support services are provided, the likely distance to services, cost of insurance, if value-added tax (VAT) is included and the excess or excess-waiver amount.

Regardless of where you rent from, check brakes, water and tyre pressure, and condition before heading off.

The easiest place to rent vehicles is on Viti Levu. Most rental agencies have offices at Nadi International Airport; the established companies also have offices in other towns and rental desks at larger hotels. Car-rental agencies on Vanua Levu and Taveuni have mostly 4WDs due to the islands' rough roads.

Although not widely available, motorcycles and scooters are not a bad way to travel in Fiji. Similar traffic rules and rental conditions as mentioned previously for car rental apply to motorcycles and scooters.

Some of the more reputable car-rental agencies on Viti Levu:

Avis Rent a Car (Map p79; www.avis.com.fj) Branches at Nadi Airport (☑672 2233), Nausori Airport (☑337 8361), Port Denarau (Map p79; ☑672 2233) and Suva (☑337 8361)

Budget Rent a Car (www.budget.com.fj) Branches at Labasa (☑881 1999), Lautoka (☑666 6166), Nadi Airport (☑672 2636), Nausori Airport (☑347 9299), Port Denarau (☑675 0888), Savusavu (Map p156; ☑881 1999), Sigatoka (Map p75; ☑650 0986) and Suva (Map p89; ☑331 5899).

Hertz (www.hertzfiji.net) Branches at Nadi Airport (☑672 3466), Pacific Harbour (☑992 3923) and Suva (Map p89; ☑338 0981).

Thrifty Car Rental (www.thrifty.com) Branches at Nadi Airport (☑672 2935) and Suva (Map p90; ☑331 4436).

INSURANCE

Third-party insurance is compulsory. Some car-rental companies include it in their daily rates, while others add it at the end (count on $25 to $30, at least). Personal accident insurance is highly recommended if you are not already covered by travel insurance. Renters are liable for the first $500 damage. Common exclusions, or problems that won't be paid for by the insurance company, include tyre damage, underbody and overhead damage, windscreen damage and theft of the vehicle.

Road Conditions

The perimeter of Viti Levu is easy to get to know by car. Both the Queens Road and the Kings Road are fully sealed. It takes about 3½ hours to drive the 200km from Nadi International Airport to Suva (via the Queens Road), depending on how many lorries you get caught behind on the hills. Roads into Viti Levu's interior are unsealed, and a 4WD is generally necessary.

There are unsealed roads around most of Vanua Levu's perimeter, but there's a sealed road from Labasa to Savusavu and the first 20km of the Hibiscus Hwy from Savusavu along the scenic coast is also paved. The remainder of the Hibiscus Hwy is quite rough.

Road Hazards

Some locals drive with a fairly heavy foot on the accelerator pedal, and many ignore the whole idea of sticking to the left-hand side when navigating bends (particularly along the Coral Coast). Local drivers also tend to stop suddenly and to overtake on blind corners, so take care, especially on gravel roads. Buses also stop where and when they please. There are lots of potholes and sometimes the roads are too narrow for two vehicles to pass so be aware of oncoming traffic.

Watch for sugar trains in the cane-cutting season because they have right of way. Dogs wandering onto the road can be a major hazard,

so observe the speed-hump-enforced 20km/h rule when driving through villages. Avoid driving at night as there are many pedestrians and wandering animals – especially along the southeast coast of Viti Levu, on Vanua Levu and on Taveuni.

Road Rules

Drive on the left-hand side of the road. The speed limit is 80km/h, which drops to 50km/h in villages. Many villages have speed humps to force drivers to slow down. Seatbelts are compulsory for front-seat passengers.

Hitching

Hitching is never entirely safe in any country, and we don't recommend it. Travellers who decide to hitch should understand that they are taking a small but potentially serious risk.

Hitching in Fiji, however, is common. Locals do it all the time, especially with carriers. It is customary to pay the equivalent of the relevant bus fare to the driver. Hitchhikers will be safer if they travel in pairs and let someone know where they are planning to go.

Crime is more prevalent around Suva, although there have been cases of hitchhikers being mugged around Nadi.

Local Transport

Many locals drive small trucks (known as carriers) with a tarpaulin-covered frame on the back. These often have passenger seating, and some run trips between Nadi and Suva. You can pick one up on Nadi's main street; they leave when they are full and are quicker and only slightly more expensive than taking the bus.

Minivans are also an increasingly common sight on the road. Popular with locals, they're also quicker and more expensive than a bus but much cheaper than a taxi. Your ride won't necessarily be more comfortable, though – it's generally a sardine-type affair. Minivans plough up and down the Queens Road around Nadi.

Taxi

You will find taxis on Viti Levu, Vanua Levu, Taveuni and Ovalau. The bus stations in the main towns usually have taxi depots, and there is often an oversupply of taxis, with drivers competing for business. Most taxi drivers are Indo-Fijians keen to discuss life and local issues. They invariably have relatives in Australia, New Zealand or Canada.

Unlike in Suva, the taxi drivers in Nadi, Lautoka and most rural areas don't use their meters. First ask locals what an acceptable rate for a particular trip is. If here is no meter, confirm an approximate price with the driver before you agree to travel. Cabs can be shared for long trips. For touring around areas with limited public transport, such as Taveuni, forming a group and negotiating a taxi fee for a half or full day may be an option.

Always ask if the cab is a return taxi (returning to its base). If so, you can expect to pay $1 per person or less, as long as the taxi doesn't have to go out of its way. To make up for the low fare, the driver will usually pick up extra passengers from bus stops. You can usually recognise a return taxi because most have the name of their home depot on the bumper bar.

Language

The majority of the local people in Fiji you're likely to come in contact with speak English, and all signs and official forms are also in English. At the same time, English is not the mother tongue of most locals – at home, indigenous Fijians speak Fijian and Indo-Fijians speak Fiji-Hindi (also known as Fijian Hindi or Fiji Hindustani).

FIJIAN

There are some 300 regional varieties of Fijian spoken in Fiji today – all descend from the language spoken by the original inhabitants and belong to the Austronesian language family. These 300 or so regional varieties of Fijian belong to two major groups: the varieties spoken to the west of an imaginary line extending north–south, with a couple of kinks, across the centre of Viti Levu belong to the Western Fijian group, while all others are Eastern Fijian.

The dialect which is based on the eastern varieties of the Bau–Rewa area is understood by Fijians throughout the islands and is considered the standard form of Fijian. It is popularly known as *vosa vakabau* (Bauan). It's used in conversation among Fijians from different areas, on the radio and in schools, and is the variety of Fijian used in this chapter.

WANT MORE?

For in-depth language information and handy phrases, check out Lonely Planet's *Fijian Phrasebook*. You'll find it at **shop.lonelyplanet.com**, or you can buy Lonely Planet's iPhone phrasebooks at the Apple App Store.

Pronunciation

Fijian pronunciation isn't particularly difficult for English speakers, since most of the sounds found in Fijian are similar to those found in English. Standard Fijian is written in the Roman alphabet, and it is phonetically consistent – each letter represents only one sound and vice versa.

There are five vowels in Fijian. They are pronounced as follows: a as in 'father', e as in 'bet', i as in 'machine', o as in 'more', and u as in 'flute'. Each vowel has a short and a long variant. In this chapter a long sound is written as a double vowel, eg aa. Vowel length is important for distinguishing the meaning of words. For example, *mama* means 'a ring' and *maamaa* means 'light' (in weight).

Most consonants are pronounced as they are in English, with a few differences: b is pronounced with a preceding nasal sound as 'mb', c as the 'th' in 'this', d with a preceding nasal sound as 'nd', g like 'ng' in 'sing', j like the 'ch' in 'charm' (without a puff of breath), k as in 'kick' (without a puff of breath), p as in 'pip' (without a puff of breath), q like 'ng' in 'angry', r is trilled, t as in 'tap' (without a puff of breath; often pronounced 'ch' before 'i'), and v is pronounced between a 'v' and a 'b'.

Occasionally on maps and in tourist publications you'll find a variation on the spelling system used in this guide – it's intended to be easier for English speakers. In this alternative system, for example, Yanuca is spelt 'Yanutha', Beqa 'Mbengga', and so on.

Basics

In Fijian, there are two ways of saying 'you', 'your' and 'yours'. When speaking to an adult stranger or someone who is your superior, you should use the longer 'polite' form. This form is easy to remember because it always ends in -*ni*. In all other situations, a shorter 'informal' address is used.

Hello.	Bula!
Hello. (reply)	Io, bula./Ia, bula. (more respectful)
Good morning.	Yadra.
Goodbye.	Moce. (if you don't expect to see them again)
See you later.	Au saa liu mada.
Where are you going?	O(ni) lai vei? (meaning 'How are you?')
Nowhere special, just wandering around.	Sega, gaade gaa. (as reply to 'How are you?')
Let's shake hands.	Daru lululu mada.
Yes./No.	Io./Sega.
Thank you (very much).	Vinaka (vakalevu).
Sorry.	(Ni) Vosota sara.
What's your name?	O cei na yacamu(ni)?
My name is ...	O yau o ...
Pleased to meet you.	Ia, (ni) bula.
Where are you from?	O iko/kemuni mai vei?
I'm from ...	O yau mai ...
How old are you?	O yabaki vica?
I'm ... years old.	Au yabaki ...
Are you married?	O(ni) vakawati?
How many children do you have?	Le vica na luvemu(ni)?
I don't have any children.	E sega na luvequ.
I have a daughter/ son.	E dua na luvequ yalewa/ tagane.
I don't speak Fijian/English.	Au sega ni kilaa na vosa vakaviti/vakavaalagi.
Do you speak English?	O(ni) kilaa na vosa vakavaalagi?
I understand.	Saa macala.
I don't understand.	E sega ni macala.
Can I take your photo?	Au tabaki iko mada?
I'll send you the photo.	Au na vaakauta yani na itaba.

Accommodation

Note that the term 'guesthouse' and its Fijian equivalent, *dua na bure ni vulagi*, can refer locally to establishments offering rooms for hire by the hour.

Where's a hotel?	I vei dua na otela?
Where's a cheap hotel?	I vei otela saurawarawa?
I'll stay for one day/ week.	Au na siga/maacawa dua.

NUMBERS – FIJIAN

1	dua
2	rua
3	tolu
4	vaa
5	lima
6	ono
7	vitu
8	walu
9	ciwa
10	tini
11	tinikadua
12	tinikarua
20	ruasagavulu
21	ruasagavulukadua
30	tolusagavulu
100	dua na drau
1000	dua na udolu

I'm not sure how long I'm staying.	Sega ni macala na dede ni noqu tiko.
Where's the bathroom/toilet?	I vei na valenisili/ valelailai?

Directions

Compass points (north, south etc) are never used. Instead, you'll hear these expressions:

on the sea side of ...	mai ... i wai
on the land side of ...	mai ... i vanua
the far side of ...	mai ... i liu
this side of ...	mai ... i muri

Emergencies

Help!	Oilei!
Go away!	Lako tani!
I'm lost.	Au saa sese.
Call the police!	Qiria na ovisa!
Call an ambulance!	Qiria na lori ni valenibula!
Call a doctor!	Qiria na vuniwai!

Where's the hospital?	I vei na valenibula?
I need a doctor.	Au via raici vuniwai.
I have a stomachache.	E mosi na ketequ.
I'm diabetic.	Au tauvi matenisuka.
I'm allergic to penicillin.	E dau lako vakacaa vei au na penisilini.

condoms	rapa/kodom
contraceptive	wai ni yalani
diarrhoea	coka
medicine	wainimate
nausea	lomalomacaa
sanitary napkin	qamuqamu

Shopping & Services

I'm looking for a/the ...	Au vaaqaraa ...
church	na valenilotu
market	na maakete
museum	na vale ni yau maaroroi
police	na ovisa
post office	na posi(tovesi)
public toilet	na valelailai
tourist office	na valenivolavola ni saravanua
What time does it open/close?	E dola/sogo ina vica?
I'm just looking.	Sarasara gaa.
How much is it?	E vica?
That's too expensive.	Au sega ni rawata.

bookshop	sitoa ni vola
clothing shop	sitoa ni sulu
laundry	valenisavasava
pharmacy	kemesi

Time & Dates

What time is it?	Saa vica na kaloko?
yesterday	nanoa
today	nikua
tonight	na bogi nikua
tomorrow	nimataka

Monday	Moniti
Tuesday	Tusiti
Wednesday	Vukelulu
Thursday	Lotulevu
Friday	Vakaraubuka
Saturday	Vakarauwai
Sunday	Sigatabu

Transport

Where's the ...?	I vei na ...?
airport	raaraa ni waqavuka
(main) bus station	basten
bus stop	ikelekele ni basi

When does the ... leave/arrive?	Vica na kaloko e lako/kele kina na ...?
boat	waqa
bus	basi
plane	waqavuka

I want to go to ...	Au via lako i ...
How do I get to ...?	I vei na sala i ...?
Is it far?	E yawa?
Can I walk there?	E rawa niu taubale kina?
Can you show me (on the map)?	Vakaraitaka mada (ena mape)?
Go straight ahead.	Vakadodonu.
Turn left.	Gole i na imawi.
Turn right.	Gole i na imatau.

FIJI-HINDI

Fiji-Hindi is the language of all Indo-Fijians. It has features of the many regional dialects of Hindi spoken by the Indian indentured labourers who were brought to Fiji from 1879 to 1916. Some people call Fiji-Hindi 'Bhojpuri', but this is the name of just one of the dialects that contributed to the language.

Many words from English are found in Fiji-Hindi (eg 'room', 'towel', 'book', 'reef'), but some have slightly different meanings. For example, the word 'book' in Fiji-Hindi also refers to magazines and pamphlets, and if you refer to a person of the opposite sex as a 'friend', it implies that he/she is your sexual partner.

Fiji-Hindi is used in all informal settings, such as in the family and among friends, but the standard Hindi of India is considered appropriate for formal contexts, eg in public speaking, radio broadcasting and writing. Hindus write in standard Hindi using the Devanagari script. Muslims use the Perso-Arabic script – when written this way, it's considered a separate language, Urdu (the language of Pakistan). Indo-Fijians learn standard Hindi or Urdu in school along with English, but they all speak Fiji-Hindi in informal situations.

Some say that Fiji-Hindi is a 'corrupted' version of standard Hindi wherehas, in fact, it is a legitimate dialect with its own grammatical rules and vocabulary unique to Fiji.

Pronunciation

Fiji-Hindi, spoken by Indo-Fijians in informal siuations, is normally written only in publications for foreigners, such as this guide, in which it is transcribed using the English alphabet. In our pronunciation guides, the vowels are pronounced as follows: a as in 'about' or 'sofa', aa as the 'a' in 'father', e as in 'bet', i as in 'police', o as in 'obey', u as in 'rule', ai as in 'hail', aai as the 'ai' in 'aisle', au as the 'o' in 'own', and oi as in 'boil'.

The consonant sounds b, ch, f, g, h, j, k, l, m, n, p, s, sh, v, y, w and z are similar to those in English. The pronunciation of d, r and t in Fiji-Hindi differs from English – however, in this chapter we've used a simplified pronunciation guide and haven't made these distinctions. If you pronounce these sounds as the English 'd', 'r' and 't', you'll be understood.

Fiji-Hindi also has 'aspirated' consonants (pronounced with a puff of air). Aspiration is important in distinguishing meaning, and it's indicated with the letter 'h' after the consonant – eg pul/phul (bridge/flower), kaalaa/khaalaa (black/valley), taali/thaali (clapping/brass plate). Other aspirated consonants are bh (as in 'grab him', said quickly), chh (as in 'church hat', said quickly), dh (as in 'mad house'), gh (as in 'slug him'), jh (as in 'bridge house') and th (as in 'out house').

Basics

There are no exact equivalents for 'hello' and 'goodbye' in Fiji-Hindi. The most common greeting is kaise (How are you?). The usual reply is tik (fine). In parting, it's common to say fir milegaa (We'll meet again). More formal greetings are: namaste (for Hindus) or salaam alaykum (for Muslims) – the reply to the latter is alaykum as-salaam.

NUMBERS – FIJI-HINDI

English is used for numbers 20 to 99.

1	ek
2	dui
3	tin
4	chaar
5	paanch
6	chhe
7	saat
8	aath
9	nau
10	das
100	sau
1000	hazaar

There are no equivalents for 'please' and 'thank you'. To make a polite request, people use the word thoraa (a little) and a special form of the verb ending in -naa, eg thoraa nimak denaa (Please pass the salt). For 'thanks', often just achhaa (good) is used. English 'please' and 'thank you' are also commonly used. The word dhanyavaad, meaning something like 'blessings be bestowed upon you', is used to thank someone who has done something special for you.

The polite form of the word 'you', ap, should be used with people you don't know well. The informal mode uses the word tum. Polite and informal modes of address are indicated in this chapter by the abbreviations 'pol' and 'inf', respectively.

Yes./No.	ha/nahi
Maybe.	saayit
I'm sorry. (used for something serious)	maaf karnaa
What's your name?	aapke naam kaa hai? (pol) tumaar naam kaa hai? (inf)
My name is ...	hamaar naam ...
Where are you from?	aap/tum kaha ke hai? (pol/inf)
I'm from ...	ham ... ke hai
Are you married?	shaadi ho gayaa?
How many children do you have?	kitnaa larkaa hai?
I don't have any children.	larkaa nahi hai
Two boys and three girls.	dui larkaa aur tin larki
Do you speak English?	aap/tum English boltaa? (pol/inf)
Does anyone here speak English?	koi English bole?
I don't understand.	ham nahi samajhtaa

Emergencies & Health

Help me!	hame madad karo!
Go away!	jaao!
Call the doctor/police.	doktaa ke/pulis ke bulaao
Where's the hospital?	aaspataal kaha hai?
I'm diabetic.	hame chini ke bimaari hai
I'm allergic to penicillin.	penesilin se ham bimaar ho jaai
I have a stomachache.	hamaar pet piraawe
I feel nauseous.	hame chhaant lage
condom	kondom/raba

contraceptive	pariwaar niyojan ke dawaai
medicine	dawaai
sanitary napkin	ped/nepkin
tampon	tampon

Time & Dates

English days of the week are generally used.

What time is it?	kitnaa baje?
It's ... o'clock.	... baje
When?	kab?
yesterday	kal
today	aaj
tonight	aaj raatke
tomorrow	bihaan

Transport & Directions

When does the ... leave/arrive?	kitnaa baje ... chale/pahunche?
car	mottar
ship	jahaaj

Where's the ...?	... kaha hai?
airport	eyapot
(main) bus station	basten
church	chech
market	maaket
mosque	masjid
shop	dukaan
temple	mandir

I want to go to ...	ham ... jaae mangtaa
Please write down the address.	thoraa edres likh denaa
Is it near/far?	nagich/dur hai?
Can I go by foot?	paidar jaae saktaa?
Go straight ahead.	sidhaa jaao

By the ...	... ke paas
coconut tree	nariyal ke per
mango tree	aam ke per
breadfruit tree	belfut ke per
sugar-cane field	gannaa khet

GLOSSARY

This glossary is a list of Fijian (F), Fijian-Hindi/Hindi (FH) and other (O) terms you may come across in Fiji.

balabala (F) – tree fern with the unique property of not igniting over hot stones; good for fire-walking rituals

bêche-de-mer (O) – elongated, leathery sea cucumber, with a cluster of tentacles at the mouth; considered a delicacy in Asia – you may find it on your menu

beka (F) – flying fox or fruit bat

bete (F) – priests of the old Fijian religion

bilibili (F) – bamboo raft

bilo (F) – drinking vessel made from half a coconut shell

bokola (F) – the dead body of an enemy

bula (F) – cheers! hello! welcome! (literally, 'life')

bure (F) – traditional thatched dwelling or whatever your resort decides it to be

bure bose (F) – meeting house

bure kalou (F) – ancient temple

bure lailai (F) – little house (toilet)

cibi (F) – death dance

copra (O) – dried coconut kernel, used for making coconut oil

dadakulaci (F) – banded sea krait, Fiji's most common snake

dakua (F) – a tree of the kauri family

dele (F) – a dance where women sexually humiliate enemy corpses and captives; also called wate

drua (F) – double-hulled canoe; traditional catamaran

FVB – Fiji Visitors Bureau

girmitiya (FH) – indentured labourer; the word comes from girmit, the Indian labourers' pronunciation of agreement

ibe (F) – a mat

ibuburau (F) – drinking vessels used in kava rites

ivi (F) – Polynesian chestnut tree

kaivalagi (F) – literally, 'people from far away'; Europeans

kava (F) – Piper methysticum (Polynesian pepper shrub); more importantly the mildly narcotic, muddy and odd-tasting drink made from its aromatic roots; also called yaqona

kerekere (F) – custom of unconditional giving based on the concept that time and property is communal; also means please

koro (F) – village headed by a hereditary chief

kula – a type of parrot, Fiji's national bird

lau toka (F) – spear hit

lovo (F) – Fijian feast cooked in a pit oven

mana (F) – spiritual power

masi (F) – bark cloth with designs printed in black and rust; also known as malo or tapa

mataqali (F) – extended family or landowning group

meke (F) – a dance performance that enacts stories and legends

naga (F) – snake

NAUI (O) – National Association of Underwater Instructors

nokonoko (F) – Casuarina; also known as ironwood

noni (F) – an evergreen that produces a warty, foul-smelling, bitter-tasting fruit gaining credibility worldwide for its ability to help relieve complaints including arthritis, chronic fatigue, high blood pressure, rheumatism and digestive disorders

ota (F) – edible fern

PADI (O) – Professional Association of Diving Instructors

pandanus (O) – a plant common to the tropics whose sword-shaped leaves are used to make mats and baskets

pelagic (O) – large predatory fish, or whale

puja (O) – Hare Krishna prayer

rara (F) – ceremonial ground

ratu (F) – male chief

sevusevu (F) – presentation of a gift to a village chief and, consequently the ancestral gods and spirits; the gift is often kava (yaqona); however, tabua is the most powerful sevusevu; acceptance of the gift means the giver will be granted certain privileges or favours

sulu (F) – skirt or wrapped cloth worn to below the knees

tabu (F) – forbidden or sacred, implying a religious sanction

tabua (F) – the teeth of sperm whales, which carry a special ceremonial value for Fijians; they are still used as negotiating tokens to symbolise esteem or atonement

tagimaucia (F) – a flower with white petals and bright red branches; Fiji's national flower

talanoa (F) – to chat, to tell stories, to have a yarn

tanoa (F) – kava drinking bowl

tapa (F) – see masi

tikina (F) – a group of Fijian villages linked together

trade winds (O) – the near-constant (and annoying) winds that buffer most of the tropics

tui (F) – king or chief

turaga-ni-koro (F) – hereditary chief

vale (F) – a family house

vale ne bose lawa (F) – parliament house

vanua (F) – land, region, place

vatu ni bokola (F) – head-chopping stone used during cannibalistic rituals

vatuni'epa (F) – rock pedestals formed by the erosion of the coral base along the coast

vilavilairevo (F) – fire-walking (literally, 'jumping into the oven')

Viti (F) – the name indigenous Fijians used for Fiji before the arrival of Europeans (whose mispronunciation gave Fiji its current name)

waka (F) – bunch of *kava* roots

wate (F) – see *dele*

waqa tabus (F) – double-hulled canoe

yaka (F) – breadfruit tree

yaqona (F) – see *kava*

yavu (F) – base for housing

Behind the Scenes

SEND US YOUR FEEDBACK

We love to hear from travellers – your comments keep us on our toes and help make our books better. Our well-travelled team reads every word on what you loved or loathed about this book. Although we cannot reply individually to your submissions, we always guarantee that your feedback goes straight to the appropriate authors, in time for the next edition. Each person who sends us information is thanked in the next edition – the most useful submissions are rewarded with a selection of digital PDF chapters.

Visit **lonelyplanet.com/contact** to submit your updates and suggestions or to ask for help. Our award-winning website also features inspirational travel stories, news and discussions.

Note: We may edit, reproduce and incorporate your comments in Lonely Planet products such as guidebooks, websites and digital products, so let us know if you don't want your comments reproduced or your name acknowledged. For a copy of our privacy policy visit lonelyplanet.com/privacy.

OUR READERS

Many thanks to the travellers who used the last edition and wrote to us with helpful hints, useful advice and interesting anecdotes:

Charlene Trestrail, Charlotte Sandes, Christian Garcia, Eduardo Gallo, Emma Dagostino, Kit Withers, Luigi Zeccardo, Mark Veale, Patti Elliott, Peter Biggs, Peter Felker, Scott Walton, William Leung

AUTHOR THANKS

Paul Clammer

In Suva, *vinaka vakalevu* to Matt Capper of Talanoa Treks, Elia Nakoro at the Fiji Museum, and Merewalesi Nailatikau for some useful cultural insights. In Kadavu, thanks to Jeanne Maillard. At LP, Tasmin Waby was an understanding editor, and Diana Von Holdt a great cartographer. Special thanks (and nerdy hugs) to Irene Fernandez, for the loan of the Macbook (and the comics) after the robbery and for being generally awesome, along with Alice Clements. Finally, as always, thanks and love to Robyn, without whom I'd never have to got to Fiji, or very far at all.

Tamara Sheward

A shower of hibiscuses and a whopping *vinaka vakalevu* to the indomitable and all-out wonderful Miri Sau, and to Lailanie Burnes, Kalo Baravilala, Michelle and Gary at Stoney Creek, Alex at Coconut Beach (we'll pack the *rakija* next time), Finau Bavadra, Tupou Moeofo, Rosie Titifanue, Bart at JMC in Savusavu, the lovely Paulina (and Elizabeth!) at Bibi's, Kit Withers and the extraordinarily helpful and resourceful Viola Koch at Dolphin Bay. Frangipanis and South Sea smooches to my two crazy coconuts, Dušan and Masha.

ACKNOWLEDGEMENTS

Climate map data adapted from Peel MC, Finlayson BL & McMahon TA (2007) 'Updated World Map of the Köppen-Geiger Climate Classification', Hydrology and Earth System Sciences, 11, 163344.

Cover photograph: Hawksbill turtle, Vanua Levu. Dave Fleetham/Getty Images ©

THIS BOOK

This 10th edition of Lonely Planet's *Fiji* guidebook was researched and written by Paul Clammer and Tamara Sheward. The previous edition was written by Dean Starnes, Celeste Brash and Virginia Jealous. This guidebook was produced by the following:

Destination Editor Tasmin Waby

Product Editors Grace Dobell, Jenna Myers, Alison Ridgway, Amanda Williamson

Senior Cartographer Diana Von Holdt

Book Designer Mazzy Prinsep

Assisting Editors Melanie Dankel, Victoria Harrison, Amy Karafin, Jeanette Wall

Cover Researcher Naomi Parker

Thanks to Liz Heynes, David Hodges, Andi Jones, Lauren Keith, Karyn Noble, Kirsten Rawlings, Dianne Schallmeiner, Angela Tinson

Index

NOTES

NOTES

NOTES

Map Legend

Sights

- Beach
- Bird Sanctuary
- Buddhist
- Castle/Palace
- Christian
- Confucian
- Hindu
- Islamic
- Jain
- Jewish
- Monument
- Museum/Gallery/Historic Building
- Ruin
- Shinto
- Sikh
- Taoist
- Winery/Vineyard
- Zoo/Wildlife Sanctuary
- Other Sight

Activities, Courses & Tours

- Bodysurfing
- Diving
- Canoeing/Kayaking
- Course/Tour
- Sento Hot Baths/Onsen
- Skiing
- Snorkelling
- Surfing
- Swimming/Pool
- Walking
- Windsurfing
- Other Activity

Sleeping

- Sleeping
- Camping

Eating

- Eating

Drinking & Nightlife

- Drinking & Nightlife
- Cafe

Entertainment

- Entertainment

Shopping

- Shopping

Information

- Bank
- Embassy/Consulate
- Hospital/Medical
- Internet
- Police
- Post Office
- Telephone
- Toilet
- Tourist Information
- Other Information

Geographic

- Beach
- Gate
- Hut/Shelter
- Lighthouse
- Lookout
- Mountain/Volcano
- Oasis
- Park
- Pass
- Picnic Area
- Waterfall

Population

- Capital (National)
- Capital (State/Province)
- City/Large Town
- Town/Village

Transport

- Airport
- Border crossing
- Bus
- Cable car/Funicular
- Cycling
- Ferry
- Metro station
- Monorail
- Parking
- Petrol station
- Subway station
- Taxi
- Train station/Railway
- Tram
- Underground station
- Other Transport

Note: Not all symbols displayed above appear on the maps in this book

Routes

- Tollway
- Freeway
- Primary
- Secondary
- Tertiary
- Lane
- Unsealed road
- Road under construction
- Plaza/Mall
- Steps
- Tunnel
- Pedestrian overpass
- Walking Tour
- Walking Tour detour
- Path/Walking Trail

Boundaries

- International
- State/Province
- Disputed
- Regional/Suburb
- Marine Park
- Cliff
- Wall

Hydrography

- River, Creek
- Intermittent River
- Canal
- Water
- Dry/Salt/Intermittent Lake
- Reef

Areas

- Airport/Runway
- Beach/Desert
- Cemetery (Christian)
- Cemetery (Other)
- Glacier
- Mudflat
- Park/Forest
- Sight (Building)
- Sportsground
- Swamp/Mangrove

OUR STORY

A beat-up old car, a few dollars in the pocket and a sense of adventure. In 1972 that's all Tony and Maureen Wheeler needed for the trip of a lifetime – across Europe and Asia overland to Australia. It took several months, and at the end – broke but inspired – they sat at their kitchen table writing and stapling together their first travel guide, *Across Asia on the Cheap*. Within a week they'd sold 1500 copies. Lonely Planet was born.

Today, Lonely Planet has offices in Dublin, Franklin, London, Melbourne, Oakland, Beijing and Delhi, with more than 600 staff and writers. We share Tony's belief that 'a great guidebook should do three things: inform, educate and amuse'.

OUR WRITERS

Paul Clammer

Paul has contributed to more than 25 guidebooks for Lonely Planet, and has worked as a tour guide in countries from Turkey to Morocco. In a previous life he may even have been a molecular biologist. When his aid-worker partner was offered a job in Suva, he leapt at the chance of being based in Fiji for an extended period, even when Tropical Cyclone Pam threw a spanner in the works. Follow @paulclammer on Twitter for updates from the road.

Tamara Sheward

Despite a hearty dislike of heat and humidity – not to mention that pesky mango allergy – Tamara not only lives in the tropics, but enjoys travelling them extensively. While researching this book, she rode in 41 boats, six aeroplanes, umpteen rattly open-air buses and one submarine; alas, no similar tally was kept on kava consumption. In addition to writing about Fiji, Tamara has covered a miscellany of countries for Lonely Planet, including the Samoas, Serbia, northern Australia, Bulgaria and Russia.

Published by Lonely Planet Global Ltd
CRN 554153
10th edition – December 2016
ISBN 978 1 78657 214 1
© Lonely Planet 2016   Photographs © as indicated 2016
10 9 8 7 6 5 4 3 2 1
Printed in China